T. W. Robertson

Six Plays

T. W. Robertson

Six Plays

with an Introduction
by Michael R. Booth

Amber Lane Press

This edition published in 1980 by
Amber Lane Press
Amber Lane Farmhouse
The Slack
Ashover
Derbyshire S45 oEB

Printed and bound in Great Britain
by Morrison and Gibb Ltd, London and Edinburgh

0 906399 16 5 (cased)
0 906399 17 3 (paper)

Contents

T. W. Robertson

THOMAS WILLIAM ROBERTSON, the eldest of (reputedly) twenty-two children, was born in Newark on 9 January, 1829, into a family that had provided the provincial stage with generations of actors. His great-grandfather was an actor; his grandfather was an actor; his father was an actor and manager of the Lincoln circuit; his sister was Madge Kendal, one of the leading actresses of the Victorian stage. In the eighteenth and nineteenth centuries the stage was amply supplied with personnel from extended theatrical families, some of them, like the Kembles and the Terrys, great dynasties of considerable theatrical influence. To be born into such a family was a sure road to the stage. A manager with an actress wife, two or three children, and a brother and sister already formed the nucleus of a circuit company or a group of strolling players.

In Robertson's youth the circuit system in the provinces was already in decline. A circuit was essentially a system of theatrical organization in which a manager based his company on at least two theatres, usually more, in the same geographical area, and moved it from one theatre to another at appropriate seasons of the year. If the company was big enough and business good enough, more than one theatre could be simultaneously open in the same circuit. The circuits were at their most extensive and most profitable in the early years of the nineteenth century. In 1827 there were forty-six provincial managements in England and Wales (a few not in circuits), but by then the circuits were already on the way down, victims of economic hard times and later of shifting patterns of entertainment and transport, to be eventually replaced by the touring company. In the 1830s the Lincoln circuit of Robertson's father (and formerly of his great uncle) included Lincoln, Boston, Grantham, Peterborough, Newark, Spalding, Wisbech, Whittlesea, Huntingdon, and Stamford, and the company would spend three or four weeks in each town at special occasions like fairs, assizes, and race meetings. At this time Robertson was playing children's parts. (At fourteen he had been taken out of school in Whittlesea to save fees, and returned to helping his father on the circuit.) He then turned his hand to all things necessary in his father's business as well as acting: scene-painting, prompting, stage-managing, singing, writing songs for low comedians and plays for the company. As an actor he specialised in what was known as eccentric comedy – a distinct line of stock company business – and in the parts of Frenchmen, many of them comic. Even in characters of this kind Robertson was by all accounts a relatively restrained and 'natural' actor. In 1848, tiring of the constant theatrical grind and wishing to take up a different career, he applied for and obtained the position of usher in a school at Utrecht, but lasted only six weeks. Poor food, low pay, and the unpleasantness of a fellow usher – viciously embodied in the character of Krux in *School* – drove him back to his old position of jack-of-all-trades in his father's company. However, the Lincoln circuit was in its death throes. In 1849 it disbanded and Robertson came to London.

Making a living in the metropolis was not at all easy, and for many years until he established himself with the Bancrofts in the 1860s Robertson lived from hand to mouth, frequently on the borderline of wretchedness and poverty. He took acting engagements at minor theatres and in the provinces, and sold the copyright of his plays for only a few pounds each to the theatrical publisher and bookseller Thomas Hailes Lacy. Some of the plays – farces, comedies, melodramas – were performed at a variety of theatres in the West End and East End; they are the standard fare of the early Victorian stage. In 1854 Robertson took a position as prompter, at £3 a week, with Madame Vestris and Charles Mathews at the Lyceum, but this management collapsed the following year. In 1856 he married a young actress, Elizabeth Burton, and the young couple went to Ireland for a year, playing in Dublin, Belfast, and other towns. Three children were born of this marriage. One, a girl, died in her infancy; of the other two, Thomas William and Maud, the former at least went on the stage. (One of the confusing aspects of the biography of the Robertson family is that so many sons over several generations were called Thomas William.)

Later in the fifties Robertson decided to give up acting, although his wife continued to perform, and concentrate on writing, both for the stage and for the press. This was the heyday of the English comic magazine and, together with W. S. Gilbert, Robertson wrote dramatic reviews for *Fun*. Among the many magazines and newspapers to which he contributed perhaps the most important was the *Illustrated Times*, where he succeeded Edmund Yates as theatre critic and wrote an interesting series of articles on 'Theatrical Types', the principal personages of a theatre company such as the Leading Lady, the Tragedian, the Low Comedian, the Light Comedian, the Burlesque Actress, the Old Man, and the Stage Manager. Other publications for which Robertson wrote included the *Welcome Guest*, the *Liverpool Porcupine*, the *Comic News*, the *Glowworm*, the *Wag*, *London Society*, *Colman's Magazine*, and *Beeton's Englishwoman's Domestic Magazine*. Like his sometimes bohemian and occasionally raffish colleagues, for whom he had great affection, Robertson was an extremely hard-working journalist. The Owl's Roost scene in *Society* was based on fact and considered a daring presentation of the bohemian club life of the day which might offend journalists; in fact they were delighted with it.

After many years of writing for the stage, Robertson's first real success came with *David Garrick* (1864), played first in Birmingham and then at the Haymarket in London. It was adapted from a French play, *Sullivan,* which Robertson had seen performed by a French company at the St James's, and has nothing to do with the stage life of the famous actor but is a love story in which Garrick, invited to the house of a City merchant, promises to dispel the infatuation the daughter has conceived for him by seeing him on stage. In order to do this Garrick acts the part of a drunken boor, much to his own disgust, since he had previously fallen in love with the very same girl, whom he once saw in the audience but whose identity he did not know. Needless to say, the play ends happily and quite unhistorically, with the selfless actor and the still-loving daughter given to each other with the blessing of the father. The success of the play probably owed more to the star acting of E. A. Sothern than to the writing of Robertson; later the part of Garrick was one of Charles Wyndham's most popular and effective roles.

Soon after *David Garrick* came Robertson's introduction to Marie Wilton through the good offices of his friend H. J. Byron, and the production of *Society* in 1865 by the new management of the Prince of Wales's Theatre. Robertson had actually written *Society* for Sothern and the Haymarket company, but the manager Buckstone disliked the play and refused to do it. Its success at the Prince of Wales's, however, was immense, and it ran for 150 nights. This year of artistic triumph for Robertson was marred by the death of his wife at the age of twenty-nine. In 1867 he married a German girl, Rosetta Feist, and a daughter, Rosy, was born. A whole series of dramatic successes now rapidly followed at the Prince of Wales's. Robertson has few real affinities with Chekhov, but in the relationship between their lives and their theatrical achievements they are very close. Chekhov's four great plays were produced by the Moscow Arts Theatre in the space of five years; toward the end of this period their author was suffering from his final illness and died at forty-four at the height of his dramatic achievement. The six consecutive successes of Robertson, from *Society* to *M.P.*, were produced by the Bancrofts within five years, the last one when the playwright was dangerously ill; he died at forty-two, also at the height of his reputation. During these few years Robertson wrote plays for other managements with varying fortune. Among them, *Progress* was successful at the Globe in 1869, but a melodrama, *The Nightingale,* failed at the Adelphi in 1870, and his last play, *War,* was badly received at the St James's less than three weeks before his death on 3 February, 1871, at his house in Chalk Farm. At the end of his life, ironically, after all the years of struggle, his income as well as his residence was eminently respectable. His nightly fees from the Bancrofts had risen from £2 to £5, and he recorded his earnings for 1870 as £3,760 – £500 less than in 1869. Robertson was buried in Abney Park Cemetery in Stoke Newington in the presence of a large number of mourners, and on the evening of his funeral the Prince of Wales's Theatre was closed.

Such a mark of respect from the Bancrofts was appropriate, since not only did they hold Robertson in great esteem and affection but also knew that he was personally responsible for their success and their profits. Squire and Marie Bancroft gave up the Prince of Wales's for the larger Haymarket in 1880, and in 1885 they retired after twenty years of management with a net profit of £180,000 – something like £2,000,000 in today's money. Almost half the number of performances they gave in those twenty years were of Robertson's six comedies. *Society* was revived in 1868, 1874, and 1881 for a total of nearly 500 performances. *Ours* (1866) received the most revivals: 1870, 1876, 1879, 1882, and 1885, totalling 700 performances. *Caste* (1867) was revived in 1871, 1879, and 1883, for 650 performances. *Play* (1868) had an initial run of 106 performances but was not revived. *School* (1869) was the Bancrofts' greatest money-spinner with 800 performances, being revived in 1873, 1880, and 1883. *M.P.* (1870) was given 156 times when it opened and was not revived; the Bancrofts considered it the weakest of the comedies, attributing this to its author's illness. Altogether they gave the six comedies approximately 2,900 performances, or about 145 a year. It is not surprising that in writing of the revival of *Ours* in 1876 Squire Bancroft believed that "We might have put the six Robertson plays upon a sort of dramatic wheel, and have gone on for years, with nothing but successive revivals of them in their turn, had neither madness nor crutches intervened." The decision of the Bancrofts to retire from management in 1885 was closely related to the fact that they had exhausted the potentialities of Robertsonian performance and that there was no new drama with anything like either Robertson's appeal or a style and content so well suited to the abilities of their company. There are hints in their autobiography that by the 1880s they were getting rather tired of doing Robertson. Certainly the last revival of *Ours* in 1885 went, according to Bancroft, at a snail's pace occasioned by ". . . the outcome of long familiarity and a consequent lack of vitality on the part of the performers." The fact that the Haymarket was much larger than the little Prince of Wales's might have also adversely affected the playing in the former house of a comedy whose intimate and quiet domesticity ideally suited the space of the latter. This is what Bancroft himself suggests; yet there were six Robertson revivals at the Haymarket, and Bancroft was pleased with the success of a short season of *Caste* in 1873 at the huge Standard Theatre in the East End.

Robertson's ideas about the performance of his plays so well accorded with the notions of the Bancrofts that the theatrical union of both parties was a perfect example of a marriage between a dramatist in search of a company and a company in search of a dramatist. One must not think, however, that the debt and the good fortune were all on Robertson's side. The playwright was well acquainted with all aspects of production from his experience on the Lincoln circuit, and had been both a prompter and a stage-manager, jobs that combined much of the function of the modern director. He had very clear ideas as to how his plays should be produced, and the principles of artistic restraint and truth to nature, which were also those of the Bancrofts, were of prime importance to him. At several points in the stage directions of his plays he warned the actor against what he considered exaggerated effect but what an actor nurtured for years on stock company stereotypes might believe to be a standard and acceptable performance. For instance, on the first appearance of the Earl of Eagleclyffe in *Birth* Robertson declares, "It is requisite that no foppery, or swelldom of dress or manner be assumed." At the final curtain of *M.P.* "DUNSCOMBE *masters his emotion.*" Robertson glosses this direction: "The actor playing Dunscombe is requested not to make too much of this situation. All that is required is a momentary memory of childhood – succeeded by the external phlegm of the man of the world. No tragedy, no tears, or pocket-handkerchief." Even in the melodrama *The Nightingale* the actor playing the sinister Eastern villain Ismael is instructed that his manner should be ". . . amiable and agreeable, perpetually smiling (no Iago-glances at the pit, and private information to the audience that he is a villain, and that they shall see what they shall see)." In his last play, *War*, the part of a French colonel is to be played ". . . with a *slight* French accent. He is not to pronounce his words absurdly or shrug his shoulders, or duck his head towards his stomach, like the conventional stage Frenchman." A German in the same piece is "to be played with a slight German accent, and not to be made wilfully comic." Robertson does not avoid caricature and comic eccentricity in his plays, for they were essential ingredients of nineteenth-century drama, but he was obviously concerned to set limits which the actor should not overstep.

In performance it is clear that at least at the Prince of Wales's Robertson had artistic control over his plays. The Bancrofts were happy to turn the stage management over to him, and the results much impressed contemporaries. Looking back from the 1880s, W. S. Gilbert thought that stage management "as now understood" – that is, the direction of plays – was absolutely invented by Robertson. Sir John Hare, who acted in all the Prince of Wales's comedies, remembered the playwright's gift in rehearsal of ". . . conveying by some rapid and almost electrical suggestion to the actor an insight into the character assigned him." Hare believed that Robertson founded a natural school of acting. To decide what was or was not "natural" on the stage is very difficult. Every apparently new "natural" actor proves to have antecedents. It is doubtful if Robertson was as much of an innovator here as Hare claimed, considering what had been done previously by actors in comedy like Charles Mathews and Alfred Wigan, but there is no doubt that together with Dion Boucicault he was the first nineteenth-century dramatist to exercise a significant influence on the staging of his plays and the performance of his actors: Gilbert, Pinero, Shaw, and Granville-Barker were followers in this respect rather than leaders.

The restraint and scaling-down of effects evident in Robertson's writing was matched by the style of the Bancrofts. The size of the Prince of Wales's with a seating capacity in 1866 of 814, one of the smallest in London, meant two things: first, that actors did not have to be much larger than life, or strain to produce an impression, and secondly, that a detailed domestic realism of setting was possible in a playhouse where all spectators could observe this detail. The critic Dutton Cook made the first point in reviewing *School:*

> "A story gains in strength and significance by being brought so close to the view of the spectators; and the players are not constrained to unnatural shouting and grimacing in order that their speeches may be heard and the expression of their faces seen from the distant portions of the house. Both author and actors are thus enabled to avoid exaggeration of language and manner which has long been a prominent failing in dramatic writing and representation."

When Robertson was too ill to attend rehearsals of *M.P.* the Prince of Wales's company came to rehearse in his house; it was their longest rehearsal period for a Robertson play – six weeks. Henry James probably did not know this, but interestingly he developed the idea of household domesticity in a disparaging remembrance in 1881 of the Prince of Wales's as a "little theatre":

> "The pieces produced there dealt mainly with little things – presupposing a great many chairs and tables, carpets, curtains, and knick-knacks, and an audience placed close to the stage. They might, for the most part, have been written by a cleverish visitor at a country house, and acted in the drawing-room by his fellow inmates. The comedies of the late Mr. Robertson were of this number, and these are certainly among the most diminutive experiments ever attempted in the drama."

The Times, reviewing *M.P.*, noted that the actors are ". . . almost at arm's length of an audience who sit, as in a drawing-room, to hear drawing-room pleasantries, interchanged by drawing-room personages." This intimacy and domesticity of decor was matched on the Bancrofts' part by an intimate and quietly domestic acting style. During rehearsals of *Caste* Bancroft (playing Hawtree) told Frederick Younge (who was playing the hero, D'Alroy) that Hawtree should be dark and D'Alroy fair. This surprised Younge, who was accustomed to the conventional dark hero and the fair eccentric swell with long flaxen whiskers and an exaggerated acting style, the sort of stereotyped character represented by E. A. Sothern as Lord Dundreary in Tom Taylor's *Our American Cousin* and by H. J. Byron in several of his own comedies. In the event, although there is something of the traditional stage fop in the character of Hawtree, Bancroft acted him as a pale man with short, straight black hair, and was praised for his quiet realism and departure from convention. The careful stage furnishing at the theatre was all the more noticed in combination with the care and restraint of the ensemble performance with which it was perfectly in accord. The real doors, the real locks, the snow blowing into the hut of *Ours* – these were not such innovations as critics like Clement Scott and Shaw claimed, since impeccable stage furnishing and realistic stage effects went back in the former case to the management of Madame Vestris at the Olympic in the 1830s and in the latter at least to the well-mounted melodramas of several managements in the fifties and early sixties. However, together with domestic realism of the writing and acting in many of the parts, the staging (after *Society*) impressed many contemporaries. It was the combination of these elements that was in some way revolutionary, not their separate existence.

"Domestic and commonplace" were the adjectives H. Barton Baker applied to Robertson's plays in 1878, plays which he believed required little more from actors than the ". . . tame emotions of everyday existence." He did not exactly mean it as a compliment, but nevertheless this very domesticity and commonplaceness is at the heart of Robertson's appeal, especially as the dramatist was able to bathe them both with washes of sentiment and charm. When Hawtree says in *Caste* that "I suppose I'm about the average standard sort of thing" he typifies much about Robertsonian character that was fundamentally attractive to ordinary, decent middle-class audiences. The juxtaposition of strong emotion and sentiment with extreme domesticity can be seen in the miraculous return from the dead of George D'Alroy in *Caste* in the middle of a front parlour tea, or the smothering of the Crimean War in a mass of detailed kitchen business, including the making of a real roly-poly pudding on stage a few yards from the battlefield, in *Ours*. In instances of this kind Robertson makes a virtue of ironing out great moments of human

emotion and great events so smoothly that they seem but wrinkles on
the brow of comedy and domestic incident.

There is, however, an aspect of Robertson completely antagonistic
to quiet sentiment and domestic restraint – although coexistent – and
that is an incipient tendency to melodrama. Robertson certainly did
not eschew the conventional plot mechanisms of the nineteenth-
century stage, the initial expositions, soliloquies, asides, and strong
curtains; the exposition at the beginning of *Caste* and *Progress*, for
example, is clumsy. It was especially with act endings that Robertson
showed his love of melodramatic effect and his adherence to the
traditional conventions of strong curtains that dictated stage
grouping and moments of both verbal and wordless climax. The Act
II curtain of *Society* is an instance of this familiar method, when
Sidney Daryl makes his speech denouncing Maud, which is followed
by a crash of music, the near collapse of Maud, and Daryl reeling
through a ballroom full of dancers as the curtain falls. Another is the
end of the second act of *Play* when the heroine Rosie badly
misunderstands the situation when Frank Price appears in the
picturesque ruins searching for a trivial box of lozenges and
"AMANDA *reels backwards, and falls fainting into his arms.* MRS
KINPECK *sees all this from her perch, and gesticulates with her parasol to
those above and below her. Enter* FANQUEHERE, ROSIE, BROWNE, *and*
TODDER, *from different points, to form picture."* Mrs. Kinpeck is,
admittedly, a comic figure, but there is no such admixture of comedy
at the end of Act II of *Progress*, when Eva staggers suicidally out into
the bitter wind and falling snow as *"music – piano"* sounds till the
curtain. Nor is it easy to accept Robertson's instruction about *Dreams*
(1869) – "The Author requests that this Drama may be played after
the style and manner of Comedy, and not after the manner of
Melodrama" – when emotionally the play is intensely melodramatic,
as at the conclusion of the first act when Rudolf departs for England,
leaving his mother and his devoted Lina on stage:

> FRAU: My son – my pride – my life! [*sobbing*] My home
> will be desolate without thee – what shall I do? I
> who have watched thee from thy childhood. My
> noble boy, away in a new world, among new
> faces, who will keep thee from harm, who watch
> over thee?
>
> > [*The stage gradually darkens. Vespers
> > sound till end of scene at intervals.
> > Organ heard until end of scene.*]
>
> LINA: Heaven! dear mother, I love him too. [*Bell. The
> women embrace and sob together.*] We are but two
> poor women, but we can pray together for his
> safety and his happiness [*falling on her knees near

chair; bell] – bear up, bear up, your Rudolf, my Rudolf is away [*bell*], but he is watched and guarded, as all are here on earth. [RITTMEISTER *appears at window*.]

RITTMEISTER: Is he gone?

> [LINA, *who is kneeling at chair, sobs and hides her face in her hands.* FRAU *points to her.* RITTMEISTER *at window. Bell at intervals as Act Drop descends.*]

Of the plays in this volume, *Birth* and *Progress* have the most overtly melodramatic character; that neither was done by the Bancrofts perhaps tells us something about their restraining influence on their author. Contrariwise, the lurid melodrama of *The Nightingale* (though apparently not lurid enough for Adelphi audiences) contains a character from pure Robertsonian comedy in Jack Chepstowe. Yet although the melodrama in the comedies performed at the Prince of Wales's may on the whole be more controlled, it is still there, and breaks out from time to time. A mixture of comedy and melodrama or strong pathetic emotion in the same play was not, however, some awkward compromise or new amalgam of dramatic form arrived at by Robertson, but inherent and traditional in comedy from the beginning of the nineteenth century. It is one illustration of Robertson's indebtedness to his predecessors, but not, as we shall see, the only one.

Robertson's domesticity, the freshness, humour, and sincerity of his writing at its best, to which is joined a genuine delicacy and restraint in feeling and expression, especially in love scenes, all this, curiously mixed with a fondness for the purple passage and the melodramatic climax, is utterly typical of the better comedies. Yet Robertson is not only interesting as the creator of a distinctive style as well as of a range of very human, amusing, and likeable characters, but he also deals in interesting ways with ideas of considerable social significance.

For the historian of attitudes to social class in entertainment, Robertson is absorbing material. The audience of the Prince of Wales's, the Haymarket, and most of the West End theatres was in the 1860s and 1870s primarily middle-class. The Prince of Wales's in particular, with its repertoire, its antimacassars on the seats, its elegance and refinement, and its ten-shilling stalls, deliberately appealed to what would now be called an up-market audience. This audience did not seek to have its comfortable middle-class values challenged, nor was it sceptical and looking for the faith of honest doubt; that sort of comic territory was uniquely the property of Gilbert, not Robertson. What it got from Robertson was reassurance, the comic exploitation but not the discrediting of an unshakeable class position, and the fulfilment of class dreams related to money, ambition, and love; there is much fantasy in Robertson. In performance style and in the handling of character and theme both the Bancrofts and Robertson were extraordinarily skilful at suiting their product to the tastes of their consumers.

The class contrasts and economic antagonisms of the first Prince of Wales's comedy, *Society,* are obvious. Sidney Daryl may be poor, but he is well-born, and by the end of the play comes into his inheritance: the lady, a title, property, and – most respectably – a seat in Parliament. The audience was therefore able to have its cake and eat it. Daryl is both beneath the audience in respectability, income, and position, and above it; he can be both patronised and admired, and his final elevation is a satisfying fantasy common to the nineteenth-century theatre. The Chodds, on the other hand, are newly moneyed vulgarians, generally the most disliked and satirised class of character in Robertson. The Chodds' only value, their only morality, is money, and this is clearly wrong. Chodd Junior declares that with his cheque-book he can purchase anything: friends, a wife, honours, a House of Commons seat. Of course he must receive his come-uppance and lose wife, seat, and possible influence and status. The third side of the triangle is the unabashed and haughty aristocrat Lady Ptarmigant. Her refusal to understand and forgive would carry more dramatic weight if it were not based on the feeble plot devices of coincidences and off-stage events which Robertson could never avoid; similarly, her partial reformation and reconciliation with Daryl is suspiciously coincident with his sudden good fortune – but that may be the point. In any case, like her comically eccentric husband she proves to be good at heart, like all the principal characters except the Chodds, and that is often the main thing in Robertson. The Ptarmigant view of wealth and luxury is little different from that of Chodd Junior, only more aristocratic, and there seems to be little satire of such a view when it is held in the right quarters.

In *Ours* the class position is somewhat more complex. The aristocracy is represented by the quarrelsome and unyielding Lady Shendryn, the brave, harassed, and altruistic Sir Alexander, and the dignified Prince Perovsky. There is no fundamental antagonism to Hugh Chalcot, the representative of a rich brewing family, because he is neither a vulgarian nor too obviously a man of commerce. All the same, his alliance is not with the heiress Blanche Haye, but with Mary Netley, a lady in reduced circumstances. "I know my place," she says, "and if I didn't, Lady Shendryn and the world would make me." The Prince of Wales's audience, one feels, would have approved that sentiment. The heiress is reserved not for the Russian prince, which would have been patriotically unthinkable, but for the brave Scottish officer who goes to war for a change of scene. To be a soldier and an officer is in Robertson to be brave, virtuous, and deserving of good fortune; he admired war and was fascinated by it. In the comedies it is glorified because it is romantic and exciting, because it proves the innate superiority and heroism of the British soldier, and because it makes a man of the likes of Hugh Chalcot. Daryl, Angus MacAlister in *Ours*, D'Alroy, Oscar de Rochevannes in *War* – these are all heroes (in the dramatic sense) and all soldiers. Mary and Blanche in *Ours* even play at soldiers, and the curtain to Act II falls on one of the most rousing and theatrically effective expressions of patriotic feeling on the nineteenth-century stage. The debate in *War* between the jingoism of Colonel de Rochevannes and Karl Hartmann's hatred of war is never resolved, but is evenly balanced while it lasts. It was the nearest Robertson came to the serious examination of a subject that colours the background of several of his plays. *War,* however, is drama, and none of the comedies has anything like even this degree of commentary on war and the concepts of honour and glory. *Ours* is much more typical of the dramatist's attitudes.

War is a remote but romantic background to *Caste,* the one play of Robertson's overtly about class and its "inexorable law". This law can be broken by love but by nothing else; at the end of the play D'Alroy says, "Caste is a good thing if not carried too far. It shuts the door on the pretentious and the vulgar: but it should open the door very wide for exceptional merit. Let brains break through its barriers, and what brains can break through love may leap over." An examination of the comedies reveals that although the door is certainly shut on the pretentious and vulgar and although love certainly leaps over barriers, the breakthrough of merit and brains is not so noticeable – only *Birth* and *Progress* deal with these aspects of ambition and achievement. In *Caste* the class war is carried on purely by comic means. The *prima donna* of the aristocracy is the arrogant Froissart-spouting Marquise, and the radical working-class agitator is the drunken Eccles; any class conflict here is merely ludicrous. More serious is the Marquise's (and initially Hawtree's) attitude to Esther and Polly and to D'Alroy's marriage into the Eccles family, but this problem is overcome by the judicious application of a warm poultice of sentiment and heroism to the wound; as in so much Robertson the main theme fritters away, unresolved and almost forgotten. The lower middle-class tradesman Sam Gerridge is also comic, and his aspirations, though as strong in their way as Chodd Junior's, are rendered socially harmless to the audience by their very nature. Men of trade and commerce are almost invariably funny in Robertson – the exception being Chalcot, who, as mentioned above, does not actually seem to work at the business and is perfectly well bred. A manufacturer like Paul Hewitt in *Birth* is different, and excepted from this kind of comic disparagement because he actually *makes* things rather than too obviously *selling* them. The class division between trade and manufacturing in nineteenth-century comedy was well established before Robertson; in Douglas Jerrold's *Retired from Business* (1851) there are even gulfs of snobbery fixed between the wholesale and retail trades: "Raw wool doesn't speak to halfpenny ball of worsted – tallow in the cash looks down upon sixes to the pound, and pig iron turns up its nose at twopenny nails." The comedy of Sam Gerridge and Polly usefully controls and sometimes ironically undercuts the elements of romantic love and the gravitation to melodrama in the D'Alroy-Esther relationship. In fact the strength of *Caste* lies in this ingenious contrapuntal structure and the rich comic vigour of situation and character, as well as in the detailed and loving observation of a lower middle-class setting used for purposes both comic and serious, ironic and tender.

The elements of dream and fantasy fulfilment in Robertson's comedies are most marked in *School*, based on the German *Aschenbrödel* by Roderich Benedix, a dramatic treatment of the Cinderella story. The eight young women are treated dreamily and sentimentally; their collective sweetness and romanticism may be cloying to our taste, but to the audience of 1869 they represented the beauty of feminine innocence and girlhood, a Victorian ideal of purity and sanctity; the fairy-tale element is strong in the dramatisation of this particular Victorian myth. (*Cinderella* was a very popular pantomime in the last half of the nineteenth century.) Marie Bancroft's reasons for preferring Naomi Tighe to all her other parts are instructive. She admired her "artless simplicity and sunny nature" and "the utter ignorance of any sadness in the whole world except what school discipline enforces, her fearless and open avowal of her romantic adoration" – qualities very necessary to the Victorian image of young womanhood. This ideal is bifurcated in Robertson; half of it was acted by Marie Bancroft: Mary Netley in *Ours*, Polly Eccles in *Caste*, Naomi Tighe in *School*, Cecilia Dunscombe in *M.P.* – characters of intelligence, spirit, activity, and fun. The other half was played by Lydia Foote or Carlotta Addison: Blanche Haye in *Ours*, Esther Eccles in *Caste*, Bella in *School*, Eva in *Progress*, Ruth Deybrooke in *M.P.* – the quieter, more passive, romantic, passionate, and domestic heroine. "I am a woman – I am a wife – a widow – a mother!" Esther Eccles tells the Marquise proudly; of course she is not a widow – the return of the noble husband untouched by war is part of the fantasy – but the other things she is constitute the entire pattern of the ideal. Bella, on the other hand, is purely a fairy-tale character, elevated and rewarded like Cinderella with a prince and a fortune. The opening scene of *School*, with all the girls distributed languorously around a woodland glade, is pure pictorial fantasy, the sort of subject matter not uncommonly found in Victorian oil paintings and watercolours. The plot of *School* is as remote from reality as anything Robertson devised, and there is no hint of contact with the real world, which is somewhere outside the bounds of the enchanted wood – even the evil Krux is a fairy-tale ogre. The appeal of the fairy-tale to the Victorian mind was extremely powerful. By 1869 dozens of editions of English translations from the brothers Grimm and Hans Christian Andersen had been published; the genre of fairy painting had flourished; several notable productions of *The Tempest* and *A Midsummer Night's Dream* had strongly emphasised the fairy elements, as did Christmas pantomime; *Giselle* and *La Sylphide* were popular romantic ballets; *The King of the Golden River*, *The Rose and the Ring*, *The Water Babies*, and *Alice's Adventures in Wonderland* had already appeared. It is not surprising that *School* had the longest initial run of any Bancroft production, 381 nights.

The two comedies acted by the Bancrofts but not in this volume, *Play* and *M.P.*, were never revived and must be counted among the weaker effusions of Robertson's pen. Repetition of character, theme, structure, and technique is obvious; despite this the Bancrofts managed to bring off a successful opening run in each case. *Play* is set in a German spa and concerns unscrupulous attempts at fraud and double-dealing which are frustrated, mostly by coincidence. The plan of an already married man to marry the heroine and obtain her fortune, which nobody but he knows she possesses, goes awry through the timely revelation of marital and financial truths. Malicious intent and dark characterisation are nullified and lightened by the sudden reformation of the pseudo-villain. The comic figure of the commercial man appears again, this time in the person of the bourgeois Todder of "Todder's Original Patent Starch", and once again there is the juxtaposition of two simultaneous but very different love scenes, a favourite technique of Robertson's and used with great skill in *Ours* and *Caste*. In the last of the comedies, *M.P.*, the upright and honourable Talbot Piers takes both the girl with a fortune and the seat in Parliament from the *nouveau-riche* schemer Isaac Skoome, whose name betrays his nastiness. Plot structure and themes echo *Society*, but *M.P.* has neither the charm nor the delicate touch of that play. From the evidence of *M.P.* it is clear that Robertson had nothing new to say in comedy, nor any new ways in which to say the old things.

Thematically, the two most potentially interesting Robertson comedies are not those the Bancrofts produced but *Progress* (1869) and *Birth* (1870). Like *Society*, the first was written for the Buckstone company at the Haymarket and, like *Society*, not performed by them. The original destination of *Progress* is indicated by the large part for Bunnythorne, the sort of character Buckstone had been playing for years, and for Bob Bunnythorne, meant for Buckstone's son. *Birth* was written for Sothern – thus the substantial and distorting part for the largely irrelevant Jack Randall – and was successful in the provinces. Sothern, however, did not have the courage to bring the play in its present form into London, and Robertson was too ill for rewriting. The first acts of both plays are promising. In *Progress*, adapted from Sardou's *Les Ganaches*, the clash is between the old aristocracy and the new technocracy, between the values of tradition and the values of technological innovation and radical social change; in *Birth* the conflict is between the aristocracy of the old landowner and the manufacturing power of the new industrialist. In *Progress* the railway and the Abbey come face-to-face; in *Birth* the castle glowers down at the new ironworks. Class antagonism is initially bitter in both plays. *Progress* also contains the character of a retired tradesman who is the object of amusement not unconnected with his devotion to all things old and tested.

Yet these striking themes dwindle into triviality after the first acts of both plays. Unlike some of his predecessors Robertson was never able to sustain the serious dramatic development of socially significant themes, despite the titles of the plays, which suggest more in content than they deliver. This did not much bother his contemporaries, although they noticed it. They frequently employed terms like "truth to nature" and "realism" to describe his achievement, but several recognised the fact that this was nature and realism on a small scale. John Oxenford praised *Caste* in *The Times* for ". . . a connection with the realities, which, perhaps, must not be too closely scrutinised, but which, to a certain extent, makes the stage reflect the world with more than usual accuracy." Baker thought that Robertson dealt only with "the superficial phases" of civilisation, and Henry James disdainfully dismissed the comedies as "infantile" and "addressed to the comprehension of infants". The problem that we can recognise, although it did not disturb Victorian audiences, is that as in so much Victorian comedy the subject matter of ambition, pride, wealth, class conflict, social position, commercialism, privilege, and so on, is finally either resolved (if one can call it a resolution) or pushed aside by the pressing claims of love and marriage. This is particularly true in Robertson, and *Birth* and *Progress* are examples of the impulse in his work to cover the initial and potentially vital social themes with a thick candy-floss of sweet sentimentality and romantic entanglements. Thus in *Progress* Ferne the engineer falls in love with the stricken Eva; there is no more talk of the subject matter of the first act, and at the end Eva says to *"music, piano,"* "My path must lead to happiness when love and hope conduct me, and affection and experience guide me – (*smiling*) – That's Progress!" – a rather different notion of progress from that propounded in the dialectic of Act I. Similarly, in *Birth* the gulf of class hostility between industry and aristocracy is easily bridged by the intermarriage of the rival families. Even in the drama *War* the theme of war itself and the antagonism of opposing views are forgotten and subordinated to romantic sentiment and the triumph of love. Economic difficulties and humble status are not overcome by effort – the people who make that sort of effort and are successful, the Chodds, the Skoomes, the Bunnythornes, the Todders of the Robertson world, are vulgarians and are to be laughed at or vanquished, or both – but by the *deus ex machina* of a fortune or a title, as in the case of Sidney Daryl, Rosie Fanquehere in *Play*, and Bella in *School*. Potentially serious themes may not exactly be abandoned, but are developed through love relationships and romantic sentiment. In this development, however, they become diluted and enervated. Yet it may be unfair to criticise Robertson in the 1860s for not writing the sort of play we might want him to write, and for not fulfilling the thematic potential of the early acts of his plays. They were, after all, light comedies written to entertain and reassure a pleasure-seeking middle-class audience; it was not Robertson's responsibility to be a Shaw a generation ahead of his time.

In using romance and endings that brought happiness, marriage, and wealth to his main characters, Robertson was only following the standard pattern of development in several preceding generations of stage comedy. Thematically he was no innovator. All his theme material is inherited from older writers. The coexistence of the melodramatic and pathetic with the ludicrous and comically satiric has already been noted, and this mixture, characteristic of English drama, had immediate antecedents in the early nineteenth-century comedy of George Colman, Thomas Morton, Frederic Reynolds, and others. The ambitious parvenu is satirised in the person of a retired stationer aspiring to Parliament and a baronetcy in Mrs. Gore's *Quid Pro Quo* (1844) and in the wife of the retired grocer in Jerrold's *Retired from Business*. The relationship of wealth to social ambition and class standing is satirically explored by a really important and influential comedy, Bulwer-Lytton's *Money* (1840), although this may have owed something to an especially savage attack upon the corruption engendered by money in Jerrold's *The Golden Calf* (1832). Several of *Money's* ideas of position and fortune and the lengths people will go to obtain them are picked up by Boucicault in *The School for Scheming* (1847), which is much concerned with the world of commerce, capitalist speculation, and "progress". The play sustains the serious themes for four acts but collapses in the fifth; Robertson was not the only Victorian playwright who would not or could not pursue his intellectual concepts to the final curtain. Another author of comedies who failed to do this was Jerrold, despite *The Golden Calf*. *Retired from Business* veers off into love and sentimentality in the same way as does Robertson. The bright ideal of womanhood, the innocence and purity of Victorian girlhood, the apotheosis of wifehood and motherhood – these shine through and dominate so many Victorian comedies and dramas before Robertson that it would be pointless to enumerate them. Idealism about life so intense that it almost becomes – and sometimes does become – fantasy is strong in Robertson as in his progenitors, and nowhere is his idealism stronger than in his depiction of young love between serious characters; it is really no wonder that love usually sinks the thematic freight of other concerns without a bubble. Robertson's skill in making this love interesting and dramatically credible through seemingly ordinary conversation and a quiet, hesitant, coming together of mutually attracted couples is considerable, and here he had no predecessors.

Since Robertson came toward the end of a long and developing tradition of English comedy, he represents an end rather than a beginning. One can easily trace the varied influences of the past upon his work, but it is harder to say how significant was his impact upon succeeding dramatists. Certainly his immediate contemporaries quickly absorbed his techniques. Tom Taylor's *New Men and Old Acres,* which appeared in the same year as *School* and *Progress,* is a less rumbustious comedy than others Taylor had written before; the love scenes are restrained and quietly sentimental somewhat in Robertson's manner. The themes of the vulgar *nouveau-riche* pitted against the proud aristocrat, of technology clashing with tradition, are close to Robertson as well as to the substance of Victorian comedy. James Albery intensifies Robertson's sweetness and sentimentality in *Two Roses* (1870), a story of idealised love as well as melodramatic intrigue and low comedy derived from the character of a travelling salesman. Gilbert was undoubtedly influenced by Robertson in his duet for two lovers, *Sweethearts* (1874), a graceful, controlled, and delicate comedy, written for the Prince of Wales's and for Mrs. Bancroft. Later he went his own way into realms of cruel satire and topsy-turvydom that Robertson could never have created.

Robertson's influence on the next generation of playwrights was probably small. Pinero drew on the techniques of French dramatists, the themes of social guilt and fear of social exposure in the Mayfair society around him, and the determinism of Ibsen. The comedies of Henry Arthur Jones were closer to Pinero than to Robertson, with a strong admixture of melodrama and the old stock company stereotypes which he and Pinero and Shaw transformed but never abandoned. (It should not be forgotten that Robertson wrote for a stock company, and there are traditional character stereotypes in his plays too.) It is true that much English comedy developed in the direction of rather ordinary middle-class domestic reality after Robertson, and this may be his most significant dramatic legacy; there were, however, firm indications of this direction before *Society.* In 1897 all that the sympathetic Shaw could really advance in favour of Robertson was the domestic reality of his settings, the novel domestic commonplaces of his dialogue, and the humanity of his observation and characterisation. This is much, but it does not constitute the *oeuvre* of an original and influential dramatist; these characteristics can be found – though not in combination – in previous drama and staging. Yet even taking into account all influences and indebtedness, conscious or unconscious, Robertson's dramatic territory is his very own and nobody else's. This makes him unique, and to be unique is to be important. The humanity to which Shaw draws attention, the charm, the domesticity, the style, the peculiar fairyland of his dramatic vision, the very Englishness of his work, all these make him a dramatist to be respected, valued and prized.

Michael R. Booth
May, 1980

Select Bibliography

In his introduction to these *Six Plays* by T. W. Robertson, Professor Booth quotes from the following:

H. Barton Baker, *Our Old Actors* (1878)

Squire and Marie Bancroft, *Mr. and Mrs. Bancroft On and Off the Stage,* 4th edn. (1888) and *The Bancrofts* (1909)

Dutton Cook, *Nights at the Play* (1883)

Sir John Hare, quoted in T. Edgar Pemberton, *The Life and Writings of T. W. Robertson* (1893)

Henry James, "The London Theatres", *Scribner's Monthly,* xxi (January 1881)

T. W. Robertson, *The Principal Dramatic Works of Thomas William Robertson* (Samuel French edition, 1889)

Publisher's Note

The text for the six plays in this volume is taken from the collected works published by Samuel French in 1889 as cited above. Certain inconsistencies and misspellings have been corrected and some extraneous stage directions omitted.

SOCIETY

Produced at the Prince of Wales's Theatre, Liverpool [under the management of Mr A. Henderson], on 8th May, 1865; afterwards performed at the Prince of Wales's Theatre, London [under the management of Miss Marie Wilton], on 11th November, 1865.

CAST OF CHARACTERS

	Liverpool	London
Lord Ptarmigant	Mr Blakeley	Mr Hare
Lord Cloudwrays, M.P.	Mr F. Cameron	Mr Trafford
Sidney Daryl [a Barrister]	Mr Edward Price	Mr Bancroft
Mr John Chodd, Sen.	Mr G. P. Grainger	Mr Ray
Mr John Chodd, Jun.	Mr L. Brough	Mr J. Clarke
Tom Stylus	Mr E. Saker	Mr F. Dewar
O'Sullivan	Mr C. Swan	Mr H. W. Montgomery
MacUsquebaugh	Mr Chater	Mr Hill
Doctor Makvicz	Mr Smith	Mr Bennett
Bradley	Mr W. Grainger	Mr Parker
Scargil	Mr Waller	Mr Lawson
Sam Stunner, P.R. [alias the Smiffel Lamb]	Mr Hill	Mr J. Tindale
Shamheart		Mr G. Odell
Doddles		Mr Burnett
Moses Aaron [a Bailiff]	Mr Davidge	Mr G. Atkins
Sheridan Trodnon	Mr Bracewell	Mr Macart
Lady Ptarmigant	Miss Larkins	Miss Larkins
Maud Hetherington	Miss T. Furtado	Miss Marie Wilton
Little Maud	Miss F. Smithers	Miss George
Mrs Churton	Miss Procter	Miss Merton
Servant		Miss Thompson

Waiters, servants, roughs, &c.

Optional characters:
Sir Farintosh Fadileaf
Colonel Browser

ACT I – SCENE I – SIDNEY DARYL'S *Chambers*. SCENE II – *A West End Square*.

ACT II – SCENE I – *A Parlour at the "Owl's Roost"*. SCENE II – *Retiring Room at* SIR FARINTOSH FADILEAF'S.

ACT III – SCENE I – *Same as 1st Scene, Act II*. SCENE II – *Apartment at* LORD PTARMIGANT'S. SCENE III – *Exterior at Springmead-le-Beau*.

Modern Costumes. Time of Representation, three hours.

TO

MY DEAR FRIEND

TOM HOOD

THIS PLAY

IS DEDICATED

SOCIETY

ACT I

SCENE I – SIDNEY DARYL's *Chambers, in Lincoln's Inn; set doorpiece* R. *and set doorpiece* L. [*to double up and draw off*]; *the room to present the appearance of belonging to a sporting literary barrister; books, pictures, whips; the mirror stuck full of cards* [*painted on cloth*]; *a table, chairs, &c. As the curtain rises a knock heard, and* DODDLES *discovered opening door*, L.

TOM: [*without*] Mr Daryl in?

DODDLES: Not up yet.

[*Enter* TOM STYLUS, CHODD, JUN., *and* CHODD, SEN.]

CHODD, JUN.: [*looking at watch*] Ten minutes to twelve, eh, guv?

TOM: Late into bed; up after he oughter; out for brandy and sobering water.

SIDNEY: [*within*] Doddles.

DODDLES: [*an old clerk*] Yes, sir!

SIDNEY: Brandy and soda.

DODDLES: Yes, sir!

TOM: I said so! Tell Mr Daryl two gentlemen wish to see him on particular business.

CHODD, JUN.: [*a supercilious, bad swell; glass in eye; hooked stick; vulgar and uneasy*] So this is an author's crib – is it? Don't think much of it, eh, guv?

CHODD, SEN.: [*a common old man, with a dialect*] Seems comfortable enough to me, Johnny.

CHODD, JUN.: Don't call me Johnny! I hope he won't be long. [*looking at watch*] Don't seem to me the right sort of thing, for two gentlemen to be kept waiting for a man they are going to employ.

CHODD, SEN.: Gently, Johnny. [CHODD, JUN., *looks annoyed.*] I mean gently without the Johnny – Mister——

TOM: Daryl – Sidney Daryl!

CHODD, SEN.: Daryl didn't know as we was coming!

CHODD, JUN.: [*rudely to* TOM] Why didn't you let him know?

TOM: [*fiercely*] How the devil could I? I didn't see you till last night. [CHODD, JUN., *retires into himself.*] You'll find Sidney Daryl just the man for you; young – full of talent – what I was thirty years ago; I'm old now, and not full of talent, if ever I was; I've emptied myself; I've missed my tip. You see I wasn't a swell – he is!

CHODD, JUN.: A swell – what a man who writes for his living?

[DODDLES *enters.*]

DODDLES: Mr Daryl will be with you directly; will you please to sit down?

[CHODD, SEN., *sits.* TOM *takes a chair* L. *of table;* CHODD, JUN., *waiting to have one given to him, is annoyed that no one does so, and sits on table.*]

CHODD, JUN.: Where is Mr Daryl?

DODDLES: In his bath!

CHODD, JUN.: [*jumping off table*] What! You don't mean to say he keeps us here while he's washing himself?

[*Enter* SIDNEY, *in morning jacket.*]

SIDNEY: Sorry to have detained you; how are you, Tom?

[TOM *and* CHODD, SEN., *rise;* CHODD, JUN., *sits again on table and sucks cane.*]

CHODD, SEN.: Not at all!

CHODD, JUN.: [*with watch*] Fifteen minutes.

SIDNEY: [*handing chair to* CHODD, JUN.] Take a chair!

CHODD, JUN.: This'll do.

SIDNEY: But you're sitting on the steel pens.

TOM: Dangerous things! pens.

[CHODD, JUN., *takes a chair.*]

SIDNEY: Yes! loaded with ink, percussion powder's nothing to 'em.

CHODD, JUN.: We came here to talk business. [*to* DODDLES] Here, you get out!

SIDNEY: [*surprised*] Doddles – I expect a lot of people this morning, be kind enough to take them into the library.

DODDLES: Yes, sir! [*aside, looking at* CHODD, JUN.] Young rhinoceros!

[*Exit* DODDLES.]

SIDNEY: Now, gentlemen, I am——

TOM: Then I'll begin. First let me introduce Mr Sidney Daryl to Mr John Chodd, of Snoggerston, also to Mr John Chodd, Jun., of the same place; Mr John Chodd, of Snoggerston, is very rich – he made a fortune by——

CHODD, SEN.: No! – my brother Joe made the fortune in Australey, by gold digging and then spec'lating; which he then died, and left all to me.

CHODD, JUN.: [*aside*] Guv! cut it!

CHODD, SEN.: I shan't – I ain't ashamed of what I was, nor what I am;

it never was my way. Well, sir, I have lots of brass!

SIDNEY: Brass?

CHODD, SEN.: Money!

CHODD, JUN.: Heaps!

CHODD, SEN.: Heaps; but having begun by being a poor man, without edication, and not being a gentleman——

CHODD, JUN.: [aside] Guv! – cut it.

CHODD, SEN.: I shan't – I know I'm not, and I'm proud of it, that is, proud of knowing I'm not, and I won't pretend to be. Johnny don't put me out – I say I'm not a gentleman, but my son is.

SIDNEY: [looking at him] Evidently.

CHODD, SEN.: And I wish him to cut a figure in the world – to get into Parliament.

SIDNEY: Very difficult.

CHODD, SEN.: To get a wife?

SIDNEY: Very easy.

CHODD, SEN.: And in short, to be a – a real gentleman.

SIDNEY: Very difficult.

CHODD, SEN.: ⎫
CHODD, JUN.: ⎭ Eh?

SIDNEY: I mean very easy.

CHODD, SEN.: Now, as I'm anxious he should be an M.P. as soon as——

SIDNEY: As he can.

CHODD, SEN.: Just so, and as I have lots of capital unemployed, I mean to invest it in——

TOM: [slapping SIDNEY on knees] A new daily paper!

SIDNEY: By Jove!

CHODD, SEN.: A cheap daily paper, that could – that will – What will a cheap daily paper do?

SIDNEY: Bring the "Court Circular" within the knowledge of the humblest.

TOM: Educate the masses – raise them morally, socially, politically, scientifically, geologically, and horizontally.

CHODD, SEN.: [delighted] That's it – that's it, only it looks better in print.

TOM: [spouting] Bring the glad and solemn tidings of the day to the labourer at his plough – the spinner at his wheel – the swart forger at his furnace – the sailor on the giddy mast – the lighthouse keeper as he trims his beacon lamp – the housewife at her pasteboard – the mother at her needle – the lowly lucifer seller, as he splashes his wet and weary way through the damp, steaming, stony streets, eh? – you know.

[Slapping SIDNEY on the knee – they both laugh.]

CHODD, SEN.: [*to* CHODD, JUN.] What are they a laughing at?

TOM: So my old friend, Johnny Prothero, who lives hard by Mr Chodd, knowing that I have started lots of papers, sent the two Mr Chodds, or the Messrs Chodd – which is it? – you're a great grammarian – to me. I can find them an efficient staff, and you are the first man we've called upon.

SIDNEY: Thanks, old fellow. When do you propose to start it?

CHODD, SEN.: At once.

SIDNEY: What is it to be called?

CHODD, SEN.: We don't know.

CHODD, JUN.: We leave that to the fellows we pay for their time and trouble.

SIDNEY: You want something——

CHODD, SEN.: Strong.

TOM: And sensational.

SIDNEY: [*rising*] I have it.

TOM: ⎫
CHODD, SEN.: ⎬ What?
CHODD, JUN.: ⎭

SIDNEY: The "Morning Earthquake"!

TOM: Capital!

CHODD, SEN.: [*rising*] First-rate!

CHODD, JUN.: [*still seated*] Not so bad.

SIDNEY: Don't you see? In place of the clock, a mass of houses, factories, and palaces tumbling one over the other; and then the prospectus! "At a time when thrones are tottering, dynasties dissolving – while the old world is displacing to make room for the new——"

TOM: Bravo!

CHODD, SEN.: [*enthusiastically*] Hurray!

TOM: A second edition at 4 o'clock, p.m. The "Evening Earthquake," eh? Placard the walls. "The Earthquake," one note of admiration; "The Earthquake," two notes of admiration; "The Earthquake," three notes of admiration. Posters: " 'The Earthquake' delivered every morning with your hot rolls." "With coffee, toast, and eggs, enjoy your 'Earthquake' "!

CHODD, SEN.: [*with pocket-book*] I've got your name and address.

CHODD, JUN.: [*who has been looking at cards stuck in glass*] Guv.

[*He takes old* CHODD *up and whispers to him.*]

TOM: [*to* SIDNEY] Don't like this young man!

SIDNEY: No.

TOM: Cub.

SIDNEY: Cad.

TOM: Never mind. The old un's not a bad 'un. We're off to a printer's.

SIDNEY: Good-bye, Tom, and thank ye.
TOM: How's the little girl?
SIDNEY: Quite well. I expect her here this morning.
CHODD, SEN.: Good morning.

[*Exeunt* CHODD, SEN., *and* TOM.]

SIDNEY: [*filling pipe, &c.*] Have a pipe?
CHODD, JUN. [*taking out a magnificent case*] I always smoke cigars.
SIDNEY: Gracious creature! Have some bitter beer? [*getting it from locker*]
CHODD, JUN.: I never drink anything in the morning.
SIDNEY: Oh!
CHODD, JUN.: But champagne.
SIDNEY: I haven't got any.
CHODD, JUN.: Then I'll take beer. [*They sit.*] Business is business – so I'd best begin at once. The present age is, as you are aware – a practical age. I come to the point – it's my way. Capital commands the world. The capitalist commands capital, therefore the capitalist commands the world.
SIDNEY: But you don't quite command the world, do you?
CHODD, JUN.: Practically, I do. I wish for the highest honours – I bring out my cheque-book. I want to go into the House of Commons – cheque-book. I want the best legal opinion in the House of Lords – cheque-book. The best house – cheque-book. The best turn out – cheque-book. The best friends, the best wife, the best-trained children – cheque-book, cheque-book, and cheque-book.
SIDNEY: You mean to say with money you can purchase anything.
CHODD, JUN.: Exactly. This life is a matter of bargain.
SIDNEY: But "honour, love, obedience, troops of friends"?
CHODD, JUN.: Can buy 'em all, sir, in lots, as at an auction.
SIDNEY: Love, too?
CHODD, JUN.: Marriage means a union mutually advantageous. It is a civil contract, like a partnership.
SIDNEY: And the old-fashioned virtues of honour and chivalry?
CHODD, JUN.: Honour means not being a bankrupt. I know nothing at all about chivalry, and I don't want to.
SIDNEY: Well, yours is quite a new creed to me, and I confess I don't like it.
CHODD, JUN.: The currency, sir, converts the most hardened sceptic. I see by the cards on your glass that you go out a great deal.
SIDNEY: Go out?
CHODD, JUN.: Yes, to parties. [*looking at cards on table*] There's my Lady this, and the Countess t'other, and Mrs somebody else. Now that's what I want to do.
SIDNEY: Go into society?

CHODD, JUN.: Just so. You had money once, hadn't you.
SIDNEY: Yes.
CHODD, JUN.: What did you do with it?
SIDNEY: Spent it.
CHODD, JUN.: And you've been in the army?
SIDNEY: Yes.
CHODD, JUN.: Infantry?
SIDNEY: Cavalry.
CHODD, JUN.: Dragoons?
SIDNEY: Lancers.
CHODD, JUN.: How did you get out?
SIDNEY: Sold out.
CHODD, JUN.: Then you were a first-rate fellow, till you tumbled down?
SIDNEY: Tumbled down?
CHODD, JUN.: Yes, to what you are.

[SIDNEY *about to speak, is interrupted by* MOSES AARON, *without.*]

MOSES: Tell you I mush't shee him.

[*Enter* MOSES AARON *with* DODDLES.]

MOSES: [*not seeing* CHODD, JUN., *going round behind table*] Sorry, Mister Daryl, but at the shoot of Brackersby and Co. [*Arrests him.*]
CHODD, JUN.: [*rising*] Je-hosophat!
SIDNEY: Confound Mr Brackersby! It hasn't been owing fifteen months! – How much?
MOSES: With exes, fifty four pun' two.
SIDNEY: I've got it in the next room. Have some beer?
MOSES: Thank ye, shir.

[SIDNEY *pours it out.*]

SIDNEY: Back directly.

[*Exit* SIDNEY.]

CHODD, JUN.: This chap's in debt. Here you!
MOSES: Shir.
CHODD, JUN.: Mr Daryl – does he owe much?
MOSES: Spheck he does, shir, or I shouldn't know him.
CHODD, JUN.: Here's half a sov. Give me your address?
MOSES: [*Gives card.*] "Orders executed with punctuality and despatch."
CHODD, JUN.: If I don't get into society now, I'm a Dutchman.

[*Enter* SIDNEY.]

SIDNEY: Here you are – ten fives – two two's – and a half-a-crown for yourself.

MOSES: Thank ye, shir. Good mornin', shir.

SIDNEY: Good morning.

MOSES: [to CHODD, JUN.] Good mornin', shir.

CHODD, JUN.: Such familiarity from the lower orders. [Exit MOSES AARON.] You take it coolly. [sitting L. of table]

SIDNEY: [sitting] I generally do.

CHODD, JUN.: [looking round] You've got lots of guns?

SIDNEY: I'm fond of shooting.

CHODD, JUN.: And rods?

SIDNEY: I'm fond of fishing.

CHODD, JUN.: And books?

SIDNEY: I like reading.

CHODD, JUN.: And whips?

SIDNEY: And riding.

CHODD, JUN.: Why you seem fond of everything?

SIDNEY: [looking at him] No; not everything.

[DODDLES enters, with card.]

SIDNEY: [reading] "Mr Sam. Stunner, P.R."

CHODD, JUN.: "P.R." What's P.R. mean? Afternoon's P.M.?

SIDNEY: Ask him in.

[Exit DODDLES.]

CHODD, JUN.: Is he an author? Or does P.R. mean Pre-Raphaelite?

SIDNEY: No; he's a prize-fighter – the Smiffel Lamb. [Enter the SMIFFEL LAMB.] How are you, Lamb?

LAMB: Bleating, sir, bleating – thankee kindly.

CHODD, JUN.: [aside to SIDNEY] Do prize-fighters usually carry cards?

SIDNEY: The march of intellect. Education of the masses – the Jemmy Masseys. Have a glass of sherry?

LAMB: Not a drain, thankee, sir.

CHODD, JUN.: [aside] Offers that brute sherry, and makes me drink beer.

LAMB: I've jist bin drinkin' with Lankey Joe, and the Dulwich Duffer, at Sam Shoulderblows. I'm a going into trainin' next week to fight Australian Harry, the Boundin' Kangaroo. I shall lick him, sir. I know I shall.

SIDNEY: I shall back you, Lamb.

LAMB: Thankee, Mr Daryl. I knew you would. I always does my best for my backers, and to keep up the honour of the science; the Fancy, sir, should keep square. [Looks at CHODD, JUN., hesitates, then walks to door, closes it, and walks sharply up to SIDNEY DARYL – CHODD, JUN., leaping up in alarm, and retiring to back – leaning on table and speaking close to SIDNEY DARYL's

ear.] I jist called in to give you the office, sir, as has always bin
so kind to me, not to *put* any tin on the mill between the
Choking Chummy and Slang's Novice. It's a cross, sir, a
reg'lar barney!

SIDNEY: Is it? Thank ye.

LAMB: That's wot I called for, sir; and now I'm hoff. [*Goes to door –
turning.*] Don't *putt* a mag on it, sir; Choking Chummy's a
cove as would sell his own mother; he once sold *me*, which is
wuss. Good-day, sir.

[*Exit* LAMB. CHODD, JUN., *reseats himself.*]

CHODD, JUN.: As I was saying, you know lots of people at clubs, and in
society.

SIDNEY: Yes.

CHODD, JUN.: Titles, and Honourables, and Captains, and that.

SIDNEY: Yes.

CHODD, JUN.: Tip-toppers. [*after a pause*] You're not well off?

SIDNEY: [*getting serious*] No.

CHODD, JUN.: I am. I've heaps of brass. Now I have what you haven't,
and I haven't what you have. You've got what I want, and I've
got what you want. That's logic, isn't it?

SIDNEY: [*gravely*] What of it?

CHODD, JUN.: This; suppose we exchange or barter. You help me to
get into the company of men with titles, and women with
titles; swells, you know, real 'uns, and all that.

SIDNEY: Yes.

CHODD, JUN.: And I'll write you a cheque for any reasonable sum you
like to name.

[SIDNEY *rises indignantly, at the same moment* LITTLE
MAUD *and* MRS CHURTON *enter.*]

LITTLE MAUD: [*running to* SIDNEY] Here I am, uncle; Mrs Churton
says I've been such a good girl.

SIDNEY: [*kissing her*] My darling. How d'ye do, Mrs Churton. [*to*
LITTLE MAUD] I've got a waggon, and a baa-lamb that squeaks,
for you. [*then to* CHODD, JUN.] Mr Chodd, I cannot entertain your very commercial proposition. My friends are my
friends; they are not marketable commodities. I regret that I
can be of no assistance to you. With your appearance,
manners, and cheque-book, you are sure to make a circle of
your own.

CHODD, JUN.: You refuse, then——

SIDNEY: Absolutely. Good morning.

CHODD, JUN.: Good morning [*aside*] And if I don't have my knife into
you, my name's not John Chodd, Jun.

[*Exeunt* SIDNEY, LITTLE MAUD, *and* MRS CHURTON, *door* R. CHODD, JUN., *door* L.]

SCENE II – *The interior of a Square at the West End. Weeping ash over a rustic chair, trees, shrubs, walks, rails, gates, &c.; houses at back. Time evening – effect of setting sun in windows of houses; lights in some of the windows, &c.; street lamps.* MAUD *discovered in rustic chair reading; street band heard playing in the distance.*

MAUD: I can't see to read any more. Heigho! how lonely it is! and that band makes me so melancholy – sometimes music makes me feel – [*rising*] Heigho! I suppose I shall see nobody to-night; I must go home. [*Starts.*] Oh! [SIDNEY *appears at gate.*] I think I can see to read a few more lines.

[*She sits again, and takes book.*]

SIDNEY: [*feeling pockets*] Confound it! I've left the key at home. [*Tries gate.*] How shall I get in! [*looking over rails*] I'll try the other.

[*He goes round at back to opposite gate.*]

MAUD: Why, he's going! He doesn't know I'm here. [*Rises, calling.*] Sid——No I won't, the idea of his – [*Sees* SIDNEY *at gate.*] Ah!

[*She gives a sigh of relief, reseats herself and reads.*]

SIDNEY: [*at gate*] Shut too! [*trying gate*] Provoking! What shall I—— [*Sees* NURSEMAID *approaching with* CHILD – *drops his hat into square.*] Will you kindly open this? I've forgotten my key. [GIRL *opens gate.*] Thanks! [SIDNEY *enters square;* GIRL *and* CHILD *go out at gate;* LIFE GUARDSMAN *enters, speaks to* GIRL; *they exeunt.* SIDNEY *sighs on seeing* MAUD.] There she is! [*Seats himself by* MAUD.] Maud!

MAUD: [*starting*] Oh! is that you? Who would have thought of seeing you here?

SIDNEY: Oh, come – don't I know that you walk here after dinner? and all day long I've been wishing it was half-past eight.

MAUD: [*coquetting*] I wonder, now, how often you've said that, this last week.

SIDNEY: Don't pretend to doubt me, that's unworthy of you. [*a pause*] Maud!

MAUD: Yes.

SIDNEY: Are you not going to speak?

MAUD: [*dreamily*] I don't know what to say.

SIDNEY: That's just my case. When I'm away from you, I feel I could talk to you for hours; but when I'm with you, somehow or other, it seems all to go away. [*getting closer to her, and taking her hand*] It is such happiness to be with you, that it makes me forget everything else. [*Takes off his gloves, and puts them on seat.*] Ever since I was that high, in the jolly old days down at Springmead, my greatest pleasure has been to be near you. [*Looks at watch.*] Twenty to nine. When must you return?

MAUD: At nine.

SIDNEY: Twenty minutes. How's your aunt?

MAUD: As cross as ever.

SIDNEY: And Lord Ptarmigant?

MAUD: As usual – asleep.

SIDNEY: Dear old man! how he does doze his time away. [*another pause*] Anything else to tell me?

MAUD: We had such a stupid dinner; such odd people.

SIDNEY: Who?

MAUD: Two men by the name of Chodd.

SIDNEY: [*uneasily*] Chodd!

MAUD: Isn't it a funny name? – Chodd.

SIDNEY: Yes, it's a Chodd name – I mean an odd name. Where were they picked up?

MAUD: I don't know. Aunty says they are both very rich.

SIDNEY: [*uneasily*] She thinks of nothing but money. [*Looks at watch.*] Fifteen to nine [*Stage has grown gradually dark.*] Maud?

MAUD: [*in a whisper*] Yes.

SIDNEY: If I were rich – if you were rich – if we were rich.

MAUD: [*drawing closer to him*] Sidney!

SIDNEY: As it is, I almost feel it's a crime to love you.

MAUD: Oh, Sidney!

SIDNEY: You who might make such a splendid marriage.

MAUD: If you had – money – I couldn't care for you any more than I do now.

SIDNEY: My darling! [*Looks at watch.*] Ten minutes. I know you wouldn't. Sometimes I feel mad about you – mad when I know you are out a smiling upon others – and – and waltzing.

MAUD: I can't help waltzing when I'm asked.

SIDNEY: No, dear, no; but when I fancy you are spinning round with another's arm about your waist. [*his arm round her waist*] Oh! – I feel——

MAUD: Why, Sidney [*smiling*] You are jealous!

SIDNEY: Yes, I am.

MAUD: Can't you trust me?

SIDNEY: Implicitly. But I like to be with you all the same.

MAUD: [*whispering*] So do I with you.

SIDNEY: My love! [*Kisses her, and looks at watch.*] Five minutes.

MAUD: Time to go?

SIDNEY: No! [MAUD, *in taking out her handkerchief, takes out a knot of ribbon.*] What's that?

MAUD: Sòme trimmings I'm making for our fancy fair.

SIDNEY: What colour is it. Scarlet?

MAUD: Magenta.

SIDNEY: Give it to me?

MAUD: What nonsense.

SIDNEY: Won't you?

MAUD: I've brought something else.

SIDNEY: For me?

MAUD: Yes.

SIDNEY: What?

MAUD: These. [*producing a small case, which* SIDNEY *opens*]

SIDNEY: Sleeve links!

MAUD: Now, which will you have, the links or the ribbon?

SIDNEY: [*after reflection*] Both.

MAUD: You avaricious creature!

SIDNEY: [*putting the ribbons near his heart*] It's not in the power of words to tell you how I love you. Do you care for me enough to trust your future with me? Will you be mine?

MAUD: Sidney?

SIDNEY: Mine, and none other's; no matter how brilliant the offer – how dazzling the position?

MAUD: [*in a whisper – leaning towards him*] Yours and yours only!

[*Clock strikes nine.*]

SIDNEY: [*with watch*] Nine! Why doesn't time stop, and Big Ben refuse to toll the hour?

[LADY *and* LORD PTARMIGANT *appear and open gate.*]

MAUD: [*frightened*] My aunt!

[SIDNEY *gets to back, round square.* LORD *and* LADY PTARMIGANT *advance.*]

LADY P: [*a very grand acid old lady*] Maud!

MAUD: Aunty, I was just coming away.

LADY P: No one in the square? Quite improper to be here alone. Ferdinand!

LORD P: [*a little old gentleman*] My love!

LADY P: What is the time?

LORD P: Don't know – watch stopped – tired of going, I suppose, like me.

LADY P: [*sitting on chair – throws down the gloves left by* SIDNEY *with her dress.*] What's that? [*picking them up*] Gloves?

MAUD: [*frightened*] Mine, aunty!

LADY P: Yours? You've got yours on! [*looking at them*] These are
Sidney Daryl's. I know his size – seven-and-a-half. I see why
you are so fond of walking in the square; for shame! [*turning to*
SIDNEY, *who has just got the gate open, and is going out*] Sidney!
[*fiercely*] I see you! There is no occasion to try and sneak away.
Come here. [SIDNEY *advances*. *With ironical politeness*] You
have left your gloves.

> [*All are standing except* LORD PTARMIGANT, *who lies at
> full length on chair and goes to sleep.*]

SIDNEY: [*confused*] Thank you, Lady Ptarm——

LADY P: You two fools have been making love. I've long suspected it.
I'm shocked with both of you; a penniless scribbler, and a
dependent orphan, without a shilling or an expectation. Do
you [*to* SIDNEY] wish to drag my niece, born and bred a lady, to
a back parlour, and bread and cheese? Or do you [*to* MAUD]
wish to marry a shabby writer, who can neither feed himself
nor you? I can leave you nothing, for I am as well bred a
pauper as yourselves. [*to* MAUD] To keep appointments in a
public square! your conduct is disgraceful – worse – it is
unladylike; and yours [*to* SIDNEY], is dishonourable, and
unworthy, to fill the head of a foolish girl with sentiment and
rubbish. [*loudly*] Ferdinand!

LORD P: [*waking up*] Yes, dear.

LADY P: Do keep awake; the Chodds will be here directly; they are to
walk home with us, and I request you to make yourself
agreeable to them.

LORD P: Such canaille.

LADY P: Such cash!

LORD P: Such cads.

LADY P: Such cash! [*authoritatively*] Pray, Ferdinand, don't argue.

LORD P: I never do. [*He goes to sleep again.*]

LADY P: I wish for no *esclandre*. Let us have no discussion in the
square. Mr Daryl, I shall be sorry if you compel me to forbid
you my house. I have other views for Miss Hetherington.

> [SIDNEY *bows. The two* CHODDS, *in evening dress,
> appear at gate; they enter.*]

LADY P: My dear Mr Chodd, Maud has been so impatient. [*The*
CHODDS *do not see* SIDNEY – *to* CHODD, SEN.] I shall take your
arm, Mr Chodd. [*very sweetly*] Maud, dear, Mr John will
escort you.

> [*Street band heard playing "Fra Poco" in distance;*
> MAUD *takes* CHODD, JUN.'s *arm; the two couples go off;*

as MAUD *turns, she looks an adieu at* SIDNEY, *who waves the bunch of ribbon, and sits down on chair in a reverie, not perceiving* LORD PTARMIGANT'S *legs;* LORD PTARMIGANT *jumps up with pain;* SIDNEY *apologises. Curtain quick.*]

END OF ACT I

ACT II

SCENE I – *Parlour at the "Owl's Roost" public-house. Cushioned seats all round the apartment; gas lighted over tables; splint boxes, pipes, newspapers, &c., on table; writing materials on* R. *table [near door]; gong bell on* L. *table; door of entrance; clock above door [hands set to half-past nine]; hat pegs and hats on walls. In the chair at* L. *table head is discovered* O'SULLIVAN; *also, in the following order,* MACUSQUEBAUGH, AUTHOR, *and* DR MAKVICZ; *also at* R. *table,* TRODNON [*at head*], SHAMHEART, BRADLEY, SCARGIL; *the* REPORTER *of "Belgravian Banner" is sitting outside the* R. *table, near the head, and with his back turned to it, smoking a cigar. The* CHARACTERS *are all discovered drinking and smoking, some reading, some with their hats on.*

OMNES: Bravo! Hear, hear! Bravo!

O'SULLIVAN: [*on his legs, a glass in one hand, and terminating a speech, in Irish accent*] It is, therefore, gintlemen, with the most superlative felicitee, the most fraternal convivialitee, the warmest congenialitee, the most burning friendship, and ardent admiration, that I propose his health!

OMNES: Hear, hear! &c.

O'SULLIVAN: He is a man, in the words of the divine bard——

TRODNON: [*in sepulchral voice*] Hear! hear!

O'SULLIVAN: Who, in "suffering everything, has suffered nothing."

TRODNON: Hear, hear!

O'SULLIVAN: I have known him when, in the days of his prosperitee, he rowled down to the House of Commons in his carriage.

MACUSQUEBAUGH: 'Twasn't his own – 'twas a job!

OMNES: Silence! Chair! Order!

O'SULLIVAN: I have known him when his last copper, and his last glass of punch, has been shared with the frind of his heart!

OMNES: Hear, hear!

O'SULLIVAN: And it is with feelings of no small pride that I inform ye that that frind of his heart was the humble individual who has now the honour to address ye!

OMNES: Hear, hear! &c.

O'SULLIVAN: But, prizeman at Trinity, mimber of the bar, sinator, classical scholar, or frind, Desmond MacUsquebaugh has always been the same – a gintleman and a scholar; and that highest type of that glorious union – an Irish gintleman and scholar. Gintlemen, I drink his health – Desmond, my long loved frind, bless ye! [*All rise solemnly and drink –* "Mr MacUsquebaugh."] Gintlemen, my frind, Mr MacUsquebaugh will respond.

OMNES: Hear, hear!

[*Enter* WAITER, *with glasses, tobacco, &c., and receives*

orders – changes O'SULLIVAN'S *glass and exits. Enter*
TOM STYLUS *and* CHODD, JUN. TOM *has a greatcoat on,*
over an evening dress.]

CHODD, JUN.: Thank you; no, not anything.

TOM: Just a wet – an outrider – or advanced guard, to prepare the way
for the champagne.

CHODD, JUN.: No.

[*As soon as the sitters see* TOM STYLUS *they give him a*
friendly nod, looking inquiringly at CHODD, *and whis-*
per to each other.]

TOM: You'd better. They are men worth knowing. [*pointing them out*]
That is the celebrated Olinthus O'Sullivan, Doctor of Civil
Laws.

[O'SULLIVAN *is at this moment reaching to the gaslight*
to light his pipe.]

CHODD, JUN.: The gent with the long pipe?

TOM: Yes; one of the finest classical scholars in the world; might have
sat upon the woolsack if he'd chosen, but he didn't.
[O'SULLIVAN *is now tossing with* MACUSQUEBAUGH.] That is the
famous Desmond MacUsquebaugh, late M.P. for
Killcrackskullcoddy, county Galway, a great patriot and
orator; might have been Chancellor of the Exchequer if he'd
chosen, but he didn't. [SCARGIL *reaches to the gaslight to light*
his pipe.] That's Bill Bradley [*pointing to* BRADLEY, *who is*
reading paper with double eye-glass], author of the famous
romance of "Time and Opportunity"; ran through ten editions. He got two thousand pounds for it, which was his ruin.

CHODD, JUN.: How was he ruined by getting two thousand pounds?

TOM: He's never done anything since. We call him "One book
Bradley." That gentleman fast asleep – [*looking towards*
AUTHOR, *at table,* L.] has made the fortune of three publishers,
and the buttoned-up one with the shirt front of beard is Herr
Makvicz, the great United German. Dr Scargil, there, discovered the mensuration of the motive power of the cerebral
organs.

[SCARGIL *takes a pinch of snuff from a box on the table.*]

CHODD, JUN.: What's that?

TOM: How many million miles per minute thought can travel. He
might have made his fortune if he'd chosen.

CHODD, JUN.: But he didn't. Who is that mild-looking party, with the
pink complexion, and the white hair! [*looking towards*
SHAMHEART]

TOM: Sam Shamheart, the professional philanthropist. He makes it his business and profit to love the whole human race. [SHAMHEART *puffs a huge cloud of smoke from his pipe.*] Smoke, sir; all smoke. A superficial observer would consider him only a pleasant oily humbug, but I, having known him two and twenty years, feel qualified to pronounce him one of the biggest villains untransported.

CHODD, JUN.: And that man asleep at the end of the table.

TOM: Trodnon, the eminent tragedian.

[TRODNON *raises himself from the table, yawns, stretches himself, and again drops head on table.*]

CHODD, JUN.: I never heard of him.

TOM: Nor anybody else. But he's a confirmed tippler, and here we consider drunkenness an infallible sign of genius – we make that a rule.

CHODD, JUN.: But if they are all such great men, why didn't they make money by their talents?

TOM: Make money! They'd scorn it! They wouldn't do it – that's another rule. That gentleman there [*looking towards a very seedy man with eye-glass in his eye*] does the evening parties on the "Belgravian Banner."

CHODD, JUN.: [*with interest*] Does he? Will he put my name among the fashionables to-night?

TOM: Yes.

CHODD, JUN.: And that we may know who's there and everything about it – you're going with me?

TOM: Yes, I'm going into *society;* thanks to your getting me the invitation. I can dress up an account, not a mere list of names, but a picturesque report of the soirée, and show under what brilliant auspices you entered the beau-monde.

CHODD, JUN.: Beau-monde. What's that?

TOM: [*chaffing him*] Every man is called a cockney who is born within the sound of the beau-monde.

CHODD, JUN.: [*not seeing it*] Oh! Order me two hundred copies of the "Belgravian"—— What's its name?

TOM: "Banner."

CHODD, JUN.: The day my name's in it – and put me down as a regular subscriber. I like to encourage high-class literature. By the way, shall I ask the man what he'll take to drink?

TOM: No, no.

CHODD, JUN.: I'll pay for it. I'll stand, you know. [*going to him,* TOM *stops him.*]

TOM: No, no – he don't know you, and he'd be offended.

CHODD, JUN.: But I suppose all these chaps are plaguy poor?

TOM: Yes, they're poor; but they are *gent*lemen.

CHODD, JUN.: [*grinning*] I like that notion – a *poor* gentleman – it tickles me.

TOM: Metallic snob!

CHODD, JUN.: I'm off now. You'll come to my rooms and we'll go together in the brougham. I want to introduce you to my friends, Lady Ptarmigant and Lord Ptarmigant?

TOM: I must wait here for a proof I expect from the office.

CHODD, JUN.: How long shall you be?

TOM: [*looking at clock*] An hour.

CHODD, JUN.: Don't be later.

> [*Exit* CHODD, JUN. *– the* REPORTER *rises, gets paper from* L. *table, and shows it to* SHAMHEART, *sitting next him.*]

O'SULLIVAN: Sit down, Tommy, my dear boy. Gintlemen, Mr. Desmond MacUsquebaugh will respond.

> [*Tapping with hammer. Enter* WAITER, *and gives* BRADLEY *a glass of grog.*]

MACUSQUEBAUGH: [*rising*] Gintlemen.

> [TOM *taking his coat off, shows evening dress.*]

TOM: A go of whisky.

WAITER: Scotch or Irish?

TOM: Irish.

> [*Exit* WAITER. *All are astonished at* TOM'S *costume – they cry* "By Jove! there's a swell," &c.]

O'SULLIVAN: Why, Tom, my dear friend – are ye going to be married to-night, that ye're got up so gorgeously?

MACUSQUEBAUGH: Tom, you're handsome as an angel.

O'SULLIVAN: Or a duke's footman. Gintlemen, rise and salute our illustrious brother.

> [*All rise and make* TOM *mock bows.*]

BRADLEY: The gods preserve you, noble sir.

SHAMHEART: May the bill of your sublime highness's washer-woman be never the less.

MACUSQUEBAUGH: And may it be paid.

> [*A general laugh.*]

O'SULLIVAN: Have you come into a fortune?

DR MAKVICZ: Or married a widow?

SHAMHEART: Or buried a relation? [*A general laugh.*] By my soul, Tom, you look an honour to humanity!

O'SULLIVAN: And your laundress.

[*A general laugh.*]

BRADLEY: Gentlemen, Mr Stylus's health and shirt front.

[*A general laugh – all drink and sit.*]

TOM: Bless ye, my people, bless ye!

[*He sits, and takes out short pipe and smokes.*]

O'SULLIVAN: Gintlemen [*rising*] My friend, Mr MacUsquebaugh, will respond.

OMNES: Hear, hear!

MACUSQUEBAUGH: [*rising*] Gintlemen——

[*Enter* SIDNEY, *in evening dress and wrapper. Enter* WAITER *with* TOM'S *grog.*]

OMNES: Hallo, Daryl!

SIDNEY: How are ye, boys? Doctor, how goes it? [*shaking hands*] Mac. How d'ye do, O'Sullivan? Tom, I want to speak to you.

O'SULLIVAN: Ah, Tom, this is the real metal – the genuine thing; compared to him you are a sort of Whitechapel would-if-I-could-be. [*to* SIDNEY] Sit down, my gorgeous one, and drink with me.

SIDNEY: No, thanks.

[SIDNEY *and* TOM *sit at* R. *table head.*]

O'SULLIVAN: Waiter, take Mr Daryl's orders.

SIDNEY: Brandy cold.

[*Exit* WAITER.]

MACUSQUEBAUGH: Take off your wrap, rascal, and show your fine feathers.

SIDNEY: No; I'm going out, and I shall smoke my coat.

[TOM *extinguishing his pipe, and puts it in his dress-coat pocket, then puts on his greatcoat with great solemnity.*]

O'SULLIVAN: Going?

TOM: No.

O'SULLIVAN: Got the rheumatism?

TOM: No; but I shall smoke my coat.

[*General laugh. Enter* WAITER. *He gives glass of brandy and water to* SIDNEY, *and glass of grog to* SHAMHEART.]

O'SULLIVAN: What news, Daryl?

SIDNEY: None, except that the Ministry is to be defeated.

[O'SULLIVAN *pays* WAITER.]

OMNES: No!

SIDNEY: I say, yes. They're whipping up everything to vote against Thunder's motion. Thunder is sure of a majority, and out they go. Capital brandy. [*coming forward*] Tom! [TOM *rises; they come down stage.*] I am off to a soirée.

TOM: [*aside*] So am I; but I won't tell him.

SIDNEY: I find I've nothing in my portmonnaie but notes. I want a trifle for a cab. Lend me five shillings.

TOM: I haven't got it, but I can get it for you.

SIDNEY: There's a good fellow, do.

[*He returns to seat.*]

TOM: [*to* MACUSQUEBAUGH, *after looking round*] Mac, [*whispering*] lend me five bob.

MACUSQUEBAUGH: My dear boy, I haven't got so much.

TOM: Then don't lend it.

MACUSQUEBAUGH: But I'll get it for you. [*to* BRADLEY – *whispers*] Bradley lend me five shillings.

BRADLEY: I haven't it about me, but I'll get it for you. [*to* O'SULLIVAN – *whispers*] O'Sullivan, lend me five shillings.

O'SULLIVAN: I haven't got it, but I'll get it for you. [*to* SCARGIL – *whispers*] Scargil, lend me five shillings.

SCARGIL: I haven't got it, but I'll get it for you. [*to* MAKVICZ – *whispers*] Doctor, lend me five shillings.

DR MAKVICZ: I am waiting for change vor a zovern; I'll give it you when de waiter brings to me.

SCARGIL: All right! [*to* O'SULLIVAN] All right!

O'SULLIVAN: All right! [*to* BRADLEY] All right!

BRADLEY: All right! [*to* MACUSQUEBAUGH] All right!

MACUSQUEBAUGH: All right! [*to* TOM] All right!

TOM: [*to* SIDNEY] All right!

O'SULLIVAN: [*tapping*] Gentlemen, my friend, Mr MacUsquebaugh will respond to the toast that——

MACUSQUEBAUGH: [*rising*] Gintlemen——

SIDNEY: Oh, cut the speechifying, I hate it! you ancients are so fond of spouting; let's be jolly, I've only a few minutes more.

BRADLEY: Daryl, sing us "Cock-a-doodle-doo."

SIDNEY: I only know the first two verses.

TOM: I know the rest.

[*Enter* WAITER, *gives glass of grog to* MAKVICZ.]

SIDNEY: Then here goes. Waiter, shut the door, and don't open it till I've done. Now then, ready.

[*Exit* WAITER. O'SULLIVAN *taps.*]

SIDNEY: [*giving out*] Political:——

[*sings*] When Ministers in fear and doubt,
That they should be from place kicked out,
Get up 'gainst time and sense to spout
A long dull evening through,
What mean they then by party clique,
Mob orators and factions weak?
'Tis only would they truth then speak
But cock-a-doodle-doo!
Cock-a-doodle, cock-a-doodle, cock-a-doodle-doo.

CHORUS: [*gravely and solemnly shaking their heads*] Cock-a-doodle, &c.

SIDNEY: [*speaking*] Commercial:—

[*sings*] When companies, whose stock of cash
Directors spend to cut a dash,
Are formed to advertise and smash,
And bankruptcy go through.
When tradesfolks live in regal state,
The goods they sell adulterate,
And puff in print, why what's their prate
But cock-a-doodle-doo?
Cock-a-doodle, cock-a-doodle, &c.

CHORUS: [*as before*] Cock-a-doodle, &c.

[*Enter* WAITER.]

O'SULLIVAN: How dare you come in and interrupt the harmony!
WAITER: Beg pardon, sir, but there's somebody says as he must see Mr Stylus.
TOM: Is he a devil?
WAITER: No, sir, he's a juvenile.

[*A general laugh.*]

TOM: Send in some whisky – Irish – and the devil.
WAITER: Hot, sir?

[*A general laugh.* TOM *nods to* WAITER, *who exits.*]

SIDNEY: Why can't you see your proofs at the office?
TOM: I'm in full fig, and can't stew in that atmosphere of steam and copperas.

[*Enter* PRINTER'S BOY; *he goes up to* TOM. *Enter* WAITER, *with tray, hot-water jug, &c.; he gives change in silver to* MAKVICZ, *who crosses to* SCARGIL. WAITER *puts hot-water jug and whisky before* TOM, *and exits.*]

DR MAKVICZ: Here! [*giving two half-crowns to* SCARGIL] Scargil!

SCARGIL: [*crossing in same manner to* O'SULLIVAN] Here, O'Sullivan.

O'SULLIVAN: [*crossing to* BRADLEY] Here, Bradley.

BRADLEY: [*crossing to* MACUSQUEBAUGH] Here, Mac.

MACUSQUEBAUGH: [*crossing to* TOM] Here, Tom.

BOY: [*to* TOM] Please, sir, Mr Duval said would you add this to it? [*giving* TOM *a proof slip*]

TOM: All right – wait outside – I'll bring it to you.

[*Exit* BOY.]

TOM: [*Draws writing pad towards him, takes his grog, and is about to pour hot water from pewter jug into it, when he burns his fingers, starts up and dances.*] Confound it!

OMNES: What's the matter?

TOM: I've scalded my fingers with the hot water.

SIDNEY: [*taking up pen*] Here, I'll correct it for you.

TOM: Thank you.

O'SULLIVAN: Gintlemen, proceed with the harmony. Mr Stylus——

TOM: One minute. [*to* SIDNEY] Just add this to it. [SIDNEY *sits down to write.* TOM *standing over him, reading slip.*] "Fashionable Intelligence. – We hear a marriage is on the tapis between Mr John Chodd, Junior, son of the celebrated millionaire, and Miss Maud Hetherington, daughter of the late Colonel Hetherington."

[SIDNEY *starts.*]

TOM: What's the matter?

SIDNEY: Nothing!

[*He goes on writing –* O'SULLIVAN *taps hammer.*]

TOM: [*speaking*] Amatory:——

[*sings*] When woman, lovely woman sighs,
  You praise her form, her hair, her eyes;
  Would link your heart by tend'rest ties,
   And vow your vows are true.
  She answers tenderly and low,
  Though from her lips the words that flow,
  So softly sweet, are nought we know
   But cock-a-doodle-doo!
     &c., &c., &c.

[TOM *throws the five shillings to* SIDNEY, *which rattle on the table.* SIDNEY *gives him back the proof; his face is deadly pale; as his head falls on the table the Chorus is singing,* "Cock-a-doodle-doo," &c. – *closed in.*]

SCENE II – *A retiring room at* SIR FARINTOSH FADILEAF'S [*2nd grooves*];
*large archway or alcove, with curtains drawn or doors leading to
ballroom; small arch or alcove, leading to supper-room, with drawn
curtain; centre opening curtains drawn; the room is decorated for a ball;
candelabra, flowers, &c.**

"LADY P: [*without*] Very pretty – very pretty indeed, Sir Farintosh; all
very nice."

> [LADY PTARMIGANT *enters with* "SIR FARINTOSH,"
> LORD PTARMIGANT, *and* MAUD, *all in evening dress.*]

"SIR F: [*an old beau*] So kind of you, Cousin Ptarmigant, to take pity
on a poor old widower, who has no womankind to receive for
him, and all that."
"LADY P: Not at all; I am only too glad to be useful."
LORD P: [*speaking off*] Bring chairs.
LADY P: Ferdinand, you can't want to go to sleep again!
LORD P: I know I can't, but I do.

> [SERVANT *brings two chairs and a small table.*]

LADY P: Besides I don't want chairs here, young men get lolling about,
and then they don't dance. [LORD PTARMIGANT *sits and closes his
eyes*] "Farintosh, [*Knocks heard.*] the arrivals are beginning."
"SIR F: But, Lady Ptarmigant, if——"
"LADY P: Remember that the old Dowager Countess of
McSwillumore has plenty of whisky toddy in a green glass, to
make believe hock."
"SIR F: But if——"
LADY P: "Now go. Oh dear me! [*Almost forces* SIR FARINTOSH *off.*"]
Now, Maud, one word with you; you have been in disgrace all
this last week about that writing fellow?
MAUD: [*indignant*] What writing fellow?
LADY P: Don't echo me if you please. You know who I mean – Daryl!
MAUD: Mr Daryl is a relation of your ladyship's – the son of the late
Sir Percy Daryl, and brother of the present Baronet.
LADY P: And when the present Baronet, that precious Percy, squan-
dered everything at the gaming table, dipped the estates, and
ruined himself, Sidney gave up the money left him by his
mother, to reinstate a dissolute beggared brother! I don't
forget that.
MAUD: [*with exultation*] I do not forget it, I never shall. To give up all
his fortune, to ruin his bright prospects to preserve his
brother, and his brother's wife and children, to keep unsullied
the honour of his name, was an act——

---

* The lines between inverted commas can be omitted.

LADY P: Of a noodle, and now he hasn't a penny save what he gets by scribbling – a pretty pass for a man of family to come to. You are my niece, and it is my solemn duty to get you married if I can. Don't thwart me, and I will. Leave sentiment to servant wenches who sweetheart the policemen; it's unworthy of a lady. I've a man in my eye – a rich one – young Chodd.

MAUD: [*with repugnance*] Such a commonplace person.

LADY P: With a very uncommonplace purse. He will have eighteen thousand a year. I have desired him pay you court, and I desire you to receive it.

MAUD: He is so vulgar.

LADY P: He is so rich. When he is your husband put him in a back study, and don't show him.

MAUD: But I detest him.

LADY P: What on earth has that to do with it? You wouldn't love a man before you were married to him, would you? Where are your principles? Ask my lord how I treated him before our marriage. [*hitting* LORD PTARMIGANT *with her fan*] Ferdinand!

LORD P: [*awakening*] My love!

LADY P: Do keep awake.

LORD P: 'Pon my word you were making such a noise I thought I was in the House of Commons. [*with fond regret*] I used to be allowed to sleep so comfortably there.

LADY P: Are you not of opinion that a match between Mr Chodd and Maud would be most desirable?

LORD P: [*looking at* LADY PTARMIGANT] Am I not of opinion – my opinion – what is my opinion?

LADY P: [*hitting him with fan*] Yes, of course.

LORD P: Yes – of course – my opinion is yes, of course. [*aside, crossing with chair*] Just as it used to be in the House. I always roused in time to vote as I was told to.

MAUD: But, uncle, one can't purchase happiness at shops in packets, like bon-bons. A thousand yards of lace cost so much, they can be got at the milliner's; but an hour of home or repose can only be had for love. Mere wealth——

LORD P: My dear, wealth, if it does not bring happiness, brings the best imitation of it procurable for money. There are two things – wealth and poverty. The former makes the world a place to live in; the latter a place to – go to sleep in – as I do. [*Leans back in chair and dozes.*]

["*Enter* SIR FARINTOSH, COLONEL BROWSER, *and* LORD CLOUDWRAYS."]

"SIR F: Have you heard the news? The division is to come off to-night. Many men won't be able to come. I must be off to vote. If the Ministry go out——"

"COLONEL B: They won't go out – there'll be a dissolution!"

"SIR F: And I shall have to go down to be re-elected. Cloudwrays, will
    you come and vote?"

"LORD C: [*languidly*] No."

"SIR F: Why not?"

"LORD C: I'm dying for a weed."

"SIR F: You can smoke in the smoking-room!"

"LORD C: So I can – that didn't occur to me!"

"SIR F: Ptarmigant, cousin, you do the honours for me. My country
    calls, you know, and all that. Come on, Cloudwrays; how slow
    you are. Hi, tobacco!"

> ["CLOUDWRAYS *rouses himself. Exeunt* SIR FARINTOSH
> *and* LORD CLOUDWRAYS. LORD PTARMIGANT *dozes.*"]

"COLONEL B: [*who has been talking to* LADY PTARMIGANT, *turns to* LORD
    PTARMIGANT] As I was saying to her ladyship——"

"LADY P: Ferdinand, do wake up!"

"LORD P: Hear, hear! [*waking*] My dear!"

> [*Enter* SERVANT.]

SERVANT: Mr Chodd, Mr John Chodd, and Mr Stylus.

> [*Enter* CHODD, JUN., CHODD, SEN. *and* TOM. *Exit*
> SERVANT.]

LADY P: My dear Mr Chodd, how late you are! Maud dear, here is Mr
    Chodd. Do you know we were going to scold you, you naughty
    men!

CHODD, SEN.: [*astonished, aside*] Naughty men! Johnny, her ladyship
    says we're naughty men; we've done something wrong!

CHODD, JUN.: No, no – it's only her ladyship's patrician fun. Don't call
    me Johnny. I'm sure I hurried here on wings of – [*crossing,
    falls over* LORD PTARMIGANT'S *feet, who rises and turns his chair
    the reverse way;* CHODD *seeing* MAUD, *repellant*] – a brougham
    and pair. Lady Ptarmigant, let me introduce a friend of mine.
    Lady Ptarmigant – Mr Stylus, whom I took the liberty of——

LADY P: Charmed to see any friend of yours!

> [TOM *advances from back, abashed; as he is backing
> and bowing he falls over* LORD PTARMIGANT'S *legs;*
> LORD PTARMIGANT *rises with a look of annoyance; they
> bow;* LORD PTARMIGANT *again turns chair and sits.*]

"LADY P: Mr Chodd, take me to the ballroom. [CHODD, SEN., *offers his
    arm.*] You will look after Maud, I'm sure. [*to* CHODD, JUN., *who
    smilingly offers his arm to* MAUD, *who, with a suppressed look of
    disgust, takes it*] Mr Si-len-us."

"TOM: Stylus – ma'am – my lady."

"LADY P: Stylus – pardon me – will you be kind enough to keep my lord awake? [*significantly*] Maud! Now, dear Mr Chodd."

"CHODD, JUN.: Guv!"

> ["*Exeunt* LADY PTARMIGANT, MAUD, *and the* CHODDS."]

"TOM: [*aside*] These are two funny old swells!"

"COLONEL B: Odd looking fellow. [*to* TOM] Nice place this!"

"TOM: Very."

"COLONEL B: And charming man, Fadileaf."

"TOM: Very. I don't know him, but I should say he must be very jolly."

"COLONEL B: [*laughing*] Bravo! Why you're a wit!"

"TOM: Yes! [*aside*] What does he mean?"

"COLONEL B: [*offering box*] Snuff! Who's to win the Leger? Diadeste?"

"TOM: I don't know – not in my department."

"COLONEL B: [*laughing*] Very good."

"TOM: [*innocently*] What is?"

"COLONEL B: You are. Do you play whist?"

"TOM: Yes; cribbage, and all fours, likewise."

"COLONEL B: We'll find another man, and make up a rubber."

"TOM: [*pointing to* LORD PTARMIGANT *asleep*] He'll do for dummy."

"COLONEL B: [*laughing*] Capital!"

"TOM: What a queer fellow this is – he laughs at everything I say."

[*Dance music.*]

"COLONEL B: They've begun."

"TOM: [*waking up* LORD PTARMIGANT] My lady said I was to keep you awake."

"LORD P: Thank you."

"COLONEL B: Come and have a rubber! Let's go and look up Chedbury."

"LORD P: Yes."

"COLONEL B: [*to* TOM] You'll find us in the card-room."

> ["*Exeunt* LORD PTARMIGANT *and* COLONEL BROWSER."]

[NOTE. – *If preceding lines be omitted, the following sentence and business.*]

LADY P: Ferdinand! [*going up to* LORD PTARMIGANT, *who awakes*] Do rouse yourself, and follow me to the ballroom.

> [*Exeunt all, but* TOM. LORD PTARMIGANT *returns, and drags chair off after him.*]

TOM: Here I am in society, and I think society is rather slow; it's much

jollier at the "Owl," and there's more to drink. If it were not
wicked to say it, how I should enjoy a glass of gin and water!

[*Enter* LADY PTARMIGANT.]

LADY P: Mr Si-len-us!

TOM: [*abashed*] Stylus, ma'am – my lady!

LADY P: Stylus! I beg pardon. You're all alone.

TOM: With the exception of your ladyship!

LADY P: All the members have gone down to the House to vote, and we
are dreadfully in want of men – I mean dancers! You dance, of
course?

TOM: [*abashed*] Oh! of course – I——

LADY P: As it is Leap-year, I may claim the privilege of asking you to
see me through a quadrille!

TOM: [*frightened*] My lady! I——

LADY P: [*aside*] He's a friend of the Chodds, and it will please them.
Come then. [*She takes his arm; sniffing*] Dear me! What a
dreadful smell of tobacco!

TOM: [*awfully self-conscious – sniffing*] Is there?

LADY P: [*sniffing*] Some fellow must have been smoking.

TOM: [*sniffing*] I think some fellow must, or some fellow must have
been where some other fellows have been smoking. [*aside*] It's
that beastly parlour at the "Owl." [*In taking out his pocket-
handkerchief his pipe falls on floor.*]

LADY P: What's that?*

TOM: [*in torture*] What's what? [*turning about and looking through eye-
glass at the air*]

LADY P: [*pointing*] That!

TOM: [*as if in doubt*] I rather think – it – is – a pipe!

LADY P: I'm sure of it. You'll join me in the ballroom.

TOM: Instantly, your ladyship. [*Exit* LADY PTARMIGANT. *Looking at
pipe, he picks it up.*] If ever I bring you into society again——
[*Drops it.*] Waiter! [*Enter* PAGE.] Somebody's dropped something. Remove the Whatsoname. [*Quadrille music in ballroom:*
PAGE *goes off and returns with tray and sugar tongs, with which he
picks up pipe with an air of ineffable disgust and goes off.*] Now to
spin round the old woman in the mazy waltz. [*Splits kid gloves
in drawing them on.*] There goes one-and-nine.

[*Exit* TOM. *Enter* SIDNEY. *He is pale and excited; one of
the gold links of his wrist-band is unfastened.*]

SIDNEY: I have seen her – she was smiling – dancing, but not with him.
She looked so bright and happy. I won't think of her. How

---

* This incident is taken from M. Emile Augier's admirable comedy of "Les
Effrontés." – T. W. R.

quiet it is here: so different to that hot room, with the crowd of fools and coquettes whirling round each other. I like to be alone – alone! I am now thoroughly – and to think it was but a week ago – one little week – I'll forget her – forget, and hate her. Hate her – Oh, Maud, Maud, till now, I never knew how much I loved you; loved you – loved you – gone; shattered; shivered; and for whom? For one of my own birth? For one of my own rank? No! for a common clown, who – confound this link – but he is rich – and – it won't hold [*trying to fasten it – his fingers trembling*] I've heard it all – always with her, at the Opera and the Park, attentive and obedient – and she accepts him. My head aches. [*louder*] I'll try a glass of champagne.

TOM: [*without*] Champagne – here you are! [*Draws curtain. Enter* TOM, *with champagne glass from supper-room; portion of supper table seen in alcove; seeing* SIDNEY] Sidney!

SIDNEY: Tom! you here!

TOM: Very much here. [*drinking*] I was brought by Mr Chodd.

SIDNEY: Chodd?

TOM: Don't startle a fella. You look pale – aren't you well?

SIDNEY: [*rallying*] Jolly, never better.

TOM: Have some salmon.

SIDNEY: I'm not hungry.

TOM: Then try some jelly, it's no trouble to masticate and is emollient and agreeable to the throat and palate.

SIDNEY: No, Tom, champagne.

TOM: [*fetching bottle from table*] There you are.

SIDNEY: I'll meet her eye to eye. [*Drinks.*] Another, Tom – and be as smiling and indifferent. As for that heavy-metalled dog – thanks, Tom. [*Drinks.*] Another.

TOM: I've been dancing with old Lady Ptarmigant.

SIDNEY: Confound her.

TOM: I did. As I was twirling her round I sent my foot through her dress and tore her skirt out of the gathers.

SIDNEY: [*laughing hysterically*] Good! good! Bravo! Tom! Did she row you?

TOM: Not a bit. She said it was of no consequence; but her looks were awful.

SIDNEY: Ha! ha! ha! Tom, you're a splendid fellow, not like these damned swells, all waistcoat and shirt front.

TOM: But I like the swells. I played a rubber with them and won three pounds, then I showed them some conjuring tricks – you know I'm a famous conjuror [*taking a pack of cards out of his pocket*] By Jupiter! look here, I've brought the pack away with me; I didn't know I had. I'll go and take it back.

SIDNEY: [*taking cards from him absently*] No, never mind, stay with me, I don't want you to go.

TOM: I find high life most agreeable, everybody is so amiable, so thoughtful, so full of feeling.

SIDNEY: Feeling! Why man, this is a flesh market where the match-making mammas and chattering old chaperons have no more sense of feeling than drovers – the girls no more sentiment than sheep, and the best man is the highest bidder; that is, the biggest fool with the longest purse.

TOM: Sidney, you're ill.

SIDNEY: You lie, Tom – never better – excellent high spirits – confound this link!

[*Enter* LORD CLOUDWRAYS *and* "SIR FARINTOSH."]

LORD C: ⎫
"SIR F": ⎭ By Jove! Ha, Sidney, heard the news?

SIDNEY: News – there is no news! The times are bankrupt, and the assignees have sold off the events.

LORD C: ⎫
"SIR F": ⎭ The Ministry is defeated.

TOM: No

LORD C: ⎫
"SIR F": ⎭ Yes; by a majority of forty-six.

SIDNEY: Serve them right.

LORD C: ⎫
"SIR F": ⎭ Why?

SIDNEY: I don't know! Why, what a fellow you are to want reasons.

LORD C: Sidney!

SIDNEY: Hullo, Cloudwrays! my bright young British senator – my undeveloped Chatham, and mature Raleigh.

TOM: Will they resign?

SIDNEY: Of course they will: resignation is the duty of every man, or Minister, who can't do anything else.

TOM: Who will be sent for to form a Government?

SIDNEY: Cloudwrays.

LORD C: How you do chaff a man!

SIDNEY: Why not? Inaugurate a new policy – the policy of smoke – free-trade in tobacco! Go in, not for principles, but for Principes – our hearths – our homes, and 'bacca boxes!

TOM: If there's a general election?

SIDNEY: Hurrah, for a general election! eh, Cloudwrays? – "eh, Farintosh?" What speeches you'll make – what lies you'll tell, and how your constituents *won't* believe you!

LORD C: ⎫
"SIR F": ⎭ How odd you are.

LORD C: Aren't you well?

SIDNEY: Glorious! Only one thing annoys me.

LORD C: ⎫
"SIR F": ⎬   What's that?.
</br>
SIDNEY: They won't give me any more champagne.

["*Enter* COLONEL BROWSER."]

LORD C: ⎫ Lady Ptarmigant sent me here to say——
"COLONEL B: ⎬ Farintosh," the ladies want partners.

["COLONEL *and* SIR FARINTOSH *go off*."]

SIDNEY: Partners! Here are partners for them – long, tall, stout, fat, thin, poor, rich. Cloudwrays, you're the man! [*Enter* CHODD, JUN. SIDNEY *sees and points to him.*] No; this is the man!

CHODD, JUN.: [*aside*] Confound this fellow!

SIDNEY: This, sir, is the "Young Lady's Best Companion," well bound, Bramah-locked, and gilt at the edges – mind, gilt only at the edges. This link will *not* hold. [*Sees the pack of cards in his hand.*] Here, Chodd, take these – no, cut for a ten-pound note.

[*He puts cards on small table.*]

CHODD, JUN.: [*quickly*] With pleasure. [*aside*] I'll punish this audacious pauper in the pocket.

LORD C: You mustn't gamble here.

SIDNEY: Only for frolic!

CHODD, JUN.: I'm always lucky at cards!

SIDNEY: Yes, I know an old proverb about that.

CHODD, JUN.: Eh?

SIDNEY: Lucky at play, unlucky in—— This link will not hold.

CHODD, JUN.: [*maliciously*] Shall we put the stakes down first?

SIDNEY: [*producing portémonnaie*] With pleasure!

LORD C: But I don't think it right—— [*advancing* – CHODD, JUN., *stays him with his arm.*]

TOM: Sidney!

SIDNEY: Nonsense! hold your tongue, Cloudwrays, and I'll give you a regalia. Let's make it for five-and-twenty?

CHODD, JUN.: Done!

SIDNEY: Lowest wins – that's in your favour.

CHODD, JUN.: Eh?

SIDNEY: Ace is lowest. [*They cut.*] Mine! Double the stakes?

CHODD, JUN.: Done!

[*They cut.*]

SIDNEY: Mine again! Double again?

CHODD, JUN.: Done!

[*They cut.*]

SIDNEY: You're done again! I'm in splendid play to-night. One hundred, I think?

CHODD, JUN.: I'd play again [*handing notes*] but I've no more with me.

SIDNEY: Your word's sufficient – you can send to my chambers – besides, you've got your cheque-book. A hundred again?

CHODD, JUN.: Yes.

[*They cut.*]

SIDNEY: Huzzah! Fortune's a lady! Again? [CHODD, JUN., *nods – they cut.*] Bravo! Again? [CHODD, JUN., *nods – they cut.*] Mine again! Again? [CHODD, JUN., *nods – they cut.*] Mine again! Again? [CHODD, JUN., *nods – they cut.*] Same result! That makes five! Let's go in for a thousand?

CHODD, JUN.: Done!

LORD C: [*advancing*] No!

CHODD, JUN.: [*savagely*] Get out of the way! [LORD CLOUDWRAYS *looks at him through eye-glass in astonishment.*]

SIDNEY: Pooh! [*They cut.*] Mine! Double again?

CHODD, JUN.: Yes.

LORD C: [*going round to back of table and seizing the pack*] No; I can't suffer this to go on – Lady Ptarmigant would be awful angry. [*going off.*]

SIDNEY: Here, Cloudwrays! What a fellow you are. [*Exit* LORD CLOUDWRAYS. *turning to* CHODD, JUN.] You owe me a thousand!

CHODD, JUN.: I shall not forget it.

SIDNEY: I don't suppose you will. Confound—— [*trying to button sleeve link*] Oh, to jog your memory, take this.

[SIDNEY *gives him sleeve link, which he has been trying to button, and goes off after* LORD CLOUDWRAYS.]

CHODD, JUN.: And after I have paid you, I'll remember and clear off the old score.

TOM: [*taking his arm as he is going*] Going into the ballroom?

CHODD, JUN.: [*aghast at his intrusion*] Yes!

TOM: I'll go with you.

CHODD, JUN.: [*disengaging his arm*] I'm engaged!

[*Exit* CHODD, JUN. *Music till end.*]

TOM: You've an engaging manner! I'm like a donkey between two bundles of hay. On one side woman – lovely woman! On the other, wine and wittles. [*taking out a sovereign*] Heads, supper – tails, the ladies. [*Tosses at table.*] Supper! sweet goddess Fortune, accept my thanks!

[*Exit* TOM *into supper-room. Enter* MAUD *and* CHODD, JUN.]

MAUD: This dreadful man follows me about everywhere.

CHODD, JUN.: My dear Miss Hetherington!

MAUD: I danced the last with you.

CHODD, JUN.: That was a quadrille. [*Enter* SIDNEY.] This is for a polka.

SIDNEY: [*advancing between them*] The lady is engaged to me.

CHODD, JUN.: [*aside*] This fellow's turned up again. [*to him*] I beg your pardon.

SIDNEY: I beg yours! [*bitterly*] I have a prior claim. Ask the lady – or perhaps I had better give her up to you.

MAUD: The next dance with you, Mr Chodd; this one——

CHODD, JUN.: Miss, your commands are Acts of Parliament. [*looking spitefully at* SIDNEY *as he crosses*] I'll go and see what Lady Ptarmigant has to say to this.

[*Exit* CHODD, JUN. *Music changes to a slow waltz.*]

SIDNEY: Listen to me for the last time. My life and being were centred in you. You have abandoned me for money! You accepted me; you now throw me off, for money! You gave me your hand, you now retract, for money! You are about to wed – a knave, a brute, a fool, whom in your own heart you despise, for money!

MAUD: How dare you!

SIDNEY: Where falsehood is, shame cannot be. The last time we met [*producing ribbon*] you gave me this. See, 'tis the colour of a man's heart's blood. [*Curtains or doors at back draw apart.*] I give it back to you. [*casting the bunch of ribbon at her feet.* LORD CLOUDWRAYS, "SIR FARINTOSH, COLONEL BROWSER," TOM, LORD PTARMIGANT, *and* LADY PTARMIGANT, CHODD, JUN., *and* CHODD, SEN., *appear at back.* GUESTS *seen in ballroom.*] And tell you, shameless girl, much as I once loved, and adored, I now despise and hate you.

LADY P: [*advancing, in a whisper to* SIDNEY] Leave the house, sir! How dare you – go!

SIDNEY: Yes; anywhere.

[*Crash of music.* MAUD *is nearly falling when* CHODD, JUN., *appears near her; she is about to lean on his arm, but recognising him, retreats and staggers.* SIDNEY *is seen to reel through ballroom full of dancers. Drop.*]

END OF ACT II

ACT III

SCENE I – *The "Owl's Roost." [same as Scene I, Act II.] Daylight; the room in order.* TOM *discovered writing at table,* R. BOY *sitting on table,* L. *and holding the placard on which is printed – "Read the 'Morning Earthquake' – a first-class daily paper,"* &c. *On the other, "The 'Evening Earthquake' – a first-class daily paper – Latest Intelligence,"* &c.

TOM: Um! It'll look well on the walls, and at the railway stations. Take these back to the office [BOY *jumps down.*] – to Mr Piker, and tell him he must wait for the last leader – till it's written. [*Exit* BOY. TOM *walks to and fro, smoking long clay pipe.*] The M.E. – that is, the "Morning Earthquake," shakes the world for the first time to-morrow morning, and everything seems to have gone wrong with it. It is a crude, unmanageable, ill-disciplined, ill-regulated earthquake. Heave the first – Old Chodd behaves badly to me. After organising him a first-rate earthquake, engaging him a brilliant staff, and stunning reporters, he doesn't even offer me the post of sub-editor – ungrateful old humbug! Heave the second – No sooner is he engaged than our editor is laid up with the gout; and then Old Chodd asks me to a literary warming-pan, and keeps his place hot, till colchicum and cold water have done their work. I'll be even with Old Chodd, though! I'll teach him what it is to insult a man who has started eighteen daily and weekly papers – all of them failures. Heave the third – Sidney Daryl won't write the social leaders. [*Sits at end of table.*] Poor Sidney! [*Takes out the magenta ribbon which he picked up at the ball.*] I shan't dare to give him this – I picked it up at the ball, at which I was one of the distinguished and illustrious guests. Love is an awful swindler – always drawing upon Hope, who never honours his drafts – a sort of whining beggar, continually moved on by the maternal police. But 'tis a weakness to which the wisest of us are subject – a kind of manly measles which this flesh is heir to, particularly when the flesh is heir to nothing else – even I have felt the divine damnation – I mean emanation. But the lady united herself to another, which was a very good thing for me, and anything but misfortune for her. Ah! happy days of youth! – Oh! flowing fields of Runnington-cum-Wapshot – where the yellow corn waved, our young loves ripened, and the new gaol now stands. Oh! Sally, when I think of you and the past, I feel that [*looking into his pot*] the pot's empty, and I could drink another pint. [*putting the ribbon in his pocket*] Poor Sidney – I'm afraid he's going to the bad. [*Enter* SIDNEY; *he strikes bell on table and sits at the head, his appearance altered.*] Ha! Sid, is that you? Talk of the – how d'e do?

SIDNEY: Quite well – how are you?

TOM: I'm suffering from an earthquake in my head, and a general printing office in my stomach. Have some beer?

[*Enter* WAITER.]

SIDNEY: No thanks – brandy——

TOM: So early?

SIDNEY: And soda. I didn't sleep last night.

TOM: Brandy and soda, and beer again.

[*Exit* WAITER, *with pint pot off* R. *table.*]

SIDNEY: I never do sleep now – I can't sleep.

TOM: Work hard.

[*Enter* WAITER.]

SIDNEY: I do – it is my only comfort – my old pen goes driving along, at the rate of—— [WAITER *after placing pint of porter before* TOM, *places tray with brandy and soda before* SIDNEY.] That's right! [WAITER *uncorks and exits.*] What a splendid discovery was brandy. [*drinks*]

TOM: Yes, the man who invented it deserves a statue.

SIDNEY: That's the reason that he doesn't get one.

TOM: [*reading paper*] "Election intelligence." There's the general election – why not go in for that.

SIDNEY: Election – pooh! what do I care for that!

TOM: Nothing, of course, but it's occupation.

SIDNEY: [*musing*] I wonder who'll put up for Springmead!

TOM: Your brother's seat, wasn't it?

SIDNEY: Yes, our family's for years. By-the-way, I'd a letter from Percy last mail; he's in trouble, poor fellow – his little boy is dead, and he himself is in such ill-health that they have given him sick leave. We are an unlucky race, we Daryls. Sometimes, Tom, I wish that I were dead.

TOM: Sidney!

SIDNEY: It's a bad wish, I know; but what to me is there worth living for?

TOM: What! oh, lots of things. Why, there's the police reports – mining intelligence – hop districts – the tallow market – ambition – Society!

SIDNEY: [*heartily*] Damn Society!

TOM: And you know, Sid, there are more women in the world than one.

SIDNEY: But only one a man can love.

TOM: I don't know about that; temperaments differ.

SIDNEY: [*pacing about and reciting*] "As the husband, so the wife is."
　　　　　"Thou art mated to a clown:
　　　　　　And the grossness of his nature
　　　　　Shall have power to drag thee down;
　　　　　　He will hold thee when his passion
　　　　　Shall have spent its novel force,
　　　　　　Something better than his dog, and
　　　　　Little dearer than his horse."
　　　I'm ashamed of such a want of spirit – ashamed to be such a
　　　baby! And you, Tom, are the only man in the world I'd show it
　　　to; but I – I can think of nothing else but her – and – and of the
　　　fate in store for her.

　　　　　　　[*He sobs and leans on table with his face in his hands.*]

TOM: Don't give way, Sid; there are plenty of things in this life to care
　　　.for.
SIDNEY: Not for me – not for me.
TOM: Oh, yes! there's friendship; and – and – the little girl, you know!
SIDNEY: That reminds me, I wrote a week ago to Mrs Churton, asking
　　　her to meet me with Mau—— with the little darling in the
　　　square. I always asked them to come from Hampstead to the
　　　square, that I might look up at her window as I passed. What a
　　　fool I've been – I can't meet them this morning! Will you go
　　　for me?
TOM: With pleasure.
SIDNEY: Give Mrs Churton this. [*wrapping up money in paper from*
　　　TOM's *case*] It's the last month's money. Tell her I'm engaged,
　　　and can't come – and – [*putting down money*] buy the baby a
　　　toy, bless her! What a pity to think she'll grow to be a woman!

　　　　　　　[*Enter* MACUSQUEBAUGH, O'SULLIVAN, *and* MAKVICZ.]

MACUSQUEBAUGH: [*entering*] A three of whisky, hot!
O'SULLIVAN: The same for me – neat.
DR MAKVICZ: A pint of stoot.
O'SULLIVAN: Tom, mee boy, what news of the "Earthquake"?

　　　　　　　[*Enter* WAITER *with orders, and gives* TOM *a note.*]

TOM: Heaving, sir – heaving. [TOM *opens note;* SIDNEY *sits abstracted.*]
　　　Who's going electioneering?
DR MAKVICZ: I am.
O'SULLIVAN: And I.
MACUSQUEBAUGH: And so am I.
TOM: Where?
MACUSQUEBAUGH: I don't know.
O'SULLIVAN: Somewhere – anywhere.
TOM: [*reading note*] From Chodd, Senior – the old villain! [*reads*]

"Dear Sir, – Please meet me at Lady Ptarmigant's at eleven
a.m." [*suddenly*] Sidney!

SIDNEY: [*moodily*] What?

TOM: [*reading note*] "I am off to Springmead-le-Beau by the train at
two-fifty. My son, Mr John Chodd, Junior, is the candidate
for the seat for the borough."

SIDNEY: [*rising*] What! – that hound! – that cur! – that digesting
cheque-book – represents the town that my family have held
their own for centuries. I'd sooner put up for it myself.

TOM: [*rising*] Why not? Daryl for Springmead – here's occupation –
here's revenge!

SIDNEY: By heaven, I will!

TOM: Gentlemen, the health of Mr Daryl, M.P. for Springmead.

OMNES: [*rising and drinking*] Hurrah!

TOM: We'll canvass for you. [*aside*] And now, Mr Chodd, Senior, I
see the subject for the last leader. I'll fetter you with your own
type.

SIDNEY: I'll do it! I'll do it! When does the next train start?

MACUSQUEBAUGH: [*taking "Bradshaw" from table,* R.] At two-fifty –
the next at five.

SIDNEY: Huzzah! [*with excitement*] I'll rouse up the tenants – call on
the tradesmen!

O'SULLIVAN: But the money?

SIDNEY: I'll fight him with the very thousand that I won of him.
Besides, what need has a Daryl of money at Springmead?

TOM: We can write for you.

O'SULLIVAN: And fight for you.

SIDNEY: I feel so happy – Call cabs.

MACUSQUEBAUGH: How many?

SIDNEY: The whole rank!

TOM: But, Sidney, what colours shall we fight under?

SIDNEY: What colours? [*Feels in his breast and appears dejected;* TOM
hands him the ribbons; he clutches them eagerly.] What colours?
Magenta!

OMNES: Huzzah!

SCENE II – *An apartment at* LORD PTARMIGANT'S. [*1st grooves*]

LADY P: [*without*] Good-bye, dear Mr Chodd. A pleasant ride, and all
sorts of success. [*Enter* LADY PTARMIGANT.] Phew! there's the
old man gone. Now to speak to that stupid Maud. [*looking off*]
There she sits in the sulks – a fool! Ah, what wise folks the
French were before the Revolution, when there was a Bastille
or a convent in which to pop dangerous young men and

obstinate young women. [*sweetly*] Maud dear! I'll marry her to young Chodd, I'm determined.

[*Enter* MAUD, *very pensive.*]

LADY P: Maud, I wish to speak to you.

MAUD: Upon what subject, aunt?

LADY P: One that should be very agreeable to a girl of your age – marriage.

MAUD: Mr Chodd again?

LADY P: Yes, Mr Chodd again.

MAUD: I hate him!

LADY P: You wicked thing! How dare you use such expressions in speaking of a young gentleman so rich?

MAUD: Gentleman!

LADY P: Yes, gentleman! – at least he will be.

MAUD: Nothing can make Mr Chodd – what a name! – anything but what he is.

LADY P: Money can do everything.

MAUD: Can it make me love a man I hate?

LADY P: Yes; at least, if it don't, it ought. I suppose you mean to marry somebody?

MAUD: No.

LADY P: You audacious girl! How can you talk so wickedly? Where do you expect to go to?

MAUD: To needlework! Anything from this house; and from this persecution.

LADY P: Miss Hetherington!

MAUD: Thank you, Lady Ptarmigant, for calling me by my name; it reminds me who I am, and of my dead father, "Indian Hetherington," as he was called. It reminds me that the protection you have offered to his orphan daughter has been hourly embittered by the dreadful temper, which is an equal affliction to you as to those within your reach. It reminds me that the daughter of such a father should not stoop to a mésalliance.

LADY P: Mésalliance! How dare you call Mr Chodd a mésalliance? And you hankering after that paltry, poverty-stricken, penny-a-liner?

MAUD: Lady Ptarmigant, you forget yourself; and you are untruthful. Mr Daryl is a gentleman by birth and breeding! I loved him – I acknowledge it – I love him still!

LADY P: You shameless girl! and he without a penny! After the scene he made!

MAUD: He has dared to doubt me, and I have done with him for ever. For the moment he presumed to think that I could break my plighted word – that I could be false to the love I had acknowledged – the love that was my happiness and pride – all between us is over.

LADY P: [*aside*] That's some comfort. [*aloud*] Then what do you intend to do?

MAUD: I intend to leave the house.

LADY P: To go where?

MAUD: Anywhere from you!

LADY P: Upon my word! [*aside*] She has more spirit than I gave her credit for. [*aloud*] And do you mean to tell me that that letter is not intended for that fellow Daryl?

MAUD : [*giving letter*] Read it.

LADY P: [*Opens it and reads.*] "To the Editor of the 'Times.' Please insert the enclosed advertisement for which I send stamps. Wanted a situation as governess by"—— [*embracing* MAUD] Oh, my dear – dear girl! you couldn't think of such a thing – and you a lady, and my niece.

MAUD: [*disengaging herself*] Lady Ptarmigant, please don't!

LADY P: [*thoroughly subdued*] But, my love, how could I think——

MAUD: What Lady Ptarmigant thinks is a matter of the most profound indifference to me.

LADY P: [*aside*] Bless her! Exactly what I was at her age [*aloud*] But, my dear Maud, what is to become of you?

MAUD: No matter what I welcome poverty – humiliation – insult – the contempt of fools – welcome all but dependence! I will neither dress myself at the expense of a man I despise, control his household, owe him duty, or lead a life that is a daily lie; neither will I marry one I love, who has dared to doubt me, to drag him into deeper poverty.

[*Enter* SERVANT.]

SERVANT: My Lady, there is a gentleman inquiring for Mr Chodd.

LADY P: Perhaps some electioneering friend. Show him here. [*Exit* SERVANT.] Don't leave the room, Maud, dear.

MAUD: I was not going – why should I?

[SERVANT *shows in* TOM *with* LITTLE MAUD.]

LADY P: It's the tobacco man!

TOM: [*to* CHILD] Do I smell of smoke? I beg your ladyship's pardon, but Mr Chodd, the old gentleman, wished me to meet him here.

LADY P: He has just driven off to the station.

TOM: I know I'm a few minutes behind time – there's the young lady. Good morning, Miss – Miss – I don't know the rest of her – I – I – have been detained by the – this little girl——

LADY P: A sweet little creature, Mr Silenus.

TOM: Stylus.

LADY P: Stylus, pardon me.

TOM: [*aside*] This old lady will insist on calling me Silenus! She'd think me very rude if I called her Ariadne.

LADY P: Sweet little thing! Come here, my dear! [LITTLE MAUD *crosses to her.*] Your child, Mr – Stylus?

TOM: No, my lady, this is Mr Sidney Daryl's protégé.

LADY P: [*moving from* LITTLE MAUD] Whose?

TOM: Sidney Daryl's.

[MAUD *advances.*]

LADY P: Nasty little wretch! How do you mean? Speak, quickly!

TOM: I mean that Sidney pays for her education, board, and all that. Oh, he's a splendid fellow – a heart of gold! [*aside*] I'll put in a good word for him, as his young woman's here. I'll make her repent!

MAUD: Come to me, child. [LITTLE MAUD *crosses to her.*] Who are you?

LITTLE MAUD: I'm Mrs Churton's little darling, and Mr Daryl's little girl.

[*She crosses to* TOM, *as* MAUD *moves away.*]

LADY P [*to* MAUD] His very image.

TOM: Bless her little tongue! I took her from the woman who takes care of her. She's going down with me to Springmead. I've bought her a new frock, all one colour, magenta. [*aside*] That was strong.

LADY P: Did I tell you Mr Chodd had gone?

TOM: I'm one too many here. I'll vamose! Good morning, my lady.

LADY P: Good morning, Mr – Bacchus.

TOM: Stylus – Stylus! I shall have to call her Ariadne. Um! they might have asked the child to have a bit of currant cake, or a glass of currant wine. Shabby devils!

[*Exeunt* TOM *and* LITTLE MAUD.]

LADY P: [*aside*] Could anything have happened more delightfully?

MAUD: [*throwing herself into* LADY PTARMIGANT'S *arms*] Oh, aunty! Forgive me – I was wrong – I was ungrateful – forgive me! Kiss me, and forgive me! I'll marry Mr Chodd – anybody – do with me as you please.

LADY P: My dear niece! [*affected*] I – I – feel for you. I'm – I'm not so heartless as I seem. I know I'm a harsh, severe old woman, but I am a woman, and I can feel for you. [*embracing her*]

MAUD: And to think that with the same breath he could swear that he loved me, while another – this child, too! [*Bursts into a flood of tears.*] There, aunt, I won't cry. I'll dry my eyes – I'll do your bidding. You mean me well, while he – oh! [*shudders*] Tell Mr Chodd I'll bear his name and bear it worthily! [*sternly*]

LADY·P: [*embracing – kissing her at each stop*] Men are a set of brutes. I
was jilted myself when I was twenty-three – and, oh, how I
loved the fellow! But I asserted my dignity, and married Lord
Ptarmigant, and *he*, and *he* only, can tell you how I have
avenged my sex! Cheer up, my darling! love, sentiment, and
romance are humbug! – but wealth, position, jewels, balls,
presentations, a country house, town mansion, society, power
– that's true, solid happiness, and if it isn't, I don't know what
is?

[*Exeunt.*]

SCENE III – *The Wells at Springmead-le-Beau. An avenue of elms,
sloping off. House with windows, &c., on to lawn; railings at back of
stage. Garden seats, chairs, lounges, small tables, &c., discovered near
house.* LORD PTARMIGANT *discovered asleep in garden chair against
house, his feet resting on another. Enter* CHODD, SEN., *down avenue.*

CHODD, SEN. Oh, dear! Oh, dear! What a day this is! There's Johnny to
be elected, and I'm expecting the first copy of the "Morning
Earthquake" – my paper! my own paper! – by the next train.
Then here's Lady Ptarmigant says that positively her niece
will have Johnny for her wedded husband, and in one day my
Johnny is to be a husband, an M.P., and part proprietor of a
daily paper! Whew! how hot it is! It's lucky that the wells are
so near the hustings – one can run under the shade and get a
cooler. Here's my lord! [*waking him*] My lord!
LORD P: [*waking*] Oh! Eh! Mr Chodd – good morning! – how d'e do?
CHODD, SEN.: [*sitting on stool*] Oh, flurried, and flustered, and
worritted. You know to-day's the election.
LORD P: Yes, I believe there is an election going on somewhere.
[*calling*] A tumbler of the waters No. 2.

[*Enter* WAITRESS *from house, places tumbler of water on
table, and exits.*]

CHODD, SEN.: Oh, what a blessing there is no opposition! If my boy is
returned——

[*Enter* CHODD, JUN., *agitated, a placard in his hand.*]

CHODD, JUN.: Look here, guv! look here!
CHODD, SEN.: What is it, my Johnny!
CHODD, JUN.: Don't call me Johnny! Look here! [*Shows electioneering
placard*, "Vote for Daryl!"]
CHODD, SEN.: What?
CHODD, JUN.: That vagabond has put up as candidate? His brother

used to represent the borough.

CHODD, SEN.: Then the election will be contested?

CHODD, JUN.: Yes.

[CHODD, SEN., *sinks on garden chair.*]

LORD P: [*rising and taking tumbler from table*] Don't annoy yourself, my dear Mr Chodd; these accidents will happen in the best regulated constituencies.

CHODD, JUN.: Guv, don't be a fool!

LORD P: Try a glass of the waters.

[CHODD, SEN., *takes tumbler and drinks, and the next moment ejects the water with a grimace, stamping about.*]

CHODD, SEN.: Oh, what filth! O-o-o-o-o-oh!

LORD P: It is an acquired taste. [*to* WAITER] Another tumbler of No. 2.

CHODD, SEN.: So, Johnny, there's to be a contest, and you won't be M.P. for Springmead after all.

CHODD, JUN.: I don't know that.

CHODD, SEN.: What d'ye mean?

CHODD, JUN.: Mr Sidney Daryl may lose, and, perhaps, Mr Sidney Daryl mayn't show. After that ball——

CHODD, SEN.: Where you lost that thousand pounds?

CHODD, JUN.: Don't keep bringing that up, guv'nor. After that I bought up all Mr Daryl's bills – entered up judgment, and left them with Aaron. I've telegraphed to London, and if Aaron don't nab him in town he'll catch him here.

CHODD, SEN.: But, Johnny, isn't that rather mean?

CHODD, JUN.: All's fair in love and Parliament.

[*Enter* COUNTRY BOY *with newspaper.*]

BOY: Mr Chodd?

CHODD, SEN.: ⎫
CHODD, JUN.: ⎬ Here!

BOY: Just arrived.

CHODD, JUN.: The "Morning Earthquake."

[*They both clutch at it eagerly; each secures a paper, and sits under a tree.*]

CHODD, SEN.: [*reading*] Look at the leader. "In the present aspect of European politics——"

CHODD, JUN.: "Some minds seem singularly obtuse to the perception of an idea."

CHODD, SEN.: Johnny!

CHODD, JUN.: Guv!

CHODD, SEN.: Do you see the last leader?

CHODD, JUN.: Yes.

CHODD, SEN.: [*reading*] "The borough of Springmead-le-Beau has for centuries been represented by the house of Daryl."

CHODD, JUN.: [*reading*] "A worthy scion of that ancient race intends to offer himself as candidate at the forthcoming election, and, indeed, who will dare to oppose him?"

CHODD, SEN.: "Surely not a Mister——"

CHODD, JUN.: "Chodd."

CHODD, SEN.: "Whoever he may be."

CHODD, JUN.: "What are the Choddian antecedents?"

CHODD, SEN.: "Whoever heard of Chodd?"

CHODD, JUN.: "To be sure, a young man of that name has recently been the cause of considerable laughter at the clubs on account of his absurd attempts to become a man of fashion."

CHODD, SEN.: "And to wriggle himself into Society."

CHODD, JUN.: [*in a rage*] Why, it's all in his favour.

CHODD, SEN.: In your own paper, too! Oh, that villain Stylus!

CHODD, JUN.: There are no more of these in the town, are there?

BOY: Yes, sir. A man came down with two thousand; he's giving them away everywhere.

CHODD, JUN.: Confound you!

[*He pushes him off – follows.*]

CHODD, SEN.: Oh, dear! oh, dear! oh, dear! Now, my lord, isn't that too bad. [*Sees him asleep.*] He's off again! [*waking him*] My lord, here's the "Earthquake"! [*half throwing him off his seat*]

LORD P: Earthquake! Good gracious! [*rising*] I didn't feel anything.

CHODD, SEN.: No, no, the paper.

LORD P: Ah, most interesting. [*Drops paper, and leisurely reseats himself.*] My dear Mr Chodd, I congratulate you.

CHODD, SEN.: Congratulate me? [*Looks at watch.*] I must be off to the committee.

[*Exit* CHODD, SEN.]

LORD P: Waiter! Am I to have that tumbler of No. 2?

[*Band heard playing "Conquering Hero," and loud cheers as* LORD PTARMIGANT *goes into house, and enter* SIDNEY, O'SULLIVAN, MACUSQUEBAUGH, *and* DR MAKVICZ. SIDNEY *bowing off as he enters. Cheers.*]

SIDNEY: So far so good. I've seen lots of faces that I knew. I'll run this Dutch-metalled brute hard, and be in an honourable minority anyhow.

[*Enter* TOM, *hastily.*]

TOM: Daryl.

SIDNEY: Yes.

TOM: Look out.

SIDNEY: What's the matter?

TOM: I met your friend Moses Aaron on the platform. He didn't see you, but what does he want here?

SIDNEY: Me, if anybody. [*musing*] This is a shaft from the bow of Mr John Chodd, Junior. I see his aim.

TOM: What's to be done? The voters are warm, but, despite the prestige of the family name, if you were not present——

SIDNEY: Besides, I couldn't be returned from Cursitor Street, M.P. for the Queen's Bench [*thinking*] Did the Lamb come down with us?

TOM: Yes – second class.

SIDNEY: Let him stop the bailiffs – Aaron is as timid as a girl. I'll go through here, and out by the grand entrance. Let in the Lamb, and——

TOM: I see.

SIDNEY: Quick!

[*Exit* TOM.]

O'SULLIVAN: Daryl, is there any fighting to be done?

MACUSQUEBAUGH: Or any drinking?

DR MAKVICZ: If so, we shall be most happy.

SIDNEY: No, no, thanks. Come with me – I've a treat for you.

OMNES: What?

SIDNEY: [*laughing*] The chalybeate waters.

[*Exeunt* OMNES *into house. Enter* CHODD, JUN., *and* MOSES AARON.]

CHODD, JUN.: You saw him go in – arrest him. The chaise is ready – take him to the next station, and all's right. I'll stay and see him captured.

[CHODD *in great triumph.*]

MOSES: Very good, shur – do it at vunsh.

[*He is going into the house, when the* LAMB *springs out;* MOSES AARON *staggers back; the* LAMB *stands in boxing attitude before the door;* TOM *and* SIX *or* EIGHT ROUGHS *enter by avenue.*]

LAMB: [*with back half turned to audience*] Now, then, where are *you* a shovin' to?

MOSES: I want to passh by.

LAMB: Then you can't.

MOSES: Why not?

LAMB: [*doggedly*] 'Cos I'm doorkeeper, and you haven't got a check.

MOSES: Now, Lamb, dooty'sh dooty, and——

LAMB: [*turning with face to audience, and bringing up the muscle of his right arm*] Feel that!

MOSES: [*alarmed*] Yesh, shur. [*Feels it slightly.*]

LAMB: You can't come in.

CHODD, JUN.: [*crossing to* LAMB *fussily*] Why not?

LAMB: [*looks at him, half contemptuously, half comically*] 'Cos that sez I mustn't let you. Feel it! [*Taps muscle.*]

CHODD, JUN.: Thank you, some other time.

> [*The* ROUGHS *surround him, jeer, and prepare to hustle him.* TOM *mounts seat.*]

TOM: Vote for Daryl!

LAMB: [*making up to* MOSES AARON *in sparring attitude, who retreats in terror*] Are yer movin'?

CHODD, JUN.: Do your duty.

> [ROUGHS *laugh.*]

MOSES: I can't -- they are many, I am a few.

> [*Cheers without.*]

CHODD, JUN. [*losing his presence of mind*] Particular business requires me at the hustings.

> [*He goes off, midst jeers and laughter of* ROUGHS.]

LAMB: [*at same time advancing upon* MOSES AARON] Are yer movin'?

MOSES: Yesh, Mr Lamb.

> [*By this time he has backed close to* TOM, *perched upon the seat, who bonnets him.*]

TOM: Vote for Daryl!

> [MOSES AARON *is hustled off by* MOB, *followed leisurely by* LAMB.]

TOM: [*on chair*] Remember, gentlemen, the officers of the law – the officers of the sheriff – are only in the execution of their duty. [*Shouts and uproar without.*] Don't offer any violence. [*Shouts.*] Don't tear them limb from limb!

> [*Shouts, followed by a loud shriek.* TOM *leaps from chair, dances down stage, and exits. Enter* LADY PTARMIGANT *and* CHODD, SEN. LADY PTARMIGANT *is dressed in mauve.* CHODD, SEN. *escorts her to house.*]

CHODD, SEN.: But if he is absent from his post?

LADY P: His post must get on without him. Really, my dear Mr Chodd, you must allow me to direct absolutely. If you wish your son to marry Miss Hetherington, now is the time – now or never.

[*Exit into house.* CHODD, SEN., *exits. Enter* CHODD, JUN., *and* MAUD, *dressed in mauve.*]

CHODD, JUN.: Miss Hetherington, allow me to offer you a seat. [*She sits under tree; aside*] Devilish awkward! Lady Ptarmigant says, "Strike while the iron's hot"; but I want to be at the hustings. I've made my speech to the electors, and now I must do my courting. She looks awfully proud. I wish I could pay some fellow to do this for me. Miss Hetherington a – a – a—— I got the speech I spoke just now off by heart. I wish I'd got this written for me, too. Miss Hetherington, I – I am emboldened by the – by what I have just been told by our esteemed correspondent, Lady Ptar – I mean by your amiable aunt. I – I——. [*boldly*] I have a large fortune, and my prospects are bright and brilliant – bright and brilliant. I – I am of a respectable family, which has always paid its way. I have entered on a political career, which always pays its way; and I mean some day to make my name famous. My lady has doubtless prepared you for the hon – I offer you my – my humble hand, and large – I may say colossal fortune.

MAUD: Mr Chodd I will be plain with you.

CHODD, JUN.: Impossible for Miss Hetherington to be plain.

MAUD: You offer me your hand; I will accept it.

CHODD, JUN.: [*endeavouring to take her hand*] Oh, joy! Oh——

MAUD: Please hear me out. On these conditions.

CHODD, JUN.: Pin money no object. Settle as much on you as you like.

MAUD: I will be your true and faithful wife – I will bear your name worthily; but you must understand our union is a union of convenience.

CHODD, JUN.: Convenience!

MAUD: Yes; that love has no part in it.

CHODD, JUN.: Miss Hetherington – may I say Maud? – I love you – I adore you with my whole heart and fortune. [*aside*] I wonder how they are getting on at the hustings.

MAUD: I was saying, Mr Chodd——

CHODD, JUN.: Call me John – your own John! [*seizing her hand; she shudders, and withdraws it.*]

MAUD: [*struggling with herself*] I was saying that the affection which a wife should bring the man she has elected as——

[*Cheers without.*]

SIDNEY: [*speaking without*] Electors of Springmead.

MAUD: We hardly know sufficient of each other to warrant——

SIDNEY: [*without*] I need not tell you who I am.

[*Cheers.* MAUD *trembles.*]

MAUD: We are almost strangers.

SIDNEY: Nor what principles I have been reared in.

CHODD, JUN.: The name of Chodd, if humble, is at least wealthy.

SIDNEY: I am a Daryl; and my politics those of the Daryls.

[*Cheers.*]

CHODD, JUN.: [*aside*] This is awkward. [*to* MAUD] As to our being
  strangers——

SIDNEY: I am no stranger. [*Cheers.*] I have grown up to be a man
  among you. There are faces I see in the crowd I am addressing, men of my own age, whom I remember as children.
  [*Cheers.*] There are faces among you who remember me when
  I was a boy. [*Cheers.*] In the political union between my family
  and Springmead, there is more than respect and sympathy,
  there is sentiment. [*Cheers.*]

CHODD, JUN.: Confound the fellow! Dearest Miss Hetherington –
  Dearest Maud – you have deigned to say you will be mine.

SIDNEY: Why, if we continue to deserve your trust, plight your
  political faith to another?

MAUD: [*overcome*] Mr Chodd, I——

CHODD, JUN.: My own bright, particular Maud!

SIDNEY: Who is my opponent?

TOM: [*without*] Nobody.

[*A loud laugh.*]

SIDNEY: What is he?

TOM: Not much.

[*A roar of laughter.*]

SIDNEY: I have no doubt he is honest and trustworthy, but why turn
  away an old servant to hire one you don't know? [*Cheers.*] Why
  turn off an old love that you have tried and proved for a new
  one? [*Cheers.*] I don't know what the gentleman's politics may
  be. [*Laugh.*] Or those of his family. [*Roar of laughter.*] I've
  tried to find out, but I can't. To paraphrase the ballad:—

> I've searched through Hansard, journals,
> Books, De Brett, and Burke, and Dodd,
> And my head – my head is aching,
> To find out the name of Chodd.

[*Loud laughter and three cheers.* MAUD *near fainting.*]

CHODD, JUN.: I can't stand this; I must be off to the hustings, Miss
  Heth——! Oh! she's fainting. What shall I do? Lady
  Ptarmigant! Oh, here she comes! Waiter, a tumbler of No. 2.

[*He runs off.*]

SIDNEY: [*without*] And I confidently await the result which will place me at the head of the poll. [*Cheers.*]

> [*Enter* LORD *and* LADY PTARMIGANT, *from house.* LADY PTARMIGANT *attends to* MAUD.]

MAUD: 'Twas nothing – a slight faintness – an attack of——

LORD P: [*aside*] An attack of Chodd, I think! What a dreadful person my lady is, to be sure. [*sits.*]

LADY P: [*to* MAUD] Have you done it?

MAUD: Yes.

LADY P: And you are to be his wife?

MAUD: Yes. [*Cheers.*]

> [*Enter* SIDNEY, O'SULLIVAN, MACUSQUEBAUGH, *and* DOCTOR MAKVICZ.]

SIDNEY: Tom, I feel so excited – so delighted – so happy – so—— [*Sees* MAUD *stops; takes his hat off;* MAUD *bows coldly.*] In my adversary's colours!

LADY P: That fellow, Sidney!

MAUD: [*aside*] It seems hard to see him there, and not to speak to him for the last time.

> [*She is about to advance when* TOM *brings on* LITTLE MAUD, *dressed in magenta.* MAUD *recedes.* LORD PTARMIGANT *goes to sleep in garden seat.*]

LADY P: The tobacco man!

TOM: Ariadne!

> [SIDNEY *kisses* LITTLE MAUD. *Enter* CHODD, JUN.]

LADY P: [*with a withering glance at* SIDNEY] Maud, my child, here's Mr Chodd.

> [CHODD, JUN., *gives his arm to* MAUD. SIDNEY *stands with* LITTLE MAUD. *All go off, except* LADY PTARMIGANT, SIDNEY, LITTLE MAUD, TOM, *and* LORD PTARMIGANT.]

SIDNEY: On his arm! Well, I deserve it! I am poor!

LADY P: Mr Daryl.

> [SIDNEY *bows.*]

TOM: Ariadne is about to express her feelings; I shall go!

> [*Exit* TOM.]

LADY P: I cannot but express my opinion of your conduct. For a long time I have known you to be the associate of prize-fighters, betting men, racehorses, authors, and other such low persons; but despite that, I thought you had some claims to be a gentleman.

SIDNEY: In what way have I forfeited Lady Ptarmigant's good opinion?

LADY P: In what, sir? In daring to bring me, your kinswoman, and a lady – in daring to bring into the presence of the foolish girl you professed to love – that child – your illegitimate offspring!

[LORD PTARMIGANT *awakes*.]

SIDNEY: [*stung*] Lady Ptarmigant, do you know who that child is?

LADY P: [*with a sneer*] Perfectly!

SIDNEY: I think not. She is the lawful daughter of your dead and only son, Charles!

LADY P: What?

SIDNEY: Two days before he sailed for the Crimea, he called at my chambers, and told me that he felt convinced he should never return. He told me, too, of his connection with a poor and humble girl, who would shortly become the mother of his child. I saw from his face that the bullet was cast that would destroy him, and I begged him to legitimatise one who, though of his blood, might not bear his name. Like a brave fellow, a true gentleman, on the next day he married.

LADY P: How disgraceful!

SIDNEY: Joined his regiment, and, as you know, fell at Balaclava.

LADY P: My poor – poor boy.

SIDNEY: His death broke his wife's heart – she, too, died.

LADY P: What a comfort!

SIDNEY: I placed the child with a good motherly woman, and I had intended, for the sake of my old friend, Charley, to educate her, and to bring her to you, and say. Take her, she is your lawful grandchild, and a lady *pur sang*; love her, and be proud of her, for the sake of the gallant son, who galloped to death in the service of his country.

LADY P: [*affected*] Sidney!

SIDNEY: I did not intend that you should know this for some time. I had some romantic notion of making it a reason for your consent to my marriage with – [LADY PTARMIGANT *takes* LITTLE MAUD.] – with Miss Hetherington – that is all over now. The ill opinion with which you have lately pursued me has forced this avowal from me.

LADY P: [*to child*] My darling! Ah! my poor Charley's very image! My poor boy! My poor boy!

LORD P: [*who has been listening, advancing*] Sidney, let my son Charley's father thank you. [*affected*] You have acted like a kinsman and a Daryl!

LADY P: Sidney, forgive me!

SIDNEY: Pray forget it, Lady Ptarm——

LADY P: I will take care that Miss Hetherington shall know——

SIDNEY: [*hotly*] What! did she, too, suspect! Lady Ptarmigant, it is my request – nay, if I have done anything to deserve your good opinion, my injunction – that Miss Hetherington is not informed of what has just passed. If she has thought that I could love another – she is free to her opinion!

[*He goes up, and comes down with the child.*]

LORD P: But *I* shall tell her.

LADY P: [*astonished*] You! [*aside*] Don't you think, under the circumstances, it would be better——

LORD P: I shall act as I think best.

LADY P: [*authoritatively*] Ferdinand!

LORD P: Lady Ptarmigant, it is not often I speak, goodness knows! but on a question that concerns my honour and yours, I shall *not* be silent.

LADY P: [*imploringly*] Ferdinand!

LORD P: Lady Ptarmigant, I am *awake*, and you will please to follow my instructions. What is my granddaughter's name?

LITTLE MAUD: Maud.

LORD P: [*playfully*] Maud, Maud – is it Maud?

[LORD PTARMIGANT *lifts her in his arms, and is carrying her off.*]

LADY P: My lord! Consider – people are looking!

LORD P: Let 'em look – they'll know I'm a *grandfather!*

[*Exit* LORD PTARMIGANT, *with* LITTLE MAUD, *and* LADY PTARMIGANT *up avenue.* TOM *runs on.*]

TOM: It's all right, Sid! Three of Chodd's committee have come over to us. They said that so long as a Daryl was not put up, they felt at liberty to support him, but now—— [*seeing that* SIDNEY *is affected*] What's the matter?

SIDNEY: Nothing.

TOM: Ah, that means love! I hope to be able to persuade the majority of Chodd's committee to resign; and, if they resign, he must too, and we shall walk over the course. [SIDNEY *goes up and sits.* TOM, *aside*] Cupid's carriage stops the way again. Confound that nasty, naughty, naked little boy! I wonder if he'd do less mischief if they put him into knickerbockers.

[*Exit* TOM.]

SIDNEY: Mr Chodd shall not have Springmead.

[*Enter* MAUD, *leading* LITTLE MAUD *by the hand.*
SIDNEY's *face is buried in his hands on the table.*]

MAUD: [*kissing the child, then advancing slowly to* SIDNEY] Sidney!

SIDNEY: [*rising*] Maud – Miss Hetherington!

LITTLE MAUD: Uncle, this is my new aunt. She's my aunt and you're
  my uncle. You don't seemed pleased to see each other, though
  – ain't you? Aunt, why don't you kiss uncle?

MAUD: [*after a pause*] Sidney, I have to beg your forgiveness for the –
  the – mistake which——

SIDNEY: Pray don't mention it, Maud – Miss Hetherington. It is not
  of the——

MAUD: It is so hard to think ill of those we have known.

SIDNEY: I think that it must be very easy! Let me take this opportunity
  of apologising personally, as I have already done by letter, for
  my misconduct at the ball. I had heard that you were about to
  – to——

MAUD: Marry! Then you were in error. Since then I have accepted Mr
  Chodd.

[*Pause.*]

SIDNEY: I congratulate you.

[*He turns his face aside.*]

MAUD: You believed me to be false – believed it without inquiry!

SIDNEY: As you believed of me!

MAUD: Our mutual poverty prevented.

SIDNEY: [*bursting out*] Oh, yes, we are poor! We are poor! We loved
  each other – but we were poor! We loved each other – but we
  couldn't take a house in a square! We loved each other – but we
  couldn't keep a carriage! We loved each other – but we had
  neither gold, purple, plate, nor mansion in the country! You
  were right to leave me, and to marry a *gentleman* – rich in all
  these assurances of happiness!

MAUD: Sidney, you are cruel.

SIDNEY: I loved you, Maud; loved you with my whole heart and soul
  since we played together as children, and you grew till I saw
  you a lovely blushing girl, and now – pshaw! this is folly,
  sentiment, raving madness! Let me wish you joy – let me hope
  you will be happy.

LITTLE MAUD: Uncle, you mustn't make my new aunt cry. Go and
  make it up with her, and kiss her.

[LADY PTARMIGANT, LORD PTARMIGANT, *and* LORD
CLOUDWRAYS *have entered during the last speech.*]

MAUD: [*holding out her hand*] Farewell, Sidney!

SIDNEY: Farewell!

LADY P: [*advancing*] Farewell! What nonsense; two young people so fond of each other. Sidney – Maud, dear, you have my consent.

SIDNEY: [*astonished*] Lady Ptarmigant!

LADY P: I always liked you, Sidney, though, I confess, I didn't always show it.

LORD P: I can explain my lady's sudden conversion – at least, Cloudwrays can.

LORD C: Well, Sid, I'm sorry to be the bearer of good news – I mean of ill news; but your brother – poor Percy – he – a——

SIDNEY: Dead!

LORD C: The news came by the mail to the club, so as I'd nothing to do, I thought I'd come down to congratulate – I mean condole with you.

LORD P: Bear up, Sidney, your brother's health was bad before he left us.

SIDNEY: First the son, and then the father.

MAUD: Sidney!

SIDNEY: [*catching her hand*] Maud!

MAUD: No, no – not now – you are rich, and I am promised.

LADY P: Why, you wicked girl; you wouldn't marry a man you didn't love, would you? Where are your principles?

> [LORD PTARMIGANT *sits on garden seat with* LITTLE MAUD.]

MAUD: But – but – Mr Chodd?

LADY P: What on earth consequence is Mr Chodd?

> [*Enter* CHODD, SEN., *and* CHODD, JUN., *up avenue.*]

CHODD, SEN.: My lady, it's all right, Johnny has been accepted!

> [MAUD *goes up and sits,* L.C. SIDNEY *and* LORD CLOUDWRAYS *also go up with her.*]

LADY P: By whom?

CHODD, SEN.: By Miss Hetherington – by Maud!

LADY P: Why, you must be dreaming, the election has turned your brain – my niece marry a Chodd!

CHODD, SEN.: ⎱
CHODD, JUN.: ⎰ My lady!

LADY P: Nothing of the sort; I was only joking, and thought you were, too. [*aside*] The impertinence of the lower classes in trying to ally themselves with us!

CHODD, JUN.: Guv.

CHODD, SEN.: Johnny!

CHODD, JUN.: We're done.

> [*Loud cheering. Enter* TOM, *who whispers and congratulates* SIDNEY. *Enter a* GENTLEMAN, *who whispers to* CHODD, SEN., *condolingly, and exits.*]

CHODD, SEN.: [*shouting*] Johnny!

CHODD, JUN.: Guv.

CHODD, SEN.: They say there's no hope, and advise us to withdraw from the contest.

> [ALL *congratulate* SIDNEY.]

LADY P: Sir Sidney Daryl, M.P., looks like old times. [*to* LORD PTARMIGANT] My lord, congratulate him.

LORD P: [*waking and shaking* CHODD, JUN., *by the hand*] Receive my congratulations.

LADY P: Oh! It's the wrong man!

CHODD, SEN.: Mr Stylus, I may thank you for this.

TOM: And yourself, you may. I brought out your journal, engaged your staff, and you tried to throw me over. You've got your reward. Morning paper!

> [*He throws papers in the air. Enter* MOSES AARON, *with hat broken and head bound up.*]

MOSES: [*to* SIDNEY] Arresht you at the shoot of——

> [*The* CHODDS *rub their hands in triumph.*]

TOM: Too late! Too late! He's a member of Parliament.

> [CHODD, JUN., *and* CHODD, SEN., *turn into* R. *and* L. *corners.*]

SIDNEY: [*to* TOM] I haven't taken the seat or the oaths yet.

TOM: They don't know that.

SIDNEY: We can settle it another way. [*taking out pocket-book and looking at* CHODD, JUN.] Some time ago I was fortunate enough to win a large sum of money; this way if you please.

> [*He goes up with* MOSES AARON, *and gives money, notes, &c.*]

CHODD, JUN.: Pays his own bills, which I'd bought up, with my money.

CHODD, SEN.: Then, Johnny, you won't get into Society.

LADY P: Never mind, Mr Chodd, your son shall marry a lady.

CHODD, JUN.: ⎫
CHODD, SEN.: ⎭ Eh!

LADY P: I promise to introduce you to one of blue blood.

CHODD, JUN.: Blue bl—— I'd rather have it the natural colour.

> [*Cheers. Enter* O'SULLIVAN *and* COMMITTEE. *Stage full. Church bells heard.*]

O'SULLIVAN: Sir Sidney Daryl, we have heard the news. In our turn we have to inform you that your adversaries have retired from the contest, and you are member for Springmead. [*Cheers.*] We, your committee, come to weep with you for the loss of a brother, to joy with you on your accession to a title and your hereditary honours. Your committee most respectfully beg to be introduced to Lady Daryl. [*With intention and Irish gallantry*]

> [SIDNEY *shows* MAUD *the magenta ribbon; she places her hand in his.*]

SIDNEY: Gentlemen, I thank you; I cannot introduce you to Lady Daryl, for Lady Daryl does not yet exist. In the meantime I have permission to present you to Miss Hetherington.

TOM: [*leaping on chair and waving handkerchief*] Three cheers for my lady!

> [*All cheer. Church bells; band plays "Conquering Hero." *GIRL* at window of house waves handkerchief, and *CHILD* a stick with magenta streamer attached. *COUNTRYMEN, *&c., wave hats; band plays, &c.*]

CURTAIN

OURS

First performed at the Prince of Wales's Theatre, in Liverpool, on 23rd August, 1866, and produced in London at the Prince of Wales's Theatre, on 15th September, 1866.

CAST OF CHARACTERS

	Liverpool	London	London, 1870
Prince Perovsky	Mr Hare	Mr Hare	Mr Hare
Sir Alexander Shendryn, Bt.	Mr J. W. Ray ...	Mr J. W. Ray ...	Mr Addison
Captain Samprey	... ...	Mr Trafford ...	Mr Herbert
Angus MacAlister	Mr Bancroft ...	Mr Bancroft ...	Mr Coghlan
Hugh Chalcot	Mr J. Clarke ...	Mr J. Clarke ...	Mr Bancroft
Sergeant Jones	Mr F. Dewar ...	Mr F. Younge ...	Mr Collette
Houghton	Mr Tindale ...	Mr Tindale	
Lady Shendryn	Miss Larkin ...	Miss Larkin ...	Miss Le Thiere
Blanche Haye	Miss L. Moore	{ Miss L. Moore Miss Lydia Foote	Miss Fanny Josephs
Mary Netley	Miss Marie Wilton	Miss Marie Wilton	Miss Marie Wilton
Servant			
Keeper			

Period – Before, and during the Crimean War.

ACT I – THE PARK – *Autumn*.

ACT II – THE DRAWING-ROOM – *Spring*.

ACT III – THE HUT – *Winter*.

TO

JOSEPH M. LEVY

THIS COMEDY IS DEDICATED

BY

HIS SINCERE AND OBLIGED FRIEND

THE AUTHOR

London, October, 1870

OURS

ACT I

SCENE I – *An avenue of trees in Shendryn Park; the avenue leading off. Seat round tree in foreground. Stumps off trees. The termination of the avenue out of sight. Throughout the Act the autumn leaves fall from the trees.* CHALCOT *discovered asleep on ground under tree, a handkerchief over his face.*

> [*Enter* SERGEANT JONES, *meeting* HOUGHTON, *who enters with gun.*]

SERGEANT: Good morning.

HOUGHTON: Good morning.

SERGEANT: [*warmly*] How are you?

HOUGHTON: Quite well; how are you?

SERGEANT: [*semi-important*] I'm – I'm as well as can be expected.

HOUGHTON: [*with dialect*] What d'ye mean?

SERGEANT: [*with importance*] I mean that last night my missus—— [*whispers* HOUGHTON]

HOUGHTON: [*surprised*] Nay!

SERGEANT: Fact.

HOUGHTON: Two! [SERGEANT *nods.*] Twins? [SERGEANT *nods.*] Well, mate, it does you credit! And I hope you'll soon get over it.

SERGEANT: Eh?

HOUGHTON: I mean I hope your missus 'ull soon get over it. Come and ha' some beer.

SERGEANT: I must go to the Hall first. I wish they'd been born at Malta.

HOUGHTON: Where?

SERGEANT: At Malta.

HOUGHTON: Malta! Be that where they make the best beer?

SERGEANT: No; it's "furrin." When a child's born in barracks there, it gets half a pound o' meat additional rations a-day.

HOUGHTON: Child does?

SERGEANT: Its parents. Twins would ha' been a pound a-day – pound o' meat you know. It's worth while being a father at Malta.

HOUGHTON: [*looking at* SERGEANT *admiringly and shouldering his gun*] Come and ha' some beer to drink this here joyful double-barrelled event.

> [*They turn up stage together, meeting* BLANCHE *and*

MARY *as they enter. Both fall back.* SERGEANT *to attention,* HOUGHTON *touching his cap as* BLANCHE *and* MARY *come down stage.* SERGEANT *and* HOUGHTON *exeunt.*]

BLANCHE: Don't walk so fast, Mary. Lady Shendryn said she'd overtake us. Let us rest here. [*They sit on seat.*] It's charming under the trees. I mean to look after the little boy. That's for him.

[*She puts portemonnaie into basket.*]

MARY: [*taking out portemonnaie*] And I mean to look after the little girl. This is for her.

[*She puts portemonnaie into basket.*]

BLANCHE: But, Mary, dear, can you afford it?

MARY: Yes; though I am poor, I must have some enjoyments. You rich people mustn't monopolise all the pleasures in the world.

BLANCHE: [*hurt*] My dear Mary, you know I didn't mean——

MARY: And *I* didn't mean; but I can't help being sensible. I know my place; and if I didn't, Lady Shendryn and the world would make me. I haven't a penny, so I'm a companion, though I don't receive wages, which the cook does. But then she's respected – she's not in a false position. I wish I hadn't been born a lady.

BLANCHE: No you don't.

MARY: Yes *I* do. I should have kept a Berlin-wool shop, and been independent and happy. And you, Blanche – you could have rolled down in your carriage, and given your orders – [*with imitation*] Miss Netley, please send me home this – or that – and so on.

BLANCHE: Mary, do talk about something else.

MARY: Well, I will, dear, to please you; but it is annoying to be a companion. Not your companion, Blanche – that's charming – to know that you're kept in the room to save another woman from rising to ring a bell, or to hand her the scissors, or to play the piano when you're ordered [*imitating*] Miss Netley – oh! – yes, a very nice person; so useful about the house. Useful – oh! – There, I beg your pardon, Blanche; but really Lady Shendryn's temper does upset me – one minute she's so tender and sentimental, and the next – Poor Sir Alick. Then there's that Mr Chalcot – I detest him.

BLANCHE: Why?

MARY: Oh, for his gloomy air, and his misanthropic eye-glass. [*imitating*] Liking nothing, and dissatisfied with everything.

BLANCHE: Despite all that, he has a very good heart.

MARY: My gentleman is rich, and thinks that every girl he speaks to is

dying for his ugly face, his stupid banknotes and his nasty
brewhouse. When I look at him I feel that I could smack his
face.

BLANCHE: For being rich!

MARY: Yes – perhaps. No, for being disagreeable.

BLANCHE: I'm rich; at least, they tell me so.

MARY: But you're not disagreeable.

BLANCHE: Do talk about something else.

MARY: Who – what?

BLANCHE: Anything – anybody.

MARY: Of the people staying at the Hall?

BLANCHE: Yes.

MARY: Prince Perovsky?

BLANCHE: If you like.

MARY: He means "you"; I can see it in his eye. I know Sir Alick would
say yes, and so would my lady. Blanche, what would you say?

BLANCHE: [*pensively*] I don't know.

MARY: That means "yes"! A Russian prince – wealthy, urbane – quite
the grand air, but dried up as a Normandy pippin. Will my
Blanche be a princess?

BLANCHE: Prince Perovsky is a little old.

MARY: Not for a prince. Princes are never old.

BLANCHE: And I'm a little young.

MARY: Not too young for a princess. Princesses are never too young.

BLANCHE: Why, Mary, you're quite worldly.

MARY: Only on your account. I should like to see you a princess.
You'd be charming as a princess.

BLANCHE: [*smilingly*] And if I were and had a court, what would you
be?

MARY: [*rising*] Mistress of the Robes, and First High Gold Parasol in
Waiting! Oh, my charming, darling Royal Highness. My
Highest, Mightiest, Most Serene Transparentissima!
[*curtseying*]

[CHALCOT *wakes up, and looks about him.*]

BLANCHE: [*laughs*] How silly!

MARY: Who – me?

BLANCHE: Yes.

MARY: Then I renounce my allegiance – turn Radical, and dethrone
you. I wish the prince would ask me.

BLANCHE: Ask you what?

MARY: To be his wife.

CHALCOT: [*aside*] Devil doubt you!

BLANCHE: How would you answer?

MARY: I'd answer – No!

CHALCOT: [*aside*] Dreadful falsehood!

MARY: Though I'd like to be a princess – a Russian princess – and
have slaves.

BLANCHE: Oh! I shouldn't like to have slaves.

MARY: I should, particularly if they were men.

CHALCOT: [aside] Nice girl that!

BLANCHE: Let's leave off talking Russian.

MARY: What shall we talk then? Scotch?

BLANCHE: What a time Lady Shendryn is!

MARY: [maliciously] About Angus MacAlister?

BLANCHE: [seeing CHALCOT] Hush!

MARY: What?

BLANCHE: There's a man.

CHALCOT: [rising] Don't be alarmed; I've heard nothing that I
oughtn't to.

MARY : [primly] Impossible you should.

CHALCOT: I fell asleep under that tree.

MARY: Why did you wake up?

BLANCHE: Asleep, just after breakfast!

CHALCOT: Humph! There was nothing else to do.

MARY: You mean nothing else that *you* could do.

CHALCOT: I thought of climbing the tree; good notion, wasn't it?

MARY: Excellent – if you'd stayed up there!

CHALCOT: Eh?

MARY: I mean, if you hadn't come down.

[*Guns fired without.*]

CHALCOT: Sir Alick might have brought me down.

BLANCHE: Mistaken you for a rook!

MARY: [aside] Or a scarecrow!

CHALCOT: [pointing to basket] What have yòu got there?

BLANCHE: Guess.

CHALCOT: Can't. Never could make out conundrums – or ladies.

MARY: Beyond your comprehension?

CHALCOT: Quite. [annoyed] Confound the girl! [aloud] But what's in
the basket?

BLANCHE: [holding up basket] Fowls, jelly, sago, tapioca, wine!

MARY: [repeating her words] Wine, tapioca, sago, jelly, fowls!

CHALCOT: That's variety! Somebody ill?

[MARY *sits. Enter* LADY SHENDRYN, *who heard the last
few words.*]

LADY S: Ill – no! Nobody. They're all doing well.

CHALCOT: All! Who?

LADY S: The Twins!

CHALCOT: Twins! What twins?

LADY S: Ours.

CHALCOT: Yours? Yours and Sir Al——

LADY S: [*a languishing, sentimental, frisky person*] Mine and – no, no. What a man you are! When I say Ours, I mean Sergeant Jones's.

CHALCOT: Sergeant Jones's!

LADY S: Ours – of Sir Alexander's regiment. Alexander is very fond of him; and I quite doat on Mrs Jones. You know the barracks are not eight miles off, and the railway drops you close to—— [*turning*] Miss Netley, I'll sit down—— [MARY *rises, and crosses to* BLANCHE. LADY SHENDRYN *sits.*] So I gave Mrs Jones the use of the Cottage – and it's – *a* most agreeable circumstance; isn't it?

CHALCOT: [*thoughtfully*] Very – for poor Jones!

MARY: [*aside to* BLANCHE] Make him give you something – subscription – you know.

CHALCOT: [*overhearing*] Make me! I should like to see anyone make me!

BLANCHE: [*rising, and crossing to* CHALCOT] By the way [*to* CHALCOT] I'm collecting for them. [*taking out pocket-book*] How much shall I put you down for?

CHALCOT: [*seeing* MARY's *eyes on him*] Nothing.

MARY: Nothing!

LADY S: Oh, Hugh!

BLANCHE: Oh, Mr Chalcot!

MARY: Oh, these men!

BLANCHE: Consider poor Mrs Jones!

LADY S: And the twins!

CHALCOT: Twins! I don't think those sort of women ought to be encouraged.

MARY: [*aside*] And that's a man worth thousands!

BLANCHE: [*coaxingly*] Let me put you down for something!

MARY: A shilling!

CHALCOT: [*to* MARY] I'm not to be put down.

LADY S: Miss Netley, pray don't interfere. How charming it is here, under the trees! – so poetical and leafy!

CHALCOT: [*throwing insect off her mantle*] And insecty!

> [LADY SHENDRYN *starts up.* Enter PRINCE, *smoking a cigarette.* CHALCOT *crosses to* L. PRINCE *seeing ladies raises his hat, and throws cigarette on ground.*]

LADY S: Ah! here's the Prince. How charming!

MARY: He'll give something.

BLANCHE: Prince, I'm begging – make a subscription.

PRINCE: Let me trust I may be permitted to become a subscriber.

BLANCHE: For any amount you please [*with pocket-book*] How much?

PRINCE: I leave that to you.

LADY S: Oh, Prince, you are so kind!

MARY: What a difference! [*to* CHALCOT] A noble nation the Russians!

BLANCHE: [*writing, and showing him*] Will that do?

PRINCE: If you think it sufficient.

[BLANCHE *joins* MARY.]

LADY S: Charmingly chivalric!

PRINCE: Shall I be indiscreet in asking the object of——

LADY S: *Objects!* There are two!

PRINCE: Two objects!

CHALCOT: Yes – babies.

LADY S: Twins.

CHALCOT: The Jones's gemini!

[*He crosses and sits under tree.*]

PRINCE: [*to* CHALCOT] Twins! Extraordinary people you English.

LADY S: We're going to take these things to the Cottage for them. Prince! will you come as far?

PRINCE: If I may be allowed to take part in so delicate a mission.

LADY S: Blanche! the Prince will escort you.

PRINCE: [*crossing to* BLANCHE] May I carry the basket?

BLANCHE: Can I trust you?

PRINCE: With what?

BLANCHE: The sago.

[*Exeunt* PRINCE *and* BLANCHE.]

LADY S: Miss Netley will be my cavalier.

MARY: [*coming from back*] What a treat!

LADY S: Unless you, Mr Chalcot——

CHALCOT: [*eye to eye with* MARY] Thanks, no. I'll stay where I am.

LADY S: We shall leave you all alone.

CHALCOT: I don't mind that.

MARY: That's just the sort of man who would pinch his wife on his wedding day.

[*Exeunt* LADY SHENDRYN *and* MARY.]

CHALCOT: That's a detestable girl! Whenever I meet her, she makes me thrill with dislike.

[SERGEANT *and* KEEPER *enter at end of avenue, carrying a large hamper. Meeting* SIR ALEXANDER *in shooting dress.* KEEPER *takes gun and exits with* SERGEANT.]

SIR A: Ah, Hugh – that you?

CHALCOT: [*seated*] Yes.

SIR A: What have you been doing here? [*He sits on stump.*]

CHALCOT: Sleeping. Shot anything?

SIR A: A brace. I'm nervous. I've been annoyed this morning.

CHALCOT: I'm annoyed every morning – and evening, regularly.

SIR A: I'd bad news by post – and then my lady – and I'm so horribly hard up.

CHALCOT: A little management——

SIR A: I know; but I've other troubles, Hugh. You're an old friend, and so was your father before you. If you only knew what was on my mind. There's my lady wrangling perpetually.

CHALCOT: People always quarrel when they're married – or single; and you must make allowances – her ladyship is much younger than you.

SIR A: She might remember how long *we* have—— But it isn't that – it isn't that.

CHALCOT: What then?

SIR A: I mustn't tell – I wish I could.

CHALCOT: I'm open to receive a confession of early murder, or justifiable matricide.

SIR A: It isn't my secret, or I'd tell it you. Oh! my lady is very wrong. The idea of her being jealous!

CHALCOT: I've heard that years ago you were a great killer.

SIR A: [*not understanding*] Killer! Of what – birds?

CHALCOT: No. Ladies.

SIR A: Oh! – like other men.

CHALCOT: That's bad – that's very bad. But surely my lady knew that before marriage you were not a Joseph?

SIR A: Not she.

CHALCOT: But she must have guessed——

SIR A: Pooh! pooh! You're talking like a bachelor.

CHALCOT: A bachelor may know——

SIR A: A bachelor can know nothing. It is only after they're married that men begin to understand the purity of women – [*aside*] – or their tempers.

CHALCOT: But do you mean to tell me – between men, you know – that Lady Shendryn has no cause.

SIR A: Has no cause? Certainly not——

CHALCOT: *Had* no cause, then?

SIR A: *Had!* Um – well – the slightest possible——

CHALCOT: Did she find it out?

SIR A: Unfortunately she did.

CHALCOT: Ah! Nuisance that – being found out. Is the cause removed now?

SIR A: The what?

CHALCOT: The cause – the slightest possible——

SIR A: Oh yes – long ago. Gone entirely.

CHALCOT: Dead?

SIR A: No – married.

CHALCOT: Better still. Further removed than ever.

SIR A: But my lady has never forgotten it. It was an absurd scrape; for I cared nothing about her.

CHALCOT: About my lady?

SIR A: [*irritably*] No – the——

CHALCOT: Slightest possible – no, no.

SIR A: Where is my lady?

CHALCOT: She has gone to the Cottage to see the interesting little Joneses. The Prince went with her – and Blanche – and – that other girl.

SIR A: Mary Netley! Charming girl that!

CHALCOT: Very.

SIR A: She's the daughter of very dear old friends, who died without leaving her a penny.

CHALCOT: Very dear old friends always do.

SIR A: What?

CHALCOT: Die without leaving pennies.

SIR A: Poor little thing! I wish I could find her a husband!

CHALCOT: What a misanthropic sentiment!

SIR A: Now, there's Blanche; she's a fortune. She, like Mary, has no guardians but us – neither father nor mother.

CHALCOT: Splendid qualification that; but Blanche is much too nice a girl to have a mother.

SIR A: She's another anxiety.

CHALCOT: All girls are anxieties.

SIR A: You were wrong to let Blanche slip through your fingers.

CHALCOT: Me marry an heiress! Ugh! [*shudders*] There's Prince Perovsky, he is very particular in his attentions.

SIR A: Yes; it would be a good match. He owns two-thirds of a Russian province.

CHALCOT: Poor devil! Isn't it rather awkward, his staying here? If war is to be declared——

[*He rises and goes up looking off.*]

SIR A: He's off in a couple of days; besides, after all, Russia may not mean fighting.

CHALCOT: There's Angus, coming down the avenue!

SIR A: [*rising*] Between you and me, Hugh, I wish he wouldn't come so often. He's too fond of teaching Blanche billiards. I'm always finding them with their heads closer together than is warranted by the rules of the game. When children, they saw a good deal of each other. Blanche is my ward, and an heiress; Angus, a distant cousin, poor as a rat – the Scotch branch of the family. I shouldn't like it to be thought that I threw them together.

CHALCOT: No, no.

SIR A: I'll go and meet the people at the Cottage. I promised to join

them. [*taking letters from his pocket, selecting one*] I daren't take
this into the house with me; eh – yes I may – this from Lady
Llandudno. She's in a terrible fright about the prospect of
war. You know her boy's in Ours. Asks me if I think the
regiment will be ordered out. I may show my lady that.
[*Replaces letter in pocket, then tears another into very small
pieces. Sighs deeply.*] Heigho! It's not much use. It is sure to be
found out at last.

> [CHALCOT *sits by stump on ground. Exit* SIR
> ALEXANDER. ANGUS MACALISTER *comes down the
> avenue.* CHALCOT *smokes incessantly; as soon as one
> cigar or pipe is out, he lights another.*]

CHALCOT: Well, Gus. Just got in?
ANGUS: Yes. Slept last night in barracks. Got leave again for to-day.

> [ANGUS *is grave and composed in manner; as he speaks,
> he looks about him, as if his thoughts were away.*]

CHALCOT: Bring down a paper with you?
ANGUS: Yes. [*Gives him newspaper, which* CHALCOT *looks over.*] Where
are all the people gone? There's nobody in the Hall.
CHALCOT: Gone to the Cottage to try on a pair of new twins – born on
the estate. My lady, Sir Alick, Miss Netley, the Prince, and
Blanche.
ANGUS: Have they been gone long?

> [*He crosses to seat and puts* R. *foot on it.*]

CHALCOT: No. I haven't quite made up my mind whether I like that
Prince Perovsky or not. Do you like him?
ANGUS: I never think about him.
CHALCOT: [*aside*] That's not true, Angus, my man. [*aloud, eyeing*
ANGUS] I wonder if we shall have war with Russia?
ANGUS: I don't know – I don't care – I wish we had!
CHALCOT: Out of sorts?
ANGUS: Yes.
CHALCOT: Have a weed. [*handing cigar-case.* ANGUS *goes to* CHALCOT
and takes cigarette.] Why want war? For the sake of change?
ANGUS: Yes.
CHALCOT: Change of scene?
ANGUS: Change of anything – change for anything – silver, copper –
anything out of this!

> [*He goes to seat and sits.*]

CHALCOT: [*puffing smoke*] Out of what?
ANGUS: Out at elbows! If there's no war I shall go to India. What use
in staying here – without a shilling or a friend? [*plucking leaf*]

What chance is there?

CHALCOT: What chance! You mean what chances? Plenty. You're young – good family – marry a fortune.

ANGUS: Marry for money! That's not the way with the MacAlisters.

CHALCOT: Umph! Marriage is a mistake, but ready money's real enjoyment; at least, so people think who haven't got it. I suppose you've made your choice?

ANGUS: I have. Perhaps you're aware of that?

CHALCOT: Yes.

ANGUS: And who it is?

CHALCOT: Yes.

ANGUS: I'm a bad hand at concealment. I'm too proud of loving her. I love to hide it. That's why I mean to go to India.

[*He crosses to tree.*]

CHALCOT: Better stop here and smoke. I feel in a confidential humour. So you're in love with Blanche?

ANGUS: Yes.

CHALCOT: I saw that long ago. You know that I proposed to her?

ANGUS: Yes.

CHALCOT: But I'm proud to say she wouldn't have me. Ah! she's a sensible girl; and her spirited conduct in saying "No!" on that occasion laid me under an obligation to her for life.

ANGUS: She declined?

CHALCOT: She declined very much. I only did it to please Sir Alick, who thought the two properties would go well together – never mind the two humans. Marriage means to sit opposite at table, and be civil to each other before company. Blanche Haye and Hugh Chalcot. Pooh! the service should have run: "I, Brewhouses, Malt-kilns, Public-houses, and Premises, take thee, Landed Property, grass and arable, farm-houses, tenements, and Salmon Fisheries, to my wedded wife, to have and to hold for dinners and evening parties, for carriage and horse-back, for balls and presentations, to bore and to tolerate, till mutual aversion do us part"; but Land, grass and arable, farm-houses, tenements, and Salmon Fisheries said "No"; and Brewhouses is free.

[*He strikes match.*]

ANGUS: At all events, you could offer her a fortune.

CHALCOT: And you're too proud to make her an offer because you're poor! [ANGUS *sighs.*] You're wrong. You're very wrong. I have more cause for complaint than you. I'm a great match. My father was senior partner in the brewery. When he died, he left me heaps. His brother, my uncle, died – left me more. My cousin went mad – bank-notes on the brain. His share fell to me; and, to crown my embarrassments, a grand-aunt, who lived in retirement in Cornwall on four hundred a year, with a faithful poodle and a treacherous companion, died too, leaving me the accumulated metallic refuse of misspent years. Mammas languished at me for their daughters, and daughters languished at me as their mammas told them. At last my time came. I fell in love – down, down, down, into an abyss where there was neither sense, nor patience, nor reason – nothing but love and hope. My heart flared with happiness as if it were lighted up with oxygen. She was eighteen – blue eyes – hair the colour of wheat, with a ripple on it like the corn as it bends to the breeze – fair as milk. She looked like china with a soul in it. Pa made much of me – ma made much of me; so did her brothers and sisters, and uncles and aunts, and cousins and cousinettes, and cousiniculings. How I hated 'em! One day I heard her speaking of me to a sister; she said – her voice said – that voice that, as I listened to it, ran up and down my arms, and gave me palpitation – she said, "I don't care much about him; but then he's so very rich!" [*His face falls.*] That cured me of marriage, and mutual affection, and the rest of the poetical lies. [*knocking ashes out of pipe*] You've youth, health, strength, and not a shilling – everything to hope for. Women can love *you* for *yourself* alone. Money doesn't poison your existence. You're not a prize pig, tethered in a golden sty. What is left for me? Purchasable charms; every wish gratified; every aspiration anticipated, and the sight of the drays belonging to the firm rolling about London with my name on them, and a fat and happy drayman sitting on the shafts, whom I envy with all my heart. Pity the poor! Pity the rich; for they are bankrupts in friendship, and beggars in love.

ANGUS: [*Crosses to* CHALCOT *and standing over him.*] So, because one woman was selfish, you fall in love with poverty, and the humiliations and insults – insults you cannot resent – heaped on you daily by inferiors. Prudent mothers point you out as dangerous, and daughters regard you as an epidemic. You are a waiter upon fortune – a man on the look-out for a wife with money – a creature whose highest aim and noblest ambition is to sell himself and his name for good rations and luxurious quarters – a footman out of livery, known as the husband of Miss So-and-so, the heiress. You talk like a spoiled child! The rich man is to be envied. He can load her he loves with proofs of his affection – he can face her father and ask him for her hand – he can roll her in his carriage to a palace, and say, This is your home, and I am your servant!

[*He goes back to seat.*]

CHALCOT: You talk like a – man in love. Couldn't you face Sir Alick?

ANGUS: No.

CHALCOT: His marriage hasn't made him happy. Poor Sir Alick! He never could have been happy with his weakness.

ANGUS: You mean Lady Shendryn?

CHALCOT: No; she's not a weakness – she's a power. No; Sir Alick's great regret in life is that he isn't tall. There's a skeleton everywhere; and his skeleton lacks a foot. He can't reach happiness by ten inches. He's a fine soldier, and an accomplished gentleman; his misery is that he is short. An odd sort of unhappiness, isn't it, from the point of view of men of our height?

ANGUS: What's that to do with the subject of money *versus* none?

CHALCOT: Nothing whatever – that's why I mentioned it.

ANGUS: Talking of money – you lent me £50. Here it is. [*giving him note from pocket-book*] I got a note for fifty, because it was portable.

CHALCOT: [*taking it reluctantly*] If it shouldn't be quite convenient—

ANGUS: Oh, quite.

> [*He goes up, cutting at leaves of tree with cane.*]

CHALCOT: [*aside*] Now this would be of use to him; it's of none to me. I know he wants it – I don't; I didn't even remember that I'd lent it to him. Confound it. [*putting it in his pocket*] It's enough to make a man hate his kind, and build a hospital.

ANGUS: [*at top of avenue*] Coming in?

CHALCOT: No; I shall stay here. [*turning, and lying on ground*] The great comfort of the country is, one can enjoy peace and quiet. [*A large wooden ball is thrown. It falls near* CHALCOT's *head. He starts up.*] "Eh!" [*Four more balls are thrown, each nearly hitting him.*] By Jove!

ANGUS: Here they are!

> [*Enter* PRINCE, BLANCHE, LADY SHENDRYN, MARY, SIR ALEXANDER, *and* CAPTAIN SAMPREY.]

PRINCE: [*looking at bowls. To* BLANCHE] Yours – that's ten. It's your first throw. Permit me.

> [*He picks up the bowl.* ANGUS *comes down between them.*]

ANGUS: Good morning.

BLANCHE: Oh, Cousin Angus, how you made me start! [*As the* PRINCE *hands her the ball, she drops it with a start.*]

LADY S: My dear child, my nerves!

> [*She leans against* SIR ALEXANDER.]

SIR A: [*aside to her*] Don't be so affected.

[LADY SHENDRYN *sits.*]

ANGUS: Good morning, Lady Shendryn; good morning, Miss Netley.
[*raising hat*] How are you, Samprey?

SAMPREY: How d'ye do, Mac ?

CHALCOT: Who threw that ball? [*pointing to the first one thrown*]

MARY: I did.

CHALCOT: It only just missed falling on my head.

MARY: I'm very sorry.

CHALCOT: That it missed me?

MARY: No; that it fell so far off.

CHALCOT: My head?

MARY: No; [*pointing to ball*] that other wooden thing.

[CHALCOT, *very wild, goes up* R. MARY, *laughing to
herself, goes up* L.]

ANGUS: May I join in the game?

SAMPREY: [*giving him bowl*] Take my hand, Mac.

LADY S: It's going to rain. We'd better get indoors.

BLANCHE: Oh no, it won't. It never rains when I wish it to be fine.
Now, where shall I throw it.

PRINCE: I would suggest this side of the hillock.

ANGUS: I would advise the other. We couldn't see what became of it
then.

BLANCHE: The other side. There!

[*She throws ball off.*]

ANGUS: [*about to throw*] Now then!

[PRINCE *and* ANGUS *both go to throw and collide.*]

LADY S: [*interposing*] It's for the Prince to throw first.

ANGUS: I beg your pardon.

PRINCE: No; after you. [ANGUS *refuses.* PRINCE *throws.*] There!

[ANGUS *throws.* PRINCE *goes to* BLANCHE *and then to*
LADY SHENDRYN *as soon as* ANGUS *has thrown, who
immediately returns to* BLANCHE. CHALCOT, *in looking
after the throwing, is in* MARY's *way when her turn
arrives. She coughs and he turns suddenly.*]

CHALCOT: [*to* MARY] Are you going to throw now?

MARY: Yes; why do you ask?

CHALCOT: That I may get out of the way.

[MARY *throws, then goes up, and sits on stump, looking
at paper.*]

PRINCE: Now, Lady Shendryn.

LADY S: Oh, I am so fatigued! My dear Prince, pray throw for me.

> [PRINCE *throws.* LADY SHENDRYN *goes up.*]

SAMPREY: All thrown. Who's won?

> [PRINCE *and* ANGUS *start together, then stop.*]

ANGUS: I beg your pardon.

PRINCE: After you.

> [*They hesitate, each unwilling to precede the other.*]

BLANCHE: Oh do go! You can't stop to behave prettily across country.

> [BLANCHE *exits, followed by* ANGUS *and the* PRINCE, *then* SAMPREY.]

LADY S: [*coming down, trying to take* SIR ALEXANDER'S *arm*] I'm so tired, Alexander.

SIR A: [*avoiding her*] Do leave me alone.

> [*Exit* SIR ALEXANDER.]

LADY S: Miss Netley, I must trouble you.

> [MARY *is seated on stump.* LADY SHENDRYN *takes her arm.* LADY SHENDRYN *and* MARY *cross and exeunt,* MARY *and* CHALCOT *exchanging looks.*]

CHALCOT: [*alone*] Serves her right. Poor Angus Mac-Moth. He'll flutter round that beautiful flame till he singes his philibeg. [*The patter of rain heard upon the leaves.*] Lady Shendryn was right. It's coming down. That'll break up the skittle party. [*The* SERGEANT *enters, puts out his hand, feels the rain, and takes shelter under tree.*] There's the Sergeant. I must tip him something in consideration of his recent domestic – affliction. [*Takes out pocket-book.*] I'll give him a fiver – eh? Here's Angus's fifty, I'll give him that. [*pausing*] No; he'll go mentioning it, and it will get into the papers, and there'll be a paragraph about the singular munificence of Hugh Chalcot, Esq., the eminent brewer! – eminent! – as if a brewer could be eminent! No; I daren't give him the fifty. [*Stands under tree, next to* SERGEANT. SERGEANT *touches his cap.*] Wet day, Sergeant. [*turning up coat collar*]

SERGEANT: Yes, sir.

CHALCOT: Glad to hear that Mrs Jones is getting over her little difficulty – I should say difficulties – so well.

SERGEANT: Thank you, sir; [*with solemnity*] she is as a person might say, sir, as well as can be expected.

[*During this scene the rain comes down more heavily, and the stage darkens.*]

CHALCOT: Have a pipe, Sergeant?

SERGEANT: Thank you, sir. [CHALCOT *gives him tobacco and fusee. They fill and light pipes.*] Thank you, sir.

CHALCOT: Sergeant, how many are you in family now?

SERGEANT: [*lighting pipe*] Eight, sir.

CHALCOT: Eight! Good gracious! [*aside, and looking at note*] If I were only sure he wouldn't mention it——

SERGEANT: Yes, sir. Six before, and two this morning – six and two are eight.

CHALCOT: Rather a large family. May I ask what your pay is?

SERGEANT: One-and-tenpence a day, sir.

CHALCOT: One-and-tenp—— [*aside*] P'raps he wouldn't mention it! [*aloud*] A small income for so large a family!

SERGEANT: Yes, sir; the family is larger than the income; but then there are other things, and Sir Alick is very kind, and so is my lady, and I hope for promotion – I may be colour-sergeant some day, and my eldest boy will soon be in the band; and so you see, sir, it's not a bad look-out, take one thing with another.

CHALCOT: [*astonished, aside*] Happiness and hope, with a wife and eight children on one-and-tenpence a day! Oh, Contentment! in what strange, out-of-the-way holes do you hide yourself? If he wouldn't mention it! [*looking at note, aloud*] Twins! – both of the same sex?

SERGEANT: No, sir – one boy, one girl.

CHALCOT: Which is the elder?

SERGEANT: Don't know, sir. Don't think Mrs Jones knows. Don't think they know themselves. We never had a baby-girl before, sir. It's quite a new invention on Mrs Jones's part. We always have boys, 'cos they make the best soldiers. There's one thing as strikes me with regard to these twins as being odd.

CHALCOT: Odd! – you mean even. What's odd?

SERGEANT: I'm their father, and so the credit of them must be half mine; and yet everybody asks after Mrs Jones, and nobody asks after me.

CHALCOT: Oh, vanity! vanity! poor human vanity! [*Rain hard.*] By Jove, it is coming down. The skittle party must be broken up. Well, Sergeant, I wish the twins all sorts of good luck, and their mamma and papa likewise. Please buy 'em something for me. [*giving note*] Good morning. [*He hurries up avenue, and goes off.*]

SERGEANT: Here's luck! [*looking at note*] Hey! Hullo! Here's some mistake! [*calling after CHALCOT*] Hi! Sir! Sir! [CHALCOT *re-*

enters.] I beg your pardon, sir, for calling you back; but you've made a mistake; you meant to give me a five-pun' note – and many thanks, sir; but this here's for fifty.

CHALCOT: [*after a pause, with suppressed rage*] Thank you, – yes – my mistake.

[*Takes bank-note, and gives* SERGEANT *the other, and goes off, biting his lips with fury.*]

SERGEANT: Five pounds. He's a trump! Who'd a thought it? – and him only a civilian. My twins is as good as promotion. I'll go and show Mrs Jones.

[*Exit* SERGEANT. *Rain and wind. Enter* BLANCHE *and* ANGUS. BLANCHE *carries the skirt of her dress over her head.*]

BLANCHE: [*under tree*] How unfortunate, the rain coming on!
ANGUS: Very.
BLANCHE: Where are all the other people gone?
ANGUS: I don't know. [*aside*] And I don't care. Your feet will get wet through on the grass. Better stand upon the seat. Allow me.

[*He helps her to get on seat.*]

BLANCHE: You're very careful of me.
ANGUS: As careful of you as if you were old——
BLANCHE: As if I were old?
ANGUS: Old china. [*He gets up on seat, and stands by her side.*] This is more comfortable, isn't it?
BLANCHE: Infinitely.

[*Enter* LADY SHENDRYN *and* SIR ALEXANDER, *at end of avenue.*]

LADY S: [*her skirt over her head*] I said it would rain.
SIR A: I didn't contradict you.
LADY S: [*sitting on stump of tree.*] No, but I understood your silence.
SIR A: Now you're under shelter, I'll leave you.
LADY S: Leave me by myself in the Park?
SIR A: Do you suppose you'll be attacked by freebooters? What are you afraid of?
LADY S: Of – of the deer!
SIR A: [*sitting down, back to back with* LADY SHENDRYN, *aside*] The deer! They're more likely to be afraid of you.
LADY S: [*sentimentally*] Ah! You would have been glad to have sat with me beneath the shelter of this verdant canopy years ago!
SIR A: Years ago, I was a fool!

[*Rain and wind.*]

ANGUS: Quite a storm! Your hair will be wet!
BLANCHE: It is already.
ANGUS: Take my hat.

> [*He takes off* BLANCHE's *hat and puts his own on her head. Then hangs* BLANCHE's *hat by ribbon on branch of tree above his head.*]

BLANCHE: How do I look in a man's hat?
ANGUS: Beautiful! Take this, too. [*He takes off his coat, and wraps it round her shoulders; puts his arm round her waist, and ties coat over her bosom by its sleeves.*] That's much better, isn't it?
BLANCHE: But you'll catch cold.
ANGUS: No; we're used to cold in Cantyre; besides, we're trained not to care for it. There's a special sort of drill that makes us almost macintosh! You've seen troops marching in the wet?
BLANCHE: Often.
ANGUS: That was rain drill!
LADY S: If you walked to the Hall, you could send me an umbrella.
SIR A: I'd rather you got wet. Just now you wished me to stay for fear of highwaymen.
LADY S: I might catch cold.
SIR A: I should be sorry for the cold that caught you.
LADY S: It might be my death.
SIR A: Lady Shendryn, the rain fertilises the earth, nourishes the crops, and makes the fish lively; but still it does not bring with it every blessing. You have no right to hold out agreeable expectations which you know you do not intend to realise.

> [*These conversations to be taken up as if they were continuous.*]

ANGUS: What was that song you sang at the Sylvesters'?
BLANCHE: Oh!
ANGUS: I wish you'd hum it to me now.
BLANCHE: Without music?
ANGUS: It won't be without music.
BLANCHE: You know the story: it is supposed to be sung by a very young man who is in love with a very haughty beauty, but dare not tell her of his love.
ANGUS: Of course he was poor.
BLANCHE: N – o.
ANGUS: What else could keep him silent?
BLANCHE: Want of – courage.
ANGUS: How does it go?
BLANCHE: [*Sings: Air, "Le Chanson de Fortunio," in Offenbach's "Maître Fortunio".*]

> If my glances have betrayed me,
>   Ask me no more,
> For I dare not tell thee, lady,
>   Whom I adore.
> She is young, and tall, and slender.
>   Eyes of deep blue,
> She is sweet, and fair, and tender,
>   Like unto you.
> Unless my lady will me,
>   I'll not reveal,
> Though the treasured secret kill me,
>   The love I feel.

LADY S: Advertising our poverty to the whole county; a filthy, old rumbling thing, not fit for a washerwoman to ride in. I won't go out in it again!

SIR A: Then stay at home.

LADY S: Why not order a new carriage?

SIR A: Can't afford it.

ANGUS: The air has haunted me ever since I heard you sing it. I've written some words to it myself.

BLANCHE: Oh, give them to me, I'll sing them.

ANGUS: Will you?

> [*He gives her verses, which he takes from pocket-book in coat pocket.*]

LADY S: Oh! I feel so faint. I think it must be time for lunch.

SIR A: I'm sure it is. [*looking at watch*] And I'm awfully hungry. Confound it!

BLANCHE: [*reading verses which* ANGUS *has given her*] They're very charming. [*sighs*]

ANGUS: You're faint. They'll lunch without us.

BLANCHE: Never mind.

ANGUS: You're not hungry?

BLANCHE: No; are you?

ANGUS: Not in the least.

BLANCHE: Cousin, do you know I rather like to see you getting wet. May I keep these?

ANGUS: If you wish it.

LADY S: Where does all your money go to then? And what is that Mr Kelsey, the lawyer always coming down for?

SIR A: You'd better not ask. You'd better not know.

BLANCHE: But tell me, cousin, have you ever been in love?

ANGUS: Yes.

BLANCHE: How many times?

ANGUS: Once.

BLANCHE: Only once?

ANGUS: Only once.

LADY S: I know where the money goes to.

SIR A: Do you? I wish I did. Where?

LADY S: I know.

SIR A: Where?

LADY S: I know.

BLANCHE: I shouldn't like a husband who was too good, he'd become monotonous.

ANGUS: No husband would be too good for you; at least, I think not!

LADY S: Isolating me from my family! Never letting me see my brother!

SIR A: Your brother——

LADY S: Poor Percy! only twenty-two, and——

SIR A: [*in a fury*] Don't mention his name to me! I won't hear of him! Infernal young villain! always in scrapes himself and dragging others into them! Don't mention his name!

LADY S: I should not have been so treated if I'd married a man of decent height. What could I expect from a little fellow of five feet two?

SIR A: [*rising, out of temper*] Lady Shendryn!

LADY S: Such violence! 'Tis the same as when years ago I discovered your falsehood. I know why we live so near. You have too many establishments to provide for!

SIR A: Madam!

LADY S: I suppose that when that woman——

SIR A: Lady Shendryn!

LADY S: That Mrs——

SIR A: Silence!

[*Distant thunder and lightning.*]

LADY S: [*rising and clinging to* SIR ALEXANDER] Alexander!

SIR A: Don't touch me!

[*Exit* SIR ALEXANDER *quickly.*]

ANGUS: [*nearing her*] Blanche!

BLANCHE: Angus!

[*The* PRINCE *enters, with umbrella up, followed by* SERVANT *with another, which he takes to* LADY SHENDRYN, *holding it over her as she exits* [*the umbrellas to be wet*]. *The* PRINCE *goes down to* BLANCHE, *and takes her off under umbrella, leaving coat in* ANGUS's *hands; at same time,* CHALCOT *and* MARY *enter, wrangling, she saying,* "I never saw such a man! You want all the umbrella," *&c., snatches it away* *from him, and runs off.* ANGUS, *who is reaching* BLANCHE's *hat from tree, drops coat over* CHALCOT's *head,* ANGUS *puts* BLANCHE's *hat on his head,* CHALCOT *pointing to it as drop descends.*]

END OF ACT I

ACT II

SCENE I – *Drawing-room at* LADY SHENDRYN'S, *in the neighbourhood of Birdcage Walk. Centre opening with folding-doors leading into inner room, with bay window, looking on to balcony. Door* L. *Oval tea-table with afternoon tea laid and gong-bell. Ottoman down stage. Sofa with small round table at side, with cup of tea upon it. Chandelier and lamps lighted. In inner room, door, piano, music-stool and chair against window. Folding-doors to be closed at rise of curtain. Small chairs head and* L. *of table.*

[MARY *discovered presiding at tea-table.* BLANCHE *on ottoman,* LADY SHENDRYN *on sofa, reading letter.*]

LADY S: My dear Blanche, I must request your attention to the subject of this letter again.

BLANCHE: I'm listening.

LADY S: Although I am all excitement at Sir Alexander's departure to-night, still, this affair must be settled, and at once; for not only Sir Alexander, but the Prince leaves town to-night. I'll read Lady Maria's letter again. [MARY *and* BLANCHE *exchange looks.*] The last side is all that I shall trouble you with. [*reads*] "It could easily be arranged, and though a formal contract could not be entered into, a mutual agreement might be ratified, and when the war is concluded – and I hear from the very *best* authority" – "Best" underlined, my dear – "that it *cannot* last long" – "Cannot" underlined, my dear – "the Prince could return to this country and renew his suit. This is *my* opinion" – "My" underlined, Blanche – "and it is also the opinion of the *Duchess*, with whom I have held counsel" – "Duchess" underlined. – "It is *most desirable*" – "Most desirable" underlined – "that the match should be *made*." – "Made" underlined. – "Ever your own ADELAIDE." There, Blanche! now you know what Lady Maria thinks! and when the Prince comes here to-night to make his adieux, you can act in accordance with the views she has so feelingly, so very feelingly, expressed.

BLANCHE: But why should I be engaged to Prince Perovsky?

LADY S: Because he's a great match.

BLANCHE: But to engage oneself to a Russian at the very time we're going to war with them!

LADY S: But when the fighting is over, you can be married.

MARY: [*aside*] And then the fighting can begin again!

BLANCHE: And Sir Alick going away this very night!

LADY S: [*with suppressed emotion*] It is my husband's duty to go.

MARY: [*aside*] And his pleasure.

LADY S: And go he must.

MARY: [*aside*] And will!

BLANCHE: Poor Sir Alick! I am so sorry.

LADY S: Duty, my child! duty!

BLANCHE: [*to* MARY] But I don't want to get married at all!

MARY: [*to her*] Duty, my pet! duty! And in this case duty ought to be a pleasure.

BLANCHE: Duty! The same as it is Sir Alick's duty to go and fight?

LADY S: Precisely.

BLANCHE: And a girl must put on her wedding-dress for the same reason a soldier puts on his regimentals?

MARY: Just so. And seek the mutual conflict at the altar.

BLANCHE: Oh, Mary – conflict!

MARY: I repeat it – conflict. And may the best man win.

LADY S: Miss Netley, I think you talk too much.

BLANCHE: Why do girls get married?

MARY: [*aside*] That's a poser!

LADY S: O——h. For the sake of society.

BLANCHE: That means for the sake of other people?

LADY S: Naturally. If people didn't marry there would be no – evening parties.

MARY: [*aside*] And what a dreadful thing that would be!

BLANCHE: But I don't want to get married.

LADY S: Then you ought to do.

BLANCHE: Ought I, Mary?

MARY: I don't know – I never was married.

LADY S: [*severely*] And never will be. With your views, Miss Netley, you don't deserve to be. Marriage is one of those – a – dear me – I want a word. Marriage is one of those——

MARY: Evils?

LADY S: [*angrily*] No.

BLANCHE: Blessings?

LADY S: Blessings – yes – blessings, which cannot be avoided.

BLANCHE: What do you think, Mary?

MARY: It is woman's mission to marry.

BLANCHE: Why?

MARY: That she may subdue man.

LADY S: Quite so.

MARY: The first step to man's subjugation is courtship. The second matrimony. Any more tea?

[*They signify* No.]

BLANCHE: [*rising and going to* MARY *sitting in chair.*] Don't talk about it any more. Think of poor Sir Alick!

MARY: [*to* BLANCHE] And Angus MacAlister.

LADY S: [*sharply*] What's that?

BLANCHE: Nothing! [*rising with* MARY *quickly*] What's what!

LADY S: Didn't I hear the name of Angus MacAlister?

BLANCHE: ⎫
MARY: ⎬ Oh, no.

BLANCHE: She doesn't believe us.

MARY: She knows better.

> [*Enter* SIR ALEXANDER, *in regimentals*. BLANCHE *and* MARY *meet him, back of ottoman.*]

SIR A: Well, girls, my time is up, and I've come to bid you good-bye.

BLANCHE: ⎫
MARY: ⎬ Oh, Sir Alexander!

SIR A: You won't see me again till I come back – if ever I do come back. One word with my lady. [*The* GIRLS *sit at tea-table as before.* SIR ALEXANDER *goes down beside* LADY SHENDRYN *on sofa.*] Diana, you know the dispositions I have made, and how I have left you – in case any – in case anything should befall me. For ready money, there is £2,000 at Coutts's in your name.

LADY S: [*dignified*] You are very kind – indeed, you are very liberal.

SIR A: With every possible allowance for your temper, and customary misapprehension of my conduct, I cannot understand why you should meet me in this way.

LADY S: £2,000! Where does the rest of the money go? I know your income. What have you done with it?

SIR A: Is this the moment – when I am about to leave you – perhaps never to return – to quarrel about money?

LADY S: Money! You know that I despise it. I only speak of the disappearance of these large sums as a proof——

SIR A: Proof! – proof of what?

LADY S: [*with tears*] Of your faithlessness – your infidelity!

SIR A: Consider the girls.

LADY S: They cannot hear me.

> [SIR ALEXANDER *back to audience.*]

BLANCHE: [*to* MARY] This is all very dreadful. I don't think I'll ever marry.

MARY: Yes, you will.

BLANCHE: To quarrel with my husband?

MARY: Think how pleasant it is to own a husband to quarrel with!

LADY S: Such large sums unaccounted for!

SIR A: [*turning*] I know it.

LADY S: Where do they go?

SIR A: I cannot tell you. You are the last person in the world I would have know.

LADY S: Doubtless!

SIR A: Diana, you are wrong – very wrong!

LADY S: Alexander Shendryn, you know how you have treated me. You know——

SIR A: I know that at one time you had just cause of complaint. I confessed my fault, and entreated your forgiveness. Instead of pardoning, you have never forgotten my indiscretion; but have dinned – dinned – dinned it into my ears unceasingly.

LADY S: And, pray, sir, what divine creature is a man, that he may be faithless to his wife with impunity? What are we women, that our lot should be that we must be deceived that we may forgive; that we may be deceived again that we may forgive again, to be deceived again? Sir Alexander, these expenses from home demand my scrutiny, and I insist on knowing why they are, and wherefore? But perhaps I am detaining you, and you have adieux to make elsewhere!

SIR A: Diana, I lose all patience!

[*Enter a* SERVANT.]

SERVANT: The orderly is below, Sir Alexander, and wishes to speak to you.

SIR A: May he come up here?

LADY S: If you wish it.

SIR A: [*after motioning to* SERVANT, *who goes off, coming to* LADY SHENDRYN] Consider, £2,000 is a large sum – more than enough for your immediate requirements!

LADY S: [*with exultation*] My requirements! All I ask is a cottage, and a loaf of bread – and all your secrets told to me!

[*Enter* SERGEANT.]

SIR A: Now, Sergeant!

SERGEANT: [*saluting*] This letter, Colonel. Mr Kelsey, the lawyer, brought it himself.

LADY S: Mr Kelsey?

SIR A: To the barracks?

SERGEANT: Yes, Colonel; he said it was of the utmost consequence, and that you was to have it directly, and that he would be back in half an hour at your quarters to receive your instructions.

[SIR ALEXANDER *goes into inner room, and reads.*]

LADY S: Mrs Jones quite well, Sergeant?

SERGEANT: Middling, my lady, thank you.

BLANCHE: And the children?

SERGEANT: Quite well, thank you, miss; all but the twins. The twins has got the twinsey!

BLANCHE: ⎫
MARY: ⎬ The what?

SERGEANT: The twinsey, inside their throats – just here – under the stock.

MARY: You mean quinsy?

SERGEANT: Very like, miss. It's a regulation infant complaint!

BLANCHE: And what does Mrs Jones think of your going away to Varna?

SERGEANT: Well, mum, she don't like it much. She is a little cut up about it, and has made me a outfit – six new shirts complete. [*piqued*] The twins don't seem to care much – but children never seem to know when you've done enough for 'em!

MARY: And how do you like it?

SERGEANT: Well, miss, I'm sorry to leave the missus and the children – 'specially them twins, who wants more looking after than the others, being two; but I shouldn't like to stay behind. I don't think the company could get along without me.

SIR A: [*violently agitated*] Good heavens!

LADY S: What's the matter?

SIR A: [*pacing stage*] Nothing!

LADY S: [*offering to take letter*] Can I——

SIR A: [*crushing letter in his hand, aside*] What's to be done? What's to be done? What's to be done? [*Looks at time-piece.*] Sergeant, take a cab, drive to the Garrick – the Garrick Club – as hard as you can go. Ask for Mr Chalcot; bring him here directly. He's dining there, I know. Lose no time, for I haven't a moment to spare.

[*Exit* SERGEANT, *after saluting.*]

LADY S: More mystery!

[*She sits on sofa.*]

BLANCHE: } You quite frighten me.
MARY: } Can I be of any——

SIR A: No, my dears – no. I must speak to your aunt again, but alone. Step into this room for a few minutes.

[*He signifies to them to go into inner room.* MARY *and* BLANCHE *go in, exchanging glances.* SIR ALEXANDER *closes door after them.*]

LADY S: What's coming now?

SIR A: [*looking at letter, then advancing*] Diana, I grieve to tell you that I cannot leave you the £2,000 I spoke of.

LADY S: What?

SIR A: [*looking at letter*] I can only leave you £500.

LADY S: This is that letter?

SIR A: Yes.

LADY S: From Mr Kelsey! Whenever that fellow shows his face, there is always trouble.

SIR A: Don't wrong poor Kelsey. He is an excellent man.

LADY S: £2,000! – £500! Why this sudden call for £1,500?

SIR A: I dare not tell you.

LADY S: Show me that letter.

SIR A: Impossible!

LADY S: Why not?

SIR A: I cannot tell you. I must ask you to have confidence.

LADY S: Confidence! – in you?

SIR A: I have sent for Chalcot to – to—

LADY S: To borrow money of him?

SIR A: Yes.

LADY S: For me?

SIR A: No.

LADY S: And I am not to know the reason of this sudden call upon your
purse?

SIR A: You must not.

LADY S: [rising] I will!

SIR A: [about to tell her] Diana – no! no! You must not know!

LADY S: [trying to snatch letter] That letter!

SIR A: [struggling] Diana!

LADY S: I am your wife. I will have it. I will know this woman's name.

[As she gets hold of the letter, it tears in half. She has
the blank side. Enter SERGEANT and CHALCOT in evening dress. BLANCHE and MARY, hearing the noise, enter
from inner room.]

LADY S: [showing blank] The blank side!

SIR A: [showing written side] Thank heaven!

CHALCOT: [aside] There's been a row.

SERGEANT: Colonel, I met Mr Chalcot as I was going to the cab-rank.

SIR A: Chalcot, a word! [speaks to SERGEANT, who salutes.] – Sergeant.
[aside] In this room, Chalcot.

CHALCOT: An awful row!

[SIR ALEXANDER and CHALCOT go off through folding-
doors.]

LADY S: [after a pause, crossing and sitting] Sergeant, I shall take care of
your wife while you are away.

SERGEANT: [dolefully] Thank you, my lady.

BLANCHE: And the children.

MARY: And the twins.

LADY S: ⎫
BLANCHE: ⎬ Oh, the twins! Certainly.

SERGEANT: [affected] Thank you, ladies. It'll make me more comfortable to know that they will be cared for, if anything should – if

anything – 'cos accidents will happen with – the best regulated enemy. She's waiting below to march with me to parade, so as to see the last of me. [*A pause.*] Thank you, ladies. Good evening.

> [*Exit* SERGEANT. *The* WOMEN *look sorrowfully and go up. Enter* SIR ALEXANDER *and* CHALCOT.]

SIR A: You understand?

CHALCOT: Perfectly!

SIR A: And you'll see that it's explained as I——

CHALCOT: Certainly.

SIR A: Thanks. [*shaking hands*] You are a friend indeed.

> [*He sits on sofa.* LADY SHENDRYN *and* BLANCHE *sitting at table,* MARY R. *of ottoman,* CHALCOT *on ottoman.*]

CHALCOT: This is a charming wind-up to a jolly evening. Parting with all my pals. I didn't know I cared at all about them; and now they're going, I find out I like them very much. Saw Sergeant Jones's wife crying in the hall. Why don't she stop at home and cry? Why does she come and cry where I am?

MARY: [*half crying*] What a world this is!

CHALCOT: Sad hole, I confess.

MARY: And what villains men are!

CHALCOT: They are! – they are!

MARY: To quarrel and fight, and bring grief upon poor women – and what fools women are——

CHALCOT: They are! – they are!

MARY: [*impatiently*] I mean, to cry about the men! How stupid you are!

CHALCOT: I am! – I am! You're quite right [*rising*] I agree with you entirely.

BLANCHE: You two don't often agree.

CHALCOT: No; but then we very seldom meet.

MARY: Thank goodness!

CHALCOT: Thank goodness!

MARY: At all events, Mr Chalcot does not deny that women are far superior to men.

CHALCOT: Pardon me. He does deny it – he denies it very much.

BLANCHE: Which, then, are the better?

CHALCOT: Neither! – both are worst.

BLANCHE: ⎱ Oh!
MARY: ⎰

CHALCOT: And, as a general axiom, this truth is manifest. Whatever is – is wrong!

SIR A: [*advancing to* LADY SHENDRYN] And now there is no more to say, but good-bye, and God bless you! [*Holds out his hand.* LADY

SHENDRYN *remains motionless. A pause.*] Won't you bid me good-bye?

LADY S: The letter!

SIR A: Impossible! It would make you more miserable.

LADY S: Doubtless.

SIR A: [*holding out his hand*] Diana!

LADY S: You are waited for elsewhere. Kiss and bid good-bye to those you love.

SIR A: It may be for the last time.

LADY S: The letter! [SIR ALEXANDER *dissents, and again holds out his hand.*] Your lady-love is waiting. Waste no more time with me.

SIR A: [*aside*] Ah! I may find peace in the campaign – I cannot find it here. I can control a regiment, but not a wife. Better battle than a discontented woman. [CHALCOT *persuades him to go back, aloud*] Good-bye, Chalcot – [*shaking hands*] – and remember! Good-bye, Blanche – Good-bye, Mary. [*kissing them*]

BLANCHE: ⎫
MARY: ⎭ [*hanging about him*] Oh, Sir Alick!

> [*They look appealingly at him, and then towards* LADY SHENDRYN, *who remains motionless.* SIR ALEXANDER *again goes to her, and offers his hand. She takes no notice of him. He bows and goes off hurriedly, followed by* BLANCHE, *crying.* MARY *turns at door to look at* LADY SHENDRYN, *and meeting* CHALCOT's *eye, stamps at him, saying,* "Go away," *and slams the door.* CHALCOT *looks with contempt at* LADY SHENDRYN, *who sinks on to ottoman.*]

LADY S: Mr Chalcot – don't leave me! Ring for Jennings, my maid. Give me some air – the heat overpowers me. Open those doors.

> [CHALCOT *opens folding-doors and rings gong bell on table. Enter* LADY'S–MAID, LADY SHENDRYN *motions her down and takes her arm.*]

LADY S: Thank you Mr Chalcot. I'm better now – much better.

> [*She is led off by* MAID, *nearly fainting.*]

CHALCOT: No better than you should be. Oh temper – temper! And that's matrimony! [BLANCHE *enters hurriedly through door in inner room, followed by* ANGUS *in regimentals. She sits at piano and begins playing the Chanson of the 1st Act.* ANGUS *leaning over her at top of piano. Immediately* CHALCOT *hears the music he gets over to door noiselessly, shaking his head.*] How people with these before their eyes can fall in love?

> [*Exit* CHALCOT *on tiptoe.* BLANCHE *sings the song of Act I. She breaks down at the last words with a sob, and lets her face and arms fall on piano. Pause.*]

ANGUS: Won't you sing the words I wrote?
BLANCHE: I can't sing to-night. I can't play.

> [*Rising, and coming forward. Sits on ottoman.*]

ANGUS: [*standing by her side*] I shall often think of that air, when I am far away.

> [*This scene to be broken by frequent pauses.*]

BLANCHE: I – I am very sorry you are going.
ANGUS: I have few reasons for wishing to remain – hardly any – only one.
BLANCHE: And that one is——
ANGUS: [*nearing her*] To be near you! [*kneeling on ottoman*]
BLANCHE: [*averting her eyes*] Oh, cousin!
ANGUS: In the old days a soldier wore a badge, bestowed on him by the lady he – he vowed was the fairest in the world! They were his own individual personal colours! Some say the days of chivalry are over! Never mind that! Give me a token, Blanche – Cousin Blanche – a ribbon – anything that you have worn!
BLANCHE: [*trembling*] But, cousin, these exchanges are only made by those who are – engaged!
ANGUS: [*standing*] And if this war had not been declared, should you have been engaged to Prince Perovsky? Should you have exchanged tokens with him?
BLANCHE: [*troubled*] Oh! How can I tell?
ANGUS: I should like to know before I go.
BLANCHE: [*rising*] And when must that be?
ANGUS: [*looking at time-piece*] In five minutes!
BLANCHE: [*approaching him*] So soon! [*pauses*]
ANGUS: Have you nothing to say to me?
BLANCHE: I – I hardly know – what would you have me say?
ANGUS: Only one word – that you care what becomes of me!
BLANCHE: You know I do.
ANGUS: Care for me?

> [*He clasps her in his arms, she recoiling.*]

BLANCHE: Yes – no—— Oh, cousin! you make me say things——
ANGUS: That you don't mean?

BLANCHE: No – yes! You confuse me so – I hardly know what I'm doing!

> [*Bugle without, at distance. Roll on side drum, four beats on big drum, then military band play "Annie Laurie" – the whole to be as if in the distance.* ANGUS *starts up, and goes to window.* BLANCHE *springs up, and stands before door.* ANGUS *goes to door, embracing* BLANCHE. *They form Millais's picture of the "Black Brunswicker."*]

BLANCHE: Oh, Angus – dear cousin Angus!

ANGUS: [*faltering*] Blanche! you are rich – an heiress. I am but a poor Scotch cadet; but Scotch cadets ere now have cut their way to fame and fortune; and I have my chance. Say, Blanche, do you love me? Say, if at some future day I prove myself not unworthy of you, will you be mine?

BLANCHE: Oh, Angus!

ANGUS: Answer, love; for every moment is precious as a look from you. May I hope?

> [*Handle of the door moves; they separate. Enter* SERVANT.]

SERVANT: Prince Perovsky!

> [*Enter* PRINCE. *Exit* SERVANT. *A pause.*]

PRINCE: I fear that I arrive inopportunely?

BLANCHE: No, Prince; my cousin is just bidding us good-bye. He is about to sail for – he is about to leave England.

PRINCE: [*smiling*] On service?

ANGUS: Yes, on service. I have the honour, Prince, to take my leave.

> [*They bow – a momentary pause –* PRINCE *takes in situation and abruptly turns his back to* ANGUS *and* BLANCHE, *taking a pinch of snuff as the following business proceeds, viz.: –* ANGUS *goes to door, turns to* BLANCHE, *calling her by name. She rushes to him, tearing the locket from her neck, and gives it to* ANGUS, *unperceived by* PRINCE. ANGUS *holds her in his arms, kisses her, and exits hurriedly. The music of band ceases as* BLANCHE *sits on ottoman. Pause.*]

PRINCE: [*turning slowly round*] Miss Haye, I am charmed to find you alone; for what I have to say could only be said *tête-à-tête*. [BLANCHE *rises.*] Pray don't rise. Both Sir Alexander and Lady Shendryn are aware of the object of my visit, and do me the honour of approving it. Have I the happiness of engaging your attention? [BLANCHE *assents.* PRINCE *sits by her side, taking chair from* L. *of table.*] I leave London for Paris to-night *en route* to Vienna. I mention that fact that it may excuse the apparent *brusquerie* of what is to follow. Have I your permission to go on? [BLANCHE *assents. He bows.*] My mission here was not, as many supposed, diplomatic, but matrimonial. I may say, as the man said when he was asked who he was, "When I am at home, I am somebody." I came to England in search of a wife – one who would be an ornament to her station and mine. I wished to take back with me, to present to my province and to my Imperial master, a princess.

BLANCHE: A princess?

PRINCE: Unhappily, this Ottoman difficulty has arisen. I thought that diplomacy would have smoothed it away. I was wrong – and so my mission, which was so eminently peaceful, must be postponed until the war is over.

BLANCHE: Until the war is over?

PRINCE: That will be in very few months.

BLANCHE: [*eagerly*] Why so?

PRINCE: Wars with Russia never last long.

BLANCHE: Why not?

PRINCE: Pardon me, if for a moment I am national and patriotic. Against Russian power, prowess and resources are useless. The elements have declared on our side, and in them we have two irresistible allies.

BLANCHE: And they are——

PRINCE: Frost and fire! If cold fails, we try heat – that is, to warm the snow, we burn our Moscows. [BLANCHE *shivers.*] But, pardon me, you are thinking of those among your relatives who hold rank in the English army? [*significantly*]

BLANCHE: [*hesitating*] Yes; Sir Alexander.

PRINCE: Of course – Sir Alexander. As I alighted, I saw troops mustering outside – a pretty sight. Fine fellows! fine fellows! But I fear I am fatiguing you; for I am – *hélas!* too many, many years your senior to hope to interest you personally. [*rising with courtliness and dignity*] Miss Haye, with the permission of your guardians, I lay my name and fortune at your feet. Should you deign to accept me, at the end of the war I shall return to England for my bride.

BLANCHE: [*rising, confused*] Prince, I am sensible——

PRINCE: Should you honour me by favourable consideration of my demand, in return for the honour of your hand, I offer you rank and power. On our own lands we hold levées – indeed, you will be queen of the province – of 400,000 serfs – of your devoted slave – my queen!

BLANCHE: [*sits on sofa*] Queen! If I should prove a tyrant?

PRINCE: [*standing*] I am a true Russian, and love despotism!

BLANCHE: [*smiling*] And could you submit to slavery?

PRINCE: At your hands – willingly. [*sits on her* R.H.] I assure you, slavery is not a bad thing!

BLANCHE: But freedom is a better! And you came to England, Prince, to seek a wife?

PRINCE: Not only to seek a wife – to find a princess!

BLANCHE: You can make a princess of anybody!

PRINCE: But I cannot make anybody a princess! Let me hope my offer is not entirely objectionable, despite the disparity of our years.

[*Music – "British Grenadiers" – drum and fife heard outside.*]

CHALCOT: [*without*] I beg your pardon.

MARY: [*without*] Beg my pardon? Couldn't you see?

CHALCOT: [*without*] I didn't.

MARY: [*without*] I was right before your eyes.

[MARY *enters.*]

CHALCOT: [*entering*, L.D.] Perhaps that was the reason.

MARY: Tearing one's dress to pieces!

CHALCOT: Really, what with the troops, and the bands and the bother, I feel I must tear something!

MARY: Poor fellows – leaving their wives!

CHALCOT: They consider that one of the privileges of the profession.

[*Music grows distant.*]

MARY: [*excitedly*] Oh, when I hear the clatter of their horses' hoofs, and see the gleam of the helmets, I – I wish I were a man!

CHALCOT: [*standing, his glass in his eye*] I wish you were!

MARY: [*opening window at back*] We can see them from the balcony.

[*Music ceases. When she opens window, the moonlight, trees, gas, &c., are seen at back. Distant bugle.*]

MARY: There's Sir Alick on horseback. [*Distant cheers, on balcony*] Do you hear the shouts?

CHALCOT: [*up at window*] Yes.

MARY: And the bands?

CHALCOT: [*on balcony*] And the chargers prancing.

MARY: And the bayonets gleaming.

CHALCOT: And the troops forming.

MARY: And the colours flying. Oh, if I were not a woman, I'd be a soldier!

CHALCOT: So would I.

MARY: Why are you not?

CHALCOT: What! – a woman!

MARY: No – a soldier. Better be anything than nothing. Better be a soldier than anything.

> [*Tramp of troops marching heard in the distance. Cheers.*]

CHALCOT: [*catching* MARY's *enthusiasm, and sitting on ottoman*] She's right! She's right! Why should a great hulking fellow like me skulk behind, lapped in comfort, ungrateful, uncomfortable, and inglorious? Fighting would be something to live for. I've served in the militia – I know my drill – I'll buy a commission – I'll go!

MARY: [*meeting him, as he goes up*] That's right. I like you for that.

> [*Music – "The girl I left behind me." Cheers and music.*]

CHALCOT: Do you? [*Distant cheers.*] Come and shout. [*to* MARY; *then to* PRINCE, *who is seated on sofa, with* BLANCHE] Come and shout. Oh, I beg pardon!

PRINCE: Not at all – not at all! [*Rises, and goes up to window, and looks out.*] In splendid condition. Fine fellows! Fine fellows! Poor fellows! [*taking snuff*] Won't you come and look at them, Miss Haye?

> [*As* BLANCHE *rises*, LADY SHENDRYN *enters.* BLANCHE *sits again on sofa.* CHALCOT *and* MARY *at window.*]

LADY S: My dear Prince, I did not know you were here!

PRINCE: I profited by your ladyship's absence to urge the suit of which you have been kind enough to approve.

LADY S: And have you received an answer?

PRINCE: Not precisely.

> [*Music stops.*]

CHALCOT: [*at balcony*] There's Sir Alick!

> [*Cheers.*]

SIR A: [*outside*] Battalion! Attention! Form fours, right! March off by companies in succession from the front! Number one, by your left, quick march.

> [*Music. Repeat, "The girl I left behind me." –* LADY SHENDRYN, *starts. Tramp loud.*]

CHALCOT: They're marching right past the window. Come here and see. There's the sergeant. [*Command outside,* "Number two, by your left, quick march."]

PRINCE: Miss Haye, may I be permitted to know if I may hope?

MARY: [*at window*] There's Angus!

        [BLANCHE *rushes up.*]

ANGUS: [*without*] Number three, by your left! Quick march!

        [*Music forte. Band plays "God save the Queen."*
        Cheers. Tramp of soldiers. Excitement. Picture.
        CHALCOT *and* MARY *waving handkerchiefs, and cheer-*
        ing at window. PRINCE, *taking snuff.* LADY SHENDRYN,
        C. BLANCHE *totters down and falls fainting at her feet.*]

END OF ACT II

ACT III

SCENE I – *Interior of a hut, built of boulders and mud, the roof built out, showing the snow and sky outside. The walls bare and rude, pistols, swords, guns, maps, newspapers, &c., suspended on them. Door, R. Window showing snow-covered country beyond; rude fireplace; wood fire burning; over-hanging chimney and shelf; small stove, very rude, with chimney going through roof, which is covered with snow and icicles; straw and rags stuffed in crevices and littered about floor; a rope stretched across back of hut, with fur rugs and horse-cloths hanging up to divide the beds off; camp and rough make-shift furniture; camp cooking utensils, &c.; arm-chair, made of tub, &c. Cupboards round containing properties; hanging lamp, a rude piece of planking before fireplace, stool, tubs, pail, &c. Portmanteau, table, rough chair, broken gun-barrel near fireplace, for poker, and stack of wood. Stage half dark, music, "Chanson," distant bugle and answer, as curtain rises.*

> [ANGUS *discovered, very shabby, high, muddy boots, beard, &c., seated at table, reading by light of candle letters which are lying on an open travelling-desk.*]

ANGUS: [*reading old note*] "Dear Cousin Angus, – Lady Shendryn desires me to ask you to come and dine on Thursday. The usual hour. Do come. – Yours, Blanche. P.S. – Which my lady does not see. Mary says that men ought not to be believed, for all they say is fable." [*Smooths note, and folds it, puts it away, reads another.*] "Dear Cousin Angus, – I shall not be at dinner, but I shall be in the drawing-room, for inspection, as you call it. I don't believe a word that you said the night before last. You know. – Blanche." – [*Folds it, and places it in a large envelope, with other letters, an old glove, a flower, which he kisses, and a ribbon, seals them up, leaving packet on top of desk.*] If the attack is ordered for the morning, Hops will find this on the table as I told him. [*taking letter from his pocket*] How much oftener shall I read this? It contains the last news of her. [*reads*] "Dear Mac, – London is terribly slow, no parties, no nothing" – um – um – um – "All the news comes to the Rag; but of course you know that before we do." [*turns over*] Here it is! "I saw the fascinating party, the thought of whom occupies your leisure hours, yesterday; she was in a carriage with Lady Shendryn, and Dick Fanshawe sat opposite. Dick has been often seen at Lady Shendryn's lately. I keep you posted up on this subject, because you told me to. Dick's uncle, the old mining-man, died two months ago, and left him a pot of money. Such is luck! My uncles never die, and when they do, they leave me dressing-cases! Damn dressing-cases! Dick's name, and that of the divine party, have been coupled,

Apropos d'amour. I am awfully hard up. Little Lucy has left
me. She bolted with a Frenchman in the cigar-trade, taking all
she could with her." [*rising*] Um – that's four months ago.
What a fool I am! Fanshawe's very rich, and not a bad fellow –
as well he as another. [*sighs*] The next six hours may lay me on
the snow, as has been the fate of many a better fellow. Oh!
when I think of her, I feel that I could charge into a troop of
cavalry, sabreproof with love. [*pause*] This won't do! – I'm
getting maudlin! [*Looks at watch, and takes fur great-coat and
cap from arm-chair, buckles on sword, buttons up his coat, &c.*]
Mustn't be maudlin here. There's work! [*smiling sadly, and
taking up packet*] If I can't live to marry Blanche, and make her
Lady MacAlister, wife of General Sir Angus MacAlister, I
can, at least, die a decent soldier. So there, Master Hops!
[*placing packet on table, and lighting pipe by candle. Exit,
singing –*]

> "Parti-t-en guerre, pour tuer l'ennemi,
> Parti-t-en guerre, pour tuer l'ennemi;
> Revint de guerre, apres six ans et demi,
> Revint de guerre, apres six ans et demi;
> Que va-t-il faire? Le Sire de Framboissey –
> Que va-t-il faire? Le Sire de Framboissey."

> [*All exits and entrances are made from door. Wind is
> heard as door opens, and snow is driven in.*]

CHALCOT: [*sneezes, then sings behind curtain*] –

> "In Liquorpond Street, London, a merchant did dwell,
> Who had one only darter – an uncommon nice young
>   gal;
> Her name it was Dinah, just sixteen years old,
> And she'd a very large fortin' in silvier and gold.
>   Ri-tiddle-um, &c."

> [*Drawing curtain, is discovered on a rude bed of straw,
> rough wrapping, &c., his appearance entirely altered,
> hair rough, long beard, face red and jolly, his whole
> manner alert and changed. He wears an old uniform
> coat; one leg is bandaged at the calf, the trouser being
> cut to the knee, and tied with strings and tape; he sits up
> in bed and yawns. Rubbing his eyes, and hitting his
> arms out with enjoyment.*]

CHALCOT: What a jolly good sleep I have had, to be sure! [*Takes flask
from under pillow, and drinks.*] Ah! What a comfort it is that in
the Crimea you can drink as much as you like without its
hurting you! The doctor says it's the rarefaction of the

atmosphere. Bravo, the rarefaction of the atmosphere! –
whatever it may be. I must turn out. [*Takes pillow, and
addresses it in song.*] "Kathleen Mavourneen, arouse from thy
slumbers." [*Hits pillow, and gets out of bed.*] *Gardez vous* the
poor dumb leg. It's jolly cold! [*Goes to fireplace and warms his
hands, then turns and holds them round the candle, whilst so doing
sees letters.*] Oh, Gus has left his love-traps to my keeping in
case he should be potted. [*Puts letters in cupboard.*] Now for
my toilette. Where's the water? [*Goes across stage, finds bucket
against barrel up stage.*] Ice, as usual! Where's the hammer?
[*As he comes down he strikes foot against old gun-barrel lying
amongst the straw on stage; he winces from pain to leg. Breaks ice
in bucket, and taking up tin basin from side of barrel, retires
behind curtain. Business of pouring out water, washing, &c.;
comes out, wiping hands and face with straw.*] If the water's
cold, the straw's warm. What luxuries those fellows in
London do enjoy to be sure, soap and towels everywhere, and
coffee for ringing for it. The sergeant left the coffee – good
[*Takes coffee-pot from stove, and pours out coffee. Drinking
coffee, and shaking his head. Sings.*]

"Oh! father, says Dinah, I am but a child,
And for to get married just yet don't feel not at all
          inclined;
If you'll let me live single for a year or two more,
My werry large fortin' I freely will give o'er."

[*getting biscuit from canister*] Oh! this poor dumb leg of mine!
Just my luck! I obtain my commission all right – get into the
same company as Angus – and wounded in my first engagement. If it hadn't been for the sergeant, I should have been
killed. He received cut number three meant by the Russian for
me. Down he went and up I got. [*Sits at head of table, on
barrel.*] And while he was down, the brute ran his bayonet into
the calf of my leg. A mean advantage to take – to stick me while
he was down. However, I split his skull [*Cracks biscuit.*] so he
didn't get the best of it; and here I am – lame for another
month. The first fortnight's dressing did my leg no good, for
that fool of a sergeant, instead of putting on the ointment
given him by the doctor, went and spread the bandages all
over orange marmalade; and I should never have found it out
if he hadn't served up the salve for breakfast along with the
anchovies. [*eating and drinking*] Now, I superintend the
cookery department – when there's anything to cook. [*Knock
at door.*] Who's there? If you're French, *Entrez*; if you're
Sardinian, *Entre*; if you're Turkish, *Itcherree*; if you're
Russian, *Vnutri*; and if you're English, Come in!

[*Enter* SERGEANT – *ragged great-coat, long beard, his
left arm in a sling, bundle slung over his* R. *shoulder,
straw bands on legs, snow on coat, boots, beard. &c.
Wind heard as door opens, and snow driven in.*]

CHALCOT: Shut the door; shut the door – it's awfully cold.

SERGEANT: [*shutting the door by placing his back against it. Saluting*]
Good morning, sir. How's your leg this morning, sir?

CHALCOT: It feels the cold, sergeant. How's your arm?

SERGEANT: Thank you, sir, it feels frosty too; but I can move it a little.
[*Moves arm, and winces.*]

CHALCOT: Gently, sergeant, gently. How about dinner?

SERGEANT: [*placing bundle on table*] Here you are, sir. Mutton, sir – for
roasting.

CHALCOT: And vegetables!

SERGEANT: Under the meat, sir.

CHALCOT: [*lifting up meat*] Capital! The muddy, but flowery potato;
the dirty milky turnip; and the humble, blushing, but diges-
tive carrot. [*putting them near cupboard*] Can you cook 'em?

SERGEANT: Not to-day, sir. I'm on hospital duty.

CHALCOT: Then I suppose I must.

SERGEANT: But I shall be able to look in, sir, now and then.

CHALCOT: Do; for your legs are indispensable. Any news outside?

SERGEANT: They say, sir, there's to be an attack shortly.

CHALCOT: Um!

SERGEANT: And the enemy was heard moving in the night.

CHALCOT: Oh!

SERGEANT: And that they're very strong in artillery.

CHALCOT: [*drinking*] Oh!

SERGEANT: Talking of artillery, sir, Captain Rawbold sent his
compliments to you, sir, and would you oblige him with the
loan of your frying-pan, a pot of anchovies, and a few rashers
of bacon.

CHALCOT: [*annoyed*] Anything else?

SERGEANT: No sir.

CHALCOT: Confound Captain Rawbold! – he's always borrowing
something. Last week I lent him our own private and
particular gridiron, and he sent it back with one of the bars
broken. [*aside*] Confound those damned gunners! – borrowing
one's *batterie-de-cuisine*. [*rising*]

[*Knock on door.*]

SERGEANT: I dare say that is Captain Rawbold come himself to——

CHALCOT: Open the door. I'll just give him a bit of my mind about that
gridiron. Well [*taking frying-pan*], you don't deserve it; but
here's your frying-pan, and—— [SERGEANT *opens door.* SIR

ALEXANDER *enters.* CHALCOT *sees him.*] Eh! – Colonel!

> [SERGEANT *salutes, shutting door with his back.*
> CHALCOT *puts frying-pan behind him. Wind heard as
> door opens. Snow.*]

SIR A: Good morning, Chalcot. I want to speak to you.

> [*He goes to fire.*]

CHALCOT: Sergeant, my c'ompliments – and frying-pan to the captain
– and – and—— [*aside to* SERGEANT] He mustn't do it again.
[*opening door for* SERGEANT. SERGEANT *salutes with frying-pan,
and exits, holding it before his face. Wind heard as door opens.*]
Did you meet MacAlister?

SIR A: [*Sits on barrel at head of table.*] Yes; and that's what I came to
speak to you about. He reminded me of the documents that I
intended to entrust to your care – should anything befall me.

> [SIR ALEXANDER *gives him packet, which* CHALCOT
> *places in portmanteau.*]

CHALCOT: Is there any news, then?

SIR A: I think we shall be ordered to the front – and I believe there is to
be a combined attack, which is likely to be decisive. Angus
told me that he had made his last will and testament, and
confided it to you. I have done the same.

CHALCOT: [*who is arranging a rude spit and string for suspending mutton
before fire*] And while you're fighting, I shall have to stop in
here, cooking – like a squaw in a wigwam.

SIR A: I'm sorry you can't go with us.

CHALCOT: Just my luck! Where's the cookery book?

> [*He gets book from mantelpiece, and goes to table.*]

SIR A: Hugh – you've been a good friend – a real friend! At that time,
when Kelsey came with that terrible news just before we
sailed——

CHALCOT: [*at table, reading, and feigning not to hear*] "Roast" – "boil"
– "bake" – "fry" – "stew"——

SIR A: [*taking book from him*] Put that down and listen to me. You
know the original cause of my quarrel – with my lady.

CHALCOT: The slightest possible—— Oh, yes.

SIR A: You know, too, how she has wronged me since by her
suspicions. I wrote a long letter to her last night – here it is.
[*showing it*] If this general engagement should give promotion
to our senior major, send it home at once. My lady will find –
when it is too late – how far she has been mistaken. [*Gives him
letter.*]

CHALCOT: [*endeavouring to hide his feelings, and looking at mutton on

table] You don't know how mutton is usually roasted, do you –
I mean, which side up? [*taking it in his hands*]

SIR A: I had more to say to you – but I must go.

CHALCOT: I'd hobble with you as far as the hill, if it wasn't for the
mutton. [*Hangs mutton at fire.*]

SIR A: And I could speak to you as we walked.

CHALCOT: [*warming himself at stove*] The sergeant will be back
directly. I can leave it for a few minutes. I have it! [*Writes on a
piece of paper, folds it, and sticks it on the point of a sword, then
fixes sword in drawer of table, so that the point is upwards.*] He
can't help seeing that. [*putting on cap and cloak*] I believe I've
hung it wrong side up. Now, Sir Alick; since my wound, this
will be my first walk. [*taking stick*]

SIR A: And perhaps my last.

> [*Wind and snow, as door opens. Exeunt* SIR ALEXANDER
> *and* CHALCOT. *Bugle. A pause.* CAPTAIN SAMPREY,
> LADY SHENDRYN, BLANCHE *and* MARY, *and* SOLDIER,
> *pass window. Knocking heard at door. Knocking
> repeated.*]

SAMPREY: [*without*] Chalcot, MacAlister – nobody at home [*Wind.
Looks in, then enters.*] This way, we have the field to ourselves.
[*Enter* BLANCHE, LADY SHENDRYN *and* MARY, *and* SOLDIER, *with
whip.*] These are their quarters.

LADY S: Oh, thank you, major – so kind of you to have escorted us
from Balaclava.

SAMPREY: So kind of you to have accepted my escort. They are out,
but I should think they're sure to be back directly. In the
meantime——

LADY S: We'll stay here. I suppose we need to be under no
apprehension.

SAMPREY: My dear Lady Shendryn, let me reassure you. Sir
Alexander is quite well – so is Chalcot – and so is MacAlister.
I'll now go and seek Sir Alexander – [*All this lively.*] and tell
him who is here.

BLANCHE: Where are they?

SAMPREY: I don't know. Pray be under no alarm – nobody will come
here. There's no fighting going on – nor is there likely to be.
We've no employment here but to keep ourselves warm – and
to go without our dinners.

> [*Exit* SAMPREY. *The* LADIES, *who are shivering with
> cold, run to fire.*]

BLANCHE: Mary, your nose is red.

MARY: So's yours.

BLANCHE: So's my lady's.

LADY S: Blanche, how can you take such a liberty?

BLANCHE: It was the frost, not me. Let us warm our noses.

> [*They go on their knees, and warm their noses at fire, rub them with handkerchiefs, &c.*]

LADY S: I wonder when Mr Chalcot will come back.

> [BLANCHE *and* MARY *examine furniture, peep behind curtain, see bed, and drop curtain, exclaiming Oh!*]

BLANCHE: [*at fire*] And this is a hut. And this is the Crimea which we have all heard about and read about so much. And neither Sir Alick, nor Mr Chalcot——

MARY: Nor Captain MacAlister——

BLANCHE: Expect us, and here we are. [*seeing sword*] What's that?

LADY S: Looks like a sword, with a note at the top of it.

MARY: Perhaps that's the Crimean method of delivering letters.

BLANCHE: [*taking* MARY'S *hand sentimentally*] Perhaps, Mary, Chalcot——

MARY: Or MacAlister——

BLANCHE: Or some comrade, has left that letter containing his last request.

MARY: Or a letter to his wife.

LADY S: More probably to his sweetheart.

BLANCHE: A few lines to his mother.

LADY S: Or his children.

MARY: Or his tailor.

BLANCHE: I wonder what *is* in it! [*crossing to sword*] I declare I feel like Blue Beard's wife at the door of the blue chamber.

MARY: So do I.

LADY S: What absurdity!

MARY: There's no address on it.

BLANCHE: Then it's intended for anybody.

MARY: Or nobody.

LADY S: Do you consider yourself nobody, Miss Netley?

MARY: Almost.

BLANCHE: My fingers tingle to know what's inside it.

LADY S: Blanche I'm surprised at you. Open a letter not addressed to you! Most un-ladylike.

MARY: [*whispering to* BLANCHE] Tell her you think it's in Sir Alick's handwriting.

BLANCHE: It's open at this end. I can read *T-h-e*, "the." I think it's Sir Alexander's handwriting.

LADY S: [*rising*] Eh?

BLANCHE: But we mustn't open it, Mary; so whether it is Sir

Alexander's or anybody else's——

LADY S: My dear Blanche, if you insist on gratifying this childish
     whim——

BLANCHE: You'll let me?

LADY S: To please you, my dear.

BLANCHE: You take it off.

MARY: No, you.

BLANCHE: No, you.

> [*Pushing each other forward.* MARY *snatches letter, the
> sword falls to the ground. All frightened.*]

OMNES: Oh!

BLANCHE: It's like the taking of Sebastopol.

MARY: Yes; only that we've got it. [MARY *opens letter, and reads.*]
     "Please to look after the mutton!"

OMNES: Oh!

> [LADY S *goes to stove.*]

LADY S: Sir Alexander never wrote that; it's not his style.

MARY: Such a stupid thing to say! Now put the sword and letter back.

BLANCHE: No; that would be mean. We'll look after the mutton
     ourselves. I feel so excited; I think it must be the air. [*twirling
     mutton*] Isn't it fun seeing it go round? [*standing with her back
     to fire*] Upon my word, Mary, I think I should make as good an
     officer as any of the men. [*imitating*] I could stand with my
     back to the fire, as they do.

MARY: But you couldn't face the fire,.as they do.

BLANCHE: I don't know that. I could talk just as they do. [*imitating
     slow swell smoking, and taking cigars from case on mantelpiece*]
     Yaas, it's a very fine cigaw – but I know a man – Bedfordshire
     man – who imports – for his own smoking, very finest cigaws
     evaw smoked. Now, Mary, you go on.

MARY: [*imitating different sort of swell, with eye-glass, and hands in
     pockets*]. Look here, old fella, if you talk of cigars – I know
     some cigars that are cigars – and such cigars as no other fella's
     got the like cigars.

BLANCHE: [*slow*] You don't say so. [*smoking*]

MARY: [*quick*] Assure you – never saw such cigars before in all my life.
     [*rising*] Oh! ain't they nasty?

> [*They put them down.*]

BLANCHE: [*snatching up sword that note was attached to*] Mary, let's
     play at soldiers.

LADY S: Oh! you stupid girls.

MARY: Oh! It's such a silly game.

BLANCHE: No, it isn't. To please me! There, take one of those guns.

[MARY *takes gun hesitatingly.*]

MARY: D'ye think it'll go off?

BLANCHE: No; it is not loaded. Now, you be the soldier, and I'll be the officer.

MARY: No; I'll be the officer.

BLANCHE: No; I'll be the officer.

MARY: No; then I shan't play.

BLANCHE: We can't both be officers.

MARY: Yes we can.

BLANCHE: Then who's to give the word of command?

MARY: Both.

BLANCHE: And who's to obey it?

MARY: Neither.

BLANCHE: Nonsense.

MARY: It's going off, Blanche.

BLANCHE: [*in tone of command*] Hi! Ho! Ha! Attention! Form hollow square! Prepare to receive cavalry!

[BLANCHE *charges upon* MARY. MARY, *somewhat frightened, retreats to the corner. Door opens;* ANGUS *and* CHALCOT *enter.*]

CHALCOT: Lady Shendryn!

ANGUS: Blanche!

CHALCOT: Miss Netley!

LADY S: How do you do, Hugh. [*General shaking of hands.*] How are you, Angus?

BLANCHE: We're so glad to see you, Mr Chalcot. [*embarrassed*] And you too, Captain MacAlister.

MARY: How do you do, Captain? How do you do, Mr Chalcot?

[*She places stock of gun in his hand. Goes up and disrobes.* CHALCOT *and* ANGUS *take off overcoats, &c.* ANGUS *helps* CHALCOT *off with coat. Puts his sword against barrel.*]

CHALCOT: [*aside*] She's looking very well. But you must have dropped from the clouds.

LADY S: It was all done in a moment. Lady Llandudno felt that she must come over here to see her boy – you know he's her only one. She sent Lord Llandudno to Southampton, where his yacht was lying, to ask the captain if the "Curlew" was big enough to make the voyage to the Crimea. The captain answered that it was, and that it could be ready in two days. During that time, Lady Llandudno called on me to bid me good-bye. I was seized with the desire to come out too. Lady

Llandudno acceded to my wish. Blanche asked to accompany me: I acceded to her wish. I brought Miss Netley as a companion for Blanche; and here we are. Major Samprey brought us from Balaclava in a cart.

CHALCOT: I saw female figures entering our hut from the top of the hill, and hobbled on as fast as I could. I took you for vivandieres.

> [ANGUS *and* BLANCHE *never take their eyes off each other.*]

LADY S:
BLANCHE: } Vivandieres!
MARY:

BLANCHE: Do vivandieres ever come here?

CHALCOT: [*exchanging glances with* ANGUS] No; but seeing petticoats – it seems a dream. By Jove! If this were put in a play, people would say it was improbable. [*knocks his wounded leg against gun, and winces.*] Oh!

MARY:
BLANCHE: } What's the matter?

CHALCOT: I'm wounded.

BLANCHE: } Wounded?
MARY:

CHALCOT: Yes.

MARY: But how?

CHALCOT: A Russian infantry man ran his bayonet in the calf of my leg.

MARY: [*hiding her face*] Oh! how horrid!

CHALCOT: I brought it away as a trophy.

BLANCHE: The leg?

CHALCOT: No – the bayonet. [*pointing to bayonet on wall*] That's the bayonet – this is the leg.

BLANCHE: What's the matter, Mary?

MARY: Nothing; but to find oneself close to the realities – to the horrors of war!

CHALCOT: Eh?

BLANCHE: [*laughing*] She says you're one of the horrors of war.

MARY: Oh! Blanche! How can you!

> [BLANCHE *and* MARY *go to* ANGUS *at table.*]

LADY S: [*aside to* CHALCOT] Are Sir Alexander's quarters near here?

CHALCOT: No. [*aside*] If he only knew who was here? At some distance.

LADY S: Is he likely to come here?

CHALCOT: I think so – shortly – yes. [*aside*] This is awkward. [LADY S *returns to stove. With fashionable air. Going up.*] Well, ladies, happy to see you in the heart of luxury and civilisation; welcome to this baronial hall, which, by the way, we built ourselves. Chalcot *fundavit* – Chalcot *pinxit* – Chalcot *carpetavit*. This is the boudoir. Won't you come upon the Turkey carpet? [*standing upon a piece of planking, which rocks to and fro*]

ANGUS: [*bringing down rude arm-chair*] Allow me to offer your ladyship a chair.

> [ANGUS *goes to arm-chair, and then to* R. *of table, facing* BLANCHE. MARY *sits at head of table, and* BLANCHE *at end.*]

CHALCOT: I made it myself; it's beautifully stuffed – put your feet on the hearthrug. Dinner will be ready, when it's done. The *menu* is substantial, but not various. *A grand gigot de mouton rôti au naturel, pas de sauce.* In the meantime, can we offer you any light refreshment – any lunch? We have an admirable tap of rum, and as for fruit, I can strongly recommend our raw onions. After dinner we can go to the Opera.

> [*Cannonade distant.*]

LADY S: What's that?

CHALCOT: [*looking at* ANGUS] The overture! May I offer you some coffee?

LADIES: Oh, yes.

> [CHALCOT *hands coffee to* LADY SHENDRYN *and* MARY; ANGUS *to* BLANCHE, *fetching cups, &c., from cupboard, then a cup for himself; crossing to* BLANCHE, *stirring coffee, with his eyes fixed on her; sees she has no spoon, gives her the fork he is using, squeezing her hand.*]

ANGUS: [*conscious that* LADY SHENDRYN'S *eyes are upon him, to* BLANCHE] I hope I have the pleasure of seeing you quite well!

BLANCHE: Quite well; and you?

ANGUS: Quite well.

MARY: I want a spoon.

> [CHALCOT *gives her the wooden one.*]

CHALCOT: Our family plate.

> [*A pause. They sigh.*]

ANGUS: Any news in London, when you left it?

BLANCHE: No; none.

> [*Pause*]

ANGUS: No news?

BLANCHE: None; none whatever.

MARY: It's so hot.

CHALCOT: Have some ice in?

BLANCHE: [*pauses*] You remember Miss Featherstonhaugh?

ANGUS: No – yes. Oh – yes.

BLANCHE: The Admiral's second daughter, the one with the nice eyes;
used to wear her hair in bands. Her favourite colour was pink?

[ANGUS *puts cup to his lips, but does not drink.*]

ANGUS: Yes.

BLANCHE: She always wears green now.

ANGUS: Good gracious!

CHALCOT: Can I offer your ladyship the spoon?

ANGUS: [*not knowing what to say*] I heard that London had been very
dull.

BLANCHE: Oh! very dull.

ANGUS: Seen anything of our friends, the Fanshawes?

BLANCHE: No.

ANGUS: Not of *Mr* Fanshawe?

BLANCHE: Oh – Dick! He's married!

ANGUS: Married?

BLANCHE: Yes; one of Sir George Trawley's girls.

ANGUS: [*with a sigh of relief*] Poor old Fanshawe! [*He empties cup at a
draught; sees that* LADY SHENDRYN *is not looking, opens his coat,
and taking out the locket shows it to* BLANCHE, *and whispers*] Do
you remember the night we parted?

BLANCHE: Yes.

LADY S: [*looking round*] Blanche, dear, are you not cold out there?

BLANCHE: No; quite warm, I assure you.

CHALCOT: Oh, they are quite warm – that's the warmest corner in the
hut.

ANGUS: You remember it?

BLANCHE: Yes.

[*Enter* SERGEANT *with order book, which he gives to*
ANGUS. *He expresses surprise at seeing* LADIES. ANGUS
takes sword and belt from barrel.]

LADY S: ⎫
BLANCHE: ⎬ Sergeant Jones!
MARY: ⎭

ANGUS: [*aside to* CHALCOT] To the front! [*to* BLANCHE, *seeing she has
observed paper*] So Miss Featherstonhaugh wears green, does
she? [*buckling on sword*] I'm afraid that I must leave you.

BLANCHE: Must you?

ANGUS: Yes.

BLANCHE: On duty?

ANGUS: Yes.

BLANCHE: Shall you be back soon?

ANGUS: I hope so. Good day, Miss Netley. Good day, Lady
Shendryn, for the present. [*Pause, to* BLANCHE, *after shaking
hands with* CHALCOT] I hope to have the pleasure of seeing you
again.

> [SERGEANT *opens door. Exit* ANGUS. *The* "Chanson" *is
> played as a march by* BAND *outide; it grows more and
> more distant. No snow or wind here.*]

BLANCHE: What band is that playing?

SERGEANT: The band of "Ours."

BLANCHE: I think I've heard that march before.

SERGEANT: We call it Captain MacAlister's march. He had it arranged
by the bandmaster. They often play it.

> [LADY SHENDRYN *speaks aside to* SERGEANT.]

CHALCOT: [*at fire, observing* BLANCHE, *sings*]

> "And a cup of cold pisen lay close by her side,
> And a billy-dow, which said as how for Villikins she died."

SERGEANT: Thank you, my lady – I'm glad to hear the missus is well,
and the children – and the twins – and the new one which I
haven't seen.

MARY: There's a letter I promised Mrs Jones to give you if I met you
[*giving it*] I saw them all the day before we left. The twins have
grown wonderfully.

SERGEANT: Have they now? Clever little things! Grown! – So like 'em
– just the sort of thing they would do!

BLANCHE: [*rising, sighing*] Has Captain Mac—— Has the regiment to
go far?

SERGEANT: "Ours," mum?

BLANCHE: Yes.

SERGEANT: We're going to the front, into——

CHALCOT: [*interrupting quickly*] To parade.

SERGEANT: [*catching his eye*] Yes; to parade.

LADY S: Will Sir Alexander be there?

SERGEANT: Yes, my lady. He wouldn't let the regiment go into——

CHALCOT: [*interrupting*] On parade.

SERGEANT: On parade – without him.

LADY S: Can we see them? [*A pause.* CHALCOT *and* SERGEANT *look at
each other embarrassed.*] I mean, can we not see the regiment

parading? You can't escort us on account of your wound; but the Sergeant could conduct us to some place where we could see them, could he not?

BLANCHE: Oh! – I should so like that!

CHALCOT: Well – if you insist – Sergeant, take the three ladies to the——

LADY S: No. Miss Netley can remain here – she is such a bad walker.

MARY: [*pouting*] No, I'm not.

LADY S: We shall not be gone long.

[LADY SHENDRYN *and* BLANCHE *put on wraps;* MARY *assisting* LADY SHENDRYN.]

CHALCOT: You'll come back to dinner?

LADY S: Yes. Miss Netley will perhaps be kind enough to assist in its preparation. We shall most likely be back before Sir Alexander or the Captain.

CHALCOT: Most likely. [*Opens door.*] It's not snowing, but you'd better stay here.

LADY S: No, no.

BLANCHE: We've made up our minds.

CHALCOT: I understand feminine discipline too well to make another observation. [*Exeunt* LADY SHENDRYN *and* BLANCHE.] Sergeant, take the ladies to Flagstaff Hill. Good-bye, for the present; and [*aside to* SERGEANT], not a word about the action! [*Exit* SERGEANT.]

CHALCOT: This is a singular *tête-à-tête* – shut up alone with this girl. I always hated her in England! Now I like her very much! Somehow, the air of the Crimea seems to improve everything. Everything has improved since I've had something to do – and a bayonet in the calf of my leg.

MARY: [*at fire*] Now, Mr Chalcot, what are we to do for dinner?

CHALCOT: Dinner?

MARY: [*attending to fire*] Yes; of course I must obey Lady Shendryn's orders.

CHALCOT: Orders! [*aside*] Lady Shendryn behaves like a perfect brute to this girl. Such a charming girl, too – [*aloud*] About dinner – shall we have a set dinner?

MARY: If you like; I'm a capital cook.

CHALCOT: Are you?

MARY: Yes.

CHALCOT: What an accomplished creature it is!

MARY: In my poor father's time, I was housekeeper. He wasn't very rich; but he always said his dinners were excellent; and he ought to know, for he was a clergyman.

CHALCOT: [*aside*] A housekeeper, too – ah! [*aloud*] Well, now for this dinner – this grand dinner; to begin at the beginning.

MARY: Soup?

CHALCOT: We've got no soup.

MARY: Fish?

CHALCOT: We're out of fish.

MARY: Entrées?

CHALCOT: I don't think we'll have any entrees to-day.

MARY: The joint?

CHALCOT: There we are strong. [*crossing to fire, singing Barcarole, "Masaniello"*] See the mutton brightly – brightly burning.

MARY: And the vegetables?

CHALCOT: [*pointing to potatoes*] Pommes-de-terre au naturel, dans leur jackets.

MARY: Game?

CHALCOT: No game.

MARY: Sweets – ices?

CHALCOT: Lots of ice outside.

MARY: Puddings?

CHALCOT: Unheard-of luxuries.

MARY: Have you no flour?

CHALCOT: [*pointing*] A barrelful.

MARY: Any preserves?

CHALCOT: Lots – pots!

MARY: I can make a pudding.

CHALCOT: [*lost in astonishment*] No!

MARY: I can – a roly-poly.

CHALCOT: A roly-poly pudding in the Crimea! It's a fairy-tale!

[*They clear table.*]

MARY: Now get the flour.

[*She turns up sleeves of her dress.* CHALCOT, *waiting on her with wonder and admiration, gets flour from barrel.*]

MARY: I declare! here's some paste ready-made; I shall want a paste-board. [*Takes up straw from floor and rubs table.*] That won't do. What have you there?

CHALCOT: The lid of the barrel?

MARY: That'll do. Now I shall want an apron.

CHALCOT: An apron? [*Looks round.*] I know, I've got an apron. This will do. It belonged to a pioneer of ours; he was shot at the Alma. [MARY *shrinks.*] But he didn't wear it that day.

[*He helps her on with pioneer's apron. She mixes pudding.*]

MARY: [*mixing pudding*] Oh! I forgot.

CHALCOT: What?

MARY: I shall want a rolling-pin.

CHALCOT: Rolling-pin? [*Looks about – then under table, sees small barrel – takes it up and rolls it up and down table.* MARY *laughs but rejects it – in putting it down again* CHALCOT *knocks three-legged stool over – after a little difficulty succeeds in pulling one of the legs out and brings it sharply down on pudding.* MARY *rolls pudding, &c.*] Beauty, accomplishments, amiability, no mother, and roly-poly pudding! [*approaching her*]

MARY: My hands are all over flour! You mustn't talk to the cook. Now, the preserves!

CHALCOT: Here.

[CHALCOT *gets preserves.*]

MARY: What's this?

CHALCOT: Strawberry.

MARY: Ah! I like strawberry. That'll do. [*Smells it.*] Take it away. Good gracious, what's that! [*Both smell it; knock heads together; business.*] Why, that's varnish!

CHALCOT: It's that damned ointment! [*Puts it in cupboard, gets another pot, breaks paper, smells it, tastes it.*] I think you'll find that right.

MARY: Now the spoon – *the* wonderful spoon.

CHALCOT: Our piece of family plate.

[*Producing spoon from pocket. –* MARY *puts preserves in pudding.*]

CHALCOT: With such a woman as that to sweeten one's path through life – to put – metaphorically speaking – the preserves into one's pudding – that's woman's mission.

MARY: Oh – I forgot!

CHALCOT: What?

MARY: A pudding-cloth. What shall we do for a pudding-cloth?

CHALCOT: Won't the leather apron do? [MARY *shakes her head.*] Then I'm afraid our resources have broken down in the moment of victory! To think that a pudding – and such a pudding – should break down for the sake of a paltry pudding-cloth. [*after a pause*] I have it!

MARY: What?

CHALCOT: I received a packet of linen a month ago from England. I've never opened it. [*Opens portmanteau, and takes out towel.*] Eureka! I have found it! A towel! – and here have I been wiping my face with straw for the last three weeks!

MARY: Now I want a bit of string.

CHALCOT: [*getting string from cupboard*] Here you are.

MARY: Now get me a saucepan.

[CHALCOT *gets saucepan and puts it on table.*]

MARY: Does it boil?

CHALCOT: [*taking lid off and throwing it on floor*] Yes, I'll take my oath it boils.

MARY: [*Ties up the ends of pudding cloth, puts it in saucepan.*] Now get the lid.

[CHALCOT *gets lid from floor, puts it first on stool, then on table, and then on to saucepan.*]

MARY: Now then stand it on the fire, just there in the right hand corner.

[*Pointing to fire with leg of stool.* CHALCOT *puts saucepan on fire, offers it to* MARY, *who puts pudding in it, and places it in saucepan,* CHALCOT *burning his hands with lid.*]

MARY: The mutton's getting on beautifully.

[*She pokes fire with leg of stool, and as she turns, hits* CHALCOT's *leg.* CHALCOT *staggers to small barrel.*]

MARY: I have hurt your wound! – pray, forgive me!

CHALCOT: It's nothing. Do it again. I like it.

MARY: I'm very, very sorry.

CHALCOT: Don't mention it – hurt me again! But speak in that tone – and look in that way again!

MARY: Shall I loosen the bandages?

[*She kneels,* L. *of* CHALCOT.]

CHALCOT: If you like; but you can't fasten them up again.

MARY: I can.

CHALCOT: With what?

MARY: A hair-pin.

[*She takes one from her hair and fastens bandages.*]

CHALCOT: [*taking her hand*] Miss Netley – Mary——

MARY: My hands are all over flour!

CHALCOT: Never mind – I like them all the better. You don't dislike me – do you, Mary?

MARY: Oh, Mr Chalcot!

CHALCOT: Not very much, I hope? I've always loved you – even when we used to quarrel. May I trust that some day I may not be indifferent to you; and, if so, that I may make you my own – my wife! [*She turns away.*] Don't let me frighten you. I won't tell the Colonel – I mean Lady Shendryn! I know you can't love me now – but I'll try to deserve your love: and perhaps if I

try hard – and I will – I may succeed. Sebastopol isn't taken in
a day; and you'll let me try – won't you, Sebastopol? – I mean
Mary? [*with great agitation*]

MARY: Mr Chalcot, you know I am a poor dependent.

CHALCOT: That's the very reason! I couldn't love a girl with money.

MARY: A man of your position – your property——

CHALCOT: For Heaven's sake don't raise up the dismal spectre of my
money! Don't let cash forbid the banns! If I am rich, don't
reproach me with it. I don't deserve it – it isn't my fault! I
never made a penny in my life – I never had the talent. Only
say you will be mine!

[*Bugle call without.*]

LADY S: [*outside*] Mr Chalcot!

[*Enter* LADY SHENDRYN, *quickly.*]

CHALCOT: [*kissing* MARY, *who rises quickly; to* LADY SHENDRYN] All
right. The mutton's doing beautifully.

LADY S: They're fighting! – And my husband is in the action! I – I –
I—— Oh! I don't know what I'm doing! Give me your hand!

[CHALCOT *supports her. Enter* BLANCHE, *hurriedly.*]

BLANCHE: [*to* MARY] Mary – he's fighting! He's gone to battle – with
two or three thousand others! I heard the officers who
galloped by say there was an engagement! He's fighting!

[CHALCOT *gathers things on table.*]

LADY S: Who? – Sir Alexander?

BLANCHE: No; Angus.

LADY S: Angus! What, then – do you love him?

BLANCHE: Yes, I do; and I don't care who knows it.

LADY S: Well, my child, I don't blame you. We can't help these
things. [*Kisses her.*]

BLANCHE: Perhaps, at this very moment – even now, as I speak – a
bullet may have reached his heart.

LADY S: Oh!

[*Both* WOMEN *horrified at the picture.* LADY SHENDRYN
and BLANCHE *pull down* CHALCOT *and hurt his leg.*
CHALCOT *has spoon in his hand.*]

LADY S: Do you think he will come back?

BLANCHE: Will he return?

CHALCOT: Of course he will! No doubt of it! How the devil should I
know?

LADY S: ⎫
BLANCHE: ⎬ If he should not!

CHALCOT: But he will – they will – they never do get killed in "Ours!"
BLANCHE: Oh, Lady Shendryn! I'm so sorry for you. [*crossing to her, and kissing her.*]
LADY S: [*kissing her*] And I for you.

> [CHALCOT *makes an offer to kiss* MARY. MARY *puts apron over* CHALCOT's *head.*]

MARY: [*repulsing him*] I'm so glad you are not fighting!
CHALCOT: Are you! [*pointing to* LADY SHENDRYN *and* BLANCHE] It's wrong of me to be so happy, isn't it.
LADY S: Think dear; it's my husband!
BLANCHE: And the man I love!
LADY S: And we parted in anger!

> [*Distant cannon and bugle calls heard throughout following scene.*]

BLANCHE: And he never knew how much I loved him! Oh! If I could see him again!

> [*Knock heard at door. All start.*]

BLANCHE: ⎱ Perhaps Angus.
LADY S: ⎰ If it is he!

> [CHALCOT *opens door, and is met by* PRINCE PEROVSKY, *who wears full Russian uniform, orders, followed by* SAMPREY.]

BLANCHE: ⎱ Prince Perovsky?
LADY S: ⎰
PRINCE: [*entering*] Miss Haye, Lady Shendryn.
LADY S: You here, Prince?
PRINCE: Yes – a prisoner – fortune of war.

> [SAMPREY *enters.* CHALCOT *assists* PRINCE *to take off cloak.*]

SAMPREY: Pardon me, Lady Shendryn, I have the honour to be the Prince's escort. Knowing that you were acquainted, I took the liberty——
LADY S: Sir Alexander——
BLANCHE: Captain MacAlister——
SAMPREY: [*very gravely*] Are in the engagement. I did not see their regiment – I could not for the smoke. Excuse me, I must go. Prince, you have given me your parole. [PRINCE *bows.*] I have the honour—— [*presenting him with his sword.* PRINCE *bows, takes sword, and sheaths it. Exit* SAMPREY.]
PRINCE: Pray, ladies, don't be alarmed; it is not a battle – a mere

affair of outposts.

LADY S: Oh, Prince, I am beyond comfort!

PRINCE: [to BLANCHE] These are strange circumstances under which to meet. You see I am always a captive in your presence.

BLANCHE: Oh, Prince, to think that battle is raging so near us!

PRINCE: Be under no alarm; my presence——

BLANCHE: It is not that, but——

PRINCE: You fear for those dear to you?

BLANCHE: Yes.

PRINCE: Sir Alexander?

BLANCHE: Yes.

PRINCE: And perhaps for some other?

BLANCHE: Yes – my cousin Angus.

PRINCE: The young gentleman I met in London?

[BLANCHE *assents*.]

BLANCHE: If he should be killed?

PRINCE: *Hélas!* Fortune of war!

BLANCHE: Or taken prisoner?

PRINCE: As I am. He would be treated with the respect and honour due to the sacred name of enemy. Reassure yourself, my dear Miss Haye; your young soldier is sheltered by your love. Oh, Youth! Inestimable, priceless treasure! Lost for ever! To be a *sous-lieutenant*, and beloved as he is – psha! Am I a child, to cry for the moon? *Pas si bête!*

CHALCOT: [to LADY SHENDRYN] If you see Sir Alexander again, of which I have but little doubt, I think what I am going to tell you will make you happy with him ever after. I am aware that you were jealous of him——

LADY S: Not without cause. Even years ago I had cause.

CHALCOT: The slightest possible. Since then he has been true and faithful. I know, for I was in his confidence. Sir Alexander's money used to go mysteriously. Do you know where it went?

LADY S: Yes; to some woman.

CHALCOT: No.

LADY S: To whom then?

CHALCOT: To your brother Percy.

LADY S: Percy!

CHALCOT: To save him – to save you and his family from dishonour. Five years ago Sir Alick discovered, by his banking account, that Percy had forged his name!

LADY S: What!

CHALCOT: You remember the night that Sir Alick left England, when Kelsey, the lawyer, sent him a letter, and he sent for me?

LADY S: And he withdrew £1,500 from my account.

CHALCOT: Yes; for fresh bills forged by Percy.

LADY S: [*hiding her face*] And he concealed this from me?

CHALCOT: Because he preferred to bear the brunt of your suspicions, rather than let you know the extent of your brother's – conduct. There is a letter, which in case of accidents, he gave to me for you; in it is contained the half of the letter you did not see, that Kelsey sent him. You need not read it now. All that I tell you is true. Sir Alick is a gallant officer, and a noble gentleman [*with emotion, then resuming his ordinary manner*], and come what may, he's sure to bring the regiment out of it creditably. So when you meet, learn to know him better.

LADY S: When we meet – oh! this suspense is terrible. Any certainty – even of the worst!

[*Enter* SERGEANT.]

SERGEANT: If you please, sir – the Colonel——

[LADY SHENDRYN *rises*.]

MARY: [*running between them*] Hush!

[BLANCHE *rises*.]

LADY S: You need not speak – I know all! – He is dead!

[*A pause.* SERGEANT *astonished*.]

BLANCHE: And Captain MacAlister?
SERGEANT: [*confounded*] Captain——

[BLANCHE *covers her face with one hand*.]

BLANCHE: You may tell me – I can bear it.

[*Enter* ANGUS.]

ANGUS: [*going to* BLANCHE *and throwing cap away*] Didn't I hear my name?
BLANCHE: [*rushing to him*] Oh! [*restraining herself*] I'm so glad to see you back!
CHALCOT: All right?
ANGUS: Quite.
BLANCHE: Unhurt?
ANGUS: Yes.

[*A pause. They look sympathetically at* LADY SHENDRYN.]

CHALCOT: And Sir Alexander?
ANGUS: Came with me. He'll be here directly.
LADY S: [*rising*] Here! Not killed?
ANGUS: No.

LADY S: Alive?

ANGUS: Yes.

[*All look at* SERGEANT.]

SERGEANT: That's just what I was going to say, only this young lady stopped me.

[*All go up but* LADY SHENDRYN.]

LADY S: Oh – my husband! [SIR ALEXANDER *appears at door.*] If I could only see you, to kneel at your feet, and ask pardon for having so wronged your noble nature! At the very time I reproached you for ruining your fortune for another, to have borne with me for the sake of the honour of my family!

SIR A: [*advancing*] Diana! These expressions of affection——

LADY S: Alexander. [*embracing; about to kneel, he prevents her.*] I know all.

SIR A: All what? [LADY SHENDRYN *shows him letter.*] Chalcot gave you this? [LADY SHENDRYN *assents.*] Hugh? What right had you to—

CHALCOT: None, whatever. That is why I did it.

LADY S: Forgive me!

SIR A: Forget it, Diana, and——

[*He staggers, and nearly falls.*]

LADY S: What's the matter?

SIR A: Nothing. I——

ANGUS: Nothing. Only a slight wound.

[*All down stage but* PRINCE. LADY SHENDRYN *attends to* SIR ALEXANDER.]

MARY: [*to* SERGEANT] Why didn't you say that he was wounded?

SERGEANT: Just what I was going to do, miss, only you stopped me.

SIR A: It is but a scratch – the affair was but a skirmish. The great event is postponed again. I came here to congratulate Angus.

CHALCOT: On what?

SIR A: [*whispering, so that* PRINCE *may not hear*] He has taken a Russian colour.

CHALCOT: Bravo, Angus! My luck; I am out of all these good things.

[*He goes up to* PRINCE.]

MARY: [*to* SERGEANT] Why didn't he mention his capturing the colours?

[*All whispering.*]

SERGEANT: We never do mention those sort of things in "Ours."

[*He goes up, and takes off overcoat.*]

PRINCE: Sir Alexander, I trust that your hurt is but slight; wounded yourself, you will have more compassion upon others.

SIR A: [*surprised*] Prince!

PRINCE: Permit me, in the hour of my adversity, to point out to you that those two young people love each other. Don't be surprised. Battle elevates as well as brutalises us. I withdraw my pretensions; I am too old.

BLANCHE: [*overhearing*] Prince!

SIR A: But Angus is so poor!

PRINCE: No man is poor while he is young. Youth is wealth – inestimable and irretrievable.

SIR A: ⎱ Well, but——
LADY S: ⎰ My dear Blanche——

BLANCHE: It's no use arguing, because I won't have anybody else; and if you don't consent, I'll wait till I'm twenty-one. You'll wait till I'm twenty-one, won't you, Angus?

SIR A: Well – well – we'll see about it.

BLANCHE: When?

SIR A: When? When the war is over.

BLANCHE: What a horrid thing is war!

ANGUS: Prince, how can I express my deep sense of obligation?

PRINCE: By silence.

> [*All go up.* SERGEANT *at fire, reading his letter. Tramp of* SOLDIERS *heard without.*]

ANGUS: [*Turns left about and runs against* CHALCOT *who has lid of barrel* [*flour*] *in his hand.* CHALCOT *takes him to* C., *and whispers.*] You engaged to Mary? By what means?

CHALCOT: Roly-poly pudding – boiling in the pot.

> [CHALCOT *and* ANGUS *go to barrel,* CHALCOT *puts flour pan and lid down and crosses to* MARY, ANGUS *to* BLANCHE.]

BLANCHE: [*aside to* MARY] You engaged to Chalcot? But he's such a little man.

MARY: You know I've no money – and I couldn't expect so big a husband as you.

ANGUS: The place is not the same now you are in it, and that you are to be mine. You illuminate it – you're a chandelier!

BLANCHE: Chandelier, indeed! A pretty compliment – all cut glass and wire!

ANGUS: Lit up by love!

CHALCOT: [*at fire*] The mutton's done!

> [*General movement. They place seats, &c. All on the alert, as at a picnic. Each person, except* LADY

SHENDRYN, SIR ALEXANDER, *and* PRINCE, *has hold of either plates, or a chair, or a saucepan, &c.* CHALCOT *places mutton on table, which has been laid by* SERGEANT *and* MARY *and others.*]

CHALCOT: *Les reines sont servies.*

[SERGEANT *waits at table. The* "Chanson" *march played, piano, without.* MEN *heard marching. Cheers.* ANGUS *opens door.*]

LADY S: What's that?

SIR A: The Russian colours. [*whispering, and pointing to* ANGUS] "Ours!"

MARY: What troops are those?

CHALCOT: [*sitting on floor*] "Ours!"

BLANCHE: [*to* ANGUS] And what are we?

ANGUS: [*her hands in his, leaning over her*] "Ours!"

CURTAIN

CASTE

Produced at the Prince of Wales's Royal Theatre, London, on 6th April, 1867.

CAST OF CHARACTERS

Hon. George D'Alroy	Mr Frederick Younge
Captain Hawtree	Mr Bancroft
Eccles	Mr George Honey
Sam Gerridge	Mr Hare
Dixon	Mr Hill
Marquise de St Maur	Miss Larkin
Esther Eccles	Miss Lydia Foote
Polly Eccles	Miss Marie Wilton

ACT I – *The Little House in Stangate.* – COURTSHIP.
A lapse of eight months.

ACT II – *The Lodgings in Mayfair.* – MATRIMONY.
A lapse of twelve months.

ACT III – *The Little House in Stangate.* – WIDOWHOOD.

TO

MISS MARIE WILTON

(MRS BANCROFT),

THIS COMEDY IS DEDICATED

BY

HER GRATEFUL FRIEND AND FELLOW LABOURER,

THE AUTHOR

CASTE

ACT I

SCENE I – *A plain set chamber, paper soiled. A window, with practicable blind; street backing and iron railings. Door practicable, when opened showing street door [practicable]. Fireplace; two-hinged gas-burners on each side of mantelpiece. Sideboard cupboard, cupboard in recess, tea-things, teapot, tea-caddy, tea-tray, &c., on it. Long table before fire; old piece of carpet and rug down; plain chairs; book-shelf back, a small table under it with ballet-shoe and skirt on it; bunch of benefit bills hanging under book-shelf. Theatrical printed portraits, framed, hanging about; chimney glass clock; box of lucifers and ornaments on mantel-shelf; kettle on hob, and fire laid; door-mats on the outside of door. Bureau.*

> [*Rapping heard at door, the handle is then shaken as curtain rises. The door is unlocked. Enter* GEORGE D'ALROY.]

GEORGE: Told you so; the key was left under the mat in case I came. They're not back from rehearsal. [*hangs up hat on peg near door as* HAWTREE *enters*] Confound rehearsal!

> [*He crosses to fireplace.*]

HAWTREE: [*back to audience, looking round*] And this is the fairy's bower!

GEORGE: Yes! And this is the fairy's fireplace; the fire is laid. I'll light it.

> [*He lights fire with lucifer from mantelpiece.*]

HAWTREE: [*turning to* GEORGE] And this is the abode rendered blessed by her abiding. It is here that she dwells, walks, talks – eats and drinks. Does she eat and drink?

GEORGE: Yes, heartily. I've seen her.

HAWTREE: And you are really spoons! – case of true love – hit – dead.

GEORGE: [*with elbow on end of mantelpiece down stage*] Right through. Can't live away from her.

HAWTREE: Poor old Dal! and you've brought me over the water to——

GEORGE: Stangate.

HAWTREE: Stangate – to see her for the same sort of reason that when a patient is in a dangerous state one doctor calls in another – for a consultation.

GEORGE: Yes. Then the patient dies.

HAWTREE: Tell us all about it – you know I've been away.

[*He sits* R. *of table, leg on a chair.*]

GEORGE: Well, then, eighteen months ago——

HAWTREE: Oh, cut that; you told me all about that. You went to a theatre, and saw a girl in a ballet, and you fell in love.

GEORGE: Yes. I found out that she was an amiable, good girl.

HAWTREE: Of course; cut that. We'll credit her with all the virtues and accomplishments.

GEORGE: Who worked hard to support a drunken father.

HAWTREE: Oh! the father's a drunkard, is he? The father does not inherit the daughter's virtues?

GEORGE: No. I hate him.

HAWTREE: Naturally. Quite so! quite so!

GEORGE: And she – that is, Esther – is very good to her younger sister.

HAWTREE: Younger sister also angelic, amiable, accomplished, &c., &c.

GEORGE: Um – good enough, but got a temper – large temper. Well, with some difficulty I got to speak to her. I mean to Esther. Then I was allowed to see her to her door here.

HAWTREE: I know – pastry-cooks – Richmond dinner – and all that.

GEORGE: You're too fast. Pastry-cooks – yes. Richmond – no. Your knowledge of the world, fifty yards round barracks, misleads you. I saw her nearly every day, and I kept on falling in love – falling and falling, till I thought I should never reach the bottom; then I met you.

HAWTREE: I remember the night when you told me; but I thought it was only an amourette. However, if the fire is a conflagration, subdue it; try dissipation.

GEORGE: I have.

HAWTREE: What success?

GEORGE: None; dissipation brought me bad health and self-contempt, a sick head and a sore heart.

HAWTREE: Foreign travel; absence makes the heart grow [*slight pause*] – stronger. Get leave and cut away.

GEORGE: I did get leave, and I did cut away; and while away, I was miserable and a gone-er coon than ever.

HAWTREE: What's to be done?

[*He sits cross-legged on chair, facing* GEORGE.]

GEORGE: Don't know. That's the reason I asked you to come over and see.

HAWTREE: Of course, Dal, you're not such a soft as to think of marriage. You know what your mother is. Either you are going to behave properly, with a proper regard for the world, and all that, you know; or you're going to do the other thing.

Now, the question is, what do you mean to do? The girl is a
nice girl, no doubt; but as to your making her Mrs D'Alroy,
the thing is out of the question.

GEORGE: Why? What should prevent me?

HAWTREE: Caste! – the inexorable law of caste! The social law, so
becoming and so good, that commands like to mate with like,
and forbids a giraffe to fall in love with a squirrel.

GEORGE: But my dear Bark——

HAWTREE: My dear Dal, all those marriages of people with common
people are all very well in novels and in plays on the stage,
because the real people don't exist, and have no relatives who
exist, and no connections, and so no harm's done, and it's
rather interesting to look at; but in real life with real relations,
and real mothers, and so forth, it's absolute bosh. It's worse –
it's utter social and personal annihilation and damnation.

GEORGE: As to my mother, I haven't thought about her.

[*He sits corner of table,* L.]

HAWTREE: Of course not. Lovers are so damned selfish; they never
think of anybody but themselves.

GEORGE: My father died when I was three years old, and she married
again before I was six, and married a Frenchman.

HAWTREE: A nobleman of the most ancient families in France, of
equal blood to her own. She obeyed the duties imposed on her
by her station and by caste.

GEORGE: Still, it caused a separation and a division between us, and I
never see my brother, because he lives abroad. Of course the
Marquise de St Maur is my mother, and I look upon her with a
sort of superstitious awe.

[*He moves chair with which he has been twisting about
during speech from* R. *of table, to corner* L.]

HAWTREE: She's a grand Brahmin priestess.

GEORGE: Just so; and I know I'm a fool. Now you're clever, Bark – a
little too clever, I think. You're paying your *devoirs* – that the
correct word, isn't it – to Lady Florence Carberry, the
daughter of a countess. She's above you – you've no title. Is
she to forget *her* caste?

HAWTREE: That argument doesn't apply. A man can be no more than a
gentleman.

GEORGE: "True hearts are more than coronets,
    And simple faith than Norman blood."

HAWTREE: Now, George, if you're going to consider this question
from the point of view of poetry, you're off to No Man's Land,
where I won't follow you.

GEORGE: No gentleman can be ashamed of the woman he loves. No matter what her original station, once his wife he raises her to his rank.

HAWTREE: Yes, he raises her – *her;* but her connections – her relatives. How about them?

ECCLES: [*outside*] Polly! Polly! [*enters*] Why the devil——

[GEORGE *crosses to* HAWTREE, *who rises.* ECCLES *sees them, and assumes a deferential manner.*]

ECCLES: Oh, Mr De-Alroy! I didn't see you, sir. Good afternoon; the same to you, sir, and many on 'em.

[*He puts hat on bureau and comes down.*]

HAWTREE: Who is this?

GEORGE: This is papa.

HAWTREE: Ah!

[*He turns up to book-shelf, scanning* ECCLES *through eye-glass.*]

GEORGE: Miss Eccles and her sister not returned from rehearsal yet?

ECCLES: No, sir, they have not. I expect 'em in directly. I hope you've been quite well since I seen you last, sir?

GEORGE: Quite, thank you; and how have you been, Mr Eccles?

ECCLES: Well, sir, I have not been the thing at all. My 'elth, sir, and my spirits is both broke. I'm not the man I used to be. I am not accustomed to this sort of thing. I've seen better days, but they are gone – most like for ever. It is a melancholy thing, sir, for a man of my time of life to look back on better days that are gone most like for ever.

GEORGE: I dare say.

ECCLES: Once proud and prosperous, now poor and lowly. Once master of a shop, I am now, by the pressure of circumstances over which I have no control, driven to seek work and not to find it. Poverty is a dreadful thing, sir, for a man as has once been well off.

GEORGE: I dare say.

ECCLES: [*sighing*] Ah, sir, the poor and lowly is often 'ardly used. What chance has the working man?

HAWTREE: None when he don't work.

ECCLES: We are all equal in mind and feeling.

GEORGE: [*aside*] I hope not.

ECCLES: I am sorry, gentlemen, that I cannot offer you any refreshment; but luxury and me has long been strangers.

GEORGE: I am very sorry for your misfortunes, Mr Eccles. [*looking round at* HAWTREE, *who turns away*] May I hope that you will allow me to offer you this trifling loan? [*giving him a half-sovereign*]

ECCLES: Sir, you're a gentleman. One can tell a real gentleman with half a sov – I mean with half a eye – a real gentleman understands the natural emotions of the working man. Pride, sir, is a thing as should be put down by the strong 'and of pecuniary necessity. There's a friend of mine round the corner as I promised to meet on a little matter of business; so, if you will excuse me, sir——

GEORGE: With pleasure.

ECCLES: [*going up*] Sorry to leave you, gentlemen, but——

GEORGE : ⎫ Don't stay on my account.
HAWTREE: ⎭ Don't mention it.

ECCLES: Business is business. [*going up*] The girls will be in directly. Good afternoon, gentlemen – good afternoon – [*going out*] – good afternoon!

        [*Exit* ECCLES. GEORGE *sits in chair corner of table* R.]

HAWTREE: [*coming down*] Papa is not nice, but [*sitting on corner of table, down stage*] –

        "True hearts are more than coronets,
        And simple faith than Norman blood."

Poor George! I wonder what your mamma – the Most Noble the Marquise de St Maur – would think of Papa Eccles. Come, Dal, allow that there *is something* in caste. Conceive that dirty ruffian – that rinsing of stale beer – that walking tap-room, for a father-in-law. Take a spin to Central America. Forget her.

GEORGE: Can't.

HAWTREE: You'll be wretched and miserable with her.

GEORGE: I'd rather be wretched with her, than miserable without her. [HAWTREE *takes out cigar case.*] Don't smoke here!

HAWTREE: Why not?

GEORGE: She'll be coming in directly.

HAWTREE: I don't think she'd mind.

GEORGE: I should. Do you smoke before Lady Florence Carberry?

HAWTREE: [*closing case*] Ha! You're suffering from a fit of the morals.

GEORGE: What's that?

HAWTREE: The morals is a disease like the measles, that attacks the young and innocent.

GEORGE: [*with temper*] You talk like Mephistopheles, without the cleverness.

        [*He goes up to window, and looks at watch.*]

HAWTREE: [*arranging cravat at glass*] I don't pretend to be a particularly good sort of fellow, nor a particularly bad sort of fellow. I suppose I'm about the average standard sort of thing, and I don't like to see a friend go down hill to the devil while I' can put the drag on. [*turning, with back to fire*] Here is a girl of very humble station – poor, and all that, with a drunken father, who evidently doesn't care how he gets money so long as he don't work for it. Marriage! Pah! Couldn't the thing be arranged?

GEORGE: Hawtree, cut that! [*at window*] She's here!

[*He goes to door and opens it. Enter* ESTHER.]

GEORGE: [*flurried at sight of her*] Good morning. I got here before you, you see.

ESTHER: Good morning.

[*She sees* HAWTREE – *slight pause, in which* HAWTREE *has removed his hat.*]

GEORGE: I've taken the liberty – I hope you won't be angry – of asking you to let me present a friend of mine to you: Miss Eccles – Captain Hawtree.

[HAWTREE *bows.* GEORGE *assists* ESTHER *in taking off bonnet and shawl.*]

HAWTREE: [*aside*] Pretty.

ESTHER: [*aside*] Thinks too much of himself.

GEORGE: [*hangs up bonnet and shawl on pegs*] You've had a late rehearsal. Where's Polly?

ESTHER: She stayed behind to buy something.

[*Enter* POLLY.]

POLLY: Hallo! [*head through door*] How de do, Mr D'Alroy? Oh! I'm tired to death. Kept at rehearsal by an old fool of a stage manager. But stage managers are always old fools – except when they are young. We shan't have time for any dinner, so I've brought something for tea.

ESTHER: What is it?

POLLY: Ham. [*showing ham in paper.* ESTHER *sits at window. Seeing* HAWTREE] Oh, I beg your pardon, sir. I didn't see you.

GEORGE: A friend of mine, Mary. Captain Hawtree – Miss Mary Eccles.

[GEORGE *sits at window.* POLLY *bows very low, half burlesquely, to* HAWTREE.]

HAWTREE: Charmed.

POLLY: [*aside*] What a swell! Got nice teeth, and he knows it. How quiet we all are; let's talk about something.

[*She hangs up her hat. She crosses to fire, round table-front.* HAWTREE *crosses and places hat on bureau.*]

ESTHER: What can we talk about?

POLLY: Anything. Ham. Mr D'Alroy, do you like ham?

GEORGE: I adore her – [POLLY *titters*.] – I mean I adore it.

POLLY: [*to* HAWTREE, *who has crossed to table, watching* POLLY *undo paper containing the ham. She turns the plate on top of the ham still in the paper, then throws the paper aside and triumphantly brings the plate under* HAWTREE's *nose,* HAWTREE *giving a little start back; very tragically*] Do you like ham, sir?

HAWTREE: Yes.

POLLY: Now that is very strange. [*getting tea-tray*] I should have thought you'd have been above ham.

HAWTREE: May one ask why?

POLLY: You look above it. You look quite equal to tongue – glazed. [*laughing*] Mr D'Alroy is here so often that he knows our ways. [*getting tea-things from sideboard and placing them on table.*]

HAWTREE: I like everything that is piquante and fresh, and pretty and agreeable.

POLLY: [*laying table all the time for tea*] Ah! you mean that for me. [*curtseying*] Oh! [*sings*] Tra, la, lal, la, la, la. [*flourishes cup in his face; he retreats a step.*] Now I must put the kettle on. [GEORGE *and* ESTHER *are at window.*] Esther never does any work when Mr D'Alroy is here. They're spooning; ugly word spooning, isn't it? – reminds one of red-currant jam. By-the-bye, love *is* very like red-currant jam – at the first taste sweet, and afterwards shuddery. Do you ever spoon?

HAWTREE: [*leaning across table*] I should like to do so at this moment.

POLLY: I dare say you would. No, you're too grand for me. You want taking down a peg – I mean a foot. Let's see – what are you – a corporal?

HAWTREE: Captain.

POLLY: I prefer a corporal. See here. Let's change about. You be corporal – it'll do you good, and I'll be "my lady."

HAWTREE: Pleasure.

POLLY: You must call me "my lady," though, or you shan't have any ham.

HAWTREE: Certainly, "my lady"; but I cannot accept your hospitality, for I'm engaged to dine.

POLLY: At what time?

HAWTREE: Seven.

POLLY: Seven! Why, that's half-past tea-time. Now corporal, you must wait on me.

HAWTREE: As the pages did of old.

POLLY: My lady.

HAWTREE: My lady.

POLLY: Here's the kettle, corporal. [*Holding out kettle at arm's length.* HAWTREE *looks at it through eye-glass.*]

HAWTREE: Very nice kettle!

POLLY: Take it into the back kitchen.

HAWTREE: Eh!

POLLY: Oh! I'm coming too.

HAWTREE: Ah! that alters the case.

> [*He takes out handkerchief and then takes hold of kettle – crosses as* GEORGE *rises and comes down, slapping* HAWTREE *on back.* HAWTREE *immediately places kettle on the floor.* POLLY *throws herself into chair by fire-side up stage, and roars with laughter.* GEORGE *and* ESTHER *laugh.*]

GEORGE: What are you about?

HAWTREE: I'm about to fill the kettle.

ESTHER: [*going to* POLLY] Mind what you are doing, Polly! What will Sam say?

POLLY: Whatever Sam chooses. What the sweetheart don't see the husband can't grieve at. Now then – Corporal!

HAWTREE: "My lady!" [*He takes up kettle.*]

POLLY: Attention! Forward! March! and mind the soot don't drop upon your trousers.

> [*Exeunt* POLLY *and* HAWTREE, HAWTREE *first.*]

ESTHER: What a girl it is – all spirits! The worst is that it is so easy to mistake her.

GEORGE: And so easy to find out your mistake. [*They cross down stage,* ESTHER *first.*] But why won't you let me present you with a piano? [*following* ESTHER]

ESTHER: I don't want one.

GEORGE: You said you were fond of playing.

ESTHER: We may be fond of many things without having them. [*leaning against end of table, taking out letter*] Now here is a gentleman says that he is attached to me.

GEORGE: [*jealous*] May I know his name?

ESTHER: What for? It would be useless, as his solicitations—— [*She throws letter into fire.*]

GEORGE: I lit that fire.

ESTHER: Then burn these too. [GEORGE *crosses to fire.*] No, not that. [*taking one back*] I must keep that; burn the others.

> [GEORGE *throws letters on fire, crosses back of table quickly – takes hat from peg and goes to door as if leaving hurriedly.* ESTHER *takes chair* R. *of table and goes* C. *with it, noticing* GEORGE's *manner.* GEORGE *hesitates at door, shuts it quickly, hangs his hat up again and comes down to back of chair in which* ESTHER *has seated herself.*]

GEORGE: Who is that from?

ESTHER: Why do you wish to know?

GEORGE: Because I love you, and I don't think you love me, and I fear a rival.

ESTHER: You have none.

GEORGE: I know you have so many admirers.

ESTHER: They're nothing to me.

GEORGE: Not one?

ESTHER: No. They're admirers, but there's not a husband among them.

GEORGE: Not the writer of that letter?

ESTHER: [*coquettishly*] Oh, I like him very much.

GEORGE: [*sighing*] Ah!

ESTHER: And I'm very fond of this letter.

GEORGE: Then, Esther, you don't care for me.

ESTHER: Don't I! How do you know?

GEORGE: Because you won't let me read that letter.

ESTHER: It won't please you if you see it.

GEORGE: I dare say not. That's just the reason that I want to. You won't?

ESTHER: [*hesitates*] I will. [*giving it to him*] There!

GEORGE: [*reads*] "Dear Madam."

ESTHER: That's tender, isn't it?

GEORGE: "The terms are four pounds – your dresses to be found. For eight weeks certain, and longer if you should suit. [*in astonishment*] I cannot close the engagement until the return of my partner. I expect him back to-day, and will write you as soon as I have seen him – Yours very," &c. Four pounds – find dresses. What does this mean?

ESTHER: It means that they want a Columbine for the pantomime at Manchester, and I think I shall get the engagement.

GEORGE: Manchester; then you'll leave London!

ESTHER: I must [*pathetically*] You see this little house is on my shoulders. Polly only earns eighteen shillings a week, and father has been out of work a long, long time. I make the bread here, and it's hard to make sometimes. I've been mistress of this place, and forced to think ever since my mother died, and I was eight years old. Four pounds a week is a large sum, and I can save out of it.

[*This speech is not to be spoken in a tone implying hardship.*]

GEORGE: But you'll go away, and I shan't see you.

ESTHER: P'raps it will be for the best. [*She rises and crosses* L.] What future is there for us? You're a man of rank, and I am a poor girl who gets her living by dancing. It would have been better that we had never met.

GEORGE: No.

ESTHER: Yes, it would, for I'm afraid that——

GEORGE: You love me?

ESTHER: I don't know. I'm not sure; but I think I do.

> [*She stops and turns half-face to* GEORGE.]

GEORGE: [*trying to seize her hand*] Esther!

ESTHER: No. Think of the difference of our stations.

GEORGE: That's what Hawtree says. Caste! caste! curse caste!

ESTHER: If I go to Manchester it will be for the best. We must both try to forget each other.

GEORGE: Forget you! no, Esther; [*seizing her hand*] let me——

POLLY: [*without*] Mind what you're about. Oh dear! Oh dear!

> [GEORGE *and* ESTHER *sit in window seat. Enter* POLLY *and* HAWTREE.]

POLLY: You nasty, great, clumsy, corporal, you've spilt the water all over my frock. Oh dear! [HAWTREE *puts kettle on ham on table.*] Take it off the ham!

> [HAWTREE *then places it on the mantelpiece.*]

POLLY: No, no; put it in the fireplace [HAWTREE *does so.*] You've spoilt my frock.

HAWTREE: Allow me to offer you a new one.

POLLY: No, I won't. You'll be calling to see how it looks when it's on. Haven't you got a handkerchief?

HAWTREE: Yes!

POLLY: Then wipe it dry.

> [HAWTREE *bends almost on one knee, and wipes dress. Enter* SAM, *whistling. Throws cap into* HAWTREE's *hat on drawers.*]

SAM: [*sulkily*] Arternoon – yer didn't hear me knock! – the door was open. I'm afraid I intrude.

POLLY: No, you don't. We're glad to see you if you've got a handkerchief. Help to wipe this dry.

> [SAM *pulls out handkerchief from slop, and dropping on one knee snatches skirt of dress from* HAWTREE, *who looks up surprised.*]

HAWTREE: I'm very sorry. [*rising*] I beg your pardon.

> [*Business;* SAM *stares* HAWTREE *out.*]

POLLY: It won't spoil it.

SAM: [*rising*] The stain won't come out.

POLLY: It's only water!

SAM: Arternoon, Miss Eccles! [*to* ESTHER] Arternoon, sir! [*to* GEORGE. POLLY *rises. to* POLLY] Who's the other swell?

POLLY: I'll introduce you. Captain Hawtree – Mr Samuel Gerridge.

HAWTREE: Charmed, I'm sure. [*staring at* SAM *through eye-glass.* SAM *acknowledges* HAWTREE'*s recognition by a "chuck" of the head over left shoulder; going up to* GEORGE] Who's this?

GEORGE: Polly's sweetheart.

HAWTREE: Oh! Now if I can be of no further assistance, I'll go.

POLLY: Going, corporal?

HAWTREE: Yaas! [*Business; taking up hat and stick from bureau he sees* SAM'*s cap. He picks it out carefully, and coming down stage* R. *examines it as a curiosity, drops it on the floor and pushes it away with his stick, at the same time moving backwards, causing him to bump against* SAM, *who turns round savagely*] I beg your pardon! George, will you – [GEORGE *takes no notice.*] Will you——?

GEORGE: What?

HAWTREE: Go with me?

GEORGE: Go? No!

HAWTREE: Then, Miss Eccles – I mean "my lady."

> [*Shaking hands and going; as he backs away bumps against* SAM, *and business repeated.* HAWTREE *close to door, keeping his eye on* SAM, *who has shown signs of anger.*]

POLLY: Good-bye, corporal!

HAWTREE: [*at door*] Good-bye! Good afternoon, Mr – Mr – er – Pardon me.

SAM: [*with constrained rage*] Gerridge, sir, Gerridge!

HAWTREE: [*as if remembering name*] Ah! Gerridge. Good day.

> [*Exit* HAWTREE.]

SAM: [*turning to* POLLY *in awful rage*] Who's that fool? Who's that long idiot?

POLLY: I told you; Captain Hawtree.

SAM: What's 'e want 'ere?

POLLY: He's a friend of Mr D'Alroy's.

SAM: Ugh! Isn't one of 'em enough?

POLLY: What do you mean?

SAM: For the neighbours to talk about. Who's he after?

POLLY: What do you mean by after? You're forgetting yourself, I think.

SAM: No, I'm not forgetting myself – I'm remembering you. What can a long fool of a swell dressed up to the nines within an inch of his life want with two girls of your class? Look at the difference of your stations! 'E don't come 'ere after any good.

> [*During the speech,* ESTHER *crosses to fire and sits before it in a low chair.* GEORGE *follows her, and sits on her* L.]

POLLY: Samuel!

SAM: I mean what I say. People should stick to their own class. Life's a railway journey, and Mankind's a passenger – first class, second class, third class. Any person found riding in a superior class to that for which he has taken his ticket will be removed at the first station stopped at, according to the bye-laws of the company.

POLLY: You're giving yourself nice airs! What business is it of yours who comes here? Who are you?

SAM: I'm a mechanic.

POLLY: That's evident.

SAM: I ain't ashamed of it. I'm not ashamed of my paper cap.

POLLY: Why should you be? I dare say Captain Hawtree isn't ashamed of his fourteen-and-sixpenny gossamer.

SAM: You think a deal of him 'cos he's a captain. Why did he call you my lady?

POLLY: Because he treated me as one. I wish you'd make the same mistake!

SAM: Ugh!

> [SAM *goes angrily to bureau,* POLLY *bounces up stage, and sits in window seat.*]

ESTHER: [*sitting with* GEORGE, *tête-à-tête, by fire*] But we must listen to reason.

GEORGE: I hate reason!

ESTHER: I wonder what it means?

GEORGE: Everything disagreeable! When people talk unpleasantly, they always say listen to reason.

SAM: [*turning round*] What will the neighbours say?

POLLY: I don't care!

SAM: What will the neighbours *think?*

POLLY: They can't think. They're like you, they've not been educated up to it.

SAM: [*going to* POLLY] It all comes of your being on the stage.

POLLY: It all comes of your not understanding the stage or anything else – but putty. Now, if you were a gentleman——

SAM: Why then, of course, I should make up to a lady!

POLLY: Ugh! [*She flings herself into chair.*]

GEORGE: Reason's an idiot! Two and two are four, and twelve are fifteen, and eight are twenty. That's reason!

SAM: [*turning to* POLLY] Painting your cheeks!

POLLY: [*rising*] Better paint our *cheeks* than paint *nasty old doors* as you do. How can you understand art? You're only a mechanic! you're not a professional. You're in trade. You are not of the same station that we are. When the manager speaks to you, you touch your hat, and say, "Yes, sir," because he's your superior.

[*She snaps fingers under* SAM's *nose.*]

GEORGE: When people love there's no such thing as money – it doesn't exist.

ESTHER: Yes, it does.

GEORGE: Then it oughtn't to.

SAM: The manager employs me same as he does you. Payment is good everywhere and anywhere. Whatever's commercial, is right.

POLLY: Actors are not like mechanics. They wear cloth coats, and not fustian jackets.

SAM: [*sneeringly, in* POLLY's *face.*] I despise play actors.

POLLY: And I despise mechanics.

[POLLY *slaps his face.*]

GEORGE: I never think of anything else but you.

ESTHER: Really?

SAM: [*goes to bureau, misses cap, looks around, sees it on floor, picks it up angrily and comes to* POLLY.] I won't stay here to be insulted. [*putting on cap*]

POLLY: Nobody wants you to stay. Go! Go! Go!

SAM: I will go. Good-bye, Miss Mary Eccles. [*He goes off and returns quickly.*] I shan't come here again!

POLLY: Don't! Good riddance to bad rubbish.

SAM: [*rushing down stage to* POLLY] You can go to your *captain!*

POLLY: And you to your *putty.*

[SAM *throws his cap down and kicks it – then goes up stage and picks it up.* POLLY *turns and rises, leaning against table, facing him, crosses to door, and locks it.* SAM, *hearing the click of the lock, turns quickly.*]

ESTHER: And shall you always love me as you do now?

GEORGE: More.

POLLY: Now you *shan't* go. [*taking out key, which she pockets and placing her back against door*] Nyer! Now I'll just show you my power. Nyer!

SAM: [*advancing to door*] *Miss Mary* Eccles, let me out!

POLLY: *Mr* Samuel Gerridge, I shan't.

[SAM *turns away.*]

ESTHER: Now you two. [*postman's knock*] The postman!

SAM: Now you must let me out. You must unlock the door.

POLLY: No, I needn't. [*opens window, looking out*] Here – postman. [*takes letter from postman, at window*] Thank you. [*Business; flicks* SAM *in the face with letter*] For you, Esther!

ESTHER: [*rising*] For me?

POLLY: Yes.

> [*She gives it to her, and closes window, and returns to door triumphantly.* SAM *goes to window.*]

ESTHER: From Manchester!

GEORGE: Manchester?

ESTHER: [*reading*] I've got the engagement – four pounds a week.

GEORGE: [*placing his arm around her*] You shan't go. Esther – stay – be my wife!

ESTHER: But the world – your world?

GEORGE: Hang the world! You're my world. Stay with your husband, *Mrs George D'Alroy.*

> [*During this* POLLY *has been dancing up and down in front of the door.*]

SAM: [*turning with sudden determination*] I *will* go out!

POLLY: You can't, and you shan't!

SAM: I can – I will!

> [*He opens window, and jumps out.*]

POLLY: [*frightened*] He's hurt himself. Sam – Sam, dear Sam!

> [*She runs to window.* SAM *appears at window.* POLLY *slaps his face and shuts window down violently.*]

POLLY: Nyer!

> [*During this* GEORGE *has kissed* ESTHER.]

GEORGE: *My wife!*

> [*The handle of the door is heard to rattle, then the door is shaken violently.* ESTHER *crosses to door; finding it locked turns to* POLLY, *sitting in window seat, who gives her the key.* ESTHER *then opens the door.* ECCLES *reels in, very drunk, and clings to the corner of bureau for support.* GEORGE *stands pulling his moustache.* ESTHER, *a little way up, looking with shame first at her father, then at* GEORGE. POLLY *sitting in window recess.*]

END OF ACT I

FOR CALL – GEORGE, *hat in hand, bidding* ESTHER *good-bye.* ECCLES *sitting in chair, nodding before fire.* SAM *again looks in at window.* POLLY *pulls the blind down violently.*

ACT II

SCENE I – D'ALROY's *lodgings in Mayfair. A set chamber. Folding-doors opening on to drawing-room. Door,* R. *Two windows, with muslin curtains. Loo-table. Sofa above piano. Two easy-chairs,* R. *and* L. *of table. Dessert – Claret in jug; two wine-glasses half full. Box of cigarettes, vase of flowers, embroidered slipper on canvas, and small basket of coloured wools, all on table. Footstool, easy-chair. Ornamental gilt work-basket on stand in window. Mahogany-stained easel with oil-painting of* D'ALROY *in full Dragoon regimentals. Davenport, with vase of flowers on it; a chair on each side; a water-colour drawing over it, and on each side of room. Half moonlight through window.*

> [ESTHER *and* GEORGE *discovered.* ESTHER *at window; when curtain has risen she comes down slowly to chair* R. *of table, and* GEORGE *sitting in easy-chair* L. *of table.* GEORGE *has his uniform trousers and spurs on.*]

ESTHER: George, dear, you seem out of spirits.

GEORGE: [*smoking cigarette*] Not at all, dear, not at all. [*rallying*]

ESTHER: Then why don't you talk?

GEORGE: I've nothing to say.

ESTHER: That's no reason.

GEORGE: I can't talk about nothing.

ESTHER: Yes, you can; you often do. [*crossing to back of table and caressing him*] You used to do before we were married.

GEORGE: No, I didn't. I talked about you, and my love for you. D'ye call that nothing?

ESTHER: [*sitting on stool,* L. *of* GEORGE] How long have we been married, dear? Let me see; six months yesterday. [*dreamily*] It hardly seems a week; it almost seems a dream.

GEORGE: [*putting his arm around her*] Awfully jolly dream. Don't let us wake up. [*aside and recovering himself*] How ever shall I tell her?

ESTHER: And when I married you I was twenty-two; wasn't I?

GEORGE: Yes, dear; but then, you know, you must have been some age or other.

ESTHER: No; but to think that I lived two-and-twenty years without knowing you?

GEORGE: What of it, dear?

ESTHER: It seems such a dreadful waste of time.

GEORGE: So it was – awful!

ESTHER: Do you remember our first meeting? Then I was in the ballet.

GEORGE: Yes; now you're in the heavies.

ESTHER: Then I was in the front rank – now I am of high rank – the Honourable Mrs George D'Alroy. You promoted me to be your wife.

GEORGE: No, dear, you promoted me to be your husband.

ESTHER: And now I'm one of the aristocracy; ain't I?

GEORGE: Yes, dear; I suppose that we may consider ourselves——

ESTHER: Tell me, George; are you quite sure that you are proud of your poor little humble wife?

GEORGE: Proud of you! Proud as the winner of the Derby.

ESTHER: Wouldn't you have loved me better if I'd been a lady?

GEORGE: You *are* a lady – you're my wife.

ESTHER: What will your mamma say when she knows of our marriage? I quite tremble at the thought of meeting her.

GEORGE: So do I. Luckily, she's in Rome.

ESTHER: Do you know, George, I should like to be married all over again.

GEORGE: Not to anybody else, I hope.

ESTHER: My darling!

GEORGE: But why over again? Why?

ESTHER: Our courtship was so beautiful. It was like in a novel from the library, only better. You, a fine, rich, high-born gentleman, coming to our humble little house to court poor me. Do you remember the ballet you first saw me in? That was at Covent Garden. "Jeanne la Folle; or, the Return of the Soldier." [*She goes to piano.*] Don't you remember the dance?

[*She plays a quick movement.*]

GEORGE: Esther, how came you to learn to play the piano? Did you teach yourself?

ESTHER: Yes. [*turning on music-stool*] So did Polly. We can only just touch the notes to amuse ourselves.

GEORGE: How was it?

ESTHER: I've told you so often.

[*She rises and sits on stool at* GEORGE's *feet.*]

GEORGE: Tell me again. I'm like the children – I like to hear what I know already.

ESTHER: Well, then, mother died when I was quite young. I can only just remember her. Polly was an infant; so I had to be Polly's mother. Father – who is a very eccentric man [GEORGE *sighs deeply* – ESTHER *notices it and goes on rapidly – all to be simultaneous in action.*] but a very good one when you know him – did not take much notice of us, and we got on as we could. We used to let the first floor, and a lodger took it – Herr Griffenhaagen. He was a ballet master at the Opera. He took a fancy to me, and asked me if I should like to learn to dance, and I told him father couldn't afford to pay for my tuition; and he said that [*imitation*] he did not vant bayment, but dat he would teach me for noding, for he had taken a fancy to me, because I was like a leetle lady he had known long years ago in de far off land he came from. Then he got us an engagement at the theatre. That was how we first were in the ballet.

GEORGE: [*slapping his leg*] That fellow was a great brick; I should like to ask him to dinner. What became of him?

ESTHER: I don't know. He left England. [GEORGE *fidgets and looks at watch.*] You are very restless, George. What's the matter?

GEORGE: Nothing.

ESTHER: Are you going out?

GEORGE: Yes. [*looking at his boots and spurs*] That's the reason I dined in——

ESTHER: To the barracks?

GEORGE: Yes.

ESTHER: On duty?

GEORGE: [*hesitatingly*] On duty. [*rising*] And, of course, when a man is a soldier, he must go on duty when he's ordered, and where he's ordered, and – and – [*aside*] why did I ever entei the service!

ESTHER: [*Rises – crosses to* GEORGE *– and twining her arm round him.*] George, if you must go out to your club, go; don't mind leaving me. Somehow or other, George, these last few days everything seems to have changed with me – I don't know why. Sometimes my eyes fill with tears, for no reason, and sometimes I feel so happy, for no reason. I don't mind being left by myself as I used to do. When you are a few minutes behind time I don't run to the window and watch for you, and turn irritable. Not that I love you less – no, for I love you more; but often when you are away I don't feel that I am by myself. [*dropping her head on his breast*] I never feel alone.

[*She goes to piano and turns over music.*]

GEORGE: [*watching* ESTHER] What angels women are! At least, this one is. I forget all about the others. [*Carriage-wheels heard off.*] If I'd known I could have been so happy, I'd have sold out when I married.

[*Knock at street door.*]

ESTHER: [*standing at table*] That for us, dear?

GEORGE: [*at first window*] Hawtree in a hansom. He's come for – [*aside*] me. I *must* tell her sooner or later. [*at door*] Come in, Hawtree.

[*Enter* HAWTREE, *in regimentals.*]

HAWTREE: How do? Hope you're well, Mrs D'Alroy? George, are you coming to——

GEORGE: No, I've dined [*gives a significant look.*]—— We dined early.

[ESTHER *plays scraps of music at piano.*]

HAWTREE: [*sotto voce*] Haven't you told her?

GEORGE: No, I daren't.

HAWTREE: But you must.

GEORGE: You know what an awful coward I am. You do it for me.

HAWTREE: Not for worlds. I've just had my own adieu to make.

GEORGE: Ah, yes – to Florence Carberry. How did she take it?

HAWTREE: Oh, [*slight pause*] very well.

GEORGE: [*earnestly*] Did she cry?

HAWTREE: No.

GEORGE: Nor exhibit any emotion whatever?

HAWTREE: No, not particularly.

GEORGE: [*surprisedly*] Didn't you kiss her?

HAWTREE: No; Lady Clardonax was in the room.

GEORGE: [*wonderingly*] Didn't she squeeze your hand?

HAWTREE: No.

GEORGE: [*impressively*] Didn't she say anything?

HAWTREE: No, except that she hoped to see me back again soon, and that India was a bad climate.

GEORGE: Umph! It seems to have been a tragic parting [*serio-comically*] – almost as tragic as parting – your back hair.

HAWTREE: Lady Florence is not the sort of person to make a scene.

GEORGE: To be sure, she's not your wife. I wish Esther would be as cool and comfortable. [*after a pause*] No, I don't – no, I don't.

[*A rap at the door. Enter* DIXON.]

GEORGE: [*Goes up to* DIXON.] Oh, Dixon, lay out my——

DIXON: I have laid them out, sir; everything is ready.

GEORGE: [*coming down to* HAWTREE – *after a pause, irresolutely*] I must tell her – mustn't I?

HAWTREE: Better send for her sister. Let Dixon go for her in a cab.

GEORGE: Just so. I'll send him at once. Dixon!

[*He goes up and talks to* DIXON.]

ESTHER: [*rising and going to back of chair* L. *of table*] Do you want to have a talk with my husband? Shall I go into the dining-room?

HAWTREE: [*going to* R. *of table and placing cap on it*] No, Mrs D'Alroy.

GEORGE: No, dear. At once, Dixon. Tell the cabman to drive like – [*Exit* DIXON.] – like a – cornet just joined.

ESTHER: [*to* HAWTREE] Are you going to take him anywhere?

HAWTREE: [GEORGE *comes to* HAWTREE *and touches him quickly on the shoulder before he can speak.*] No. [*aside*] Yes – to India. [*crossing to* GEORGE] Tell her now.

GEORGE: No, no. I'll wait till I put on my uniform.

[*The door opens, and* POLLY *peeps in.*]

POLLY: How d'ye do, good people – quite well?

[POLLY *kisses* ESTHER.]

GEORGE: Eh? Didn't you meet Dixon?
POLLY: Who?
GEORGE: Dixon – my man.
POLLY: No.
GEORGE: Confound it! he'll have his ride for nothing. How d'ye do, Polly?

[*They shake hands.*]

POLLY: How d'ye do, George?

[ESTHER *takes* POLLY'S *things.* POLLY *places parasol on table.*]

POLLY: Bless you, my turtles. [*blessing them, ballet fashion*] George, kiss your mother. [*He kisses her.*] That's what I call an honourable brother-in-law's kiss. I'm not in the way, am I?
GEORGE: Not at all. I'm very glad you've come.

[ESTHER *shows* POLLY *the new music.* POLLY *sits at piano and plays comic tune.*]

HAWTREE: [*back to audience, and elbow on easy-chair, aside to* GEORGE] Under ordinary circumstances she's not a very eligible visitor.
GEORGE: Caste again. I'll be back directly.

[*Exit* GEORGE.]

HAWTREE: [*looking at watch*] Mrs D'Alroy, I——
ESTHER: [*standing over* POLLY *at piano*] Going?
POLLY: [*rising*] Do I drive you away, captain?

[*She takes her parasol from table.*]

HAWTREE: No.
POLLY: Yes, I do. I frighten you, I'm so ugly. I know I do. You frighten me.
HAWTREE: How so?
POLLY: You're so handsome. Particularly in those clothes, for all the world like an inspector of police.
ESTHER: [*half-aside*] Polly!
POLLY: I will! I like to take him down a bit.
HAWTREE: [*aside*] This is rather a wild sort of thing in sisters-in-law.
POLLY: Any news, captain?
HAWTREE: [*in a drawling tone*] No. Is there any news with you?
POLLY: Yaas; [*imitating him*] we've got a new piece coming out at our theatre.
HAWTREE: [*interested*] What's it about?

POLLY: [*drawling*] I don't know. [*to* ESTHER] Had him there! [HAWTREE *drops his sword from his arm;* POLLY *turns round quickly, hearing the noise, and pretends to be frightened.*] Going to kill anybody to-day, that you've got your sword on?

HAWTREE: No.

POLLY: I thought not. [*sings*]

> "With a sabre on his brow,
>   And a helmet by his side,
> The soldier sweethearts servant-maids,
>   And eats cold meat besides."

> [*She laughs and walks about waving her parasol. Enter* GEORGE, *in uniform, carrying in his hand his sword, sword belt, and cap.* ESTHER *takes them from him, and places them on sofa.*]

POLLY: [*clapping her hands*] Oh! here's a beautiful brother-in-law. Why didn't you come in on horseback, as they do at Astley's? – gallop in and say [*imitating soldier on horseback and prancing up and down stage during the piece*], Soldiers of France! The eyes of Europe are a-looking at you! The Empire has confidence in you, and France expects that every man this day will do his – little utmost! The foe is before you – more's the pity – and you are before them—— worse luck for you! Forward! Go and get killed; and to those who escape the Emperor will give a little bit of ribbon! Nineteens, about! Forward! Gallop! Charge!

> [*Galloping, imitating bugle, and giving point with parasol, she nearly spears* HAWTREE'S *nose.* HAWTREE *claps his hand upon his sword-hilt. She throws herself into chair, laughing, and clapping,* HAWTREE'S *cap* [*from table*] *upon her head. All laugh and applaud. Carriage-wheels heard without.*]

POLLY: Oh, what a funny little cap, it's got no peak. [*A peal of knocks heard at street-door.*] What's that?

GEORGE: [*who has hastened to window*] A carriage! Good heavens – my mother!

HAWTREE: [*at window*] The Marchioness!

ESTHER: [*crossing to* GEORGE] Oh, George!

POLLY: [*crossing to window*] A Marchioness! A real, live Marchioness! Let me look! I never saw a real live Marchioness in all my life.

GEORGE: [*forcing her from window*] No, no, no. She doesn't know I'm married. I must break it to her by degrees. What shall I do?

> [*By this time* HAWTREE *is at door* R.H., ESTHER *at door* L.H.]

ESTHER: Let me go into the bedroom until——

HAWTREE: Too late! She's on the stairs.

ESTHER: [at C. *doors, opens them*] Here then!

POLLY: I want to see a real, live March——

> [GEORGE *lifts her in his arms and places her within folding-doors with* ESTHER – *then shutting doors quickly, turns and faces* HAWTREE, *who, gathering up his sword, faces* GEORGE. *They then exchange places much in the fashion of soldiers "mounting guard."* GEORGE *opens door and admits* MARQUISE.]

GEORGE: [*with great ceremony*] My dear mother, I saw you getting out of the carriage.

MARQUISE: My dear boy [*kissing his forehead*], I'm so glad I got to London before you embarked. [GEORGE *nervous.*] Captain Hawtree, I think. How do you do?

HAWTREE: [*coming forward a little*] Quite well, I thank your ladyship. I trust you are——

MARQUISE: [*sitting in easy-chair*] Oh, quite, thanks. [*slight pause*] Do you still see the Countess and Lady Florence? [*looking at him through her glasses*]

HAWTREE: Yes.

MARQUISE: Please remember me to them—— [HAWTREE *takes cap from table, and places sword under his arm.*] Are you going?

HAWTREE: Ya-a-s. Compelled. [*He bows, crossing round back of table to* GEORGE.] I'll be at the door for you at seven. We must be at the barracks by the quarter. Poor devil! This comes of a man marrying beneath him!

[*Exit* HAWTREE.]

MARQUISE: I'm not sorry that he's gone, for I wanted to talk to you alone. Strange that a woman of such good birth as the Countess should encourage the attentions of Captain Hawtree for her daughter Florence. [*During these lines* D'ALROY *conceals* POLLY's *hat and umbrella under table.*] Lady Clardonax was one of the old Carberrys of Hampshire – not the Norfolk Carberrys, but the direct line. And Mr Hawtree's grandfather was in trade – something in the City – soap, I think – Stool, George! [*Points to stool.* GEORGE *brings it to her. She motions that he is to sit at her feet;* GEORGE *does so with a sigh.*] He's a very nice person, but *parvenu*, as one may see by his languor and his swagger. My boy [*kissing his forehead*], I am sure, will never make a *mésalliance*. He is a D'Alroy, and by his mother's side *Planta-genista*. The source of our life stream is royal.

GEORGE: How is the Marquis?

MARQUISE: Paralysed. I left him at Spa with three physicians. He always is paralysed at this time of the year; it is in the family. The paralysis is not personal, but hereditary. I came over to see my steward; got to town last night.

GEORGE: How did you find me out here?

MARQUISE: I sent the footman to the barracks, and he saw your man Dixon in the street, and Dixon gave him this address. It's so long since I've seen you. [*Leans back in chair.*] You're looking very well, and I dare say when mounted are quite a "beau cavalier." And so, my boy [*playing with his hair*], you are going abroad for the first time on active service.

GEORGE: [*aside*] Every word can be heard in the next room. If they've only gone upstairs.

MARQUISE: And now, my dear boy, before you go I want to give you some advice; and you mustn't despise it because I'm an old woman. We old women know a great deal more than people give us credit for. You are a soldier – so was your father – so was his father – so was mine – so was our royal founder; we were born to lead! The common people expect it from us. It is our duty. Do you not remember in the Chronicles of Froissart? [*with great enjoyment*] I think I can quote it word for word; I've a wonderful memory for my age. [*with closed eyes*] It was in the fifty-ninth chapter – "How Godefroy D'Alroy helde the towne of St. Amande duryng the siege before Tournay. It said the towne was not closed but with pales, and captayne there was Sir Amory of Pauy – the Seneschall of Carcassoune – who had said it was not able to hold agaynste an hooste, when one Godefroy D'Alroy sayd that rather than he woulde depart, he woulde keep it to the best of his power. Whereat the souldiers cheered and sayd, 'Lead us on, Sir Godefroy.' And then began a fierce assault; and they within were chased, and sought for shelter from street to street. But Godefroy stood at the gate so valyantly that the souldiers helde the towne until the commyng of the Earl of Haynault with twelve thousande men."

GEORGE: [*aside*] I wish she'd go. If she once gets on to Froissart, she'll never know when to stop.

MARQUISE: When my boy fights – and you will fight – he is sure to distinguish himself. It is his nature to – [*Toys with his hair.*] – he cannot forget his birth. And when you meet these Asiatic ruffians, who have dared to revolt, and to outrage humanity, you will strike as your ancestor Sir Galtier of Chevrault struck at Poictiers. [*changing tone of voice as if remembering*] Froissart mentions it thus – "Sir Galtier, with his four squires, was in the front of that battell, and there did marvels in arms. And Sir Galtier rode up to the Prince, and sayd to him – 'Sir, take your horse and ryde forth, this journey is yours. God is this day in your hands. Gette us to the French Kynge's batayle. I think verily by his valyantesse he woll not fly. Advance banner in the name of God and of Saynt George!' And Sir Galtier galloped forward to see his Kynge's victory, and meet his own death."

GEORGE: [*aside*] If Esther hears all this!

MARQUISE: There is another subject about which I should have spoken to you before this; but an absurd prudery forbade me. I may never see you more. I am old – and you – are going into battle – [*kissing his forehead with emotion*] – and this may be our last meeting. [*A noise heard within folding-doors.*] What's that?

GEORGE: Nothing – my man Dixon in there.

MARQUISE: We may not meet again on this earth. I do not fear your conduct, my George, with men; but I know the temptations that beset a youth who is well born. But a true soldier, a true gentleman, should not only be without fear, but without reproach. It is easier to fight a furious man than to forego the conquest of a love-sick girl. A thousand Sepoys slain in battle cannot redeem the honour of a man who has betrayed the confidence of a trusting woman. Think, George, what dishonour – what stain upon your manhood – to hurl a girl to shame and degradation! And what excuse for it? That she is plebeian? A man of real honour will spare the woman who has confessed her love for him, as he would give quarter to an enemy he had disarmed. [*taking his hands*] Let my boy avoid the snares so artfully spread; and when he asks his mother to welcome the woman he has chosen for his wife, let me take her to my arms and plant a motherly kiss upon the white brow of a lady. [*Noise of a fall heard within folding-doors; rising*] What's that?

GEORGE: [*rising*] Nothing.

MARQUISE: I heard a cry.

> [*Folding-doors open, discovering* ESTHER *with* POLLY, *staggering in, fainting.*]

POLLY: George! George!

> [GEORGE *goes up and* ESTHER *falls in his arms.* GEORGE *places* ESTHER *on sofa.*]

MARQUISE: Who are these *women?*

POLLY: Women!

MARQUISE: George D'Alroy, these persons should have been sent away. How could you dare to risk your mother meeting women of their stamp?

POLLY: [*violently*] What does she mean? How dare she call me a woman? What's she, I'd like to know?

GEORGE: Silence, Polly! You mustn't insult my mother.

MARQUISE: The insult is from you. I leave you, and I hope that time may induce me to forget this scene of degradation. [*turning to go*]

GEORGE: Stay, mother. [MARQUISE *turns slightly away.*] Before you go [GEORGE *has raised* ESTHER *from sofa in both arms.*] let me present to you Mrs George D'Alroy. *My wife!*

MARQUISE: Married!

GEORGE: Married.

> [*The* MARQUISE *sinks into easy-chair.* GEORGE *replaces* ESTHER *on sofa but still retains her hand. Three hesitating taps at door heard.* GEORGE *crosses to door,* R.H., *opens it, discovers* ECCLES, *who enters.* GEORGE *drops down back of* MARQUISE's *chair.*]

ECCLES: They told us to come up. When your man came Polly was out; so I thought I should do instead. [*calling at door*] Come up, Sam.

> [*Enter* SAM *in his Sunday clothes, with short cane and smoking a cheroot. He nods and grins –* POLLY *points to* MARQUISE *–* SAM *takes cheroot from his mouth and quickly removes his hat.*]

ECCLES: Sam had just called; so we three – Sam and I, and your man, all came in the 'ansom cab together. Didn't we, Sam?

> [ECCLES *and* SAM *go over to the girls, and* ECCLES *drops down to front of table – smilingly.*]

MARQUISE: [*with glasses up, to* GEORGE] Who is this?

GEORGE: My wife's father.

MARQUISE: What is he?

GEORGE: A – nothing.

ECCLES: I am one of nature's noblemen. Happy to see you, my lady – [*turning to her*] – now, my daughters have told me who you are – [GEORGE *turns his back in an agony as* ECCLES *crosses to* MARQUISE.] – we old folks, fathers and mothers of the young couples, ought to make friends. [*holding out his dirty hand*]

MARQUISE: [*shrinking back*] Go away! [ECCLES *goes back to table again, disgusted.*] What's his name?

GEORGE: Eccles.

MARQUISE: Eccles! Eccles! There never was an Eccles. He don't exist.

ECCLES: Don't he, though! What d'ye call this?

> [*He goes up again to back of table as* SAM *drops down. He is just going to take a decanter when* SAM *stops him.*]

MARQUISE: No Eccles was ever born!

GEORGE: He takes the liberty of breathing notwithstanding. [*aside*] And I wish he wouldn't!

MARQUISE: And who is the little man? Is he also Eccles?

> [SAM *looks round.* POLLY *gets close up to him, and looks with defiant glance at the* MARQUISE.]

GEORGE: No.

MARQUISE: Thank goodness! What then?

GEORGE: His name is Gerridge.

MARQUISE: *Gerridge!* It breaks one's teeth. Why is he here?

GEORGE: He is making love to Polly, my wife's sister.

MARQUISE: And what is he?

GEORGE: A gasman.

MARQUISE: He looks it. [GEORGE *goes up to* ESTHER.] And what is she – the – the – the sister?

> [ECCLES, *who has been casting longing eyes at the decanter on table, edges towards it, and when he thinks no one is noticing, fills wine-glass.*]

POLLY: [*asserting herself indignantly*] I'm in the ballet at the Theatre Royal, Lambeth. So was Esther. We're not ashamed of what we are! We have no cause to be.

SAM: That's right, Polly! Pitch into them swells! – who are they?

> [ECCLES *by this time has seized wine-glass, and, turning his back, is about to drink, when* HAWTREE *enters.* ECCLES *hides glass under his coat, and pretends to be looking up at picture.*]

HAWTREE: [*entering*] George! [*Stops suddenly, looking round.*] So, all's known!

MARQUISE: [*rising*] Captain Hawtree, see me to my carriage; I am broken-hearted!

> [*She takes* HAWTREE'S *arm, and is going up.*]

ECCLES: [*who has tasted the claret, spits it out with a grimace, exclaiming*] – Rot!

> [POLLY *goes to piano, sits on stool –* SAM *back to audience, leaning on piano –* ECCLES *exits through folding-doors.*]

GEORGE: [*to* MARQUISE] Don't go in anger. You may not see me again.

> [ESTHER *rises in nervous excitement, clutching* GEORGE'S *hand.* MARQUISE *stops.*]

ESTHER: [*with arm round his neck*] Oh, George! must you go?

GEORGE: Yes.

ESTHER: I can't leave you! I'll go with you!

GEORGE: Impossible! The country is too unsettled.

ESTHER: May I come after you?

GEORGE: Yes.

ESTHER: [*with her head on his shoulder*] I may.

MARQUISE: It is his duty to go. His honour calls him. The honour of his family – *our* honour!

ESTHER: But I love him so! Pray don't be angry with me!

HAWTREE: [*looking at watch*] George!

GEORGE: I must go, love!

[HAWTREE *goes up to door again.*]

MARQUISE: [*advancing*] Let me arm you, George – let your mother, as in the days of old. There is blood – and blood, my son. See, your wife cries when she should be proud of you!

GEORGE: My Esther is all that is good and noble. No lady born to a coronet could be gentler or more true. Esther, my wife, fetch me my sword, and buckle my belt around me.

ESTHER: [*clinging to him*] No, no; I can't!

GEORGE: Try. [*whispers to* ESTHER] To please my mother. [*to* MARQUISE] You shall see. [ESTHER *totters up stage*, POLLY *assisting her, and brings down his sword. As* ESTHER *is trying to buckle his belt, he whispers*] I've left money for you, my darling. My lawyer will call on you to-morrow. Forgive me! I tried hard to tell you we were ordered for India; but when the time came, my heart failed me, and I——

[ESTHER, *before she can succeed in fastening his sword-belt, reels, and falls fainting in his arms*. POLLY *hurries to her.* SAM. *standing at piano, looking frightened;* HAWTREE *with hand upon handle of door;* MARQUISE *looking on.*]

END OF ACT II

FOR CALL – GEORGE *and* HAWTREE *gone.* ESTHER *in chair, fainting;* POLLY *and* SAM *each side of her*, POLLY *holding her hands and* SAM *fanning her with his red handkerchief. The folding-doors, thrown open, and* ECCLES *standing at back of table offering glass of claret.*

ACT III

SCENE I – *The Room in Stangate [as in Act I.]. Same furniture as in Act I. with exception of piano, with roll of music tied up on it in place of bureau. Map of India over mantelpiece. Sword with crape knot, spurs, and cap, craped, hanging over chimney-piece. Portrait of* D'ALROY *[large] on mantelpiece, Berceaunette, and child, with coral, in it.* POLLY's *bonnet and shawl hanging on peg. Small tin saucepan in fender, fire alight, and kettle on it. Two candles [tallow] in sticks, one of which is broken about three inches from the top and hangs over. Slate and pencil on table. Jug on table, bandbox and ballet skirt on table.*

> [*At rise of curtain* POLLY *discovered at table, back of stage. She comes down and places the skirt in bandbox. She is dressed in black.*]

POLLY: [*placing skirt in box, and leaning her chin upon her hand*] There – there's the dress for poor Esther in case she gets the engagement, which I don't suppose she will. It's too good luck, and good luck never comes to her, poor thing. [*Goes up to back of cradle.*] Baby's asleep still. How good he looks – as good as if he were dead, like his poor father; and alive too, at the same time like his dear self. Ah! dear me; it's a strange world. [*Sits in chair* R. *of table, feeling in pocket for money.*] Four and elevenpence. That must do for to-day and to-morrow. Esther is going to bring in the rusks for Georgey. [*Takes up slate.*] Three, five – eight, and four – twelve, one shilling – father can only have twopence. [*This all to be said in one breath.*] He must make do with that till Saturday, when I get my salary. If Esther gets the engagement, I shan't have many more salaries to take; I shall leave the stage and retire into private life. I wonder if I shall like private life, and if private life will like me. It will seem so strange being no longer Miss Mary Eccles – but Mrs Samuel Gerridge. [*Writes it on slate.*] "Mrs Samuel Gerridge." [*Laughs bashfully*] La! to think of my being Mrs Anybody. How annoyed Susan Smith will be! [*writing on slate*] "Mrs Samuel Gerridge presents her compliments to Miss Susan Smith, and Mrs Samuel Gerridge requests the favour of Miss Susan Smith's company to tea, on Tuesday evening next, at Mrs Samuel Gerridge's house." [*pause*] Poor Susan! [*beginning again*] "P.S. – "Mrs Samuel Gerridge——"

> [*Knock heard at room door;* POLLY *starts.*]

SAM: [*without*] Polly, open the door.
POLLY: Sam! Come in.
SAM: [*without*] I can't.

POLLY: Why not?

SAM: I've got somethin' on my 'ead.

> [POLLY *rises and opens door.* SAM *enters, carrying two rolls of wallpaper, one in each hand, and a small table on his head, which he deposits down stage, then puts rolls of paper on piano, as also his cap.* SAM *has a rule-pocket in corduroys.*]

POLLY: [*Shuts door.*] What's that?

SAM: [*pointing to table with pride*] Furniture. How are you, my Polly? [*kissing her*] You look handsomer than ever this morning. [*Dances and sings.*] "Tid-dle-di-tum-ti-di-do."

POLLY: What's the matter, Sam? – are you mad?

SAM: No, 'appy – much the same thing.

POLLY: Where have you been these two days?

SAM: [*all excitement*] That's just what I'm goin' to tell yer. Polly, my pet, my brightest batswing and most brilliant burner, what do yer think?

POLLY: Oh, do go on, Sam, or I'll slap your face.

SAM: Well, then, you've 'eard me speak of old Binks, the plumber, glazier, and gasfitter, who died six months ago?

POLLY: Yes.

SAM: [*sternly and deliberately*] I've bought 'is business.

POLLY: No!

SAM: [*excitedly*] Yes, of 'is widow, old Mrs Binks – so much down, and so much more at the end of the year. [*dances and sings*]

> "Ri-ti-toodle
> Roodle-oodle
> Ri-ti-tooral-lay."

POLLY: La, Sam!

SAM: [*pacing stage up and down*] Yes; I've bought the goodwill, fixtures, fittin's, stock, rolls of gas-pipe, and sheets of lead. [*Jumps on table quickly facing* POLLY.] Yes, Polly, I'm a tradesman with a shop – a master tradesman. [*coming to* POLLY *seriously*] All I want to complete the premises is a missus.

> [*He tries to kiss her. She pushes him away.*]

POLLY: Sam, don't be foolish!

SAM: [*arm round her waist*] Come and be Mrs Sam Gerridge, Polly, my patent-safety-day-and-night-light. You'll furnish me completely.

> [SAM *watching* POLLY *admiringly, then sees slate, snatches it up and looks at it. She snatches it from him with a shriek, and rubs out writing, looking daggers at him,* SAM *laughing.*]

SAM: [*putting arm round her waist,* POLLY *pouting*] Only to think now.

POLLY: Don't be a goose.

SAM: [*going towards table*] I spent the whole of yesterday lookin' up furniture. Now I bought that a bargain, and I brought it 'ere to show you for your approval. I've bought lots of other things, and I'll bring 'em all here to show yer for your approval.

POLLY: I couldn't think what had become of you.

SAM: Couldn't yer? Oh, I say, I want yer to choose the new paper for the little back parlour just behind the shop, you know. [*fetching a pattern from piano and unrolling it*] Now what d'yer think o' this?

POLLY: No. I don't like that. [SAM *fetches the other, a flaming pattern.*] Ah! that's neat.

SAM: Yes, that's neat and quiet. I'll new-paper it, and new-furnish it, and it shall all be bran-new.

[*He puts paper on top of piano.*]

POLLY: But won't it cost a lot of money?

SAM: [*bravely*] I can work for it. With customers in the shop, and you in the back-parlour, I can work like fifty men. [*He beckons* POLLY *to him, she comes and he puts his arm round her, sentimentally.*] Only fancy, at night, when the shop's closed, and the shutters are up, counting out the till together! [*changing his manner*] Besides, that isn't all I've been doin'. I've been writin', and what I've written I've got printed.

POLLY: No!

SAM: True.

POLLY: [*delighted*] You've been writing – about me?

SAM: No – about the shop. [POLLY *disgusted*] Here it is. [*Takes roll of circulars from pocket of his canvas slop.*] Yer mustn't laugh – you know – it's my first attempt. I wrote it the night before last; and when I thought of you the words seemed to flow like – red-hot solder. [*reads*] Hem! "Samuel Gerridge takes this opportunity of informin' the nobility, gentry, and inhabitants of the Borough-road——"

POLLY: The Borough-road?

SAM: Well, there ain't many of the nobility and gentry as lives in the Borough-road, but it pleases the inhabitants to make 'em believe yèr think so [*resuming*] – "of informin' the nobility, gentry, and inhabitants of the Borough-road, and its vicinity," and "its vicinity." [*looking at her*] Now I think that's rather good, eh?

POLLY: Yes. [*doubtfully*] I've heard worse.

SAM: I first thought of saying neighbour'ood; but then vicinity sounds so much more genteel [*resuming*] – "*and* its vicinity, that 'e has entered upon the business of the late Mr Binks, 'is relict, the present Mrs B., 'avin' disposed to 'im of the same" – now listen, Polly, because it gets interestin' – "S. G.——."

POLLY: S. G. Who's he?

SAM: [*looking at* POLLY *with surprise*] Why me. S. G. – Samuel Gerridge – me, us. We're S. G. Now don't interrupt me, or you'll cool my metal, and then I can't work. "S. G. 'opes that, by a constant attention to business, and" – mark this – "by supplyin' the best articles at the most reasonable prices, to merit a continuance of those favours which it will ever be 'is constant study to deserve." There! [*turning triumphantly*] Stop a bit – there's a little bit more yet. "Bell-'angin', gas-fittin', plumbin', and glazin', as usual." There! – it's all my own.

[*He puts circular on mantelpiece and contemplates it.*]

POLLY: Beautiful Sam. It looks very attractive from here, don't it?

[*Postman's knock.*]

SAM: There's the postman. I'll go. I shall send some of these out by post.

[*He goes off and returns with letter.*]

POLLY: [*taking it*] Oh, for Esther. I know who it's from. [*She places letter on mantelpiece.* SAM *sits corner of table, reading circular. Seriously*] Sam, who do you think was here last night?

SAM: Who?

POLLY : Captain Hawtree.

SAM: [*deprecatingly*] Oh, 'im! – come back from India, I suppose.

POLLY: Yes; luckily, Esther was out.

SAM: I never liked that long swell. He was a 'uppish, conceited——

POLLY: Oh, he's better than he used to be – he's a major now. He's only been in England a fortnight.

SAM: Did he tell yer anything about poor De Alroy?

POLLY: [*leaning against table end*] Yes; he said he was riding out not far from the cantonment, and he was surrounded by a troop of Sepoy cavalry, which took him prisoner, and galloped off with him.

SAM: But about 'is death?

POLLY: Oh! [*hiding her face*] – that he said was believed to be too terrible to mention.

SAM: Did 'e tell yer anything else?

POLLY: No; he asked a lot of questions, and I told him everything. How poor Esther had taken her widowhood and what a dear, good baby the baby was, and what a comfort to us all, and how Esther had come back to live with us again.

SAM: [*sharply*] And the reason for it?

POLLY: [*looking down*] Yes.

SAM: How your father got all the money that 'e'd left for Esther.

POLLY: [*sharply*] Don't say any more about that, Sam.

SAM: Oh! I only think Captain 'awtree ought to know where the money *did* go to, and you shouldn't try and screen your father, and let 'im suppose that you and Esther spent it all.

POLLY: [*angrily*] I told him – I told him – I told him.

SAM: Did you tell 'im that your father was always at 'armonic meetin's at taverns, and 'ad arf cracked 'isself with drink, and was always singin' the songs and makin' the speeches 'e 'eard there, and was always goin' on about 'is wrongs as one of the workin' classes? 'E's a pretty one for one of the workin' classes, 'e is! 'Asn't done a stroke o' work these twenty year. Now, I *am* one of the workin' classes, but I *don't* 'owl about it. I work, I don't spout.

POLLY: Hold your tongue, Sam. I won't have you say any more against poor father. [*sighing*] He has his faults, but he's a very clever man.

SAM: Ah! What else did Captain Hawtree say?

POLLY: He advised us to apply to Mr D'Alroy's mother.

SAM: What! the Marquissy? And what did you say to that?

POLLY: I said that Esther wouldn't hear of it. And so the Major said that he'd write to Esther, and I suppose this is the letter.

SAM: Now, Polly, come along and choose the paper for the little back parlour.

> [*He goes towards table and takes it up to wall behind door.*]

POLLY: [*rising*] Can't! Who's to mind baby?

SAM: The *baby?* Oh, I forgot all about 'im. [*Goes to cradle.*] I see yer! [*Goes to window casually.*] There's your father comin' down the street. Won't 'e mind 'im?

POLLY: I dare say he will. If I promise him an extra sixpence on Saturday. [SAM *opens window.*] Hi! Father!

> [POLLY *goes to cradle.*]

SAM: [*aside*] 'E looks down in the mouth, 'e does. I suppose 'e's 'ad no drink this mornin'. [*He goes to* POLLY.]

> [*Enter* ECCLES *in shabby black. Pauses on entering, looks at* SAM, *turns away in disgust, takes off hat, places it on piano, and shambles across to* L. *Taking chair, places it and sits before fire.*]

POLLY: [*goes to* ECCLES] Come in to stop a bit, father?

ECCLES: No; not for long. Good morning, Samuel. Going back to work? that's right, my boy – stick to it. [*Pokes fire.*] Stick to it – nothing like it.

SAM: [*aside*] Now, isn't that too bad! No, Mr Eccles. I've knocked off for the day.

ECCLES: [*waving poker*] That's bad! That's very bad! Nothing like work – for the young. I don't work so much as I used to, myself, but I like to see the young 'uns at it. It does me good, and it does them good too. What does the poet say? [*rising, impressively, and leaning on table*]

> "A carpenter said tho' that was well spoke,
> It was better by far to defend it with hoak.
> A currier, wiser than both put together,
> Said say what you will, there is nothing like *labour*.
> For a' that, an' a' that,
> Your ribbon, gown, an' a' that,
> The rank is but the guinea stamp,
> The working man's the gold for a' that."

[*He sits again, triumphantly wagging his head.*]

SAM: [*aside*] This is one of the public-house loafers, that wants all the wages and none of the work, an idle old――

[*He goes in disgust to piano, puts on cap, and takes rolls of paper under his arm.*]

POLLY: [*to* ECCLES] Esther will be in by-and-by. [*persuasive*] Do, father!

ECCLES: No, no. I tell you I won't!

POLLY: [*whispering, arm round his neck*] And I'll give you sixpence extra on Saturday.

[ECCLES' *face relaxes into a broad grin.* POLLY *gets hat and cloak.*]

ECCLES: Ah! you sly little puss, you know how to get over your poor old father.

SAM: [*aside*] Yes, with sixpence.

POLLY : [*putting on bonnet and cloak at door*] Give the cradle a rock if baby cries.

SAM: [*crossing to* ECCLES] If you should 'appen to want employment or amusement, Mr Eccles, just cast your eye over this. [*Puts circular on table, then joins* POLLY *at door.*] Stop a bit, I've forgot to give the baby one.

[*He throws circular into cradle. Exeunt,* POLLY *first.*
ECCLES *takes out pipe from pocket, looks into it, then*

*blows through it making a squeaking noise and finishes
by tenderly placing it on the table. He then hunts all his
pockets for tobacco, finally finding a little paper packet
containing a screw of tobacco in his waistcoat pocket,
which he also places on table after turning up the corner
of the tablecloth for the purpose of emptying the
contents of his pocket of the few remnants of past screws
of tobacco on to the bare table and mixing a little out the
packet with it and filling pipe. He then brushes all that
remains on the table into the paper packet, pinches it
up, and carefully replaces it in his waistcoat pocket.
Having put the pipe into his mouth, he looks about for a
light, across his shoulder and under table, though never
rising from the chair; seeing nothing his face assumes an
expression of comic anguish. Turning to table he angrily
replaces tablecloth and then notices* SAM's *circular. His
face relaxes into a smile, and picking it up tears the
circular in half, makes a spill of it, and lighting it at
fire, stands with his back to fireplace and smokes
vigorously.*]

ECCLES: Poor Esther! Nice market she's brought her pigs to – ugh!
Mind the baby indeed! What good is he to me? That fool of a
girl to throw away all her chances! – a *honourable-hess* – and her
father not to have on him the price of a pint of early beer or a
quartern of cool, refreshing gin! Stopping in here to rock a
young honourable! Cuss him! [*Business; puffs smoke in baby's
face, rocking cradle.*] Are we slaves, we working men? [*Sings
savagely.*]

"Britons never, never, never shall be——"

[*nodding his head sagaciously*] I won't stand this, I've writ to
the old cat – I mean to the Marquissy – to tell her that her
daughter-in-law and her grandson is almost starving. That
fool Esther's too proud to write to her for money. I hate pride
– it's *beastly!* [*rising*] There's no beastly pride about me.
[*smacking his lips*] I'm as dry as a lime-kiln. [*Takes up jug.*]
Milk! – [*with disgust*] – for this young aristocratic pauper.
Everybody in the house is sacrificed for him! [*at foot of cradle,
with arms on chair back*] And to think that a *working man*, and a
member of the Committee of the Banded Brothers for the
Regeneration of Human Kind, by means of equal diffusion of
intelligence and equal division of property, should be thusty,
while this cub – [*Draws aside curtain, and looks at child. After a
pause*] That there coral he's got round his neck is *gold*, real
gold! [*with hand on knob at end of cradle*] Oh, Society! Oh,

Governments! Oh, Class Legislation! – *is this right?* Shall this
mindless wretch enjoy himself, while sleeping, with a jewelled
gawd, and his poor old grandfather want the price of half a
pint? *No!* it shall not be! Rather than see it, I will myself resent
this outrage on the rights of man! and in this holy crusade of
class against class, of the weak and lowly against the *powerful
and strong* – [*pointing to child*] – I will strike one blow for
freedom! [*Goes to back of cradle.*] He's asleep. It will fetch ten
bob round the corner; and if the Marquissy gives us anythink
it can be got out with some o' that. [*Steals coral.*] Lie still, my
darling! – it's grandfather's a-watching over you –

> "Who ran to catch me when I fell,
> And kicked the place to make it well?
> My grandfather!"

[*rocking cradle with one hand; leaves it quickly, and as he takes
hat off piano* ESTHER *enters. She is dressed as a widow, her face
pale, and her manner quick and imperious. She carries a parcel
and paper bag of rusks in her hand; she puts parcel on table, goes
to cradle, kneels down and kisses child.*] My lovey had a nice
walk? You should wrap yourself up well – you're so liable to
catch cold!

ESTHER: My Georgy? – Where's his coral? [ECCLES, *at the door, fumbles
with the lock nervously, and is going out as* ESTHER *speaks.*]
Gone! – Father! – [*rising –* ECCLES *stops.*] The child's coral –
where is it?

ECCLES: [*confused*] Where's what, ducky?

ESTHER: The coral! You've got it – I know it! Give it me! – [*quickly and
imperiously*] – *Give it me!* [ECCLES *takes coral from his pocket
and gives it back.*] If you *dare* to touch *my* child——

[*She goes to cradle.*]

ECCLES: Esther! [*going quickly to piano and banging his hat on it*] Am I
not your father?——

[ESTHER *gets round to front of cradle.*]

ESTHER: And I am his mother!

ECCLES: [*coming to her*] Do you bandy words with me, you pauper!
you pauper!! you pauper!!! to whom I have given shelter –
shelter to you and your brat! [*raising his clenched fist*] I've a
good mind——

ESTHER: [*confronting him*] If you dare! I am no longer your little
drudge – your frightened servant. When mother died –
[ECCLES *changes countenance and cowers beneath her glance.*] –
and I was so high, I tended you, and worked for you – and you
beat me. That time is past. I am a woman – I am a wife – a

widow – a *mother!* Do you think I will let you outrage *him!*
[*pointing to cradle*] *Touch me if you dare!* [*advancing a step*]

ECCLES: [*bursting into tears*] And this is my own child, which I nussed
when a babby, and sung "Cootsicum Coo" to afore she could
speak. [*gets hat from piano, and returns a step or two.*] Hon. Mrs
De Alroy [ESTHER *drops down behind chair.*] I forgive you for
all that you have said. I forgive you for all that you have done.
In everything that I have done I have acted with the best
intentions. May the babe in that cradle never treat you as you
have this day *tret* a grey 'aired father. May he never cease to
love and *honour* you, as you have ceased to love and *honour*
me, after all that I have done for you, and the position to which
I 'ave raised you by my own *industry.* [*goes to door.*] May he
never behave to you like the bad daughters of King Lear; and
may you never live to feel how much more sharper than a
serpent's [*slight pause as if remembering quotation*] scale it is to
have a thankless child!

[*Exit* ECCLES.]

ESTHER: [*kneeling back of cradle*] My darling! [*arranging bed and
placing coral to the baby's lips, and then to her own*] Mamma's
come back to her own. Did she stay away from him so long?
[*Rises, and looks at the sabre, &c.*] My George! to think that
you can never look upon his face or hear his voice. My brave,
gallant, handsome husband! My lion and my love! [*pacing the
stage*] Oh! to be a soldier, and to fight the wretches who
destroyed him – who took my darling from me! [*Action of
cutting with sabre.*] To gallop miles upon their upturned faces.
[*Crossing, with action – breaks down sobbing at mantelpiece – sees
letter.*] What's this? – Captain Hawtree's hand. [*Sitting in
chair, reads, at left hand of table.*] "My dear Mrs D'Alroy, – I
returned to England less than a fortnight ago. I have some
papers and effects of my poor friend's, which I am anxious to
deliver to you, and I beg of you to name a day when I can call
with them and see you; at the same time let me express my
deepest sympathy with your affliction. Your husband's loss
was mourned by every man in the regiment. [ESTHER *lays the
letter on her heart, and then resumes reading.*] I have heard with
great pain of the pecuniary embarrassments into which
accident and the imprudence of others have placed you. I trust
you will not consider me, one of poor George's oldest
comrades and friends, either intrusive or impertinent in
sending the enclosed [*She takes out a cheque.*] and in hoping
that, should any further difficulties arise, you will inform me
of them, and remember that I am, dear Mrs D'Alroy, now,
and always, your faithful and sincere friend, Arthur

Hawtree." [ESTHER *goes to cradle, and bends over it.*] Oh, *his* boy, if you could read it!

[*She sobs, with head on head of cradle. Enter* POLLY.]

POLLY: Father gone!

ESTHER: Polly, you look quite flurried.

[POLLY *laughs, and whispers to* ESTHER.]

ESTHER: [*near head of table. taking* POLLY *in her arms and kissing her*] So soon? Well – my darling, I hope you may be happy.

POLLY: Yes. Sam's going to speak to father about it this afternoon. [*putting rusks in saucepan*] Did you see the agent, dear?

ESTHER: Yes; the manager didn't come – he broke his appointment again.

POLLY: Nasty, rude fellow!

ESTHER: The agent said it didn't matter, he thought I should get the engagement. He'll only give me thirty shillings a week, though.

POLLY: But you said that two pounds was the regular salary.

ESTHER: Yes, but they know I'm poor, and want the engagement, and so take advantage of me.

POLLY: Never mind, Esther. I put the dress in that bandbox. It looks almost as good as new.

ESTHER: I've had a letter from Captain Hawtree.

POLLY: I know, dear; he came here last night.

ESTHER: A dear, good letter – speaking of George, and enclosing me a cheque for thirty pounds.

POLLY: Oh, how kind! Don't you tell father.

[*Noise of carriage-wheels without.*]

ESTHER: I shan't.

[ECCLES *enters, breathless.* ESTHER *and* POLLY *rise.*]

ECCLES: It's the Marquissy in her coach. [ESTHER *puts on the lid of bandbox.*] Now, girls, do be civil to her, and she may do something for us. [*Places hat on piano.*] I see the coach as I was coming out of the "Rainbow."

[*He hastily pulls an old comb out of his pocket, and puts his hair in order.*]

ESTHER: The Marquise!

[ESTHER *comes down to end of table,* POLLY *holding her hand.*]

ECCLES: [*at door*] This way, my lady – up them steps. They're rather awkward for the like's o' you; but them as is poor and lowly must do as best they can with steps and circumstances.

[*Enter* MARQUISE. *She surveys the place with aggressive astonishment.*]

MARQUISE: [*half aside*] What a hole! And to think that my grandson should breathe such an atmosphere, and be contaminated by such associations! [*to* ECCLES] Which is the young woman who married my son?

ESTHER: I am Mrs George D'Alroy, widow of George D'Alroy. Who are you?

MARQUISE: I am his mother, the Marquise de Saint Maur.

ESTHER: [*with the grand air*] Be seated, I beg.

[ECCLES *takes chair, which* ESTHER *immediately seizes as* SAM *enters with an easy-chair on his head, which he puts down, not seeing* MARQUISE, *who instantly sits down in it, concealing it completely.*]

SAM: [*astonished*] It's the Marquissy! [*looking at her*] My eye! These aristocrats are fine women – plenty of 'em – [*describing circle*] quality and quantity!

POLLY: Go away, Sam; you'd better come back.

[ECCLES *nudges him, and bustles him towards door. Exit* SAM. ECCLES *shuts door on him.*]

ECCLES: [*rubbing his hands*] If we'd a know'd your ladyship had bin a-coming we'd a had the place cleaned up a bit.

[*He gets round behind* MARQUISE, *who turns the chair slightly from him.*]

POLLY: Hold your tongue, father!

[ECCLES *crushed.*]

MARQUISE: [*to* ESTHER] You remember me, do you not?

ESTHER: Perfectly, though I only saw you once. [*seating herself en grande dame*] May I ask what has procured me the honour of this visit?

MARQUISE: I was informed that you were in want, and I came to offer you assistance.

ESTHER: I thank you for your offer, and the delicate consideration for my feelings with which it is made. I need no assistance.

[ECCLES *groans and leans on piano.*]

MARQUISE: A letter I received last night informed me that you did.

ESTHER: May I ask if that letter came from Captain Hawtree?

MARQUISE: No – from this person – your father, I think.

ESTHER: [*to* ECCLES] How dare you interfere in my affairs?

ECCLES: My lovey, I did it with the best intentions.

MARQUISE: Then you will not accept assistance from me?

ESTHER: No.

POLLY: [*aside to* ESTHER, *holding her hand*] Bless you, my darling!

MARQUISE: [*with emotion*] But you have a child – a son – my grandson.

ESTHER: Master D'Alroy wants for nothing.

POLLY: [*aside*] And never shall.

[ECCLES *groans and turns on to piano.*]

MARQUISE: I came here to propose that my grandson should go back with me.

[POLLY *rushes up to cradle.*]

ESTHER: [*rising defiantly*] What! Part with my boy! I'd sooner die!

MARQUISE: You can see him when you wish. As for money, I——

ESTHER: Not for ten thousand million worlds – not for ten thousand million marchionesses!

ECCLES: Better do what the good lady asks you, my dear; she's advising you for your own good, and for the child's likewise.

MARQUISE: Surely you cannot intend to bring up my son's son in a place like this?

ESTHER: I do.

ECCLES: It *is* a poor place, and we are poor people, sure enough. We ought not to fly in the faces of our pastors and masters – our pastresses and mistresses.

POLLY: [*aside*] Oh, hold your tongue, do!

ESTHER: [*before cradle*] Master George D'Alroy will remain with his mother. The offer to take him from her is an insult to his dead father and to him.

ECCLES: [*aside*] He don't seem to feel it, stuck-up little beast!

MARQUISE: But you have no money – how can you rear him? – how can you educate him? – how can you live?

ESTHER: [*tearing dress from bandbox*] Turn columbine – go on the stage again and dance!

MARQUISE: You are insolent – you forget that I am a lady.

ESTHER: You forget that I am a mother. Do you dare to offer to buy my child – *his* breathing image, *his* living memory – with money? [*Crosses to door and throws it open.*] There is the door – go!

ECCLES: [*to* MARQUISE, *who has risen, aside*] Very sorry, my lady, as you should be tret in this way, which was not my wishes.

MARQUISE: Silence! [ECCLES *retreats, putting back chair,* MARQUISE *goes up to door.*] Mrs D'Alroy, if anything could have increased my sorrow for the wretched marriage my poor son was *decoyed* into, it would be your conduct this day to his mother.

[*Exit* MARQUISE.]

ESTHER: [*falling in* POLLY's *arms*] Oh, Polly! Polly!

ECCLES: [*looking after her*] To go away, and not to leave a sov. behind her! [*running up to open door*] Cat! Cat! Stingy old cat!

> [*He almost runs to fire, sits, and pokes it violently; carriage-wheels heard without.*]

ESTHER: I'll go to my room and lie down. Let me have the baby, or that old woman may come back and steal him.

> [*Exit* ESTHER, POLLY *follows with the baby.*]

ECCLES: Well, women is the obstinatest devils as never wore horse-shoes. Children? Beasts! Beasts!

> [*Enter* SAM *and* POLLY.]

SAM: Come along, Polly, and let's get it over at once. [SAM *places cap on piano and goes to table.* POLLY *takes bandbox from table and places it in corner.*] Now, Mr Eccles [ECCLES *turns suddenly, facing* SAM.] since you've been talkin' on family matters, I'd like to 'ave a word with yer, so take this opportunity to——

ECCLES: [*waving his hand grandly*] Take what you like, and then order more [*rising, and leaning over table*], Samuel Gerridge. That hand is a hand that never turned its back on a friend, or a bottle to give him. [*Sings, front of table.*]

> I'll stand by my friend,
> I'll stand by my friend,
> I'll stand by my friend,
> If he'll stand to me – me, genelmen!

SAM: Well, Mr Eccles, sir, it's this——

POLLY: [*aside*] Don't tell him too sudden, Sam – it might shock his feelings.

SAM: It's this: Yer know that for the last four years I've been keepin' company with Mary – Polly.

> [*Turning to her and smiling.* ECCLES *drops into chair as if shot.*]

ECCLES: Go it! go it! strike home, young man! Strike on this grey head! [*sings*] "Britons, strike home!" Here [*tapping his chest*], to my heart! Don't spare me. Have a go at my grey hairs. Pull 'em – pull 'em out! A long pull, and a strong pull, and a pull all together!

> [*He cries, and drops his face on arms, upon table.*]

POLLY: Oh, father! [*patting his head*] I wouldn't hurt your feelings for the world.

SAM: No; Mr Eccles, I don't want to 'urt your feelin's, but I'm a-goin' to enter upon a business. [*offering one*] Here's a circ'lar.

ECCLES: [*indignantly*] Circ'lars. What are circ'lars compared to a father's feelings?

SAM: And I want Polly to name the day, sir, and so I ask you——

ECCLES: This is 'ard, this is 'ard. One of my daughters marries a soger. The other goes a-gasfitting.

SAM: [*annoyed*] The business which will enable me to maintain a wife is that of the late Mr Binks, plumber, glazier, &c.

ECCLES: [*rising, sings. Air, "Lost Rosabelle."*]

"They have given thee to a plumber,
    They have broken every vow,
  They have given thee to a plumber,
    And my heart, my heart is breaking now."

[*He drops into chair again.*]

Now, genelmen!

[SAM *thrusts circulars into his pocket, and turns away angrily.*]

POLLY: You know, father, you can come and see me.

SAM: [*sotto voce*] No, no.

ECCLES: [*looking up*] So I can, and that's a comfort. [*shaking her hand*] And you can come and see me, and that's a comfort. I'll come and see you often – very often – every day [SAM *turns up stage in horror.*] and crack a fatherly bottle [*rising*] and shed a friendly tear.

[*He wipes eyes with dirty pocket-handkerchief, which he pulls from breast pocket.*]

POLLY: Do, father, do.

[*She goes up and gets tea-tray.*]

SAM: [*with a gulp*] Yes, Mr Eccles, do.

[*He goes to* POLLY *and gesticulates behind tray.*]

ECCLES: I will. And this it is to be a father. I would part with any of my children for their own good, readily – if I was paid for it. [*sings*] "For I know that the angels are whispering to me" – me, genelmen!

[POLLY *gets tea-things.*]

SAM: I'll try and make Polly a good husband, and anything that I can do to prove it [*lowering his voice*], in the way of spirituous liquors and tobacco [*slipping coin into his hand, unseen by* POLLY] shall be done.

ECCLES: [*lightening up and placing his* L. *hand on* SAM's *head*]

> "Be kind to thy father,
>   Wherever you be,
> For he is a blessing
>   And credit to thee – thee, genelmen."

Well, my children – bless you, take the blessing of a grey 'air'd father. [POLLY *looking from one to the other,* ECCLES *to* SAM.] Samuel Gerridge, she shall be thine. [*mock heroically, looking at money*] You shall be his wife [*looking at* POLLY], and you [*looking at* SAM], shall be her husband – for for a husband I know no fitter – no "gas-fitter" man. [*Runs to piano and takes hat; goes to door, looks comically pathetic at* SAM *and* POLLY, *puts on hat.*] I've a friend waiting for me round the corner, which I want to have a word with; and may you never know how much more sharper than a serpent's tooth it is to have a marriageable daughter. [*sings*]

> "When I heard she was married
>   I breathed not a tone,
> The h'eyes of all round me
>   Was fixed on my h'own;
> I flew to my chamber
>   To hide my despair,
> I tore the bright circlet
>   Of gems from my hair.
> When I heard she was married,
>   When I heard she was married——"

[*He breaks down. Exit.*]*

POLLY: [*drying her eyes*] There, Sam. I always told you that though father had his faults, his heart was in the right place.

SAM: Poor Polly.

[*He crosses to fireplace. Knock at door.*]

POLLY: Come in!

[*Enter* HAWTREE.]

POLLY: Major Hawtree.

[SAM *turns away as they shake hands.*]

HAWTREE: I met the Marquise's carriage on the bridge. Has she been here?

---

* This Exit was afterwards abandoned with the author's permission, being somewhat of an anti-climax. The Exit is usually made at the words "marriageable daughter," Eccles breaking down in a comically hysterical manner and going out quickly.

POLLY: Yes.

HAWTREE: What happened?

POLLY: Oh, she wanted to take away the child.

SAM: In the coach.

[POLLY *sets tea things.*]

HAWTREE: And what did Mrs D'Alroy say to that?

SAM: Mrs D'Alroy said that she'd see her blow'd first! [POLLY *pushes* SAM.] – or words to that effect.

HAWTREE: I'm sorry to hear this; I had hoped – however that's over.

POLLY: Yes, it's over; and I hope we shall hear no more about it. Want to take away the child, indeed – like her impudence! What next! [*getting ready tea things*] Esther's gone to lie down. I shan't wake her up for tea, though she's had nothing to eat all day.

SAM: Shall I fetch some shrimps?

POLLY: No. What made you think of shrimps?

SAM: They're a relish, and consolin' – at least I always found 'em so.

[*Check lights, gradually.*]

POLLY: I won't ask you to take tea with us, major – you're too grand.

[SAM *motions approbation to* POLLY, *not wanting* HAWTREE *to remain.*]

HAWTREE: [*placing hat on piano*] Not at all. I shall be most happy. [*aside*] 'Pon my word, these are very good sort of people. I'd no idea——

SAM: [*points to* HAWTREE] He's a-going to stop to tea – well, I ain't.

[*Goes up to window and sits.* HAWTREE *crosses and sits* R. *of table.*]

POLLY: Sam! Sam! [*pause – he says* Eh?] Pull down the blind and light the gas.

SAM: No, don't light up; I like this sort of dusk. It's unbusiness-like, but pleasant.

[SAM *cuts enormous slice of bread, and hands it on point of knife to* HAWTREE. *Cuts small lump of butter, and hands it on point of knife to* HAWTREE, *who looks at it through eye-glass, then takes it.* SAM *then helps himself.* POLLY *meantime has poured out tea in two cups, and one saucer for* SAM, *sugars them, and then hands cup and saucer to* HAWTREE, *who has both hands full. He takes it awkwardly, and places it on table.* POLLY, *having only one spoon, tastes* SAM's *tea, then stirs* HAWTREE's, *attracting his attention by so doing. He looks into his tea cup.* POLLY *stirs her own tea, and drops spoon into* HAWTREE's *cup, causing it to spurt in his eye. He drops eye-glass and wipes his eyes.*]

POLLY: [*making tea*] Sugar, Sam!

[SAM *takes tea and sits facing fire.*]

POLLY: Oh, there isn't any milk – it'll be here directly it's just his time.

VOICE: [*outside; rattle of milk-pails*] Mia-oow!

POLLY: There he is. [*Knock at door.*] Oh, I know; I owe him fourpence. [*feeling her pockets*] Sam, have you got fourpence?

[*Knock again, louder.*]

SAM: No [*his mouth full*] – I ain't got no fourpence.

POLLY: He's very impatient. Come in!

[*Enter* GEORGE, *his face bronzed, and in full health. He carries a milk-can in his hand, which, after putting his hat on piano, he places on table.*]

GEORGE: A fellow hung this on the railings, so I brought it in.

[POLLY *sees him, and gradually sinks down under the table. Then* SAM, *with his mouth full, and bread and butter in hand, does the same.* HAWTREE *pushes himself back a space, in chair, remains motionless.* GEORGE *astonished. Picture.*]

GEORGE: What's the matter with you?

HAWTREE: [*rising*] George!

GEORGE: Hawtree! You here?

POLLY: [*under table*] O-o-o-o-oh! the ghost! – the ghost!

SAM: It shan't hurt you, Polly. Perhaps it's only indigestion.

HAWTREE: Then you are not dead?

GEORGE: Dead, no. Where's my wife?

HAWTREE: You were reported killed.

GEORGE: It wasn't true.

HAWTREE: Alive! My old friend alive!

GEORGE: And well. [*Shakes hands.*] Landed this morning. Where's my wife?

SAM: [*who has popped his head from under table-cloth*] He ain't dead, Poll – he's alive!

[POLLY *rises from under table slowly.*]

POLLY: [*pause; approaches him, touches him, retreats.*] George! [*He nods.*] George! George!

GEORGE: Yes! Yes!

POLLY: Alive! – My dear George! – Oh, my dear brother! – [*looking at*

him intensely] – Alive! – [*going to him*] Oh, my dear, dear,
brother! – [*in his arms*] – how could you go and do so? [*She
laughs hysterically.*]

> [GEORGE *places* POLLY *in his arms.* SAM *goes to* POLLY.
> SAM *kisses* POLLY's *hand violently.* HAWTREE *comes up,*
> *stares – business.* SAM *goes with a stamp of his foot.*]

GEORGE: Where's Esther?
HAWTREE: Here – in this house.
GEORGE: Here! doesn't she know I'm back?
POLLY: No; how should she?
GEORGE: [*to* HAWTREE] Didn't you get my telegram?
HAWTREE: No; where from?
GEORGE: Southampton! I sent it to the Club.
HAWTREE: I haven't been there these three days.
POLLY: [*hysterically*] Oh, my dear, dear, dear dead-and-gone! – come
    back all alive oh, brother George!
SAM: Glad to see yer, sir.
GEORGE: Thank you, Gerridge. [*Shakes hands.*] Same to you – but
    Esther?
POLLY: [*back to audience, and 'kerchief to her eyes*] She's asleep in her
    room.

> [GEORGE *is going to door;* POLLY *stops him.*]

POLLY: You mustn't see her!
GEORGE: Not see her! – after this long absence? – why not?
HAWTREE: She's ill to-day. She has been greatly excited. The news of
    your death, which we all mourned, has shaken her terribly.
GEORGE: Poor girl! poor girl!
POLLY: Oh, we all cried so when you died! – [*crying*] – and now you're
    alive again, I want to cry ever so much more!
HAWTREE: We must break the news to her gently and by degrees.
SAM: Yes. If you turn the tap on to full pressure, she'll explode!

> [SAM *turns to* HAWTREE, *who is just raising cup to his*
> *lips and brings it down on saucer with a bang; both*
> *annoyed.*]

GEORGE: To return, and not to be able to see her – to love her – to kiss
    her! [*He stamps.*]
POLLY: Hush!
GEORGE: I forgot! I shall wake her!
POLLY: More than that – you'll wake the baby!
GEORGE: Baby! – what baby?
POLLY: Yours.
GEORGE: Mine?——— mine?

POLLY: Yes—— yours and Esther's! Why, didn't you know there was a baby?

GEORGE: No!

POLLY: La! the ignorance of these men!

HAWTREE: Yes, George, you're a father.

GEORGE: Why wasn't I told of this? Why didn't you write?

POLLY: How could we when you were dead?

SAM: And 'adn't left your address.

[*He looks at* HAWTREE, *who turns away quickly.*]

GEORGE: If I can't see Esther, I will see the child. The sight of me won't be too much for its nerves. Where is it?

POLLY: Sleeping in its mother's arms. [GEORGE *goes to door; she intercepts him.*] Please not! Please not!

GEORGE: I must. I will.

POLLY: It might kill her, and you wouldn't like to do that. I'll fetch the baby; but oh, please don't make a noise. You won't make a noise – you'll be as quiet as you can, won't you? Oh! I can't believe it.

[*Exit* POLLY.]

[SAM *dances break-down and finishes up looking at* HAWTREE, *who turns away astonished.* SAM *disconcerted; sits on chair;* GEORGE *at door.*]

GEORGE: My baby; my ba—— It's a dream! You've seen it. [*to* SAM] What's it like?

SAM: Oh! it's like a – like a sort of – infant – white and – milky, and all that.

[*Enter* POLLY, *with baby wrapped in shawls.* GEORGE *shuts door and meets her.*]

POLLY: Gently, gently – take care! Esther will hardly have it touched.

[SAM *rises and gets near to* GEORGE.]

GEORGE: But I'm its father!

POLLY: That don't matter. She's very particular.

GEORGE: Boy or girl?

POLLY: Guess.

GEORGE: Boy! [POLLY *nods.* GEORGE *proud.*] What's his name?

POLLY: Guess.

GEORGE: George? [POLLY *nods.*] Eustace? [POLLY *nods.*] Fairfax? Algernon? [POLLY *nods; pause.*] My names!

SAM: [*to* GEORGE] You'd 'ardly think there was room enough in 'im to 'old so many names, would yer?

[HAWTREE *looks at him – turns to fire.* SAM *disconcerted again; sits.*]

GEORGE: To come back all the way from India to find that I'm dead, and that you're alive. To find my wife a widow with a new love aged – How old are you? I'll buy you a pony to-morrow, my brave little boy! What's his weight? I should say two pound nothing. My – baby – my – boy! [*Bends over him and kisses him.*] Take him away, Polly, for fear I should break him.

[POLLY *takes child, and places it in cradle.*]

HAWTREE: [*Crosses to piano. Passes* SAM *front – stares – business.* SAM *goes round to fire-place, flings down bread and butter in a rage and drinks his tea out of saucer.*] But tell us how it is you're back? – how you escaped? [*leaning up against piano*]

GEORGE: By-and-by. Too long a story just now. Tell *me* all about it. [POLLY *gives him chair.*] How is it Esther's living here?

POLLY: She came back after the baby was born, and the furniture was sold up.

GEORGE: Sold up? What furniture?

POLLY: That you bought for her.

HAWTREE: It couldn't be helped, George – Mrs D'Alroy was so poor.

GEORGE: Poor! but I left her £600 to put in the bank!

HAWTREE: We "*must*" tell you. She gave it to her father, who banked it in his own name.

SAM: And lost it in bettin' – every copper.

GEORGE: Then she's been in want?

POLLY: No – not in want. Friends lent her money.

GEORGE: [*seated*] What friends? [*Pause; he looks at* POLLY, *who indicates* HAWTREE.] You?

POLLY: Yes.

GEORGE: [*rising, and shaking* HAWTREE's *hand*] Thank you, old fella.

[HAWTREE *droops his head.*]

SAM: [*aside*] Now who'd ha' thought that long swell 'ad it in 'im? 'e never mentioned it.

GEORGE: So Papa Eccles had the money? [*sitting again*]

SAM: And blued it!

POLLY: [*pleadingly*] You see, father was very unlucky on the race-course. He told us that if it hadn't been that all his calculations were upset by a horse winning, who had no business to, he should have made our fortunes. Father's been unlucky, and he gets tipsy at times, but he's a very clever man, if you only give him scope enough.

SAM: I'd give 'im scope enough!

GEORGE: Where is he now?

SAM: Public-house.

GEORGE: And how is he?

SAM: Drunk!

> [POLLY *pushes him off table.* SAM *sits at fire-place up stage.*]

GEORGE: [*to* HAWTREE] You were right. There is "*something*" in caste. [*aloud*] But tell us all about it.

POLLY: Well, you know, you went away; and then the baby was born. Oh! he was such a sweet little thing, just like – your eyes—— your hair.

GEORGE: Cut that!

POLLY: Well, baby came; and when baby was six days old, your letter came, Major [*to* HAWTREE]. I saw that it was from India, and that it wasn't in your hand [*to* GEORGE]; I guessed what was inside it, so I opened it unknown to her, and I read there of your capture and death. I daren't tell her. I went to father to ask his advice, but he was too tipsy to understand me. Sam fetched the doctor. He told us that the news would kill her. When she woke up, she said she had dreamt there was a letter from you. I told her, No; and day after day she asked for a letter. So the doctor advised us to write one as if it came from you. So we did. Sam and I and the doctor told her – told Esther, I mean, that her eyes were bad, and she mustn't read, and we read our letter to her; didn't we Sam? But, bless you! she always knew it hadn't come from you! At last, when she was stronger, we told her all.

GEORGE: [*after a pause*] How did she take it?

POLLY: She pressed the baby in her arms, and turned her face to the wall. [*A pause.*] Well, to make a long story short, when she got up, she found that father had lost all the money you left her. There was a dreadful scene between them. She told him he'd robbed her and her child, and father left the house, and swore he'd never come back again.

SAM: Don't be alarmed – 'e did come back.

POLLY: Oh, yes; he was too good-hearted to stop long from his children. He has his faults, but his good points, when you find 'em, are wonderful!

SAM: Yes, when you find 'em!

> [SAM *rises, gets bread and butter from table, and sits corner of table.*]

POLLY: So she had to come back here to us; and that's all.

GEORGE: Why didn't she write to my mother?

POLLY: Father wanted her; but she was too proud – she said she'd die first.

GEORGE: [*rising, to* HAWTREE] There's a woman! Caste's all humbug.
[*Sees sword over mantelpiece.*] That's my sword and a map of
India, and that's the piano I bought her – I'll swear to the silk!
POLLY: Yes; that was bought in at the sale.
GEORGE: [*to* HAWTREE] Thank ye, old fella!
HAWTREE: Not by me; – I was in India at the time.
GEORGE: By whom then?
POLLY: By Sam. [SAM *winks to her to discontinue.*] I shall! He knew
Esther was breaking her heart about any one else having it, so
he took the money he'd saved up for our wedding, and we're
going to be married now – ain't we, Sam?
SAM: [*rushing to* GEORGE *and pulling out circulars from pocket*] And
hope by constant attention to business to merit——

[POLLY *pushes him away.*]

POLLY: Since you died it hasn't been opened, but if I don't play it to-
night, may I die an old maid?

[GEORGE *crosses to* SAM, *and shakes his hand, then goes
up stage, pulls up blind, and looks into street.* SAM *turns
up and meets* POLLY *top of table.*]

HAWTREE: [*aside*] Now who'd have thought that little cad had it in
him? He never mentioned it. [*aloud*] *Apropos*, George, your
mother – I'll go to the square, and tell her of—— [*He takes hat
from piano.*]
GEORGE: [*at cradle*] Is she in town?
HAWTREE: Yes. Will you come with me?
GEORGE: And leave my wife? – and such a wife!
HAWTREE: I'll go at once. I shall catch her before dinner. Good-bye,
old fellow. Seeing you back again, alive and well, makes me
feel quite – that I quite feel—— [*Shakes* GEORGE'*s hand. Goes
to door, then crosses to* SAM, *who has turned* POLLY'*s tea into his
saucer, and is just about to drink; seeing* HAWTREE, *he puts it
down quickly, and turns his back.*] Mr Gerridge, I fear I have
often made myself very offensive to you.
SAM: Well, sir, yer 'ave!
HAWTREE: I feared so. I didn't know you then. I beg your pardon. Let
me ask you to shake hands – to forgive me, and forget it.
[*offering his hand*]
SAM: [*taking it*] Say no more, sir; and if ever I've made myself
offensive to you, I ask your pardon; forget it, and forgive me.
[*They shake hands warmly; as* HAWTREE *crosses to door, recovering from* SAM'*s hearty shake of the hand,* SAM *runs to him.*] Hi,
sir! When yer marry that young lady as I know you're engaged
to, if you should furnish a house, and require anything in my
way——

[*Bringing out circular; begins to read it.* POLLY *comes and pushes* SAM *away, against* HAWTREE. SAM *goes and sits in low chair by fire-place, down stage, disconcerted, cramming circulars into his pocket.*]

HAWTREE: Good-bye, George, for the present. [*at door*] Bye, Polly. [*Resumes his Pall Mall manner as he goes out.*] I'm off to the square.

[*Exit* HAWTREE.]

GEORGE: [*at cradle*] But Esther?

POLLY: Oh, I forgot all about Esther. I'll tell her all about it.

GEORGE: How?

POLLY: I don't know; but it will come. Providence will send it to me, as it has sent you, my dear brother. [*embracing him*] You don't know how glad I am to see you back again! You must go. [*pushing him.* GEORGE *takes hat off piano.*] Esther will be getting up directly. [*at door with* GEORGE, *who looks through keyhole*] It's no use looking there; it's dark.

GEORGE: [*at door*] It isn't often a man can see his own widow.

POLLY: And it isn't often that he wants to! [*pushing him off*] Now, you must go.

GEORGE: I shall stop outside.

SAM: And I'll whistle for you when you may come in.

POLLY: Now – hush!

GEORGE: [*opening door wide*] Oh, my Esther, when you know I'm alive! I'll marry you all over again, and we'll have a second honeymoon, my darling.

[*Exit* GEORGE.]

POLLY: Oh, Sam! Sam! [*Commences to sing and dance.* SAM *also dances; they meet in* C. *of stage, join hands, and dance around two or three times.*] Oh, Sam, I'm so excited, I don't know what to do. What shall I do – what shall I do?

SAM: [*taking up* HAWTREE's *bread and butter*] 'ave a bit of bread and butter, Polly.

POLLY: Now, Sam, light the gas; I'm going to wake her up. [*opening door*] Oh, my darling, if I dare tell you! [*whispering*] He's come back! He's come back! He's come back! Alive! Alive! Alive! Sam, kiss me!

[SAM *rushes to* POLLY, *kisses her, and she jumps off,* SAM *shutting the door.*]

SAM: [*Dances shutter dance.*] I'm glad the swells are gone; now I can open my safety valve and let my feelin's escape. To think of 'is comin' back alive from India, just as I am goin' to open my shop. Perhaps he'll get me the patronage of the Royal Family. It would look stunnin' over the door, a lion and a unicorn a-standin' on their 'ind legs, doin' nothin' furiously, with a lozenge between 'em – thus. [*Seizes plate on table, puts his left foot on chair and imitates the picture of the Royal arms.*] Polly said I was to light up, and whatever Polly says must be done. [*Lights brackets over mantelpiece, then candles; as he lights the broken one, says*] Why this one is for all the world like old Eccles! [*Places candles on piano, and sits on music-stool*] Poor Esther! to think of my knowin' 'er when she was in the ballet line – then in the 'onourable line; then a mother – no, *h*onourables is "mammas" – then a widow, and then in the ballet line again! – and 'im to come back [*growing affected*] – and find a baby, with all 'is furniture and fittin's ready for immediate use [*crossing back of table during last few lines, sits in chair*] – and she, poor thing, lyin' asleep, with 'er eye-lids 'ot and swollen, not knowin' that that great, big, 'eavy, 'ulking, overgrown dragoon is prowlin' outside, ready to fly at 'er lips, and strangle 'er in 'is strong, lovin' arms – it – it – it——

> [*He breaks down and sobs with his head upon the table. Enter* POLLY.]

POLLY: Why, Sam! What's the matter?
SAM: [*Rises and crosses.*] I dunno. The water's got into my meter.
POLLY: Hush! here's Esther.

> [*Enter* ESTHER. *They stop suddenly.*]

SAM: [*singing and dancing*] "Tiddy-ti-tum," &c.
ESTHER: [*sitting near fire, taking up costume and beginning to work*] Sam, you seem in high spirits to-night?
SAM: Yes; yer see Polly and I are goin' to be married – and – and 'opes by bestowing a merit – to continue the favour——
POLLY: [*who has kissed* ESTHER *two or three times*] What are you talking about?
SAM: I don't know – I'm off my burner.

> [*He brings music-stool.* POLLY *goes round to chair, facing* ESTHER.]

ESTHER: What's the matter with you to-night, dear? [*to* POLLY] I can see something in your eyes.
SAM: P'r'aps it's the new furniture! [*He sits on music-stool.*]
ESTHER: Will you help me with the dress, Polly?

> [*They sit,* ESTHER *upper end, back of table,* POLLY *facing her, at lower end.*]

POLLY: It was a pretty dress when it was new – not unlike the one

Mdlle Delphine used to wear. [*suddenly clapping her hands*] Oh!

ESTHER: What's the matter?

POLLY: A needle! [*Crosses to* SAM, *who examines finger.*] I've got it!

SAM: What – the needle – in your finger?

POLLY: No; an idea in my head!

SAM: [*still looking at finger*] Does it 'urt?

POLLY: Stupid! [SAM *still sitting on stool. Aloud*] Do you recollect Mdlle Delphine, Esther?

ESTHER: Yes.

POLLY: Do you recollect her in that ballet that old Herr Griffenhaagen arranged? – "Jeanne la Folle; or, the Return of the Soldier"?

ESTHER: Yes; will you do the fresh hem?

POLLY: What's the use? Let me see – how did it go? How well I remember the scene! – the cottage was on that side, the bridge at the back – then ballet of villagers, and the entrance of Delphine as Jeanne, the bride – tra-lal-lala-lala-la-la, [*Sings and pantomimes,* SAM *imitating her.*] Then the entrance of Claude, the bridegroom – [*to* SAM, *imitating swell*] How-de-do, how-de-do?

SAM: [*rising*] 'ow are yer? [*imitating* POLLY, *then sitting again*]

POLLY: Then there was the procession to church – the march of the soldiers over the bridge – [*Sings and pantomimes.*] – arrest of Claude, who is drawn for the conscription [*Business;* ESTHER *looks dreamily.*] and is torn from the arms of his bride, at the church porch. *Omnes* broken-hearted. *This is Omnes* broken-hearted.

ESTHER: Polly, I don't like this; it brings back memories.

POLLY: [*Going to table, and leaning her hands on it, looks over at* ESTHER.] Oh, fuss about memories! – one can't mourn for ever. [ESTHER *surprised.*] Everything in this world isn't sad. There's bad news, and – and there's good news sometimes – when we least expect it.

ESTHER: Ah! not for me.

POLLY: Why not?

ESTHER: [*anxiously*] Polly!

POLLY: Second Act! [*This to be said quickly, startling* SAM, *who has been looking on the ground during last four or five lines.*] Winter – the Village Pump. This is the village pump [*pointing to* SAM, *seated by piano, on music-stool.* SAM *turns round on music-stool, disgusted.*] Entrance of Jeanne – now called Jeanne la Folle, because she has gone mad on account of the supposed loss of her husband.

SAM: The supposed loss?

POLLY: The supposed loss!

ESTHER: [*dropping costume*] Polly!

SAM: [*aside to* POLLY] Mind!

POLLY: Can't stop now! Entrance of Claude, *who isn't dead*, in a captain's uniform – a cloak thrown over his shoulders.

ESTHER: Not dead?

POLLY: Don't you remember the ballet? Jeanne is mad, and can't recognise her husband; and don't, till he shows her the ribbon she gave him when they were betrothed! A bit of ribbon! Sam, have you got a bit of ribbon? Oh, that crape sword-knot, that will do!

> [SAM *astonished.*]

ESTHER: [*rising*] Touch that!

POLLY: Why not? – it's no use *now!*

ESTHER: [*slowly, looking into* POLLY's *eyes*] You have heard of George – I know you have – I see it in your eyes. You may tell me – I can bear it – I can indeed – indeed I can. [*violently agitated*] Tell me – he is not dead?

POLLY: No!

ESTHER: No?

POLLY: No!

ESTHER: [*whispers*] Thank Heaven! [SAM *turns on stool, back to audience.*] You've seen him – I see you have! – I know it! – I feel it! I had a bright and happy dream – I saw him as I slept! Oh, let me know if he is near! Give me some sign – some sound – [POLLY *opens piano.*] – some token of his life and presence!

> [SAM *touches* POLLY *on the shoulder, opens piano, takes hat and exits. All to be done very quickly.* POLLY *sits immediately at piano and plays air softly – the same air played by* ESTHER *Act II., on the treble only.*]

ESTHER: [*in an ecstasy*] Oh, my husband! come to me! for I know that you are near! Let me feel your arms clasp round me! – Do not fear me! – I can bear the sight of you! – [*Door opens showing* SAM *keeping* GEORGE *back.*] – it will not kill me!—— George – love – husband – come, oh, come to me!

> [GEORGE *breaks away from* SAM, *and coming down behind* ESTHER *places his hands over her eyes; she gives a faint scream, and turning, falls in his arms.* POLLY *plays the bass as well as treble of the air, forte, then fortissimo. She then plays at random, endeavouring to hide her tears. At last strikes piano wildly, and goes off into a fit of hysterical laughter, to the alarm of* SAM, *who, rushing down as* POLLY *cries "Sam! Sam!" falls on his knees in front of her. They embrace,* POLLY *pushing him contemptuously away afterwards.* GEORGE

gets chair, sits, and ESTHER *kneels at his feet – he snatches off* ESTHER'S *cap, and throws it up stage.* POLLY *goes* L. *of* GEORGE, SAM *brings music-stool, and she sits.*]

ESTHER: To see you here again – to feel your warm breath upon my cheek – is it real, or am I dreaming?

SAM: [*rubbing his head*] No; it's real.

ESTHER: [*embracing* GEORGE] My darling!

SAM: My darling! [POLLY *on music-stool, which* SAM *has placed for her.* SAM, *kneeling by her, imitates* ESTHER – POLLY *scornfully pushes him away.*] But tell us – tell us how you escaped.

GEORGE: It's a long story; but I'll condense it. I was riding out, and suddenly found myself surrounded and taken prisoner. One of the troop that took me was a fella who had been my servant, and to whom I had done some little kindness. He helped me to escape, and hid me in a sort of cave, and for a long time used to bring me food. Unfortunately, he was ordered away; so he brought another Sepoy to look after me. I felt from the first this man meant to betray me, and I watched him like a lynx during the one day he was with me. As evening drew on, a Sepoy picket was passing. I could tell by the look in the fella's eyes, he meant to call out as soon as they were near enough; so I seized him by the throat, and shook the life out of him.

ESTHER: You strangled him?

GEORGE: Yes.

ESTHER: Killed him – dead?

GEORGE: He didn't get up again.

[*He embraces* ESTHER.]

POLLY: [*to* SAM] You never go and kill Sepoys.

[*She pushes him over.*]

SAM: No! I pay rates and taxes.

GEORGE: The day after, Havelock and his Scotchmen marched through the village, and I turned out to meet them. I was too done up to join, so I was sent straight on to Calcutta. I got leave, took a berth on the P. and O. boat; the passage restored me. I landed this morning, came on here, and brought in the milk.

[*Enter the* MARQUISE; *she rushes to embrace* GEORGE. *All rise,* SAM *putting piano stool back.*]

MARQUISE: My dear boy! – my dear, dear boy!

POLLY: Why, see, she's crying! She's glad to see him alive, and back again.

SAM: [*profoundly*] Well! There's always some good in women, even when they're ladies. [*He goes up to window.*]

    [POLLY *puts dress in box, and goes to cradle, then beside* SAM.]

MARQUISE: [*crossing to* ESTHER] My dear daughter, we must forget our little differences. [*kissing her*] Won't you? How history repeats itself! You will find a similar and as unexpected a return mentioned by Froissart in the chapter that treats of Philip Dartnell——

GEORGE: Yes, mother – I remember. [*He kisses her.*]

MARQUISE: [*to* GEORGE, *aside*] We must take her abroad, and make a lady of her.

GEORGE: Can't, mamma – she's ready-made. Nature has done it to our hands.

MARQUISE: [*aside, to* GEORGE] But I won't have the man who smells of putty [SAM *business at back. He is listening, and at the word "putty" throws his cap irritably on table.* POLLY *pacifies him, and makes him sit down beside her on window.*] nor the man who smells of beer.

    [*She goes to* ESTHER, *who offers her chair, and sits in chair opposite to her.* MARQUISE *back to audience.* ESTHER *facing audience. Enter* HAWTREE, *pale.*]

HAWTREE: George! Oh, the Marchioness is here.

GEORGE: What's the matter?

HAWTREE: Oh, nothing. Yes, there is. I don't mind telling you. I've been thrown. I called at my chambers as I came along and found this.

    [*He gives* GEORGE *a note; sits on music-stool.*]

GEORGE: From the Countess, Lady Florence's mother. [*reads*] "Dear Major Hawtree, – I hasten to inform you that my daughter Florence is about to enter into an alliance with Lord Saxeby, the eldest son of the Marquis of Loamshire. Under these circumstances, should you think fit to call here again, I feel assured——" Well, perhaps it's for the best. [*returning letter*] Caste! you know. Caste! And a marquis is a bigger swell than a major.

HAWTREE: Yes, best to marry in your own rank of life.

GEORGE: If you can find *the* girl. But if ever you find *the* girl, marry her. As to her station –

    "True hearts are more than coronets,
      And simple faith than Norman blood."

HAWTREE: Ya-as. But a gentleman should hardly ally himself to a nobody.

GEORGE: My dear fella, Nobody's a mistake – he don't exist. Nobody's nobody! Everybody's somebody.

HAWTREE: Yes. But still – Caste.

GEORGE: Oh, Caste's all right. Caste is a good thing if it's not carried too far. It shuts the door on the pretentious and the vulgar; but it should open the door very wide for exceptional merit. Let brains break through its barriers, and what brains can break through love may leap over.

HAWTREE: Yes. Why George, you're quite inspired – quite an orator. What makes you so brilliant? Your captivity? The voyage? What then?

GEORGE: I'm in love with my wife!

[*Enter* ECCLES, *drunk, a bottle of gin in his hand.*]

ECCLES: Bless this 'appy company. May we 'ave in our arms what we love in our 'earts [*Goes to head of table.* ESTHER *goes to cradle, back to audience.* POLLY *and* SAM *half amused, half angry.* MARQUISE *still sitting in chair, back to audience.* HAWTREE *facing* ECCLES. GEORGE *up stage leaning on piano in disgust.*] Polly, fetch wine-glasses – a tumbler will do for me. Let us drink a toast. Mr Chairman [*to* MARQUISE], ladies, and gentlemen – I beg to propose the 'elth of our newly returned warrior, *my son-in-law.* [MARQUISE *shivers.*] The Right Honourable George De Alroy. Get glasses, Polly, and send for a bottle of sherry wine for my ladyship. *My* ladyship! My ladyship! M'lad'ship. [*She half turns to him.*] You and me'll have a drain together on the quiet. So delighted to see you under these altered circum – circum – circum – stangate.

[POLLY, *who has shaken her head at him to desist, in vain, very distressed.*]

SAM: Shove 'is 'ead in a bucket!

[*Exit* SAM, *in disgust.*]

HAWTREE: [*aside to* GEORGE] I think I can abate this nuisance – at least, I can remove it.

[*He rises and crosses to* ECCLES, *who has got round to* R. *side of table, leaning on it. He taps* ECCLES *with his stick, first on* R. *shoulder, then on* L., *and finally sharply on* R. ECCLES *turns round and falls on point of stick –* HAWTREE *steadying him.* GEORGE *crosses behind, to* MARQUISE, *who has gone to cradle – puts his arm round*

ESTHER *and takes her to mantelpiece.*]

HAWTREE: Mr Eccles, don't you think that, with your talent for
liquor, if you had an allowance of about two pounds a week,
and went to Jersey, where spirits are cheap, that you could
drink yourself to death in a year?

ECCLES: I think I could – I'm sure I'll try.

[*He goes up,* L. *of table, steadying himself by it, and sits
in chair by fire, with the bottle of gin.* HAWTREE
standing by fire. ESTHER *and* POLLY *stand embracing.
As they turn away from each other –*]

GEORGE: [*coming across with* ESTHER] Come and play me that air that
used to ring in my ears as I lay awake, night after night, captive
in the cave – you know.

[*He hands* ESTHER *to piano. She plays the air.*]

MARQUISE: [*bending over the cradle*] My grandson!

[ECCLES *falls off the chair in the last stage of drunkenness, bottle in hand.* HAWTREE, *leaning one foot on chair
from which* ECCLES *has fallen, looks at him through eye-
glass.* SAM *enters, and goes to* POLLY, *behind cradle,
and, producing wedding-ring from several papers,
holds it before her eyes.* ESTHER *plays until curtain
drops.*]

CURTAIN

PROGRESS

Produced at the Globe Theatre, London, on 18th September, 1869.

CAST OF CHARACTERS

Lord Mompesson	... Mr Collette
Hon. Arthur Mompesson	... Mr H. Neville
Dr Brown	... Mr J. Clarke
Mr Bunnythorne	... Mr Parselle
Bob Bunnythorne	... Mr E. Marshall
John Ferne	... Mr J. Billington
Mr Danby	... Mr Westland
Wykeham	
Eva	... Miss Lydia Foote
Miss Myrnie	... Mrs Stephens

ACT I – *Drawing-room in Mompesson Abbey.*

ACT II – *The Tapestry Chamber in the Abbey.*

ACT III – *Scene same as Act II.*

Modern Costumes. Time of Representation, two hours and three-quarters.

SCENE – *Mompesson Abbey.*

PROGRESS

ACT I

SCENE I – *Drawing-room in Mompesson Abbey. Door* C. *Small door* R. *Old-fashioned large fireplace. Scene enclosed. Window; outside window, garden and park seen. The trees covered with snow. Large fire burning. Pictures on walls, &c. Sofas, chairs, couches, tables, all old-fashioned. An air of great antiquity, and tumble-down comfort about everything. Vestiges of feudalism ranged here and there.*

[*Enter* DANBY *and* FERNE, *conducted by* WYKEHAM. FERNE *carries a portfolio.*]

WYKEHAM: [*an old servant, of about sixty-six*] If you'll be good enough to sit down, gentlemen, Mr Arthur will see you directly.

[*Exit* WYKEHAM.]

FERNE: A fire – a lovely fire. My fingers are almost frozen.

DANBY: So odd that I should find you sketching and planning as I drove past. It's more than two years since we met.

FERNE: I was going to call here when I'd finished my plan. I have business with Lord Mompesson.

DANBY: With old Lord Mompesson? You'll find it difficult to transact business with him.

FERNE: Why?

DANBY: He never attends to business. He's too old.

FERNE: Too old? A man of fifty?

DANBY: Fifty! Why, he's over eighty!

FERNE: What! Is not the old lord dead yet?

DANBY: No. I suppose you're thinking of his only son, the Honourable Arthur. Do you know him?

FERNE: I did some years ago.

DANBY: How was that?

FERNE: My grandfather was a tenant.

DANBY: Oh, yes; I remember. Before '32?

FERNE: Yes. They quarrelled with my father about his vote on that occasion. My father left the farm.

DANBY: And took to scientific drainage; lucky for you, for thanks to that, here you are, at thirty years of age, a rising engineer, making a fortune and a name.

FERNE: Never mind that. Tell me about the Mompesson family. But, first, how is it I find you here?

DANBY: Don't you know? Since my father-in-law retired from practice I'm the family lawyer.

FERNE: And the old lord is still living?

DANBY: Yes, – that is, he lives a little, preparatory to dying a great deal.

FERNE: He was a very old man when I was quite a boy.

DANBY: Of course! You know the story, don't you? The old lord – always a poor man – had hopes for his son in Parliament, so in '29 he bought a rotten borough – Wapshot-cum-Chuddock.

FERNE: Which in '32 was disfranchised.

DANBY: Just so – and the family was ruined. However, there was but one son – this Arthur – who at that time was in the Guards, a fine, handsome, young officer. Well, father and son took this misfortune so to heart that young Arthur left the army, and, with his father, settled down here in the old Abbey, on their own estate, near Stickton-le-Clay, and have given no attention to politics or public life ever since. This, they say, is a degenerate, peddling age, and they will have none of it; they have cut the world – a slight of which the world is quite unconscious.

FERNE: And what sort of a man has the Honourable Arthur crusted into?

DANBY: A country gentleman of the old school. Urbane, refined, polished, and prejudiced. A great man at Quarter Sessions – and at the County Ball. A crystallised Quixote, doing battle with everything new.

FERNE: Is he clever?

DANBY: He has a gentlemanly intellect, somewhat narrow-minded – and large-hearted. He is a noble fellow despite his prejudices. High-minded, chivalric, brave, and courteous. He would have made a splendid crusader, if he'd had the ill-luck to have been born six hundred years ago. Chop him into mincemeat, and every atom would be gentleman.

FERNE: And such a man can shut himself up in this hole of a village?

DANBY: With his father – to whom he is devoted. He has also another attached friend, who almost lives in the house. One Dr Brown – a most amusing inconsistency – moral, political, and medical. A Radical – a Chartist – a Republican of the reddest dye; a materialist of the old French revolutionary type; an adorer of Cromwell, Voltaire, Robespierre, and William Cobbett; a man who wants to root up thrones and pull down churches – behead kings and burn clergymen – in the cause of order, law, liberty, equality, and fraternity. But with all this old-world folly the Doctor is an excellent man; high-minded and straightforward; a most skilful physician; indeed, it is he who keeps the old lord alive.

FERNE: But how does the Doctor – this acid of Radicalism, agree in the same house with the alkali of aristocracy?

DANBY: Meaning the Honourable Arthur? Admirably. They used to hate each other, but when Arthur Mompesson fell from his horse in the hunting-field and broke his leg, the Doctor attended him, and, ever since, their personal attachment has been equal to their political antagonism. They discuss and quarrel over their wine. Let me tell you the Doctor is a teetotaller. Oh! how they discuss. Then there are two other people here, quite characters.

FERNE: Who are they?

DANBY: Old Bunnythorne, a retired contractor: – supplied provisions for the Navy; his father made a fortune at Portsmouth during the war.

FERNE: And what is he like?

DANBY: Oh! he too grumbles at everything new, and growls a perpetual chorus of compliments to the good old times. Not that he has much cause to grumble. Oh, yes, I forgot. He has one.

FERNE: What's that?

DANBY: His son, – his only son, – Bob, a conceited young lout, who, because his father won't give him money to go up to London to waste his time and health there, gets drunk at the "Mompesson Arms" here every night in the society of Miss Brill the barmaid and one Jack Topham, a man much looked up to in these parts by ostlers and stable boys. Bob, too, considers himself quite a literary character.

FERNE: Why?

DANBY: I don't know. I suppose because he can't spell properly, or because he's thoroughly impracticable, and never understands the poetry he reads.

FERNE: A very singular family group. And are there no women in the house?

DANBY: Yes, two. One a Miss Myrnie, a detestable old maid – scandal-loving, mischief-making, snuff-taking, poodle-doggy, and generally disagreeable. She is some sixteenth cousin, and remains here out of——

FERNE: Charity?

DANBY: No; – kinsmanship. She has, perhaps, five drops of the Mompesson blood in her, and that is quite enough for my lord and for his son.

FERNE: And the other lady?

DANBY: Oh! a girl of eighteen, – also some distant cousin. I don't know much about her, except that her mother made some *mésalliance*, and married a man in business. The father and mother dying, the girl was received here. I have been told that at first neither my lord nor his son cared much about her presence, they were both so indignant at her mother's conduct, but now they are both very much attached to her. Poor girl! she has been very ill, and is only just recovering.

FERNE: [*looking at watch*] Time that I should go, and so I must leave my card [*Leaves card in basket.*] and call again when I am here in two months' time.

DANBY: Won't you drive back with me and dine?

FERNE: Impossible. I must finish my plan, and sleep in London to-morrow night, to meet the Board the next morning.

DANBY: Well, good-bye. Stop! You're doing well, and making your fortune. Why don't you get married?

FERNE: [*smiling*] Married! I never have the time. You must meet a girl at least three or four times before you propose to her, and what with one thing and the other——

DANBY: Have you never met anyone who——

FERNE: Well – yes, – [*reflecting*] – I did think: but no, it was nothing. [*looking at watch*] Matrimony doesn't go well with engineering, so I must die a bachelor. [*Looks at watch.*] Good-bye!

DANBY: [*shaking hands*] Good-bye. [*Exit* FERNE.] How that young fellow has got on since I first knew him; but no wonder – clever, sober, industrious—— [*Enter* BOB, *followed by* WYKEHAM. DANBY, *seeing him*] Ah! this is quite another sort of thing.

WYKEHAM: Really, sir, you must not smoke anywhere but in the smoking-room: my lord don't like it.

BOB: Old fool!

WYKEHAM: Mr Arthur don't like it.

BOB: Old fool!

WYKEHAM: And your father don't like it, sir.

BOB: Another old fool! There! [*putting up his pipe in case*] That's gone out, and now you can go out! [*Exit* WYKEHAM.] Another old fool! Everybody here's an old fool – except me. Eh! Danby, is that you? I thought it was my guv'nor.

DANBY: I have not the good fortune to be your guv'nor.

BOB: You're lucky!

DANBY: I think so.

[BOB *to be got up like the conventional poet; but dirty and slovenly, velvet coat, long black hair, pale face, spectacles, a sort of pot-house Manfred.*]

BOB: My father's as much behind the age as I am above these wretched, stupid surroundings. I rust here – rust – regularly rust. I'm like a bright sword steeped in ditch water.

DANBY: [*aside*] More like a soft spoon steeped in beer.

BOB: [*spouting*]

> "My thoughts from 'mid the vulgar herd gyrate
> from pole to pole;
> Patience, my heart, oh rest, my brain, oh wait,
> my weary soul!"

Did you ever read my poems! My "Thoughts in a Crater"?

DANBY: No.

BOB: I'll lend 'em to you. They're in manuscript.

DANBY: [*quickly*] Thanks. I have no time.

BOB: The guv'nor won't let me publish. He won't give me the money. Could you lend me a sovereign?

DANBY: I'd rather not, if it's all the same to you.

BOB: Like the rest of 'em! O world! world!

> "Patience, my heart, oh rest, my brain, oh wait,
> my weary soul!"

DANBY: Why not thirsty soul?

BOB: Danby! To the calm and dispassionate observer it is curious to think what an infernal old fool my father is! If my poems were published in London, I should realise a fortune; then, with his capital, I could start a new magazine or a daily newspaper!

DANBY: And does he refuse to indulge you to that trifling extent?

BOB: He does! Oh, these fathers! what misfortunes they are to men of genius.

BUNNYTHORNE: [*without*] The horse is right enough – never mind the horse! Look after me! I think I've broken something somewhere!

BOB: There he is!

> [*Enter* BUNNYTHORNE, *his hat smashed; hat and coat covered with snow.*]

BUNNYTHORNE: [*as he enters*] Send for the doctor!

DANBY: ⎫ What is the matter?
BOB: ⎬ What's happened, guv'nor?

BUNNYTHORNE: I was driving back – everything was white with snow – and, I suppose, I got off the road into the ditch. Down we went – and then on one side – b-r-r-r-r. What weather! There never used to be any snow in the winter when I was a young man!

BOB: No snow!

BUNNYTHORNE: At least, if there was, the snow wasn't cold, and it never filled up the ditches. Everything has degenerated, even the snow!

BOB: Guv'nor, the fact is, if you don't know how to drive, you should get somebody to drive you.

BUNNYTHORNE: Hold your tongue! It was that beast of a horse; but there are no horses nowadays! No beasts worth their straw!

BOB: No beasts?

BUNNYTHORNE: Except you! Why didn't you come home last night?

BOB: I slept at Jack Topham's.

BUNNYTHORNE: Jack Topham's! A nice acquaintance for a young man of fortune!

BOB: Pretty fortune! Ten bob a week for pocket-money!

BUNNYTHORNE: With your prospects!

BOB: Pretty prospects! Stickton-le-Clay and its neighbourhood!

BUNNYTHORNE: Hold your tongue!

BOB: Can't I speak?

BUNNYTHORNE: No! Not when your father's been thrown out of a gig!

BOB: I wish to console you.

BUNNYTHORNE: Console – humbug! Hold your tongue!

BOB: I shan't!

> [*Enter* DR BROWN. *Blue coat, brass buttons, dark drab breeches and gaiters, all loose and easy, spotlessly clean; very loose large white neckerchief; red healthy face; a homely grandeur about the man; long white hair flowing over the coat collar.*]

DOCTOR: Now, what's all this fuss about?

BOB: The guv'nor's spilt himself.

BUNNYTHORNE: I didn't – it was the gig. The gigs never used to spill in my time.

DOCTOR: [*feeling his arms, &c.*] Stand up. Move your arms – so.

BOB: [*to* DANBY] The gig spilt him, – reasonable, isn't it? Nice lot of old fools I'm condemned to waste my burning youth among.

DOCTOR: You're all right. [*to* BUNNYTHORNE] Perhaps a bruise or two. I'll make you up an embrocation.

BOB: You're not hurt.

> "For the linnet loves its egglets ere a feather
>   deck their wings;
>   And the love-birds peck their mother, as their
>   lullaby she sings."

DOCTOR: [*to* BOB] What, ain't you dead yet?

BOB: Doctor!

DOCTOR: At the rate you're going it, I give you eighteen months longer. You're as white as a sheet. Look at your liver, sir! – look at it! I should like you to see your own liver.

BUNNYTHORNE: I shouldn't.

BOB: Really, if I'm treated in this way, I'll go——

BUNNYTHORNE: Do – do – and don't come back.

BOB: Such language to your own son——

DOCTOR: Pooh! Parentage is a mere accident.

BUNNYTHORNE: Accident! In this case it's an offence.

BOB: Of all the ignorance——

> [*Enter the* HON. ARTHUR MOMPESSON. *Morning dress of the late Duke of Wellington, blue frock coat, buff waistcoat, black stock, grey trousers, grey hair.*]

ARTHUR: Good morning, my dear Mr Danby. I fear I've kept you waiting.

DANBY: I have some leases that want renewing, and a few other papers to submit to Lord Mompesson.

ARTHUR: He will be here directly. Bunnythorne, I hear you've had a bad fall.

BUNNYTHORNE: All falls are bad nowadays. Augh! I've no patience. When I used to fall, thirty years ago, I didn't feel it half so much.

BOB: You were younger then.

BUNNYTHORNE: I was not. [*in a passion*] Don't talk to me.

DOCTOR: Don't excite yourself. You'll bruise your – intellect.

BOB: [*aside*] He won't feel it in that quarter.

> [*Enter* MISS MYRNIE, *an old maid of fifty-three, rusty black silk, and mortified manner of a pew-opener. She carries in her arms a little lap-dog.*]

MISS MYRNIE: [*carneying*] Good morning, dear Mr Arthur. I was not down soon enough to meet you at breakfast. [*to* DOG] Wish Mr Arthur good morning, Pamela. Dear Mr Bunnythorne, how do you do?

BUNNYTHORNE: Black and blue all over.

MISS MYRNIE: And dear Robert, too. [BOB *nods sulkily.*] And the Doctor. [*aside*] An irreligious wretch. [*to* DOG] Never mind him, Pamela; he shall not harm us. Oh, Mr Bunnythorne, here's your newspaper. [*giving it*]

BUNNYTHORNE: [*unfolding paper*] And a pretty thing a newspaper is nowadays. Why, they sell some of 'em for a penny. Nice news they must contain for a penny!

DOCTOR: Ay, indeed; Cobbett's Weekly Register——

BUNNYTHORNE: Bother Cobbett!

DOCTOR: Don't abuse Cobbett.

ARTHUR: Why not? He abused everybody.

DOCTOR: You must not touch giants. Respect the ashes of the great Cobbett, and of Cromwell, and——

ARTHUR: Cromwell – a butcher!

BUNNYTHORNE: No; a brewer.

DANBY: [aside] Now they've begun.

BUNNYTHORNE: I always liked Cromwell.

DOCTOR: Why?

BUNNYTHORNE: Because he *was* a brewer.

ARTHUR: And rose from his malt-tubs to usurp a throne. A regicide!

DOCTOR: That was his great merit. He taught indignant people to kill kings.

MISS MYRNIE: [to DOG] Listen to him, Pamela, and bite him when he's not looking.

DOCTOR: The three great epochs of modern times were '89, '32, and '48; since then the world has ceased to move. Cromwell showed the French the way to deal with despots.

BOB: I don't think much of Cromwell.

DOCTOR: *You* don't think much of Cromwell? You! I wonder what Cromwell would have thought of you.

BOB: His killing of Charles——

ARTHUR: Assassination!

DOCTOR: ⎫ Righteous execution!

ARTHUR: ⎭ Infamous assassination!

BOB: His suppression of his breathing apparatus. There! Cromwell was only an imitator; Brutus killed Caesar in the Capitol long ago.

BUNNYTHORNE: In the good old times!

DOCTOR: What the devil——

ARTHUR: [pointing to MISS MYRNIE] Hush! Hush!

BUNNYTHORNE: [who has been reading paper] Another railway accident. Go it! go it! nineteenth century!

ARTHUR: Not a fatal accident, I hope.

BUNNYTHORNE: One woman killed!

DOCTOR: Only a woman!

MISS MYRNIE: Only a woman!

DOCTOR: I meant only *one* woman.

ARTHUR: Are you disappointed that a dozen were not sacrificed to this modern scientific apparatus for swift slaughter?

DOCTOR: Woman, considered from the point of view of reason, is an inferior animal to man.

MISS MYRNIE: The villain! [to DOG] You hear what he says of us, my dear?

DOCTOR: Anatomy proves it.

ARTHUR: Anatomy! What has the mutilation and desecration of the dead to do with the beauty of a life? What has the grace, charm, goodness, heroism, patience, the *mind*, the soul, to do with anatomy?

DOCTOR: Nothing whatever. I speak as a materialist. Woman——

MISS MYRNIE: [*rising*] Doctor, if you are going to use bad language we will retire.

DOCTOR: Miss Myrnie, when I said woman I meant nothing personal to you.

> [MISS MYRNIE, *appeased, sits down again; the door is opened by* WYKEHAM, LORD MOMPESSON *led by* EVA *enters.* LORD MOMPESSON, *an old man of eighty, in a dressing-gown and skull-cap.*]

LORD M: Good morning, good folks, good morning. Mr Danby, how do you do? Excuse me for having kept you waiting. Arthur, have you made my excuses to Mr Danby? My good Doctor, you don't know how much I am indebted to my good nurse. She's been reading to me this morning. She is quite my *gouvernante*.

MISS MYRNIE: Good morning, my lord! [*to* EVA] Good morning, dear! [*aside*] He never asks me to read to him. Ah, [*to* DOG] Pamela, we have none of the beauty of the serpent when the serpent's an egg!

DOCTOR: Miss Eva is the best nurse in the world.

LORD M: Why – why – why did you not come here sooner, Eva? You've not been here – no, not twelve months; and we're all in love with you, aren't we, eh?

MISS MYRNIE: [*aside*] I'm not in love with her. Ah, these men! They never will understand women!

EVA: Oh! Don't talk in that way. You'll make me so vain! You'll spoil me!

BUNNYTHORNE: [*to* BOB] Go and talk to her. If you are a poet, behave as such.

> [BOB *gets near to* EVA.]

ARTHUR: [*to* LORD MOMPESSON] Mr Danby has some business – if you could see him.

BOB: [*aside*] She is not a patch upon Miss Brill at the "Arms" [*to* EVA] Eva, you've never read my poems?

EVA: No; I've been so well lately, and the weather's been so fine.

BOB: Then you don't know my lines——

> "When the white-winged wind woos winter, and the robin flees the wold,
> And the lover leaves his lyre, lest his fire turn to cold."

Pretty lines, aren't they?

EVA: Very. What do they mean?

LORD M: Mr Danby, come with me. Come into my room.

ARTHUR: Shall I——

LORD M: No, no. When we want you, we'll send for you.

> [ARTHUR *opens door*. DANBY *offers his arm to* LORD
> MOMPESSON. *They both go out.*]

BOB: [*pursuing* EVA]

> "For the Mayflies live in summer, though their
>   life last but a day:
> And the summer of a lover is as one eternal May."

EVA: [*turning over card-basket*] This young man always smells so
    dreadfully of tobacco. [*Sees* FERNE'S *card; starts.*] Oh!
ARTHUR: What's the matter?
EVA: Nothing. [*aside*] Has he been here?
BUNNYTHORNE: Pretty couple, aren't they?
MISS MYRNIE: I don't know. I never recognise couples. I consider
    them improper.
DOCTOR: Why so? There's you and Pamela.
ARTHUR: I don't consider Bob pretty.
BUNNYTHORNE: But he will be – he will be. I was just the same at his
    age.
ARTHUR: That hardly reassures me. But what do you mean?
BUNNYTHORNE: I mean, – why not marry them?
ARTHUR:
MISS MYRNIE: } [*astounded*] What?
DOCTOR:
BUNNYTHORNE: Make 'em man and wife. Bob would turn steady,
    and——
MISS MYRNIE: I don't like marriages, unless they are contracted in a
    Christian spirit.
ARTHUR: [*his pride wounded*] A member of my family.
BUNNYTHORNE: Exactly! Family on your side, money on mine.
ARTHUR: Money.
EVA: [*aside*] Can he have been here?
DOCTOR: Pooh! pooh! Eva can't marry.
ARTHUR:
MISS MYRNIE: } Certainly not!
BUNNYTHORNE: Why not?
DOCTOR: Why not? She is hardly convalescent. She has not entirely
    got over her last illness. Look at her now; – her eyes dilated;
    the nostrils distended; the short, catchy breathing, – all signs
    of poor, thin, weak, bad blood.
ARTHUR: Bad blood! My cousin!
BUNNYTHORNE: We Bunnythornes have always had good, rich blood!
    Look at the spots on Bob's face.
ARTHUR: The blood of the Mompessons!
BUNNYTHORNE: The blood of the Bunnythornes!

DOCTOR: Blood! [*contemptuously*] What *is* blood?

BUNNYTHORNE: ⎫ Oh! don't begin——
ARTHUR: ⎪ For goodness' sake——
MISS MYRNIE: ⎬ Never mind them, Pamela!
BOB: ⎭ [*spouting*] "When the watch-dog barks his welcome."

[*Enter* WYKEHAM.]

WYKEHAM: Lunch is on the table, sir.

ARTHUR: I have lunched.

BUNNYTHORNE: [*rising*] I have not; – but I will.

MISS MYRNIE: [*rising*] So will I.

DOCTOR: [*rising*] And I.

BOB: Eva! – may I——

EVA: [*thinking of card*] No, thanks, I never lunch.

BOB: Nor I. I've no appetite.

DOCTOR: I should think not, the life you lead. Go back to the public-house.

BUNNYTHORNE: Leave the boy alone; you're always at him.

DOCTOR: So are you.

BUNNYTHORNE: But I'm his father.

BOB: And I wish you weren't.

"Patience, my heart, oh rest, my brain, oh wait,
    my weary soul!"

MISS MYRNIE: A set of brutes!

[*Exeunt all but* EVA *and* ARTHUR.]

EVA: How could that card find its way here?

ARTHUR: [*looking at her*] 19, – 19 from 50; 9 from 10, 1; 2 from 53,—— 31; 31 years. It's a long time to look forward to, but a short time to look back on. I feel as young as ever, – younger; for I can appreciate the love of a good woman, as no lad of twenty knows how. [*mournfully*] Perhaps because I can no longer inspire it. A wasted life. A wasted life! And Arthur Mompesson, the dandy Guardsman, has sunk into an old bachelor with a talent for whist. Augh! [*sighs*] That cub, Bob! Old Bunnythorne to dare to—— Why not! Bob is her own age. Oh, youth! youth! To think that Bob should be so young and I should be so old. Eva! [EVA *starts.*] What are you thinking of?

EVA: [*placing card in basket*] Thinking of – nothing.

ARTHUR: Why, your eyes are quite animated; and there is a flush on your cheek that gives you an expression as of a rose surprised.

EVA: Oh, cousin, you're very complimentary!

ARTHUR: Has anything happened?

EVA: No!

ARTHUR: You are looking much better these last few weeks.

EVA: Yes; I think my illness has passed. Everybody was very kind to me – you especially.

ARTHUR: And are you really happy with us?

EVA: Very happy!

ARTHUR: And have no regrets – no thoughts of those you have left?

EVA: Oh, yes! I sometimes think of them. They were very good people.

ARTHUR: Very good sort of people, no doubt, for tradespeople.

EVA: But tradespeople are as good as anybody else?

ARTHUR: [*doubtfully*] Humph!

EVA: You know papa died so suddenly that he left mamma very poor; and as mamma was not noticed by her family, she was forced to work.

ARTHUR: [*aside*] A Mompesson work?

EVA: And the Dobbses took a great deal of notice of her.

ARTHUR: The Magasin des Modes people?

EVA: Yes; and were very kind to her and to me, and paid my doctor's bill, and waited on me. Oh! so tenderly!

ARTHUR: No doubt the Dobbses are very good people, and must have expended a considerable sum of money on your account. I'll write to them to thank them, and enclose them a cheque for a hundred pounds. I suppose that will be enough?

EVA: Oh, you mustn't do that!

ARTHUR: Why not?

EVA: You'll offend them! The Dobbses are very proud.

ARTHUR: Oh, the Hobbses are proud, are they? To think that pride could find a residence among the Hobbses.

EVA: Not Hobbses – Dobbses.

ARTHUR: Dobbses?

EVA: They are truly noble people!

ARTHUR: Noble?

EVA: Not by descent, but feeling.

ARTHUR: Feeling?

EVA: Heart!

ARTHUR: Heart? Then you think that the qualities of the heart level all distinctions?

EVA: I do.

ARTHUR: *All* distinctions?

EVA: Yes!

ARTHUR: Rank – birth?

EVA: Yes!

ARTHUR: Genius – talent – wealth?

EVA: Yes!

ARTHUR: [*changing his voice*] Age? – youth?

EVA: Yes! [*a pause*] Youth and age are only accidents. If one is good and kind and tender, what does it matter in what year one was born?

ARTHUR: [*quickly*] Not a bit! – not a bit! I like the liberality of your sentiments, and – and – if – if – a – a – man – or a woman – I should say girl – were to fall in love – with – with – each other – the question of age need not——

[*Enter* WYKEHAM.]

WYKEHAM: My lord wishes to see you for a few minutes.

ARTHUR: Yes. I'll come – I—— Excuse me, cousin. [*taking her hand*] I was just going to say something which—— I'll be back directly.

[*Exeunt* ARTHUR *and* WYKEHAM.]

EVA: I cannot help wondering how that card came here. He must have called; and if he called he must—— [*looking into card basket.* MISS MYRNIE *opens the little door and watches* EVA.] The card looks quite new. [*going to window*] It's more than a year since I saw him. [*At window, starts.*] Why, there he is, sketching! No! I'm right! it is he! [*trying to open window*] Oh, these nasty old windows. [*Opens window and beckons.*] He doesn't see me. I'll send to him. Now he sees me! Here – here! Go round there to the left – to the door. How d'ye do? how d'ye do? I am so glad to see you. [*Coughs and places her hand on her chest, then shuts window.*] Oh, the cold air. I've not recovered yet.

[*Enter* FERNE. MISS MYRNIE *closes door.*]

FERNE: Somebody certainly beckoned me in. [*seeing* EVA] Eh, Eva! you here?

EVA: Yes, me. Didn't you see me at the window?

FERNE: Was that you?

EVA: But why did you not come in without waiting to be asked? My uncle, Lord Mompesson, would be very glad to see you.

FERNE: Your uncle, Lord——

EVA: My grand-uncle.

FERNE: Lord Mompesson?

EVA: Yes. My mother's uncle. Since I saw you in London I've come to live with them.

FERNE: You surprise me! I knew that your mamma was of good family, but not——

EVA: I've been here eight months, and they're all so kind to me. How are the Dobbses?

FERNE: The Dobbses? I haven't seen them since I last saw you there. I've been abroad.

EVA: Where?

FERNE: In Russia principally.

EVA: Engineering?

FERNE: Engineering.

EVA: I had a letter from Mrs Dobbs last week. I saw your card there just now. So kind of you to call and see me.

FERNE: To call and see you. [*aside*] She will have it I came to see her; though I did not know she lived here.

EVA: How came you to be in this neighbourhood?

FERNE: Eh? oh, business! [*aside*] I came to knock the house down.

EVA: However, I must present you to my uncle; then you can call when you please. Oh! I forgot! just now he's engaged with Mr Danby.

FERNE: Mr Danby?

EVA: Yes. Do you know him?

FERNE: I called here with him this morning.

EVA: Oh! you called with *him?*

FERNE: Yes. How well you're looking. Do you remember at the Dobbses when I used to call and see you, and you sat in that big old arm-chair, by the fireside, propped up by pillows?

EVA: Oh, yes! – yes! That was a nice time!

FERNE: But now the colour has returned to your cheeks.

EVA: Come with me, and I'll show you over the Abbey, and by that time my uncle will be disengaged.

FERNE: But——

EVA: It's a wonderful place, the Abbey, one of the oldest in the kingdom. There are secret staircases and walls, and places I shudder as I pass, and down below – I've never been there, I'm too frightened – there are dungeons and cells, where, they say, poor people were shut up and tortured. Oh, horrible! is it not? [*lowering her voice*] Skeletons of the victims have been found within the last three years, and beneath where we are now standing is a crypt, in which are niches where living women were walled up alive, and left to die in the dark of thirst and hunger. [*frightening herself with the recital*] I cannot understand. The rulers of those days were good men, holy abbots, and pious pastors. Why were they so cruel? Thumbscrews, racks, dungeons, and burning stakes. Why – why – why did they brick up breathing, living women?

FERNE: Because – because they lived in the good old times.

[*Exeunt* FERNE *and* EVA. MISS MYRNIE *opens little door.*]

MISS MYRNIE: Oh, dear me! – oh, dear me! This is very bad! – this is very bad! I never see a young man and a young woman together but I suspect they care for each other. The wretches! And that Arthur! Oh, that Arthur! I know he's fond of the girl. Old fool! Why can't he seek a wife among his own connections

– a woman of his own time of life – of ripe experience – mature charms, and pious feeling. A blessing on the heavenly side of forty; but, no! Mr Arthur likes youth, and a slim waist, and a child's complexion, and baby tattle about ribbons and rubbish. But men are like that. The idiots! It is so ridiculous, the fuss they make in praise of youth. Why, everybody's had it once, and nobody can keep it long. Then it is so perishable. Youth soon fades away, but age lasts us to the latest hour.

[*Enter* ARTHUR, *quickly.*]

ARTHUR: Now, Eva, as I was—— [*Sees* MISS MYRNIE – *disappointed.*] Oh! it is you, is it?

MISS MYRNIE: Yes; I take that liberty. Did you expect to find Eva?

ARTHUR: Yes.

MISS MYRNIE: She's not here.

ARTHUR: Where is she?

MISS MYRNIE: She is showing the Abbey to a young gentleman.

ARTHUR: A young gentleman! Bob?

MISS MYRNIE: No, not Bob. Ah! [*sighing*] Would it were Bob!

ARTHUR: Eh, why?

MISS MYRNIE: The young man is a stranger.

ARTHUR: A stranger!

MISS MYRNIE: A perfect stranger. She saw him at that window. He made signs to her, and she made signs to him. Then she opened the window and beckoned him to come in, and he came in.

ARTHUR: [*astonished*] Impossible. How came you to know all this?

MISS MYRNIE: I saw them from behind that door.

ARTHUR: Then you were watching – listening.

MISS MYRNIE: Heaven forbid! I hope I know my duty better. But – sometimes – one happens to open a door – by accident – when something is happening by accident, which we see by accident; or, one is behind a door by accident, and one hears something – entirely by accident and accidentally. It's happened to me often.

ARTHUR: But to speak to a stranger from a window!

MISS MYRNIE: [*crossing and closing window*] Why, the sash is still open! I thought there was a draught.

ARTHUR: I can't believe it! Eva, so good – so truthful!

MISS MYRNIE: So she is; that's what I always say.

ARTHUR: To accuse her——

MISS MYRNIE: Accuse her! Heaven forbid; Christian charity forbids that I should accuse anyone. I'm defending her.

ARTHUR: Defending her?

MISS MYRNIE: Yes; she can't help it.

ARTHUR: Can't help——

MISS MYRNIE: Running after a young man – after a *young* man – no – it's in her blood.

ARTHUR: In her blood?

MISS MYRNIE: Yes; do you not remember twenty-four years ago, when her mother ran away with that low plebeian fellow Summers? It was at this very window that they used to meet. [ARTHUR *sinks in chair.*] Romeo and Juliet over again; and it was like that villain Shakespeare to put it in a play.

ARTHUR: [*rising*] Do me the favour to ask the Doctor and Mr Bunnythorne to come here.

MISS MYRNIE: With pleasure. As to dear Eva, I'm sure she's innocence itself. So youthful, so truthful – there's the pity. Innocence and youth are so apt to betray us, ain't they? But, as I often tell my Pamela, she's a darling girl. Bless her! Bless her! Bless her!

[*Exit* MISS MYRNIE.]

ARTHUR: Eva beckon to a strange man! Impossible! She must have known him. Some intrusive shop-boy from those people she was with – the – the Nobbses. A 'prentice? I – I – I—— At this very window, too, where her mother—— it would seem as if there were a fate in it.

[*Enter* DOCTOR *and* BUNNYTHORNE. BUNNYTHORNE *in night-cap and dressing-gown.*]

DOCTOR: Arthur, you sent for us.

BUNNYTHORNE: The Doctor was sending me to bed, so I came as I am.

ARTHUR: I wanted your advice. I find that there is a young man here – a stranger – come after Eva.

DOCTOR: ⎫
BUNNYTHORNE: ⎬ Eva!

ARTHUR: Now should his intentions be matrimonial——

BUNNYTHORNE: Matrimonial! Then what's to become of my boy Bob?

ARTHUR: [*out of patience*] Bob! You can't think of Eva and Bob.

BUNNYTHORNE: Why not? They're both young.

ARTHUR: Eva is too young.

DOCTOR: And too delicate.

BUNNYTHORNE: Well, Bob's delicate, too.

ARTHUR: But a stranger coming here without introduction, and *sans cérémonie*——

DOCTOR: Insolent!

BUNNYTHORNE: Kick him out!

[EVA *and* FERNE *appear at door*, ARTHUR, BUNNYTHORNE, *and* DOCTOR *with their backs to the*

audience, MISS MYRNIE *at door. A pause, during which*
MISS MYRNIE *crosses at back door and goes off.*]

EVA: [*somewhat surprised at their aggressive attitude*] Cousin, let me
    present——

ARTHUR: Not now. Your uncle wishes to see you upstairs.

EVA: But before——

ARTHUR: Don't keep him waiting. Go at once, dear.

[*Exit* EVA. *Pause.*]

FERNE: I presume that I must introduce myself, as Miss Eva——

ARTHUR: [*stiffly*] That ceremony will not be unnecessary. Whom have
    I the honour of receiving at Mompesson Abbey?

FERNE: My name is John Ferne, civil engineer.

ARTHUR: [*aside*] Ferne! A relation of the Snobbses, no doubt.

FERNE: May I now inquire whom I have the honour of addressing?

ARTHUR: Certainly! Dr Brown.

DOCTOR: W. N. Brown. No final E.

ARTHUR: Mr Bunnythorne.

BUNNYTHORNE: Late of Bunnythorne and Bingham, contractors,
    Gosport.

ARTHUR: I am Mr Arthur Mompesson.

BUNNYTHORNE: The Honourable Arthur Mompesson.

DOCTOR: What the devil's the Honourable to do with it? A man's a
    man, isn't he?

BUNNYTHORNE: Not invariably. Sometimes he's a gentleman.

ARTHUR: [*aside*] Not often.

BUNNYTHORNE: He gave you your title of Doctor, didn't he? – why not
    give him his title of Honourable?

DOCTOR: My son wouldn't be a doctor, would he?

BUNNYTHORNE: What nonsense you talk – you haven't got a son.

DOCTOR: There I have the advantage of you – you have.

ARTHUR: Chut! chut! Mr Ferne, pray take a chair. [*They all sit.*] Your
    name is not unfamiliar to me!

FERNE: My grandfather was a tenant on this estate, and I remember
    you, Mr Arthur, as we called him, perfectly.

ARTHUR: [*aside*] A tenant! [*aloud*] If I remember rightly, your
    grandfather had an old-fashioned name. Let me see – Jabez –
    Jabez, was it not?

[FERNE *assents.*]

DOCTOR: Jabez Ferne! Any relation to the Jabez Ferne who patented
    the invention for drainage by means of——

FERNE: His son! My father!

DOCTOR: [*rising and shaking hands with* FERNE] He was an honour to
    science and his country.

BUNNYTHORNE: [*crossing and shaking hands too*] So he was, for we bought the patent, and sold it in the colonies to an enormous profit.

DOCTOR: Profit! Think of making two blades of grass grow in place of one. Think of benefiting your fellow-man!

BUNNYTHORNE: Think of benefiting yourself.

ARTHUR: May I inquire if you follow the same career of sewerage your father did? Do drains run in your family?

DOCTOR: Drains don't! Brains do!

FERNE: But then brains are not always hereditary. I have already told you I am an engineer.

ARTHUR: Pardon me! I had forgotten.

FERNE: [*aside*] They're very disagreeable.

ARTHUR: An engineer! Well, engineers are the heroes of the hour – I should say of the minute – for the present age goes so fast that we have to count by minutes.

FERNE: The present age is, certainly, the age of progress.

ARTHUR: Progress! Yes! That is the word. That is the modern slang for the destruction of everything high and noble, and the substitution of everything base and degrading. Progress! progress which pushes painting aside to make room for photography. But painting is old-fashioned; and photography – which makes men uglier than they are by nature – that's progress! Citric acid – and heaven knows what other abominations – have superseded grapes; – you literally *make* wine – that is science! Horses, which in my youth were considered noble animals, are abolished for engines that smash, for trains that smash, for velocipedes that smash; and the débris of broken wheels, boilers, bones, and shattered human beings, you call progress!

BUNNYTHORNE: ⎫
⎬ [*enthusiastically*] Bravo! bravo! beautiful.
DOCTOR: ⎭

ARTHUR: As to manners, progress has indeed altered them. Everyone is too much occupied to think, to feel, to love, or to improve. Progress does not permit sleep, or sentiment, or accomplishment, or leisure. To misquote Shakespeare – another illusion of my youth, and, doubtless, an impostor – "Whatever is done must be done quickly." Nowadays you eat rapidly, you drink rapidly, you make love rapidly, you marry rapidly, you go through the Divorce Court still more rapidly. Luxury everywhere; comfort nowhere. Look at your young men! cynical, sarcastic – without faith in anything; without warmth of heart, without generous enthusiasm – *blasé* and brutal – they puff the smoke of their foul cigars in the faces of their mothers, or swear before their sisters. Their talk is slang; their morals those of betting-men. Their aim to dazzle for a moment – their end bankruptcy of person, fortune, mind, heart, brain, body, and soul.

> [DOCTOR *and* BUNNYTHORNE *rise and shake hands with* ARTHUR, *then seat themselves again.*]

BUNNYTHORNE:
DOCTOR: } [*shaking their heads*] Too true! too true!

DOCTOR: The world is going to the devil.

BUNNYTHORNE: At express speed (limited). And it used to be so good. We used to be so good! Didn't we, Doctor?

BUNNYTHORNE:
DOCTOR: } We did! – we did! We used to be so good. Ah!

> [*They sigh.*]

DOCTOR: These modern fellows, with their modern fashions, their beards and moustaches!

BUNNYTHORNE: Too lazy to shave themselves. Hairy beasts!

ARTHUR: So un-English – pah!

BUNNYTHORNE: And their floppy clothes, and their eye-glasses stuck so. [*imitating*] Ah! – ah! – ah!

DOCTOR: And their cigars.

BUNNYTHORNE: [*imitating*] Ah! – ah! – ah!

DOCTOR: Ah! The good old times!

BUNNYTHORNE:
DOCTOR: } Ah! The good old times.

DOCTOR: The men of old!

ARTHUR: Alfred! the Black Prince! the Fifth Henry!

DOCTOR: Pooh! Jack Cade – Cromwell!

ARTHUR: Pooh! Claverhouse – Marlborough!

BUNNYTHORNE: Whittington, Lord Mayor of London!

FERNE: Why not his cat?

DOCTOR: Bacon!

BUNNYTHORNE: Milton! Guy Fawkes! Mrs Fry!

DOCTOR: Thistlewood!

ARTHUR: Pitt!

DOCTOR: Fox – Cobbett – Horne Tooke!

ARTHUR: Junius!

BUNNYTHORNE: Cock-eyed Wilkes!

DOCTOR: Walter Scott!

ARTHUR: Byron!

BUNNYTHORNE: Old Parr! Where do you find such pills now? I mean, where do you find such men now?

ARTHUR: Where indeed?

ARTHUR:
DOCTOR: } Ah!
BUNNYTHORNE:

[They shake their heads mournfully over the bright past and degenerate present.]

FERNE: Do I understand the meaning of this combined attack to be because I, as an engineer, represent modern progress? If so, I accept the challenge. All that you have said is but to contrast the vices of the present with the virtues of the past. I cannot think that we are so bad as you would make us out. Vice is vice, no matter in what epoch it exists, and I readily admit that we are not as good as we should be. But, to combat your examples. We are guilty of moustaches; that, you say, is un-English. How about Shakespeare, and Bacon, and Sir Walter Raleigh? They wore beard and moustache, and they were somewhat of Englishmen. We smoke cigars. Johnson and Goldsmith smoked pipes. What difference? If we smoke more, we snuff less than our grandfathers. You have recalled the names of men dead for centuries, to ask me if I could show a parallel to them in this year of grace? Alfred, the Black Prince, Marlborough, and Pitt. Why not Pericles, Lycurgus, Alcibiades, or Solomon, or David, or Noah? For our manners, our cynicism, and lassitude, let it be remembered that we no longer beat watchmen, or steal knockers and bell-pulls for the sake of showing our wit. If we use slang, at least we are not guilty of the brutal oaths that, in the last century, made the name of Englishman a by-word over Europe. On one point, too, I must claim superiority even for our poor, weak, little modern selves – we keep sober. Men do not now reel into a drawing-room and bend over our mothers, wives, sisters, and daughters, to pump out compliments with a breath reeking of fiery port, with a faltering articulation, and unsteady step, and a tongue so loose and unguarded that it can scarce refrain from insult. From the usual degradation of daily drunkenness we are freer than our fathers, and——

BUNNYTHORNE: *[rising in indignant fury]* Who the devil are you to turn up your nose at a man that gets drunk? Let me tell you, young sir, that I got drunk before you were born. Everybody got drunk before you were born. A parcel of stuck-up sober puppies! To get drunk properly and like a gentleman is a very good thing; it's – it's – it's English – thoroughly English, and old-fashioned – and – and – all right!

[He sits down, blowing the steam off.]

FERNE: You have sneered at this age because it is an age of progress; I prefer to call it a period of transition. We have changed from the worst to the better – we are changing still, from bad to best; and during this transition – I am proud to know that it is I – the engineer, the motive-power – who leads the way. 'Tis I who bring industry, invention, and capital together; 'tis I who introduce demand to supply. 'Tis I who give the word – 'tis I who direct the train that flies over valleys, through mountains, across rivers – that dominates the mighty Alps themselves. 'Tis I – the engineer – who exchanges the wealth of one country against the poverty of another. I am broad, breathing humanity, that whirls through the air on wings of smoke to a brighter future. I spread civilisation wherever I sit a-straddle of my steed of vapour, whom I guide with reins of iron and feed with flames. As for the tumbledown old ruins I knock down in passing, what matter? Where I halt towns rise, and cities spring up into being. 'Tis the train that is the master of the hour. As it moves it shrieks out to the dull ear of prejudice, "Make room for me! I must pass and I will! and those who dare oppose my progress shall be crushed!" Its tail of smoke is like the plume of a field-marshal; and the rattle and motion of its wheels are as the throb and pulsations of the progress of the whole world.

ARTHUR: Possibly you are right, sir. [*rising*] Coal smoke is better than pure air; – the shriek of an engine is the sweetest harmony, and rapid motion is the sole secret of truth and happiness; but in my time it was not considered the act, I will not say of a gentleman, but of an honest man, to make signs to a young lady at a window, or to enter the house where she lived to speak to her clandestinely.

FERNE: [*rising*] What!

DOCTOR: [*rising*] You have been observed, sir.

BUNNYTHORNE: [*rising*] The whole morning – drawing, writing, and making signs at this window.

FERNE: To Eva?

ARTHUR: Eva! [*aside; to* FERNE] To Miss Mompesson, my cousin!

FERNE: I am compelled to contradict you most emphatically. Eva – Miss Mompesson – whom I met in London, called me in from that window. Until she did so, I was not aware that she lived here.

ARTHUR: Then why write?

FERNE: Write! I was not writing; I was sketching.

DOCTOR: Sketching?

ARTHUR: In this weather?

FERNE: Yes, a bird's-eye view of this place and the neighbourhood, by order of the company of which I am chief engineer.

ARTHUR: Eh?

FERNE: Yes! [*showing portfolio*] We are going to make a branch line from Stapleton, through Broxborough and Wainthorpe to Stickton-le-Clay.

DOCTOR:
ARTHUR: } A railway here?
BUNNYTHORNE:

FERNE: Yes. [*showing drawing*] Yes, here is the line; you see it cuts this park and the house in two——

DOCTOR:
ARTHUR: } The Abbey?
BUNNYTHORNE:

FERNE: Yes! The station will be built on this site. We must pull the Abbey down.

ARTHUR: Pull down the Abbey! Do I hear rightly? Pull down the Abbey! where my family for centuries have been born, lived, and died. Where I first saw the light; where, when my time shall come, I hope my eyes shall darken to this world, to open in a brighter and a purer. Pull down the Abbey! The royal gift of a king to my ancestor for faithful services in council and in field. A home where generations of knightly gentlemen and high-bred ladies have gone forth to rule the world and live in honour! A church, beneath whose aisles saints have spoken and martyrs have been buried. A holy shrine, reverenced by every passing peasant, where hospitality and every earthly charity, as every spiritual good were sanctified in stone. Pull down the Abbey! Sooner than see it trampled to dust and scattered to the winds, its stones shall fall and crush its master. [*giving way, sinking into chair*]

DOCTOR: [*going to him*] Arthur!

FERNE: I am very sorry——

ARTHUR: We fly their cursed civilisation – their genius of smoke – their factory palaces – their spinning-jennies – printing presses, and inventions of the devil. My father and I are not left even this retreat.

BUNNYTHORNE: Here, here, here. This can soon be settled. [*taking portfolio*] Look here; by letting the line diverge here, at the park gates, it comes round here, knocks down old Brewster's new house, and there you are for your station; and any compliment that you may consider your due, for altering your plans, we shall be most happy to pay money down.

FERNE: [*taking portfolio*] It only needed such a suggestion to recall me to a sense of my duty. I shall recommend this route. [*to ARTHUR*] At the same time I shall be glad for your sake, Mr Mompesson, if the company in considering the matter should modify my instructions, and the park and Abbey should remain intact.

ARTHUR: [*rising*] You are right, sir; and I beg your pardon for having for a moment doubted you. I recognise you as a perfect man of honour, in your way – your railway; but I shall go to London –

I will appeal against this invasion of my rights. [*During this last speech* EVA *enters, overhearing the last words;* BOB *appears;* MISS MYRNIE *at door.*] I have friends, and powerful ones; I will see whether a railway company can uproot the home of a country gentleman.

[*Music – piano till end of Act.*]

EVA: You are going away, cousin?
ARTHUR: Yes; to London.
DOCTOR:
BUNNYTHORNE:
MISS MYRNIE: } To London!
BOB:

[*Picture.* FERNE *bowing to take his leave.* ARTHUR *indignant.* BUNNYTHORNE *and* DOCTOR *sympathetic.* EVA *looking at* FERNE. BOB *contemptuous.* MISS MYRNIE *watching.*]

END OF ACT I

ACT II

SCENE I – *The Tapestry Chamber in the Abbey. Large window. Balcony and staircase seen behind it – covered with snow. Doors* R. *and* L. *Scene enclosed. Large old-fashioned fire-place. Large fire burning. The stage furnished somewhat sparely. Old-fashioned tapestry on walls. Table and invalid chair near fire-place. Sofa.*

> [*Enter* DOCTOR *from door* [EVA'S *room*], *meeting* WYKEHAM, *on whose arm* LORD MOMPESSON, *in dressing-gown, is leaning.*]

LORD M: Good morning, Doctor: good morning. How is our invalid?

DOCTOR: Much the same.

LORD M: Poor child! poor child! I miss her very much. She was so kind and thoughtful for me – so kind and thoughtful – so – so – Wykeham takes care of me now – don't you, Wykeham?

WYKEHAM: Yes, my lord.

LORD M: But you're too old; ain't you, Wykeham – too old?

WYKEHAM: Yes, my lord.

LORD M: So am I. In fact, we're both too old – ain't we, Wykeham?

WYKEHAM: Yes, my lord.

LORD M: [*to* DOCTOR] Do you think we shall have Arthur back to-day?

DOCTOR: I think so.

LORD M: Dear! dear! dear! And he thought to be only away a week, and he has been more than two months – such a long time – when one is old. Take me back to my room, Wykeham. Let me know if Arthur comes back.

DOCTOR: Of course.

LORD M: My love to Eva. Is she asleep?

DOCTOR: Aleep? Yes.

LORD M: Ay, ay! A good thing sleep. Good morning. Now, Wykeham.

> [LORD MOMPESSON *and* WYKEHAM *totter off.*]

DOCTOR: Asleep! ah! [*sighing*] If she only could sleep.

> [*Enter* EVA. *She looks very ill, and half delirious. During the scene she excites herself so as to exhibit all the symptoms of delirious fever; she coughs at intervals.*]

DOCTOR: Have you got up, dear?

EVA: Yes; don't scold me; I was so tired of the sick room.

DOCTOR: [*with great sympathy, all his rough manner gone, and the fine delicate nature rising to the surface*] Feel better?

EVA: [*languidly*] Just the same.

DOCTOR: And your head?

EVA: Heavy. And my bones all ache.

DOCTOR: [*arranging pillows and armchair for her*] Sit down by the fire.

EVA: I'm always cold. My long illness began just in this way – but this time it will not last long.

DOCTOR: Chut! chut! my dear. Come, you're more comfortable there.

EVA: I should like to be near the window.

DOCTOR: The window is too far from the fire.

EVA: But I like to see——

DOCTOR: There's nothing to see, my pet, but the snow that has fallen during the night.

EVA: I like to see the snow – the fantastic forms it seems to carve upon the trees – as if the whole world were made of white coral; or as if some good person were dead, and a shroud of ice had fallen upon the earth. [*rising*] Let me go to the window?

DOCTOR: No, no; there is too much draught. It's a crazy old casement, and you mustn't catch cold. The slightest chill – an open door – or a current of air upon you in your state——

EVA: And I should die?

DOCTOR: [*bothered*] Die! No, my love: nobody dies! it's out of date.

EVA: But it *might* kill me!

DOCTOR: Well, it might, if it were fatal. If you must move, walk about with me – so – within range of the fire.

[*She rises, takes his arm, and they walk to and fro.*]

EVA: Tell me, is it true that there are people in the world who believe, that when we die, all is finished – all is over – and that we do not meet those we love again in a better, higher sphere?

DOCTOR: I – I believe that there are such people. The world is full of varieties.

EVA: [*growing delirious*] But how is it possible they can believe it? How can they believe it – at night – when the sky is full of stars? What are the stars but beacon-fires of immortality? lamps, lighting us on the Heavenly road to future and Eternal Life? Doctor, did you ever, on a bright night, see a star – fall?

DOCTOR: Yes, often. I've seen many things fall at night.

EVA: And did you not think, as you watched it out on its bright path, through its host of shining sisters, did you not think that *you* were that star – falling, falling, falling through tremendous space – and have you not felt here, at your heart, a sense of sublime emotion – a sort of wonder and awe, but yet not fear?

DOCTOR: No; I never felt anything of the sort. We doctors, you know, have to deal with material ailments – broken collar-bones, and not erratic nebulae.

EVA: I saw my mother die! When I die I shall meet her again! I shall cleave through the air and see the white frosty earth below me, as I aspire to a bright Heaven and her warm heart. She, above, cannot forget her poor child who, even in her earthly clay, remembers her. [*coughs*]

DOCTOR: My child, you're feverish, go back to your room [*seating her in armchair*] Your head is hot, and——

EVA: Yes, I feel I am very ill, but I think that when the poor body is weak the mind is clearer. [*suddenly*] Doctor, why do you never go to church?

DOCTOR: [*staggered*] Eh?

EVA: Why do you never go to church?

DOCTOR: Me – a – a man – at my time of life.

EVA: [*slowly*] If I were to die——

DOCTOR: Eva!

EVA: If it were Heaven's will, and I should die, you would pray for me, would you not?

DOCTOR: I – I – I – you really must go to bed, my child.

EVA: God bless you for all your goodness to me.

DOCTOR: [*awfully affected*] My love!

[*Music, piano.*]

EVA: [*after a pause, taking* DOCTOR's *hand*] They sent him away on my account; did they not?

DOCTOR: Him? Who?

EVA: John – Ferne. You remember, I told you. They sent him away; Miss Myrnie told me so; because he was in love with me, and they did not think him good enough to be my husband.

DOCTOR: Miss Myrnie told you so, did she?

EVA: Yes.

DOCTOR: [*aside*] The damned old——, I'll give her some physic that will make her so ill. [*to her, soothingly*] My dear, Miss Myrnie told you a lie. So far from sending him away, your cousin Arthur likes him very much, and wishes him to marry you.

EVA: [*overjoyed*] What?

DOCTOR: Miss Myrnie is a mischief-making old——. With your permission, I will think the rest in Latin. Your cousin Arthur has gone to London——

EVA: [*eagerly*] To inquire about him?

DOCTOR: Yes; yes. [*aside*] What an infernal liar I am; but it's a pious fraud. [*to her*] And when he comes back——

EVA: He will be my husband?

DOCTOR: Yes.

[*She sinks into chair. A pause.*]

EVA: [*after a deep sigh of relief*] Doctor, I think I'll go back to my room. I can sleep now.

DOCTOR: Do, dear, do.

[*She takes his arm.*]

EVA: Will he come soon to see me?

DOCTOR: I – I think so; but how do I know? I'm not in his secrets.

EVA: [*as they are nearing door*] It's two months since I saw him; two months and three days.

DOCTOR: Yes, dear, so it is. I make it out to be just two months and three days.

EVA: [*at door*] Good-night.

DOCTOR: You mean good morning.

EVA: I shall sleep well, I'm sure I shall. [*going; returns*] If he comes while I'm asleep, you'll rouse me, will you not?

DOCTOR: I'll come and rouse you up that instant.

EVA: Do. Oh! Doctor, why did you not tell me this good news before. I am so happy.

[*Exit* EVA.]

DOCTOR: [*his handkerchief to his eyes*] Poor child! poor child!

[*Enter* BUNNYTHORNE, *all over snow. Skates in his hand.*]

DOCTOR: [*angrily and brusquely*] What the devil do you come in like that for? Don't you know that I've got an invalid there? [BUNNYTHORNE *is writhing in pain.*] What are you doing?

BUNNYTHORNE: I'm trying to get my back-bone straight again. I've been skating on the lake.

DOCTOR: More fool you – at your time of life.

BUNNYTHORNE: And I tumbled down.

DOCTOR: Of course – and hurt yourself?

BUNNYTHORNE: Yes.

DOCTOR: Where?

BUNNYTHORNE: Where I fell – on my back.

DOCTOR: Fall on your head next time, it won't hurt you there.

BUNNYTHORNE: Arthur Mompesson's come back from London.

DOCTOR: No! When?

BUNNYTHORNE: This moment. Here he is.

[*Enter* ARTHUR, *followed by* MISS MYRNIE. ARTHUR *is dressed in a modern morning suit, turn-down collar, modern cravat, &c.; his whole manner changed; he seems younger and brighter, and radiant with high spirits.*]

ARTHUR: Ah, Doctor, how dy'e do? Where is my father? Where is Eva?

DOCTOR: Not yet up.

ARTHUR: Still asleep [*looking at watch*] and past ten. The lazy creatures!

DOCTOR: [*with his watch.* BUNNYTHORNE *and* MISS MYRNIE *take out their watches, big ones.*] Past ten! Why it's not half-past nine.

ARTHUR: You're all slow here – behind time. It's past ten by the Horse Guards.

BUNNYTHORNE: The Horse Guards at Stickton-le-Clay?

ARTHUR: No; the Horse Guards in London.

MISS MYRNIE:
DOCTOR: } [*with contempt*] Oh, London!
BUNNYTHORNE:

BUNNYTHORNE: [*dogmatically*] Our time is Stickton-le-Clay time; that's good enough for us.

ARTHUR: Well, Doctor, congratulate me, I've won.

DOCTOR: Won.

ARTHUR: Yes; I went to the Commons – the Lords – I saw many old friends – I argued – I fought – and conquered – the line is to branch off at Broxborough. Wainthorpe is to be left to the right, and the railway line does not come here.

MISS MYRNIE: [*rising and shaking hands with him*] Bless you!

DOCTOR:
BUNNYTHORNE: } Hurray!

ARTHUR: [*looking round with rapture*] These dear old walls; I have preserved them! They will stand – a glorious relic of past ages – an architectural beacon to the future. Progress, with its hot oil and steam vulgarity, shall not reach us here.

DOCTOR:
BUNNYTHORNE: } Bravo!

ARTHUR: But let us be just even to our enemies; the railway is very comfortable.

DOCTOR: [*astonished*] The railway?

BUNNYTHORNE: [*disgusted*] Did you travel by railway?

MISS MYRNIE: [*horrified*] Good gracious!

ARTHUR: As far as Stapleton. [*all aghast*] Why not? It was the nearest and the quickest.

MISS MYRNIE. You travelled
BUNNYTHORNE: By rail?

[*A pause.*]

ARTHUR: Yes, by rail; nice carriage – padded – tins full of hot water for your feet – very comfortable. When you stop at a station, man shouts out, Staple – ton, Staple – ton, bell, whistle, off you go – very nice indeed. [*They all sigh.*] I didn't care much for the coach – the old "Perseverance" – afterwards. Not pleasant inside. Commercial man asleep on my shoulder, a good snorer; woman opposite with baby with whom travelling

disagreed. Damp, bad-smelling straw, the roads awful. Had to
get out and walk up the hills. Cold, wet feet – after the
comfortable first-class carriage – horrible!

[*A pause.* DOCTOR, BUNNYTHORNE, *and* MISS MYRNIE
exchange glances.]

BUNNYTHORNE: Where did you get those clothes?

ARTHUR: Oh! a tailor in Bond Street. I was so shabby. I ordered them
and he sent them to Long's.

BUNNYTHORNE: I never saw such an object in all my life. Why not wear
moustaches?

DOCTOR: And an eye-glass?

MISS MYRNIE: Or smoke a cigar?

ARTHUR: Ah! You're prejudiced! I've brought presents for all of you –
and as for Eva, I've ordered fresh furniture for this room.

MISS MYRNIE: Fresh furniture?

ARTHUR: Yes; I mean to make it into a boudoir. Poor child! after the
luxury of London, to be condemned to pass her days among
these mouldy old chairs and tables. They're only fit for an
outhouse.

BUNNYTHORNE: And what are we fit for? An outhouse, too?

ARTHUR: My dear friends, my trip to London has made me twenty
years younger. We'll make the old Abbey as gay as any place in
the country. I mean to give a ball in honour of my victory over
the railway.

MISS MYRNIE:
DOCTOR: } A ball!
BUNNYTHORNE:

BUNNYTHORNE: Do you expect me to dance?

MISS MYRNIE: Or me?

ARTHUR: Why not?

MISS MYRNIE: Is the ball, too, to be in honour of Eva?

ARTHUR: Yes.

MISS MYRNIE: Why not marry her?

ARTHUR: Why not?

MISS MYRNIE: [*rising*] Balls, Cousin Arthur, are wicked things – all sin
and shoulders. If a ball is given in the Abbey I shall quit the
place for ever.

BUNNYTHORNE:
DOCTOR: } [*congratulating each other*] Hurray!

MISS MYRNIE: [*hearing them, and more exasperated*] I dare say you'll be
very glad.

BUNNYTHORNE: We shall, indeed.

MISS MYRNIE: I will not countenance such scandals with my presence.
[*Drops her spectacles.*] Cousin Arthur, the place of future
punishment is paved with——

DOCTOR: With good intentions.

MISS MYRNIE: No, sir! with bare necks and shoulders, with false hair and paint, and other Babylonian abominations. Arthur, you went out from the country pure and unsullied. You have returned reeking with smoke, railways, impiety, and London. In time you will have ceased to be a single country gentleman, and sink into a married cockney!

[*Exit* MISS MYRNIE.]

BUNNYTHORNE: [*after a pause of astonishment, seeing her spectacles on the carpet*] She's left her green spectacles. [*Crushes them with his foot, then picking up the pieces.*] Here, Miss Myrnie, you've dropped your spectacles.

[*Exit* BUNNYTHORNE.]

ARTHUR: Upon my word, if Miss Myrnie were not——

DOCTOR: Never mind the old woman – she's jealous.

ARTHUR: Jealous!

DOCTOR: You said you'd ordered fresh furniture for Eva, and——

ARTHUR: Eva – yes – [*looking at watch*] Not up yet – lazy – I'll knock at her door. [*going to door.* DOCTOR *stops him.*]

DOCTOR: No.

ARTHUR: Eh? Why not? [*Seeing the serious expression of* DOCTOR's *face.*] Is she ill? [DOCTOR *nods.*] Very ill? Why did you not tell me? Why did you not write?

DOCTOR: What use? She fell ill two days after you left, and she has got worse and worse.

ARTHUR: Is it a return of – a relapse? [DOCTOR *nods.* ARTHUR *sinks into chair.*] But what cause?

DOCTOR: What cause? [*putting both hands in his pockets and looking* ARTHUR *full in the face*] Love!

ARTHUR: [*rising, astonished*] Love!

DOCTOR: Yes; for that young man – Ferne – the engineer.

ARTHUR: Impossible! He is not in love with her.

DOCTOR: No; he is not in love with her, but she is in love with him.

ARTHUR: How do you know?

DOCTOR: I heard her name him when she was delirious. [ARTHUR *resumes his seat.*] I questioned her, and she confessed it. She fell in love with him more than a year ago – when they were both in London. See here – [*producing letter*], from the physician who attended her. Read.

ARTHUR: [*reading*] "If the fever returns in its full force, nothing can save her." [*rising*] But it shall not return. You are here. You can battle with the disease. You can save her!

DOCTOR: Save her! How? Give me a body in pain, and I can try. Show me a diseased organ, and I know what I'm about. I can treat. I

can reduce. I have something material to fight with. But a
mind in trouble – a spirit diseased – a soul in agony – how can I
treat that? I can't give her a dose of resignation or tablespoon-
fuls of hope. I can't cure a love-sick girl, dying of love.

ARTHUR: But no girl ever died of love. You've told me so a thousand
times.

DOCTOR: And I was right. They don't die of love, but love brings on
fever, and they die of that.

[*Enter* BUNNYTHORNE *hastily.*]

DOCTOR: [*angrily*] How often am I to tell you to come in quietly?

BUNNYTHORNE: [*angrily*] I shall come in as I like.

DOCTOR: [*pointing to door*] What, when——

BUNNYTHORNE: [*softly*] Oh, I forgot. But I'm annoyed! That young
fellow – that stokineer – engineer – what is it?

ARTHUR: Ferne?

BUNNYTHORNE: Yes, Ferne – is downstairs in the drawing-room, and
wants to see you. I told Wykeham to send him away.

DOCTOR: You did?

BUNNYTHORNE: Yes.

DOCTOR: You fool.

BUNNYTHORNE: [*indignant*] Doctor Brown!

DOCTOR: Go down again – ask him to take a glass of sherry; be
attentive, polite, and bring him upstairs here in ten minutes.

BUNNYTHORNE: ⎱ [*both astonished*] Upstairs?
ARTHUR: ⎰ Here?

BUNNYTHORNE: But I don't understand——

DOCTOR: Of course you don't. I don't expect that of you. [*forcing him
off*] Now go.

BUNNYTHORNE: [*as he goes*] Ask that stokineer fellow——

DOCTOR: Yes.

[BUNNYTHORNE *is forced off.*]

ARTHUR: I don't understand——

DOCTOR: Eva must see him. Miss Myrnie told her that Ferne was
ordered from the house on her account, because you and your
father would not consent to the match. His presence will
contradict the old serpent.

ARTHUR: But she must not believe——

DOCTOR: Let her believe what she likes, so long as I can but save her.

ARTHUR: But it will be a lie to——

DOCTOR: Yes, it will be a lie. Consider the lie physic, and swallow it
with or without a wry face – as you please; but swallow it.

ARTHUR: But to-morrow we shall be forced to undeceive her.

DOCTOR: Let us save her for to-day. We can think of something else
to-morrow.

ARTHUR: But I will not consent——

DOCTOR: You must! – you shall! Damn it, sir! Who commands by the sick bed-side – you or me? Give me the chance of saving her. Don't tie my hands. I'll snatch her from death if I can.

ARTHUR: [*terrified*] Death!

DOCTOR: Yes. Send this young man away, and I'll not answer for her life eight-and-forty hours.

ARTHUR: [*despairingly*] Let him come! Let him come! Only save her, and I'll turn Radical! [*shaking hands with* DOCTOR]

DOCTOR: Hush! [*going to door*] I hear her moving – place the sofa here.

> [ARTHUR *moves sofa near fire.* EVA *opens door,* ARTHUR *offers her his arm.*]

ARTHUR: My poor girl. I'm so sorry to see you ill again.

EVA: I'm so glad to see you back.

> [*She coughs. They place her on sofa.*]

DOCTOR: Keep yourself well wrapped up – the slightest cold – the smallest draught – and the consequences might be serious.

EVA: What a long time you've been away.

DOCTOR: Arthur has been busy. [*motioning to* ARTHUR] He has just been bothering me about a matter, which I fear you have hardly strength enough to talk of.

EVA: [*trembling*] About——

DOCTOR: Yes – about that – about Mr Ferne.

> [*During the Act,* EVA *coughs at frequent intervals.*]

EVA: [*trembling*] Did you see him in London?

DOCTOR: Yes. [*looking at* ARTHUR] You saw him in London?

ARTHUR: [*embarrassed*] Oh, yes.

EVA: Then you're not – you're not – angry – with him?

> [DOCTOR *and* ARTHUR *are at back of sofa, so that* EVA *cannot see their by-play. The red light of fire on* EVA's *face.*]

DOCTOR: Angry with him – ha, ha! What for? [*aside to* ARTHUR] Say what for?

ARTHUR: [*mechanically*] What for?

EVA: For – for – Then Miss Myrnie was mistaken – and you did not—

DOCTOR: No, you didn't, did you? [*aside to* ARTHUR] Say you didn't! I'm not going to tell all the lies – you tell your share.

ARTHUR: [*to* EVA] Did not what?

EVA: You did not – decline his offer.

DOCTOR: I should think not! [*to* ARTHUR] Say no!

ARTHUR: [*embarrassed*] No!

EVA: Then you consent?

[*She is almost fainting.* DOCTOR *applies eau-de-Cologne to her forehead.*]

ARTHUR: [*taking* DOCTOR *up stage*] What are you about? She believes that I consent to her marrying this fellow!

DOCTOR: All the better.

ARTHUR: How can I undeceive her?

DOCTOR: *Don't* undeceive her!

ARTHUR: You've done it, Doctor! You've done it!

EVA: [*recovering*] What are you saying?

DOCTOR: I was saying that Ferne is such a fine young fellow – make such a capital husband. He'll be here directly!

EVA: [*excited*] Directly! – When? – To-morrow?

DOCTOR: When, Arthur? To-morrow; or, perhaps, sooner.

EVA: [*sitting up*] Hush! I hear his step! There are two people ascending the stairs; he is one of them. He is here. [*Sinks on sofa.*]

[*Enter* BUNNYTHORNE *and* FERNE.]

BUNNYTHORNE: [*aloud*] Here's Mr Ferne. [*to* DOCTOR] Now you've got him – what do you want with him?

ARTHUR: [*going to* FERNE *and shaking hands with him with feigned cordiality*] My dear Mr Ferne – delighted to see you – delighted.

DOCTOR: Delighted! [*shaking hands*] Delighted!

BUNNYTHORNE: [*to* FERNE] Eh! delighted? Why this is that fellow who was going to——

ARTHUR: ⎱ [*to* BUNNYTHORNE] Do hold your tongue!
DOCTOR: ⎰ Keep quiet, can't you? [BUNNYTHORNE *bothered.*]

FERNE: [*surprised at the warmth of his reception*] I called partly to congratulate you on your success before the committee.

DOCTOR: [*interrupting him*] And to inquire after Eva.

FERNE: Eva!

[*All this takes place near* L.H. *door up stage.* EVA, *who is on sofa, not hearing it.*]

BUNNYTHORNE: Eva! [*to* DOCTOR *and* ARTHUR] But I thought you didn't like the notion of——

ARTHUR: ⎱ Do hold your tongue.
DOCTOR: ⎰ Silence, you dreadful old magpie, silence.

BUNNYTHORNE: [*aside*] They're both gone off their heads. London has sent one mad; and living among physic has driven the other lunatic.

ARTHUR: [*aside to* FERNE] For Heaven's sake, don't contradict a word we say.

DOCTOR: [*aside to* FERNE] We'll explain to you by-and-by.

[FERNE *astonished.*]

ARTHUR: [*leading* FERNE *to sofa*] She is very ill – very ill indeed.

FERNE: I am very sorry, Miss Summers, to find you suffering. So ill.

EVA: I have been ill, but I am better now.

BUNNYTHORNE: [*following* DOCTOR *and* ARTHUR; *to them, aside*] Now perhaps you'll tell me.

DOCTOR: ⎱ Do keep quiet.
ARTHUR: ⎰ By-and-by, by-and-by.

EVA: And did you come down all the way here to see me?

FERNE: No. I came to see——

DOCTOR: Yes; to see you, dear, of course – and Arthur – and all of us. [*aside to* BUNNYTHORNE] Say as I do – make much of him.

BUNNYTHORNE: [*mechanically crossing to* FERNE, *and shaking hands with him, quite bothered*] Yes, all of us – me particularly – always glad to see my dear friend, what's your name? Come often, and bring your steam-engine – I mean——

EVA: [*to* FERNE] When you saw my cousin in London, he didn't know I was ill?

FERNE: [*mystified*] When I saw——

ARTHUR: [*interrupting*] Yes, when we met in London. They never wrote and told me. [*aside to* FERNE] For Heaven's sake don't betray us.

DOCTOR: [*aside to* FERNE] It is life or death.

ARTHUR: We'll explain some other time.

FERNE: [*to* BUNNYTHORNE] Eh?

BUNNYTHORNE: [*with importance*] Yes, I'll explain some other time, [*aside*] when I know what I've got to explain. [*aloud*] By-the-way, lunch is ready – so if you, my dear friend, will lunch with us, I'm sure Mr Mompesson will be——

ARTHUR: Delighted – yes, delighted.

EVA: No, you can lunch without him. He will stay with me. You're not hungry, are you? No; he is not hungry. Besides, I want to talk to him alone.

BUNNYTHORNE: ⎱ [*astonished*] Eh?
FERNE: ⎰ [*astonished*]

DOCTOR: Yes. We'll go to lunch, and——

ARTHUR: [*aside to him*] Leave them together?

DOCTOR: What is there to fear? He doesn't love her!

ARTHUR: No – but——

DOCTOR: Do you want to murder her?

ARTHUR: No, no. There – there [*to them*] – I shan't be long.

EVA: Don't hurry on our account.

ARTHUR: [*to* DOCTOR] We're done, Doctor, we're decidedly done.

[*Exit* ARTHUR.]

BUNNYTHORNE: [*to* DOCTOR] Now tell me why——

DOCTOR: Don't bother now – only make much of him.

[*Exit* DOCTOR.]

BUNNYTHORNE: [*bothered*] All right. [*going to* FERNE *and shaking hands mechanically*] Sorry you don't lunch with us, dear Mr——what's your name? – but you must drop in some other time – drop in often – in a friendly way – devilish glad——

[*He goes off talking to himself.* FERNE *astonished.*]

FERNE: What can they mean?
EVA: [*smiling*] Well, won't you come and sit beside me?
FERNE: With pleasure.

[*He sits on sofa.* EVA *near fire.* FERNE L. *of her*]

EVA: Oh! I am so glad to see you!
FERNE: [*embarrassed*] I, too, am delighted to have the opportunity. [*formally*]
EVA: And they never told you how ill I was – and I might have died——
FERNE: Died! Oh, Eva. How can you talk in that way?
EVA: You would have mourned me – would you not? [FERNE *embarrassed.*] But tell me – after you had seen Cousin Arthur in London – why did you not write to me?
FERNE: Write to you?
EVA: Yes; you knew the address!
FERNE: [*still more puzzled*] Oh, yes; I knew the address.
EVA: Well, then. Why not send me word of the good news immediately?
FERNE: I – I hardly felt – justified.
EVA: Why not? There was no need of any persuasion after Cousin Arthur had given his consent.
FERNIE: Given his consent?
EVA: Yes.
FERNE: To – to – what?
EVA: [*blushing*] To – you know very well – why do you want to make me say it?
FERNE: Of course I know very well – but I should like to hear you say it, because then I might have an idea of what it was.
EVA: What a tyrant you are!
FERNE: Do say it, Eva. [*repeating*] Arthur Mompesson has given his consent——
EVA: To our – correspondence?
FERNE: Correspondence!
EVA: Had given his consent – to our loving each other. There! now are you satisfied?

FERNE: [*aside*] Good heavens! Does she love me?

EVA: So you could have written. Surely a man has the privilege of writing to his future wife?

FERNE: Wife? Then have they told you——

EVA: The Doctor told me everything; so it is no use your trying to conceal it. [*joyously – then sadly*] I know why you and the others have tried to keep it from me.

FERNE: Why?

EVA: Because I was so ill, they feared the emotion – the excitement of the news might kill me.

FERNE: [*aside*] I understand.

EVA: But instead of increasing my malady it has improved my health. I feel stronger; I can breathe more easily. I can weep more freely. [*She weeps.*] Don't be frightened, these tears do me good. They are cool, refreshing tears – not like the hot scalding drops that burnt me yesterday.

> [*During this scene the sky seen through the window becomes darker as if before a storm. At the same time the glow of the fire increases in colour on the faces of* EVA *and* FERNE.]

FERNE: But, Eva, if – if events had not turned out so happily; that is, if I had not loved you, or if I had only loved you with the affection of a brother——

EVA: Oh! I shouldn't have liked that; that would not have been enough.

FERNE: Or, if – mind I say if – if I had loved another.

EVA: [*shaking her head confidently*] Impossible!

FERNE: Impossible! Why?

EVA: I loved you so much, you could not help loving me in return. These things are fostered by fate – or, no! I should not say fate, for mutual love is the work of Heaven.

FERNE: Heaven! [*He rises and walks from sofa. aside*] I can hardly believe my senses. [*returning to sofa and bending over her*] And my love makes you happy, Eva?

EVA. Happy? Oh, infinitely!

FERNE: [*with fervour, taking her hand*] And I, too, dearest Eva, am happy.

EVA: Now sit down here, and tell me one thing. [FERNE *sits by her side again*] Candidly, now – quite candidly.

FERNE: Tell you what?

> [*This scene to be played slowly.*]

EVA: When did you first discover – that is, when did your heart first tell you that you loved me?

FERNE: When?

EVA: Yes. When? [*a pause*] Ah! you can't remember. That's like men. Now, I'll tell you when I loved you for the first time. [*with child-like confidence*] It was on the twenty-eighth of September – on a Sunday. You called at the Dobbs's, and after dinner you walked out with me in the garden. It was the first time I had left the house since my illness. I was still in mourning, and you talked to me, and I fell in love with you from that moment.

FERNE: [*with fervour*] Yes – yes, I remember.

EVA: You remember what you said.

FERNE: [*trying to remember*] No, not exactly.

EVA: I remember every word, because, you know, I was obliged to *guess* that you were in love with me.

FERNE: Why?

EVA: Because you never told me.

FERNE: Because I was a fool – absorbed in my idiotic business, and disregardful of the good, kind, warm, gentle heart that beats for me. I remember now your sweet looks, your pious resignation, your soft voice, and thousand charms. I observed them then, though not with the rapture I recall them now.

EVA: [*entranced*] Go on – go on. I love to hear you talk in this way. It is the first time your heart has declared its feeling to me.

FERNE: [*his emotion mastering him*] I remember all. I am again walking by your side in that glorious sunshine. Again I see your pale face looking into mine – I see your black dress – I feel your thin white hand upon my arm – I hear your voice – that voice that death had so nearly silenced for ever, but which returned to earth laden with music as of another sphere. I recall all – and the sunstroke that vivified my heart as your dear head rested there a moment – and the tears dimmed your eyes in memory of your mother. Eva, I loved you then, though I did not know it. I love you now, that you can be mine – my own, my partner through life – my wife for ever.

> [*During this speech* EVA *has risen and stood by the side of* FERNE *as his speech reaches its climax; overpowered with emotion she falls unconscious on the sofa; at the same moment* ARTHUR *enters.*]

ARTHUR: [*angrily*] And I thought you were a man of honour.

FERNE: [*not seeing that* EVA *has fainted*] In what have I forfeited that title?

ARTHUR: In what? [*seeing* EVA *is unconscious*] She has fainted. [*to* FERNE] Leave this house this instant.

FERNE: Leave this house! Who brought me into it, and welcomed me,

and took me by the hand, and led me to hear her confession of
love [*his tone rising with his words*], and to make my avowal of
love to her?

ARTHUR: [*violently*] I order you to quit this house!

FERNE: [*placing his finger on his lip to indicate that* EVA *might hear them;
    scornfully*] I obey your order; but I will return – return,
    despite of you, or all the world – to take away the bride I love –
    the wife who loves me – the woman to whom you have
    betrothed me!

[*Exit* FERNE.]

ARTHUR: Curses on the time I first saw you! – and oh! my punishment
    for taking the advice that brought him to her side! Eva! – still
    unconscious!

[*Going to bell-rope, he sees* MISS MYRNIE, *who enters.*]

MISS MYRNIE: What is the matter?

ARTHUR: Wait here with Eva, while I fetch the Doctor.

MISS MYRNIE: [*crossing to sofa*] He's not in the dining-room!

ARTHUR: [*as he goes off*] I'll find him.

MISS MYRNIE: [*seating herself by* EVA's *side*] Poor child! What a state
    they've put her into!

EVA: [*recovering*] Ah! How bright my future! How happy I feel! [*seeing*
    MISS MYRNIE] Miss Myrnie, where is he? He was here just now!

MISS MYRNIE: Do you mean Mr Ferne?

EVA: Yes.

[*The sky becomes darker outside window.*]

MISS MYRNIE: He's gone!

EVA: Gone!

MISS MYRNIE: Yes; just this moment left the Abbey.

EVA: You are deceiving me, madam – deceiving me as you did before,
    when you told me that Cousin Arthur would not permit our
    union.

MISS MYRNIE: [*enraged*] I deceive you, my child! It is they who are
    deceiving you; I heard them during lunch. Mr Ferne's love for
    you is all a pretence.

EVA: What?

MISS MYRNIE: A plan – a scheme got up between them to comfort you
    because you are ill, and as soon as you are better they will
    undeceive you. My poor child, I speak the truth, I never speak
    anything but truth.

EVA: His love a pretence – a plan!

MISS MYRNIE: Yes, my poor child; they're treating you as if you were a
    baby, and I can't bear to see it; my sense of truth revolts at it;

so I was resolved to tell you of it, that you might assert your sex's dignity.

EVA: [*half convinced*] And yet but now he told me that – he – loved me.

MISS MYRNIE: He said that, my dear – out of pity for you.

EVA: [*stricken*] Pity!

MISS MYRNIE: Yes, dear; the wretches to deceive you! – but I've unmasked them, and now you know the truth – the beautiful, the sublime, the glorious, the eternal truth!

EVA: [*after a pause*] Please leave me, I wish to be alone.

MISS MYRNIE: [*rising*] Yes, dear; thank goodness, I have done my duty. [*as she goes*] To dare to insinuate that I could tell a lie. No! It's the men! Men are all liars! All! They lie to deceive us, but they have never deceived me, and they never shall! never! never! never! never!

> [*Exit* MISS MYRNIE. *The snow begins to fall outside window, at first slightly, then more thickly towards end of Act.*]

EVA: [*after a pause*] Pity! His pity! and all that he said as he sat here by my side. I remember. "If I had not loved you!" and, "If I had only loved you with the affection of a brother!" and, "If I had loved another!" [*rising from sofa*] I see it all. He does not love me, and his bright words were lies. Oh! I am accursed! cursed like my poor dead mother! Why did I come here to this house from which she was banished – where I have been deceived? [*coughs*] Oh! air! air! [*Approaches window.*] I cannot breathe! No! [*returning*] I must not. The cold will kill me! [*raising her head*] Well, why not? Life is tasteless! Let me die!

> [*Music – piano till end of Act. She opens window and steps out into balcony amid the thick falling snow. Noise of wind heard as the casement is opened.* EVA *throws off the wrappings from her neck and shoulders so that she stands exposed to the snow in her petticoat body. She coughs frequently and places her hands on her chest.* FERNE *appears on balcony, and as she faints catches her, and brings her into the room again. At the same moment* ARTHUR *and the* DOCTOR *enter.* MISS MYRNIE *stands in* L. *doorway. The* DOCTOR *rushes to window and closes it. Picture.*]

Drop, Quickly.

END OF ACT II

ACT III

SCENE I – *The same as* ACT II. *Night. Stage dark. On table, near fire, bottle and tumblers, and sugar. Small copper kettle on fire.*

[*Enter* BUNNYTHORNE, *in dressing-gown and night-cap. He carries a lighted bed-candle in his hand. He is slightly intoxicated. Clock strikes five.*]

BUNNYTHORNE: Five! and that boy isn't home yet. I've been to his room, and there's his bed as smooth as a – brickbat. Oh, that boy! When I was a boy, what a charming boy I was! – innocent, ingenuous, good-tempered, brave, handsome, sober. I've taken too much brandy! The Doctor asked me to sit up in case he might want me, as Arthur is knocked up, and Miss Myrnie is in the dumps; and so I – brought the brandy – to rouse me – just to pass the time pleasantly – and then I fell asleep; and I suppose that in my sleep I – [*growing maudlin sentimental*] Poor child! poor child! [*drinking neat brandy*] Oh, that boy! [*He puts candle on table, near sofa. The candlestick falls, and the light is extinguished. Stage dark.*] Confound it! In my time these sort of things never happened; but nowadays – [*with disgust*] – Augh! [*He feels for candle; finds it; contemplates it moodily.*] Oh, that boy! [*Places candle in stick, and then places the candlestick on table, then feeling on floor.*] Luckily the lucifers were in the – ah! [*Finds lucifers on floor. During the following speech he strikes lucifers on box. They do not ignite. Irritably*] Clever! [*throwing lucifers away*] Clever! clever! That's modern science! Only a penny a-box! But they don't light! [*throwing lucifers away*] Go it! [*fondly*] And when I remember in my time how pleasant it used to be with the dear old flint-and-steel and tinder-box, and those nice wooden matches, with the brimstone at the top – and you used to hit the steel on the flint, like a harmonious blacksmith – and after the fifteenth or sixteenth stroke the spark would fall upon the tinder, and then the flames would spread about – "parson and clerk" we called 'em, in my innocent childhood – and then the match used to light – and ah! [*sighing*] The good old days! the good old days! [*A lucifer lights.*] Ah! at last! [*He lights candle. Stage light. Crossing stage to* L. *door*] I wonder where the Doctor is? I'll go and see. [*As he reaches* L. *door, enter* BOB. *The draught from the door extinguishes the light. Stage dark again.*] Oh, those boys! [*angrily*] Why did you open the door when you came in?

BOB: How could I come in without opening it?

[BOB's *boots and clothes give evidence that he has been*

walking in the snow. He is shivering with cold. He is partially intoxicated. To just the same extent as BUNNYTHORNE. *His greatcoat and general appearance should resemble* BUNNYTHORNE's *in his dressing-gown.*]

BUNNYTHORNE: What d'ye mean by coming in at this time of night? – I mean morning!

BOB: I've been sitting up at the "Arms."

BUNNYTHORNE: [*with disgust*] The "Arms"! – a tavern? When I was a young man there were no taverns, and those there were closed early.

BOB: We were talking litera-too.

BUNNYTHORNE: Talking what?

BOB: [*with an effort*] Litera-*ture*.

BUNNYTHORNE: [*aside*] The boy's drunk – drunk as a fidd-l-l-l-er!

BOB: [*aside*] The guv'nor's tight – tight as a drum.

> [*Both assume an air of excessive sobriety and dignity.* BUNNYTHORNE *goes to sofa near fire.* BOB *follows him. As they cross, their resemblance to each other must be carried out by the actors' gestures and manners being arranged so as to be identical. Whatever action is used by* BUNNYTHORNE *is also used inadvertently and unconsciously by* BOB.]

BUNNYTHORNE: Why did you not go up to your room?

BOB: I wanted to inquire after poor Cousin Eva! How is she?

BUNNYTHORNE: I don't know – no better – just the same.

BOB: [*spouting*]

> "She was doomed ere we were wedded, and I never saw her more.
> Flame the lightnings, bray the thunders, bid the smoky torrents pour!
> Bid the smoky torrents pour——"

Oh! smoky torrents – fine image, isn't it?

BUNNYTHORNE: [*not heeding him*] Nothing to what it used to be in my time.

BOB: Eh?

BUNNYTHORNE: What's fine?

BOB: My poetry – my "Thoughts in a Crater"!

BUNNYTHORNE: Thoughts in a coal-hole! I hate poetry – I consider it ungentlemanlike. There never used to be any poetry in my time.

BOB: [*spouting*] "Flame the lightnings——"

BUNNYTHORNE: Flame the devil! Where are the lucifers? On the table somewhere – find 'em. [*He finds them as he is speaking, and hands them to* BOB.] Here's the box – take it, can't you?

> [*As* BUNNYTHORNE *holds box,* BOB *takes brandy bottle, helps himself, and drinks.*]

BUNNYTHORNE: Got it?

BOB: [*drinking*] Yes, I've got it.

BUNNYTHORNE: You haven't – ah! [*Lights lucifer.* BOB *puts down glass.*] Hold the candle steady.

> [*As* BOB *holds candle unsteadily,* BUNNYTHORNE *lights it also unsteadily. Stage light. They sit down again.*]

BOB: [*after looking at* BUNNYTHORNE, *aside*] Tight! He's tight.

BUNNYTHORNE: [*aside*] I'm sorry I didn't keep it dark.

> [*During the scene, at intervals, they both endeavour to take the bottle at the same time, so that their hands meet; they withdraw them immediately.*]

BOB: Do you know, governor, I'm getting tired of this sort of life?

BUNNYTHORNE: I should think so.

BOB: I feel I'm wasting my abilities, and the best years of my life in – in——

BUNNYTHORNE: In getting drunk at the "Mompesson Arms."

BOB: No, governor, *I* am not drunk; but I know who is!

BUNNYTHORNE: [*indignant*] Who is?

BOB: Never mind.

BUNNYTHORNE: Who do you mean, sir?

BOB: [*evading the question*] Never mind – Jack Topham.

BUNNYTHORNE: [*sneering*] Jack Topham – a pretty friend.

BOB: Oh! he's no friend of mine now – we've had a row.

BUNNYTHORNE: Bravo! What about?

BOB: About Miss Brill, the barmaid; I think Jack's going to marry her. However, he cut up rough about her, and we had a row. [*taking bottle.* BUNNYTHORNE *stops him.*]

BUNNYTHORNE: No; you've had enough already. Talking of Miss Brill, Bob, I used to be afraid that you were sweet upon her.

BOB: Me! no, governor. My mind is fixed upon Cousin Eva. [*Stage gets gradually lighter at window.*] And if it were not for this engineer——

BUNNYTHORNE: Those beastly railways! [*amiably*] Bob, my boy, I'd give the world to see you grow steady, and settle with your cousin Eva.

BOB: [*affectionately*] Yes – guv – I should like to settle down. I've been stirred up enough already.

> "For 'tis weary, weary, wasting mind and body
>   at the oar,
>   Rest thee——"

BUNNYTHORNE: Yes – Yes – Bob. I like you in your good humours.

BOB: Married to Eva. She'll have money.

BUNNYTHORNE: Yes, yes. [*aside*] He is a good affectionate boy with all his faults.

BOB: And you'd allow me something if I was married.

BUNNYTHORNE: Of course I would, Bob.

BOB: And with that capital I could go to London, and – start a new monthly magazine.

BUNNYTHORNE: [*horrified*] What!

BOB: There is a great want of new monthly magazines in London, and I could publish my own poetry in it, and——

BUNNYTHORNE: [*in a passion*] You idiot – do you want to ruin me? [*rising*] You're no son of mine! I disown you. Ah! Get out!

BOB: There you go, you never will listen to reason.

[*Enter* DOCTOR.]

BUNNYTHORNE: Not a shilling do you ever get——

DOCTOR: [*interrupting*] Hallo! Hallo! Will you never learn to keep quiet near an invalid? Has she stirred?

BUNNYTHORNE: No.

DOCTOR: [*seeing* BOB] What! Not dead yet?

BOB: Doctor!

DOCTOR: As I was looking from the window I saw your friend, Mr Topham, and three other blackguards outside, so I went down to ask Topham what he wanted there, and he asked me to deliver this to you. [*Gives* BOB *letter.*] There it is. Topham, I believe, is waiting for an answer.

[*Exit* DOCTOR, *cautiously.*]

BOB: [*Rises and reads letter by light of candle.*] "Robert Bunnythorne, Esq. Dear sir, – Understanding from a lady" (Oh! that's Miss Brill!) "that you have spoken of me disrespectfully, I demand the satisfaction due from one gentleman to another – some mutual friends are with me who will see that all is conducted fairly – I am waiting outside for you, to punch your damned head; so come down quickly, or I'll fetch you in two two's. Dear sir, ever yours sincerely, – JOHN TOPHAM."

BUNNYTHORNE: [*rising*] Eh! a fight with Topham! he's too much for you.

BOB: [*buttoning up his coat, and taking up his hat determinedly*] The infernal impudence! I'll thrash him till I can't stand over him.

[*He goes off briskly.*]

BUNNYTHORNE: [*agitated*] Bob! Bob! my boy, I forbid you to fight with him. He's two stun too heavy for you. Bless the boy! Just like his father. [*proudly*] My boy! my boy! Me all over! Every inch of him. Bob! [*calling*] I forbid it! I'll come and back you.

> [*Exit* BUNNYTHORNE *hastily. Stage lighter at window.*
> *Enter the* DOCTOR.]

DOCTOR: Phew! There's no use in prescribing anything – but the Engineer. He's got my note by this time, and will be here soon. It's the only hope. Then there's Arthur. He's as hot-headed as a boy, and as obstinate as an old man. All the inconveniences of youth without its pliability, and the hardness of age without its obedience to the law of compromise. Here he is!

> [*Enter* ARTHUR.]

ARTHUR: Well – what news?

DOCTOR: She sleeps – for the present.

ARTHUR: Tell me, candidly – candidly – will she recover?

DOCTOR: I don't know. [ARTHUR *sinks in chair. aside.*] Now for it. [*aloud*] I have no faith in my treatment – nor in anybody else's.

ARTHUR: Is there no hope?

DOCTOR: Yes, one.

ARTHUR: [*rising*] What is it?

DOCTOR: Ferne.

ARTHUR: Ferne!

DOCTOR: Don't fly at the mention of his name.

ARTHUR: He has killed her.

DOCTOR: No; 'tis you who will kill her by sending him away.

ARTHUR: Me?

DOCTOR: Yes. He, a plebeian, has dared to fall in love with the niece of a Mompesson. Off with his head – eh? Let the poor devil die of despair; but no Mompesson must make a *mesalliance*, particularly with a rival——

ARTHUR: A rival?

DOCTOR: Yes; a rival. I repeat it – rival. If you haven't yet confessed it to yourself, learn it from me; you've dreamt of making this dear cousin your wife – of refurnishing the Abbey, of the comforts, the joys of domesticity.

ARTHUR: [*indignant*] Doctor!

DOCTOR: Ah! I've found the wound, then. Confess you are jealous!

ARTHUR: [*loudly*] No!

DOCTOR: Ah! ah! On your honour – on your honour?

ARTHUR: Oh! you're the devil!

DOCTOR: I wish I was! For if I were, I'd bribe you to do what's right, by giving you the youth [*with intention*], the appearance, and the attractions you possessed thirty years ago.

ARTHUR: But let us seek other advice – the London doctor who attended her during her last illness.

DOCTOR: [*his hands in his pockets*] I'd give the world to consult with him.

ARTHUR: I'll write to him.

DOCTOR: Your letter will not reach London until to-morrow evening.

ARTHUR: I'll send – I'll go myself!

DOCTOR: There's no railway nearer than Stapleton, and that's eight hours from here.

ARTHUR: We'll telegraph!

DOCTOR: No telegraph nearer than Stapleton.

ARTHUR: No rail! – no telegraph! – no anything in this damned hole! We're in a desert, and miles away there are contrivances that annihilate time and space. [*stopping with sudden conviction*] And it was I who crushed the project that would have brought communication with the world up to this very spot. [*bitterly*] Congratulate me on my victory! I have saved the Abbey, and I have killed Eva!

DOCTOR: [*aside*] At last! [*aloud*] You see, then, this young man's calling has its noble, as well as its common tradesman side. Science commands time and space. King Canute couldn't command the tide, but the engineer can build a breakwater that compels the roaring ocean to keep within its proper bounds!

ARTHUR: But of what use is all this?

DOCTOR: Of every use. Ferne is not, I will say, a man of good family. Well, he'll found a family, for he is a young and already distinguished man. He has that natural patent that is the commencement of distinction and nobility.

ARTHUR: And what may that be?

DOCTOR: Brains – that coronet worn inside the skull, that no revolution can deprive him of.

ARTHUR: But do I understand that you wish me to——

DOCTOR: To give her up to this young man? Yes, I do.

ARTHUR: [*after a pause*] You are asking me to make a sacrifice – to exhibit a heroism which——

DOCTOR: Of course I'm asking a heroism – a self-sacrifice. What else should I ask of you? Now take it from your own point of view, not mine. I'm a Republican – a Radical – in modern slang, a Red. I want to see some of this real nobility I hear you talk of. I want to see it, out of a picture, or a genealogical chart. I want to see it framed in flesh and blood. In this sad business I don't ask you to act like a common man; I don't ask you to act like a gentleman – that's easy to you – you can't help it. I ask you to act like a Mompesson! Do you remember some time ago, in the year fourteen hundred and something, how your ancestor Raoul de Mompesson took service in Germany, and when the

Archduchess Something-or-other-stein, with whom Raoul
was in love, was pursued with her husband and children, by
her enemies, your ancestor put on the Archduke's armour and
alone met the foemen, who mistook him for his rival, and he
fell pierced by their swords, and while he held the hilts of their
blades to him the woman he loved gained the castle in safety;
and, don't you remember, how she and the children he had
saved offered up prayers for the chivalric lover, who had died
so true a knight, a gentleman, and soldier? Well, then, Raoul
de – I mean Arthur de Mompesson, remember your race, your
blood, your antecedents. Cast all small selfishness aside,
receive this young man. Give up Eva! Save her life! Honour
commands! Humanity insists. *Noblesse oblige!*

ARTHUR: [*after a pause, rising*] You are right. Send for Mr Ferne. I'll
do it.

DOCTOR: You will?

ARTHUR: [*extending his hand*] Upon my honour.

DOCTOR: [*shaking hand*] Mompesson, all over. Raoul redivivus! [*and
chuckling at his success*] There's always some good in a
gentleman, even when he's a nobleman! [*Knock at door, aloud*]
Doubtless, that's him.

ARTHUR: Ferne? [DOCTOR *nods.*] Already? [*mastering himself*] Come in!

[FERNE *opens door and appears on threshold. He does
not advance into room.*]

FERNE: [*after a pause*] Pardon me. I received a note from Doctor
Brown, which——

ARTHUR: [*offering his hand*] Mr Ferne, I have to ask your pardon for
what I said yesterday. I was wrong, violent, unjust. I trust that
you will accept my apology.

FERNE: [*hardly comprehending*] Mr Mompesson, I——

ARTHUR: We must talk seriously. Will you sit down?

DOCTOR: [*aside to* ARTHUR] Bravo!

FERNE: My position here is so peculiar. But I hardly know how I
should act.

ARTHUR: There is, I admit, a difficulty; but no difficulty that cannot
be overcome.

[*During* ARTHUR's *last lines* EVA *enters.*]

EVA: [*at door*] There need be no difficulty; or if there be, it is one in
which I am concerned and have a right to speak.

ARTHUR: [*advancing to her*] Eva!

DOCTOR: Hush! Leave them alone.

[ARTHUR *and* DOCTOR *retire to window.* EVA *advances
to sofa.* FERNE *approaches her.*]

EVA: Mr Ferne, let me be candid. Yesterday you told me that you loved me.

FERNE: And I spoke the truth.

EVA: No. You saw me ill – as you thought dying – and you spoke from pity. I cannot accept your love as alms.

FERNE: Alms!

EVA: I should have been proud of your affection, I must decline your compassion.

ARTHUR: [aside] She rejects him. [with pride] She is a Mompesson.

DOCTOR: [aside, at back] Wait a bit. All the Mompessons on the female side were women, and women are fondest of their sweethearts when they quarrel with them. "It is their nature to."

EVA: You and my cousin, and the Doctor, and the rest of my kind friends, have treated me as if I were a child, and——

FERNE: Eva, will you hear the truth – the honest truth – the truth that a man should tell to the woman he loves – the woman he hopes to share his life with? I came here absorbed with the small cares of the outer world – unthinking of you. I saw you – and the love that I had never dreamt of – leaped up at my heart. I remembered the old days in London, when I saw you as I see you now, pale – weak – beautiful – and a new feeling came over me. The love I feel for you throngs my veins, and I speak as I think when alone, and you are not near to dazzle me, and make me forget all but the sweet intoxication of your presence. Eva, I have the consent of your cousin, I dare to believe I have the consent of your own heart; you love me – your own sweet lips have avowed it. I love you wholly, solely, and truly. Do you believe me?

ARTHUR: [advancing] Yes, I believe him, and you may.

EVA: Are you sure you speak the truth?

FERNE: Let your heart answer for mine. My lips are silent.

EVA: [after a pause, giving him her hand] Yes, I believe you!

ARTHUR: It's all over, Doctor. It's all over. What shall I do?

DOCTOR: [advancing] Do! Congratulate them!

EVA: But Miss Myrnie told me——

[MISS MYRNIE appears.]

DOCTOR: Miss Myrnie is a deceitful old – but no – why should I libel a harmless, necessary cat, by comparing it to a spiteful unnecessary old woman? Miss Myrnie——

MISS MYRNIE: [advancing] Miss Myrnie has heard every word, and Miss Myrnie does not think it necessary to defend either what she said to Miss Summers yesterday, or what she has said to Lord Mompesson this morning. Miss Myrnie has done her duty to her own conscience, to her religion, and to her family.

[*speaking at door*] Your lordship will find every word that I
have told you to be true.

DOCTOR: ⎫ Lord Mompesson!
ARTHUR: ⎬ My father!
DOCTOR: ⎭ The old devil.

[*Enter* LORD MOMPESSON.]

ARTHUR: [*speaking to* DOCTOR *as* LORD MOMPESSON *enters, and takes a
chair*] He will never consent. I know his prejudices. Now all is
over!

LORD M: Arthur – Eva – Miss Myrnie has been telling me of
something that has been kept a secret from me.

ARTHUR: Only since yesterday.

MISS MYRNIE: I have told his lordship everything.

DOCTOR: [*aside*] And a little over. The truth made piquant with Miss
Myrnie's sauce.

LORD M: Eva, my grandniece, is it true that you have received the
attentions of a young gentleman?

EVA: Of Mr Ferne, – quite true. [*rising*] Mr Ferne, let me present you
to my grand-uncle, Lord Mompesson.

[*They bow, &c.*]

DOCTOR: [*aside*] Bravo!

LORD M: And, Doctor, is it true that in order not to contradict Eva's
whims or wishes while she was so critically ill, that you and
Arthur told her that Mr Ferne might visit the Abbey as her
accepted suitor?

ARTHUR: ⎫ Quite true.
DOCTOR: ⎭

MISS MYRNIE: As I told your lordship, they trumped up a story——

LORD M: [*interrupting*] One moment, dear Miss Myrnie. Mr Ferne,
you told me, was not exactly a – a man of family.

MISS MYRNIE: No family whatever! No blood, that is, no real blood.
His veins are plebeian as potato peelings. He is connected with
the railroads. I believe he is a railway guard, and his grandfather was a labourer on your lordship's estate.

FERNE: Permit me to correct you. I am an engineer. My grandfather
held the Branxley Farm, close to Woodside.

MISS MYRNIE: A mere question of detail.

LORD M: Aye! – aye! – aye! Ferne. I remember.

FERNE: If I may be allowed to offer a remark, I would suggest that I
was asked here, and that I offer marriage to your niece, Lord
Mompesson; that I do so from myself, and with no doubt of
my own worthiness. I court inquiry as to my character and
circumstances.

MISS MYRNIE: Such impudence!

LORD M: Is my niece attached to you?

EVA: Let me answer that! I am!

MISS MYRNIE: [*scandalised*] Well, if ever!

DOCTOR: It's so many years since she felt anything of the sort she has forgotten all about it!

ARTHUR: [*to* DOCTOR] My father will never consent. We're done, Doctor, we're done!

LORD M: Have you any relations, Mr Ferne?

FERNE: None! I am alone in the world!

DOCTOR: Oh! he's much too good a fellow to have relations!

LORD M: [*rising and going to* ARTHUR] Arthur, what is your opinion?

ARTHUR: [*the* DOCTOR's *eyes fixed upon him*] They are worthy of each other.

LORD M: And you would have me consent?

ARTHUR: Yes!

LORD M: Mr Ferne, Miss Myrnie has done us all a great service in facilitating our meeting, and understanding each other on this very serious subject. I must inquire into many details. We need not enter upon that now. In the meantime, and until we know more of you – which I make a condition – visit the Abbey in the capacity of my dear grandniece's suitor. I am an old man. I shall not be here much longer. I would not see her mother after her marriage [*mournfully*], and I never set eyes on her again. Let me make those about me as happy as I can. [EVA *takes* LORD MOMPESSON's *hand.*] Dear Miss Myrnie here, I am sure, will be pleased that her kind intervention has had so happy a result. [MISS MYRNIE *astonished.*]

DOCTOR: Dear Miss Myrnie, I congratulate you.

FERNE: [*crossing to her*] How can I find words to thank you?

EVA: [*to* MISS MYRNIE] And I was foolish enough to think that you were not my friend. Thanks!

FERNE: Thanks!

LORD M: Thanks!

DOCTOR: Thanks!

MISS MYRNIE: [*speechless with rage, masters herself*] Don't mention it – you're quite welcome. I – I will retire to my room.

DOCTOR: Do – do! and don't come out again!

> [DOCTOR *opens door. Enter* BUNNYTHORNE *in coat and hat, followed by* BOB. BOB *has a green shade over both eyes.*]

MISS MYRNIE: Good gracious!

DOCTOR: What's all this?

BUNNYTHORNE: [*leading* BOB *to chair*] Bob's been having a tooth out.

Topham on the eyes – but he licked him – I saw the fight – Bob licked him. [*with pride*] The very image of me when I was his age. When Eva gets better he's the husband for her.

BOB: [*spouting*]

"In the rapture of the battle, when whirls wild
    the foeman's glaive.
Shall thy image aye be present to the bosom of
    the brave."

MISS MYRNIE: [*coming down to* BUNNYTHORNE] Miss Eva is engaged to Mr Ferne by my lord's consent.

BOB: What?

BUNNYTHORNE: Bob!

BOB: Never mind, guv'nor; the brave heart accepts its doom. You can make me the allowance all the same. [*reseating himself moonily*]

"Though I loved her, yet she left me – it is
    years and years ago,
Once my eyes were dimmed with weeping,
    now my locks are white as snow."

[*to* DOCTOR] I should like to know why——

DOCTOR: Not now – some other time.

LORD M: [*as if concluding a conversation*] Yes – yes – yes. And if all turns out satisfactory, of which I have no doubt——

ARTHUR: I will give the bride away.

MISS MYRNIE: [*sneering*] With all your differences of opinion you seem quite agreed on one point, that Miss Eva must be married.

DOCTOR: Yes, we're all agreed on that. [*pointing to* ARTHUR] Aristocrat.

ARTHUR: [*smiling and pointing to* DOCTOR] Red Republican.

DOCTOR: [*pointing to* BUNNYTHORNE] Man of business.

BUNNYTHORNE: [*leaning over* BOB] And warrior!

DOCTOR: Lords!

BUNNYTHORNE: [*pointing to himself*] Commons!

DOCTOR: [*pointing to himself*] The people!

BUNNYTHORNE: [*pointing to* BOB] And the army.

DOCTOR: Very good! Let's try again! [*to* ARTHUR] High! [*pointing to himself*] Low! [*indicating* BUNNYTHORNE] Jack!

BUNNYTHORNE: [*pointing to* BOB's *black eye, and slapping him on the shoulder*] And game!

DOCTOR: Come, my patient, no more excitement to-day, or it will be too much for you. Let me take you to your room.

[*He crosses to her. Music, piano, during* EVA's *speech.*]

EVA: A few more minutes to thank you so much for all your goodness to me. I shall get better; I feel I shall! When the snow melts from the grass, I shall be stronger; and when the summer covers those black branches with green leaves I shall be able to walk down the avenue.

FERNE: With me by your side?

LORD M: You, on one side – me on the other. Left to yourself your pace would be too fast, and mine would be too slow. You have youth, strength, and speed; I have age, judgment, and experience. Let Eva walk between us.

EVA: [*as they are going round door*] My path must lead to happiness when love and hope conduct me, and affection and experience guide me – [*smiling*] – That's Progress! [*movement of all the characters. Music ceases*]

BUNNYTHORNE: Now, in my time, we should have all stood in a pleasant half-circle round the stage, and thanked our friends, the public, for their kind applause; but nothing is as it should be nowadays, everything is going to the——

CURTAIN QUICKLY

NOTE. – The last speech of Bunnythorne's was written for the late J. B. Buckstone, for whom the part was originally intended, but is never spoken.

SCHOOL

Produced for the first time on 16th January, 1869, at the Prince of Wales's Royal Theatre, London, under the management of Miss Marie Wilton.

CAST OF CHARACTERS

Lord Beaufoy	Mr H. J. Montague
Dr Sutcliffe	Mr Addison
Beau Farintosh	Mr Hare
Jack Poyntz	Mr Bancroft
Mr Krux	Mr F. Glover
Vaughan	Mr Hill
Mrs Sutcliffe	Mrs B. White
Bella	Miss Carlotta Addison
Naomi Tighe	Miss Marie Wilton
Tilly	Miss Augusta Wilton
Milly	Miss George
Laura	Miss Phillips
Clara	Miss Unah
Kitty	Miss Hutton
Hetty	Miss Atkins
Little Girl	
Footmen, keepers, servants	

Scene – In and near Cedar Grove House. Time – The Present.

ACT I – THE GLADE. – *A Glade in a Forest.* – RECREATION.

ACT II – THE HOUSE. – *A School-room.* – EXAMINATION.

ACT III – THE GROUNDS. – *A School-yard.* – FLIRTATION.

ACT IV – THE GROUNDS. – *Same as* ACT III – REALISATION.

Modern Costumes. Time of Representation, two-hours and three-quarters.

Between the first and second Acts eight days are supposed to elapse.

Between the second and third, two hours.

Between the third and fourth, six weeks.

[For the outline of the Plot of this Comedy the Author is indebted to a German Play by Mr Roderich Benedix, called "Aschenbrödel."]

SCHOOL

ACT I

Music from "La Cenerentola" before the Curtain rises.

SCENE I – *A Glade. All the* GIRLS *discovered in various positions.* BELLA *standing. The* GIRLS *have wild flowers, ivy, &c., in their laps.* NAOMI TIGHE *has a long string of wild flowers in her lap, which she is engaged in weaving together.* BELLA *has a small branch, which she uses as a wand.*

BELLA: And her two haughty sisters stepped into a beautiful carriage and drove towards the palace, and when they were out of sight, Cinderella sat down in a corner and began to cry. Her godmother asked her what ailed her. "I wish – I wish –," said Cinderella, but she sobbed so she couldn't say another word. The godmother said, "You wish to go to the ball." Now this godmother was a fairy.

NAOMI: I wish my godmother had been a fairy.

GIRLS: Hush! silence!

NAOMI: Girls without fathers or mothers ought to have fairies for godmothers, to make up for the loss.

BELLA: "Be a good girl," said the fairy godmother, "and you shall go." "But," said poor Cinderella, "I can't go, for I've no things fit to go in."

GIRLS: [*with deep sympathy*] Poor girl!

NAOMI: If I hadn't nice dresses I should die.

GIRLS: Hush!

BELLA: "Run into the garden," said the fairy godmother, "and bring me a pumpkin." Cinderella brought a pumpkin, and her godmother scooped out the inside.

HETTY: [*eagerly*] Was it nice?

BELLA: The godmother scooped out the inside, leaving nothing but ˌthe rind. She then touched it with her wand, and the pumpkin instantly turned into a fine coach, gilded all over with gold.

NAOMI: Bravo, pumpkin.

GIRLS: Hush! Go on, Bella.

BELLA: Then Cinderella looked into the mousetrap, where she found six mice all alive and kicking.

NAOMI: [*with a shudder*] I hate mice.

[*All shudder slightly.*]

LAURA: [*waking up*] Whenever I think of mice they make me feel quite
— sleepy.

[*She goes to sleep.*]

BELLA: Cinderella lifted the door of the trap very gently and the fairy
godmother touched the mice, and they turned into beautiful
horses of a fine dapple-grey mouse-colour.

GIRLS: Oh!

BELLA: Then the fairy turned two rats into postillions.

GIRLS: Oh!

BELLA: And six lizards into six footmen.

GIRLS: Six! my!

BELLA: "There," said the godmother, "there is an equipage." "Yes,"
said Cinderella, crying, and pointing to her nasty ugly grey
dress, "but I cannot go in these filthy rags." Then the
godmother touched her with her wand, and her rags instantly
became the most magnificent ball-dress that ever was seen.

GIRLS: Oh!

BELLA: Covered with the most costly jewels.

GIRLS: Oh!

NAOMI: I should like to be godmothered in that way.

BELLA: To these were added a beautiful pair of glass slippers. Then
Cinderella, seated in her beautiful coach, drove off to the
palace.

NAOMI: Gee up, gee oh!

[*She sings "Post Horn Galop".*]

BELLA: As soon as she arrived, the King's son——

GIRLS: The King's son?

BELLA: A most beautiful young man——

KITTY: This is interesting.

BELLA: Presented himself at the door of her carriage, and helped her
to alight.

HETTY: I should like to be helped twice to King's son.

GIRLS: Silence!

BELLA: The Prince then conducted her to the place of honour, and
soon after took her out to dance with him.

GIRLS: Oh!

CLARA: Think of that – a Prince.

NAOMI: Hetty would like to eat a Prince; wouldn't you?

TILLY: So should I.

CLARA: So should we all.

BELLA: The Prince fell in love with her.

GIRLS: Oh!

TILLY: Why shouldn't he? I suppose princes fall in love the same as
common people.

KITTY: But they don't do it in the same way.

NAOMI: [*repeating*] Go on, Bella. The Prince fell in love——

CLARA: What is love?

MILLY: You silly thing!

TILLY: Such ignorance!

KITTY: That stupid Clara!

CLARA: I don't believe any of you know, not even you big girls.

TILLY: Everybody knows what love is!

CLARA: Then what is it?

NAOMI: Who's got a dictionary? – you're sure to find it there.

TILLY: My eldest sister says it's the only place in which you can find it.

KITTY: Then she's been jilted!

MILLY: My pa says love is moonshine.

NAOMI: Then how sweet and mellow it must be!

MILLY: Particularly when the moon is at the full!

NAOMI: And there is no eclipse!

TILLY: It seems that nobody knows what love is.

KITTY: I despise such ignorance!

CLARA: Then why don't they teach it us? We've a music-master to teach music, why not a love-master to teach love?

NAOMI: You don't suppose love is to be taught like geography or the use of the globes, do you? No, love is an extra.

TILLY: Perhaps it comes naturally. Ask Laura what love is.

CLARA: [*rousing* LAURA, *who is asleep*] Laura, what is love?

LAURA: [*waking suddenly*] J'aime, I love; tu aimes, we lovest; il aime, they love; nous aimons——

[*All laugh.*]

BELLA: Hush, here's governess.

[*Enter* MRS SUTCLIFFE. *All rise, curtsey to* MRS SUTCLIFFE, *and surround her, except* LAURA.]

MRS S: Well, young ladies, what is the cause of your merriment? What is the subject under discussion?

NAOMI: Governess, we wish you to tell us something.

MRS S: What is it, dear?

GIRLS: What is love?

LITTLE GIRL: Yes, what is love?

MRS S: [*dumbfounded*] What is love? I – I – here is the Doctor!

[*Enter* DR SUTCLIFFE. GIRLS *curtsey to the* DOCTOR. MRS SUTCLIFFE *a woman of sixty; the* DOCTOR *a man over sixty-five years of age – scholastic, genial, and a cross of the clergyman in his manner.*]

MRS S: Doctor, I have just had a most extraordinary question proposed to me.

DR S: Indeed, dear!

MRS S: Yes, Doctor – What is love?

NAOMI *and* GIRLS: Yes, Doctor – What is love?

LITTLE GIRL: Yes, Doctor – What is love?

DR S: [*for a moment puzzled*] What is love? The cuneiform inscriptions on the Babylonian marbles have only been recently deciphered, so I will answer according to the comparatively modern notions of the Greeks. By them love was called Eros, but there were three separate Erotes. There was the Eros of the ancient cosmogonies. Hesiod, the earliest author who mentions him, calls him the cosmogonic Eros. In Plato's "Symposium," he is described as the eldest of the gods. Then there was the Eros of the philosophers, and, lastly, the Eros of the later degenerate Greek poets, who said, erroneously, that he was the youngest of the gods. The parentage of Eros or Cupid is doubtful. It is generally assumed that he was the son of Zeus, that is Jupiter, and of Aphrodite, that is Venus—— [MRS SUTCLIFFE *coughs.*] – so that he was both the son and grandson of – [MRS SUTCLIFFE *coughs, and arranges her dress. The* DOCTOR *takes the hint.*] That is love! I mention these facts because I am about to say no more upon the subject.

NAOMI: I know what love is.

MRS S: [*aside*] Goodness forbid!

DR S: How forward the child is!

NAOMI: [*fondling* BELLA] I love Bella – and Bella loves me; don't you, Bella?

[BELLA *afraid and constrained before* MRS SUTCLIFFE.]

DR S: [*taking* BELLA's *hand*] We all love Bella. It is impossible to know her without loving her. Goodness and amiability must command affection and esteem.

NAOMI: He talks just like a copy-book, don't he?

DR S: And I suppose, Bella, my child – [MRS SUTCLIFFE *coughs and arranges her dress*] – that you are going to aid the young ladies in their botanical researches?

MRS S: Yes; young ladies, if you have sufficiently reposed yourselves from your walk across the meadow, you can resume your self-imposed labours.

[*All the* GIRLS *go off, singing.* BELLA *standing on platform until all are off except* NAOMI, *who crosses behind* MRS SUTCLIFFE *to* LAURA *and wakes her – they follow the others.*]

GIRLS: "Through the wood, through the wood, follow and find me,
Search every hollow, and dingle, and dell,

I leave not the print of a footstep behind me,
So they who would search for must look for me well."

[*Singing dies away in the distance.*]

MRS S: It is an extraordinary thing, Doctor, that, despite all my
remonstrances, you will constantly show your too obvious
preference for that girl Bella. It has a most injurious effect
upon the other pupils.

DR S: My dear, she is an orphan, without friends or protectors,
dependent entirely on us; that sad social anomaly, a pupil-
teacher, less self-reliant than a servant, and only half a lady.
Then, poor Bella is so pretty, and so young.

MRS S: Ah! – [*Sits on branch of tree, under large tree.* DOCTOR *sits on her
R.*] – there it is – so young. [*nearly weeping*] Cruel Theodore, to
remind me of my lost youth.

DR S: Amanthis, my love, that was far from my intention. You are too
sensitive.

MRS S: Your thoughts are ever fixed on the fleeting and unsubstantial
charms of youth and beauty.

DR S: No, no, no, no!

MRS S: Yes, yes, yes, yes! Do you not remember five-and-thirty years
ago?

DR S: Amanthis! to recall that error of my youth.

MRS S: It is always present to my mind.

DR S: My love, I only danced with her three times, and it is five-and-
thirty years ago.

MRS S: I remember! We had scarcely been married seven years.

DR S: Since then you have been constantly reproaching me.

MRS S: It seems but as yesterday.

DR S: It seems to me much longer.

MRS S: Ah, Theodore, unfeeling.

DR S: No, no, Amanthis. I did not mean that. I meant that thirty-five
years' conjugal serenity ought to compensate for dancing with
a young lady three times at a ball; where, from the fault of
hosts too hospitable, the negus had been made too strong.
Come, Amanthis, don't be hard on Theodore. Think what
Jason says: "Credula res amor est."

MRS S: Utinam temereria dicar. Criminibus falsis insimula visse.

[*Enter* KRUX. *He is reading a book.*]

DR S: [*correcting her*] Insimulasse virum. The contraction for the
pentameter. [*They join hands.* KRUX *comes down.* DOCTOR *rises.*]
Ah! Mr Krux! Enjoying this beautiful day?

KRUX: No, sir; I was enjoying this beautiful book.

MRS S: [*rises*] What is it?

KRUX: "Hervey's Meditations among the Tombs."

DR S: Rather a serious work.

KRUX: Not to my taste, sir. This splendid sky, the plashing brook, the verdant meadow, these rustling trees and sweetly singing birds – all turn my thoughts unto the grave.

MRS S: Good gracious!

DR S: [*indignant*] It turns my thoughts to nothing of the sort. On the contrary, it sends them back to years when——

MRS S: [*aside to him*] Not thirty-five years, Theodore.

DR S: No, Amanthis, not thirty-five; to thirty-four or thirty-six, but not to thirty-five. Come, let us join the pupils. [*taking her arm*] For the present, Mr Krux. [*bows; aside*] Prig! I can't bear prigs, particularly young prigs.

[*Exeunt* DOCTOR *and* MRS SUTCLIFFE.]

KRUX: Upstarts! I hate those people. But then, I hate most people; I think I hate most things – [*crushing beetle with his foot*] – except Bella, and when I look at her, I feel that I could bite her. Here she is. [*Enter* BELLA. *She crosses, reading a book.*] Bella, where are you going?

BELLA: Mrs Sutcliffe has sent me to fetch her goloshes.

KRUX: Stay one moment. Sit down.

[*Seating himself left of* BELLA, *on large branch, under tree.*]

BELLA: Mrs Sutcliffe told me I was not to loiter.

KRUX: What are you reading?

BELLA: A fairy tale. What are you reading?

KRUX: "Hervey's Meditations." A different sort of literature. Do sit down.

[BELLA *sits on branch of tree.*]

BELLA: [*reading*] "The King's son, the handsome young Prince, was continually by her side, and said to her the most obliging things imaginable."

KRUX: What a beastly world this is, Bella, isn't it? Attend to me for a short time. I want to speak to you particularly.

BELLA: Be quick, then.

KRUX: Mr and Mrs Sutcliffe are getting very old.

BELLA: They are not *getting* old; they *are* old.

KRUX: And, therefore, must soon die.

BELLA: [*shocked*] Oh, Mr Krux, what a dreadful notion.

KRUX: We are all worms; particularly Doctor and Mrs Sutcliffe. All men must die some time, the Doctor and Mrs Sutcliffe included.

BELLA: Mrs Sutcliffe isn't a man.

KRUX: She ought to have been. But as I was saying, Bella, when they are dead and buried——

BELLA: Mr Krux!

KRUX: They will be no longer able to keep on the school, will they? Then who is to keep on the school, eh?

BELLA: I don't know; I don't like to think of such things.

KRUX: I do. I repeat, who is to keep on the school? I am the only resident master; I am known to all the pupils.

BELLA: Alas, yes!

KRUX: I am known and, I hope, loved.

BELLA: No; feared.

KRUX: It's the same thing in a school. Bella, you're a very good scholar.

BELLA: No, I'm not.

KRUX: Yes, you are; and you understand all about the kitchen – pies, and coals, and vegetables, and the like. You're an orphan.

BELLA: [*sighing*] Yes.

KRUX: So am I. You have no relations?

BELLA: No.

KRUX: Nor friends?

BELLA: Oh, yes; Mr and Mrs Sutcliffe, and the school, and the people in the village.

KRUX: I don't count them. I have no friends.

BELLA: No, not one?

KRUX: When the Sutcliffes [BELLA *looks at him*] go – why shouldn't we keep on the school?

BELLA: [*astonished*] We?

KRUX: Yes, you and I; we are quite capable; I am clever, so are you; we could enlarge the connection. You could manage the girls, I could manage the boys. Think how pleasant to make money – take in pupils, teach them and correct them. I should like to correct them, particularly the boys. We should get on, Bella, if we got married——

BELLA: Got married! – who got married?

KRUX: You to me – me to you! Mr and Mrs Krux, of Cedar Grove House. I love you, Bella.

BELLA: [*Rises suddenly, drops her book, and hides her face in her hands.*] Oh, don't; on such a nice day as this.

KRUX: Eh?

BELLA: Poor dear Mr and Mrs Sutcliffe, to think of their dying, it makes me cry – [*crying*] – so kind as they've been to me.

KRUX: She's a fool – [*rises*] – Bella.

BELLA: Go away, you bad man, do – to think of death and marriage, and such dreadful things.

KRUX: You won't tell the Sutcliffes, Bella, will you? I proposed it all for your good, and because I love you – [BELLA *shudders.*] – you won't tell 'em, will you, dear, and get me into trouble? Promise me you won't tell 'em! [*carneying*] Promise me; do, do!

BELLA: I won't tell 'em, if you'll promise me never to mention such subjects again.

KRUX: I won't – I'll take my oath I won't. Take your oath you won't tell them of me, Bella; take your oath, dear, will you?

BELLA: No – I give you my word. To think of our kind benefactors dying. You wicked man, I wonder that something doesn't happen to you. I wonder—— [*Two shots heard without.*] Oh! [KRUX *frightened.*] I won't stay any longer.

KRUX: Where are you going?

BELLA: To fetch the goloshes.

[*Exit* BELLA.]

KRUX: A bad girl! a bad girl! a bad girl! She'll come to no good, if I can help it; an ungrateful beast – after the offer I made her. What is she? A nobody, a foundling, a pauper – [*Enter* LORD BEAUFOY *and* JACK POYNTZ, *in shooting dress, followed by two* KEEPERS.] – brought up on charity. Oh, if she were a man, I'd——

[LORD BEAUFOY *comes down on* KRUX'S L., *and touches him with gun, before he speaks.*]

LORD B: Have you seen anybody pass this way?

KRUX: A young girl, sir, [*meekly*] with a book?

LORD B: No – an old gentleman and two servants?

KRUX: No, sir.

JACK: [*aside*] What a mangy looking cur!

KRUX: [*aside*] Two young puppies.

LORD B: [*to* KEEPERS] Are you sure this was the place where lunch was to meet us?

JACK: [*looking off*] Yes – for here it comes.

[*Enter* TIGER, *carrying two small folding chairs; two* SERVANTS, *one with picnic case, with lunch plates, knives and forks. The other has a tray-stand and butler's tray. They spread the lunch.*]

JACK: [*seeing* KRUX] Good morning.

KRUX: [*servilely*] Good morning, sir. [*aside*] Upstart beasts!

[*Exit* KRUX. *Enter* BEAU FARINTOSH, *led on by* VAUGHAN, *who carries a camp stool, which he places at table for the* BEAU; FARINTOSH *is a thin old man of seventy, dressed in the latest fashion, wigged, dyed, padded, eye glassed, a would-be young man, blind as a bat – peering into everything.*]

FARINTOSH: [*shaking hands with* JACK] My dear boy – my dear boy, how d'ye do? The very image of my poor sister – so glad to see you.

JACK: Thank you, Mr Farintosh, but my mamma had not the happiness of being your sister. That is Lord Beaufoy.

FARINTOSH: Ten thousand pardons, but my eyes are so – so – so – which is him, where is he? [*going to and shaking hands with* LORD BEAUFOY] My dear Arthur, quite well, eh? Strong, yes – you look so – very image of my poor sister.

LORD B: I'm quite well, Beau; you, too, I hope.

FARINTOSH: Never better – never better – strong, active, fine condition – fine condition. [*striking himself on chest*] Bellows to mend, eh – bellows to mend – ha! ha! ha! Sit down.

LORD B: Let me introduce my friend – Mr Poyntz – Mr Percy Farintosh.

FARINTOSH: Poyntz! Worcestershire Poyntzes?

JACK: Worcestershire Poyntzes!

FARINTOSH: Knew your grandfather. I mean your father – well – he was my second in Paris just after the battle of – no – no – sit down.

[*They sit.*]

LORD B: May I – [*helping lunch*] You may go. [*to* SERVANTS, *who exeunt.*]

FARINTOSH: Nothing before dinner, thanks.

LORD B: When we arrived at your place last night, you had gone to bed.

FARINTOSH: Yes, early to bed – late up, my way.

LORD B: And your man gave us your message; told us to shoot this morning – and that you——

FARINTOSH: Would meet you here to lunch, if fine. Pleasant in the open air. [*to* JACK] You appear to have a good appetite, Mr——

LORD B: Poyntz.

JACK: Yes – I'm quite a celebrity that way. It is my principal talent.

FARINTOSH: Ah! a very enviable one.

JACK: It is convenient at dinner time.

LORD B: Your last letter said that you had some business?

FARINTOSH: Yes, yes, yes!

JACK: Shall I and the lunch retire, and amuse ourselves together?

LORD B: No, no – Jack is an old friend. I presume it is on the old subject?

JACK: [*eating*] Ah, debt!

LORD B: No; marriage!

JACK: Oh, family troubles – shall I——

FARINTOSH: No, no, no, Mr——

LORD B: Poyntz.

FARINTOSH: Mr Poyntz, my nephew and I are at loggerheads. You shall judge between us.

JACK: Most happy.

FARINTOSH: I wish him to marry.

JACK: Hard, very; but some uncles are like that.

FARINTOSH: Have you ever been married?

JACK: Never; but once I was in quarantine ten days off Malta.

FARINTOSH: [*downcast*] I have been married.

JACK: There I have the advantage of you – I am the singlest young person possible; open to competition, and to be influenced only by money.

LORD B: [*in answer to a look from* FARINTOSH] You mustn't mind Jack, it's his humour to talk in that way.

FARINTOSH: My poor wife died early; had she lived I should have been a different man – a different man.

JACK: [*aside*] Ah – dead most likely.

LORD B: It's a melancholy story, Jack, and I shall get over it quicker than the Beau. My uncle's wife died, leaving a son: this son married——

FARINTOSH: Against my wishes.

LORD B: And he died——

FARINTOSH: Without seeing me, that I might ask his pardon and forgive him.

LORD B: He, too, left a child; of this child and her mother, my uncle has been unable to find the least trace.

FARINTOSH: I would give thousands to find them.

JACK: Try the second column of the *Times*. If you were to put in an advertisement, "Wanted, a young person to adopt, by a gentleman of fortune," you'd have lots of applicants. Indeed, why go further than this present spot? Here am I, ready to be adopted. I should like to be adopted by any gentleman or lady of means. Here you are, a strong, healthy, useful orphan, with good appetite and expensive habits all ready laid on; no objection to travel, or to go in single or double harness.

FARINTOSH: Your friend has a very singular humour.

LORD B: Yes, and it sometimes runs away with him.

JACK: And sometimes puts me down when I least expect it. Pray forgive me.

FARINTOSH: But revenons a nos – fleurs d'oranges. I want Arthur to marry.

JACK: But Arthur would rather not.

LORD B: I won't marry.

FARINTOSH: Did you ever hear such infatuation? It's tremendous. What was man invented for, but to marry?

LORD B: My tastes are so singular; I should not want such a singular wife.

JACK: What sort? Give particulars – name your age, weight, and colour.

LORD B: My wife must be a woman.

JACK: Plenty about.

LORD B: Aye, but I mean a real woman.

JACK: That's difficult.

LORD B: Not a regulation doll of the same pattern as the other dolls – the same absence of thought, the same simper, same stupid dove-like look out of the eyes. [*imitating*] "I love papa, I love mamma. I go to church on Sunday; I can walk, and talk, and play. Je suis une jolie poupée et je veux bien un bon petit mari pour m'acheter des toilettes et me faire promener au bois."

FARINTOSH: Did you ever hear? It's profane – quite profane.

JACK: [*lighting cigar*] Do you?

FARINTOSH: I don't smoke. [*taking snuff*] Do you?

JACK: [*taking snuff*] I do everything.

FARINTOSH: How you must enjoy life.

JACK: [*smoking hard*] Sir, for sensual enjoyment I would give Caligula six, and distance him. It's a great comfort having no intellect.

FARINTOSH: Many people find it so. Your language, Arthur, is blasphemy, perfect blasphemy, against the loveliest portion of creation.

LORD B: What is loveliness? Something to be bought in bottles and put on with a brush?

FARINTOSH: You don't dislike beauty?

LORD B: No; but I hate paint.

FARINTOSH: Paint?

LORD B: Paint! Shall I promise to love and cherish a plaister cast? Shall I promise to cleave only unto a living fresco, decked out in dead hair? I want a young wife, not an old master; I want charms that won't rub off on my coat sleeve if I touch them before they're dry. Pigments and spices are for Egyptian mummies; not for breathing flesh and blood. Can I exchange words of love with one who, before she has spoken, is a built up falsehood? I choose men friends who don't tell lies; I choose women who don't look them.

JACK: Which means that when you're eighty you'll marry your cook, because she doesn't use pearl powder when on active service.

LORD B: The charms of my love must be warranted to wash.

JACK: You mean not to wash off.

FARINTOSH: Arthur, I'm shocked; your opinions are – are – atheistic.

LORD B: It's not only cosmetics I do battle with. Some women would kill gallantry and chivalry by something called equality with

men. What is equality with men? Having their clothes made
by a he tailor instead of a she milliner. How pleasant for man
and wife to be measured together; or, at an election, for him to
walk arm-in-arm to the hustings with a wretched, half-mad,
whole mannish creature, who votes for the candidate you wish
to exclude.

JACK: I agree with you there; if women were admitted to electoral
privileges, they'd sell them for the price of a new chignon;
man, as the nobler animal, has the exclusive right to sell his
vote – for beer!

LORD B: Give me simplicity. I'm one of the old school.

FARINTOSH: [*rising*] And I'm one of the new. Give me chignons,
cosmetics, perfumes – in short, civilisation. I do not see why
beings endowed with immortal souls should not repair the
ravages of time by the appliances of art. As you say, it all
depends upon the school one has been reared in. [*Sits.*]

JACK: What does it matter? Indeed, in this world, what does anything
matter – after dinner?

FARINTOSH: Your sentiments are revolting, and remind me of the
works of Burke and Hare, and Tom Paine and Voltaire, and
other persons out of the social pale. Knowing your singular
views, I had prepared a splendid *parti* for you, an heiress.

LORD B: I don't want money.

JACK: Not want money! you should be photographed. The man who
don't want money deserves to be put into an album, and kept
there.

FARINTOSH: Miss Naomi Tighe – a West Indian heiress, without
father or mother.

JACK: No father and no mother, and an heiress. It's a gorgeous thing
in matrimonials. But why offer it to Arthur? He don't want it.
I do.

FARINTOSH: She's at school close by here, with some old friends of
mine. I was asked to go and see the preliminary examination of
the young ladies before the holidays. I thought it would be an
excellent thing to take you with me, that you might see Miss
Tighe, and, as I hoped, approve of her, for her guardians are
also my oldest friends.

LORD B: I'd rather not go.

[*He rises and beckons on* SERVANTS. *Enter* KEEPERS *and*
VAUGHAN. *They remove table, &c., off.*]

FARINTOSH: The examination is to-day week.

LORD B: I'll go, uncle, to please you.

FARINTOSH: Will your friend accompany us?

JACK: Thanks, I'll go to please myself.

FARINTOSH: Here's Vaughan to take me home. I always sleep before I dress for dinner. Till then——

> [JACK *sees something in the bushes.* Motions KEEPER *for a gun.* KEEPER *gives it him.*]

JACK: No; the rifle.

> [KEEPER *gives* JACK *breech-loader, which* JACK *loads, and goes off.*]

FARINTOSH: What's he doing?

LORD B: He's going to kill a bird with a bullet. He's a wonderful shot.

FARINTOSH: Now give me your arm. [*taking* VAUGHAN's *arm*] Ah, there you are; till dinner, Arthur——

> [*Exeunt* FARINTOSH, VAUGHAN, *and* KEEPERS.]

LORD B: Marry me to a young lady, all bread and butter and boarding-school. Time enough for marriage when I'm forty-five, and wear a waist belt. Marriage! Tut – a pile of boxes when you travel. Female friends to tell your wife what happened or what didn't happen before she was your wife. Hysteria when she's contradicted. Tears when you're cruel – that is, when you won't let her have her own way. Mild accents of mother-in-law. "Is this the lot, sir, you have prepared for my dear child? Come home, love, come home." By Jove, she might go home for me; there's always something the matter – a pain here or there, a sinking, or a swimming, or a floating, or a darting, or a shooting. [*Turns up stage. Shot heard without.* BELLA *runs across stage, frightened, and loses her shoe. Exit.* LORD BEAUFOY *does not see her.*] Then the brothers! What a horror is the brother of the girl you're spooning, particularly if he is like her; the thought will come that she might have been him, or he might have been her. No; love is a species of lunacy, of which marriage is the strait waistcoat. [*Kicks against shoe left by* BELLA.] What's this? Shoe! Child's shoe? No! Woman's shoe? No! Girl's shoe? [*Picks it up.*] Pretty little shoe; must belong to a pretty little foot, very pretty little foot. Now, why on earth could any young girl come into this wood for the purpose of losing her shoe? I should like to know who it belongs to? I feel quite a curiosity to—— [NAOMI *screams outside.*] Eh, perhaps this is the fair and shoeless owner.

> [NAOMI *runs on,* R. *and* BELLA *from* L. *She runs to* NAOMI, *meeting her* R.C.]

BELLA: Oh, my darling, there you are.

> [*They embrace.*]

NAOMI: Oh! I thought we were both killed – that dreadful cow!

LORD B: Quite girls, both. Now to which does this belong? It is the very tiniest shoe. [*loudly*] Ahem!

NAOMI: Oh, it's the gentleman who shot him. Oh, sir, so many, many, many thanks.

BELLA: Sir, you saved our lives; pray accept our gratitude.

LORD B: Gratitude for what? [*aside*] Surely not for finding——

BELLA: I was walking across the meadow.

NAOMI: And I saw her, and ran to meet her, when a great big ugly cow——

BELLA: Ran at us, and wanted to trample us to death——

NAOMI: When you shot him.

LORD B: I shot him!

NAOMI: And we ran away.

BELLA: We might have lost our lives.

LORD B: Haven't you lost anything else?

BELLA:
NAOMI: [*feeling her chignon*] } No!

LORD B: } Not——?
BELLA: } No.
NAOMI: } Nothing.

LORD B: [*disappointed*] I thought you had.

[*Enter* JACK POYNTZ, *with gun.*]

LORD B: Jack, was it you fired just now?

JACK: Yes.

LORD B: What have you got there – birds?

JACK: No; [*producing a pair of goloshes*] boots.

LORD B: Good gracious! [*producing shoe*] Does it rain boots about here?

JACK: Just now I was going to pot a bird, when I saw two girls running away like mad from – what the newspapers call an infuriated animal; so I sighted him, and hit him just between the horns; out of compliment to my shooting he fell down dead, and the two girls ran away; I walked up to the scene of slaughter, and at first I thought that these [*showing goloshes*] belonged to the defunct, but of course that was quite impossi*bull.*

NAOMI: [*crossing to* JACK] Then, sir, it was you who shot the cow?

JACK: Yes; I shot the cow. The cow was a bull; but that is a detail.

NAOMI: It was you, and not this gentleman!

JACK: If a bull is shot, what does it matter who shot him, particularly to the bull!

LORD B: [*aside*] I wish I'd shot him. Confound that Jack, what luck he has.

JACK: May I ask if you know the owner of these [*showing goloshes*] trophies from the field of battle?

BELLA: [*advancing*] Oh, they're mine!

LORD B: [*astounded*] Yours?

BELLA: Yes; at least, I was carrying them to Mrs Sutcliffe.

LORD B: [*relieved*] Mrs Sutcliffe!

NAOMI: Yes; our governess!

[BELLA *takes goloshes*.]

LORD B: [*to* BELLA] Then, I presume, that these belong to Mrs Sutcliffe.

BELLA: Yes.

LORD B: Then Mrs Sutcliffe's foot is somewhat large; and who does this belong to?

BELLA: [*seeing her foot is unshod*] Oh, that's mine.

LORD B: [*relieved*] I'm so glad.

BELLA: I didn't know I'd lost it, I was so frightened. [*taking it*] Thank you so much, sir, for saving my—— shoe. [*Puts it on*.]

JACK: May I know who I have the pleasure of addressing?

NAOMI: My name is Naomi Tighe.

JACK: [*aside*] The heiress——

LORD B: [*to* BELLA] And your name?

BELLA: Bella!

LORD B: Bella?

NAOMI: We're both pupils at Mrs Sutcliffe's.

BELLA: That is, I'm not quite a pupil – I'm only a pupil-teacher.

JACK: [*pointing to the red portion of* NAOMI's *dress*] It was this attracted the bull.

NAOMI: Oh, don't look at me. I can't bear to be looked at. [*She puts her handkerchief over her face*.]

JACK: How singular. [*to* LORD BEAUFOY] This is the very girl your uncle spoke of.

LORD B: Yes; do you think her handsome?

JACK: Not bad for an heiress. And the other?

LORD B: Charming.

BELLA: If you please, gentlemen, don't mention to Mrs Sutcliffe that we have been attacked. She is so nervous; it would make her ill.

[GIRLS *without, singing* "Through the Wood".]

NAOMI: Here's governess.

LORD B: Let us go; our staying may embarrass.

JACK: No; let's stop and see them take their gallops.

[*The School passes across the stage, singing,* "Through the Wood," &c.; *the* DOCTOR *and* MRS SUTCLIFFE *last*. BELLA *offers* MRS SUTCLIFFE *her goloshes*. NAOMI *is on platform when* DOCTOR *appears, waving handkerchief to* JACK *and laughing. The* DOCTOR *touches her on the shoulder; the expression on her face alters suddenly, and she runs off, followed by* DOCTOR. MRS SUTCLIFFE *signifies to* BELLA *to retain goloshes, and exits, followed by* BELLA, *who looks at* LORD BEAUFOY. *As soon as she is off,* JACK *runs on to platform and waves his cap on his gun,* LORD BEAUFOY *watching* BELLA *from below.*]

Song –

"When the red sun sets at eve you may hear me,
    Singing farewell to his rays as they fade;
But as soon as the step of a mortal is near me,
    I take to my wings and fly off to the shade."

[*Singing dies in the distance, as curtain falls quickly.*]

END OF ACT I

ACT II

SCENE I – *The Schoolroom. Shelves with books. Scene enclosed. Window* R. *and* L. *Door. Desks, desk for Master, &c. Maps. Music from "La Cenerentola" as drop rises.* BELLA *discovered, seated at small table near open window, shelling peas.*

BELLA: [*humming*]

> Said the Prince unto the maiden,
>> "There is none I love but thee";
> "Let me hence, then," said the maiden,
>> "You are not of my degree."
> "Love can raise thee to a lady,
>> Say, my Princess wilt thou be?"
> Faster, faster, flew the maiden,
>> Faster, faster followed he.

> [NAOMI, *in a hat and shawl, appears outside window; she touches* BELLA *on the shoulder.*]

BELLA: Nummy, is that you?

NAOMI: Yes, dear; what are you doing?

BELLA: Shelling peas, and——

NAOMI: Yes.

BELLA: And thinking——

NAOMI: [*in a whisper*] About the goloshes?

> [BELLA *nods.*]

BELLA: But only a little – only a little.

NAOMI: Bella, dear, I dreamt last night, and this morning I feel as if something were going to happen; that is, I feel quite hysterical, as if I should like somebody to hug or to scratch at. I dressed myself quickly, on purpose that I might come out into the garden and have a good think. It is nice to think in the shrubbery.

BELLA: I'm afraid we are too young to have a right to think upon such subjects.

NAOMI: Not a bit: one is always old enough for a sweetheart. I'm eighteen. How old are you?

BELLA: I don't know.

NAOMI: Then, perhaps you're twenty. I knew two girls who were married before they were nineteen; but then some people have such luck! Ain't you going to dress yourself for this examination, like the other girls?

BELLA: This is my Sunday frock.

NAOMI: But you can have my pink, my darling; you can wear anything of mine.

[*She kisses* BELLA *through window, and steals peas and eats them.*]

BELLA: You mustn't eat the peas, dear.

NAOMI: Why not?

BELLA: They're not nice.

NAOMI: Yes, they are, if you eat them when nobody's looking.

[*Enter* MRS SUTCLIFFE, *dressed for dinner.* NAOMI *starts from window.*]

MRS S: Bella, what are you doing there?

BELLA: Shelling peas, ma'am.

MRS S: Shelling peas in the school-room!

BELLA: They are so busy, and so pushed for room in the kitchen with the dinner, that I brought them here; I can take them back. [*rising and taking basin*]

MRS S: [*looking at watch*] It is nearly time that Mr Farintosh and his friend should be here. Bella, if the young ladies are dressed, you can tell them that I will inspect them in this apartment.

[*Door opens.*]

BELLA: Here are the young ladies.

MRS S: Good!

[BELLA *resumes her pea-shelling. Enter all the* GIRLS *(dressed for the examination) one by one in the following order:* – MILLY, CLARA, HETTY, KITTY, LITTLE GIRL. MRS SUTCLIFFE *turns them round, signifying approval or the reverse; they take their respective seats at the two desks,* – NAOMI *last but one.*]

MRS S: [*to* LITTLE GIRL] You shall be examined with the others to please you. What are you going to answer?

LITTLE GIRL: They condemned him to shoot——

MRS S: Yes, yes, that's right. [CHILD *goes to her seat.*] Why Naomi, my dear, you've been crying.

NAOMI: No, I haven't.

MRS S: Miss Tighe! Miss Tighe! you should say I was mistaken.

NAOMI: Then you are; and if I have been crying it's only a few tears. [*She goes to her seat.*]

TILLY: [*to* NAOMI] What could you cry but tears! You couldn't cry cucumbers, could you?

[*Enter* LAURA, *sleepy, her dress badly put on.*]

MRS S: Now then, Laura, you're last again.

LAURA: Somebody must be last.

[*She goes to her place.* BELLA *goes off, with peas, and*

returns immediately.]

MRS S: The Doctor will put you through an examination on the arrival of our friends. It will be an excellent bit of practice for the grand examination at the end of the half-year. The musical examination will take place in the drawing-room after dinner. Mr Farintosh brings a friend with him, Lord Beaufoy [*excitement of* GIRLS], the owner of half a county.

TILLY: Half a county? Which half?

CLARA: And which county?

NAOMI: Is he a real lord?

MRS S: Real? Yes.

NAOMI: But I mean a real, real, lord. When I get near him I'll pinch him, and see if he is flesh and blood, like other people.

TILLY: Oh, I daresay lords are very flesh.

NAOMI: And very blood – very good blood. I mean.

[*Gate bell.*]

MRS S: Hush! [*awful silence*] They are here.

NAOMI: Oh, I feel so nervous. I should like to scream.

MRS S: Young ladies, I have only time to say that I rely on you with every confidence.

[GIRLS *rise, curtsey, and seat themselves. Enter* DR SUTCLIFFE, *followed by* BEAU FARINTOSH, LORD BEAUFOY, *and* JACK POYNTZ, *dressed for dinner* [*not evening dress*]. *The* GIRLS *all rise.* BEAU FARINTOSH *and* LORD BEAUFOY *speak to* DR *and* MRS SUTCLIFFE. JACK POYNTZ *wanders down row of desks until he comes to* NAOMI.]

NAOMI: [*recognising* JACK] It's the cow.

[*She sinks on chair, blushing and giggling; then rises again, trying to restrain herself.*]

JACK: [*seeing her*] It's the little thing in red, who had the attack of bullock – the heiress. [*to* LORD BEAUFOY]

MRS S: Young ladies, let me have the honour – Lord Beaufoy.

BELLA: [*at back*] He Lord Beaufoy!

[MRS SUTCLIFFE *presenting them.* GIRLS *curtsey.*]

MRS S: Mr Percy Farintosh, Mr——

[NAOMI *giggles again, and is silenced by a look from* MRS SUTCLIFFE.]

LORD B: Poyntz.

MRS S: Mr Poyntz.

NAOMI: [*whispering to herself, and writing it on slate*] Poyntz, Poyntz, Poyntz, Poyntz!

FARINTOSH: A friend who was staying with me, and whom I have taken the liberty——

MRS S: ⎱ Charmed.
DR S: ⎰ Delighted. [*shaking hands with* JACK]

FARINTOSH: [*going towards desks*] My dear young ladies, permit me to say how highly I feel honoured by being permitted, by the kindness of my friends, Mrs Sutcliffe and – and Theodore – and the Doctor, to be present at this charming a – a——

LORD B: ⎱ Inspection!
JACK: ⎰ Review!

FARINTOSH: Inspection – review – whatever it may be.

DR S: Examination.

FARINTOSH: Examination. Indeed, this is one of the proudest privileges of my life.

MRS S: My dear Mr Farintosh!

DR S: Percy, my old friend.

FARINTOSH: [*fumbling for his eye-glass*] To see so much grace and beauty, 'tis like gazing on a parterre of beautiful flowers, whose colours are audible and whose perfume is melody.

DR S: Bravo! Very elegant.

MRS S: Flowing.

LORD B: Like Tom Moore.

JACK: Broken-winded.

MRS S: The old school.

FARINTOSH: Vieille école! Bonne école!

JACK: Good show of girls.

FARINTOSH: That is new school – short, pithy, ungraceful——

JACK: And meaning what it says.

> [*They talk in group.* BELLA, *who during this has been unobserved, crosses to door.* LORD BEAUFOY *turns and recognises her.*]

LORD B: My fairy in the wood.

NAOMI: [*aside*] It's the shoe-horn.

DR S: Bella, my dear, you are not going?

BELLA: [*faltering*] I – I——

MRS S: Miss Tighe, let me introduce you to Mr Percy Farintosh.

FARINTOSH: [*mistaking* BELLA *for* NAOMI] Miss Tighe, I knew your guardians intimately. I have——

MRS S: That is not Miss Tighe; that is Bella. [BELLA *and* BEAU FARINTOSH *scrutinise each other. During this* GIRLS *whisper.*] A little thing I took in out of charity. Makes herself very useful about the house.

DR S: [*coming down to* BELLA] The best scholar we can boast of; the pupil of whom I am most proud. Take your accustomed place, Bella, at the head of the class.

[BELLA *goes to her place, followed by* DR SUTCLIFFE.]

NAOMI: Bravo!

MRS S: [*looks at* NAOMI.] Pray be seated. [*to* GENTLEMEN]

NAOMI: [*looking at* JACK] I can't answer a single question if he looks at me.

LORD B: Handsome girls!

FARINTOSH: Delightful! Can't see a single feature.

[*He fumbles for his eye-glass, which is at his back.* BEAUFOY *finds it for him. All seated.* NAOMI *makes eyes at* JACK, *who has been gazing at her steadfastly, and then laughs.*]

MRS S: Hush, hush! Miss Tighe.

DR S: [*standing at desk*] The ancient Romans——

MRS S: [*coughs*] Doctor, as we are rather late and dinner will be punctual, if you would kindly make the preliminaries to the examination as short as possible.

DR S: I will so, my dear. We will begin with Roman history. [*As he asks the question, he indicates with a rule the* GIRL *he means, who rises as she answers.*] There were different forms of government in Rome. Please to inform me in what order these forms of government ruled the Roman people.

TILLY: First the regal power, that is the kings; next the consuls, until the first dictator was chosen; then the power of the decemviri; consular government again; imperial dictatorship; then the emperors.

FARINTOSH: My dear Mrs Sutcliffe, let me congratulate you on your fair charges.

JACK: How the *propria quae maribus* they can remember it I can't make out.

LORD B: I suppose it's cram.

DR S: After Romulus had appointed the lictors, what other royal or civic guard did he appoint?

MILLY: The Celeres.

DR S: Who were they?

MILLY: A guard of young men, numbering three hundred, who accompanied Romulus for the purpose of defending him.

LORD B: Sort of Life Guards!

JACK: Yes, without boots or breeches.

LORD B: Cool to fight in.

JACK: And convenient for fording rivers.

DR S: Name the reign and date rendered illustrious by Belisarius?

NAOMI: The reign of Justinian, in the year 561.

DR S: Who was Belisarius?

TILLY: Belisarius was a Roman general, who rendered the highest services to his country.

DR S: How was he rewarded?

CLARA: They deprived him of his dignities, and put his eyes out.

JACK: That must have been done by a Committee of the Period!

[MRS SUTCLIFFE *coughs*.]

DR S: Now for English history. With regard, now, to the ancient Druids. In what garments were the ancient Druids clothed when they offered—— [MRS SUTCLIFFE *coughs; all the* GIRLS *hide their heads behind their slates or on the desks.* FARINTOSH, BEAUFOY, *and* JACK *laugh among themselves, and the* DOCTOR *mops his forehead. General discomfiture.*] – I should say – ahem – In what reign was the ceremony of marriage first solemnised in churches?

ALL THE GIRLS: [*all rising*] In the reign of Henry III.

JACK: They all know that.

FARINTOSH: Wonderful, wonderful; and all single girls, too.

DR S: What is the difference between the political parties, Whig and Tory?

TILLY: None whatever.

DR S: By whom were the Britons first conquered?

NAOMI: [*with fire*] They never were conquered – they'd sooner die.

JACK: Girl of spirit, by Jove!

DR S: In what reign was the famous Gunpowder Plot discovered?

CLARA: In the reign of November the 5th.

FARINTOSH: Wonderful! My dear Mrs Sutcliffe——

[LORD BEAUFOY *nudges* FARINTOSH.]

BELLA: In the reign of James the First.

DR S: Who was the chief instigator, criminal, and author of that atrocious plot?

CLARA: Oliver Cromwell.

TILLY: Guy Fawkes.

DR S: How was Guy Fawkes punished?

LITTLE CHILD: They condemned him to shoot an apple off the head of his own son.

DR S: Hum! Astronomy. How far distant is the moon from the earth?

NAOMI: [*after a pause*] It depends on the weather. I knew I couldn't do it.

DR S: Bella, dear.

BELLA: The mean distance of the moon from the earth is 236,847 miles.

JACK: Good gracious!

FARINTOSH: Wonderful!

DR S: I told you Bella was our best pupil. And the diameter of the moon?

BELLA: Its apparent diameter is variable according to her distance from the earth. Her real diameter is 2,144 miles.

NAOMI: [*whispering*] What do they call the moon "her" for?

TILLY: Because the moon's a lady.

NAOMI: The more shame for her to be out so late at night. What would they say if we did it?

TILLY: Consider her age.

DR S: And the magnitude of the moon?

BELLA: About one-fiftieth of the magnitude of the earth.

FARINTOSH: Tremendous! In astronomical knowledge that young lady is a perfect Sir Isaac—— Davy.

[*Enter* KRUX, *dressed for dinner.*]

KRUX: [*to* MRS SUTCLIFFE] Pardon my interruption, but the servant didn't like to mention that dinner was ready, and——

MRS S: Oh, thank you. [*rising*] I fear we cannot proceed with the examination further. [*All rise except* GIRLS.] Mr Krux, as Mr Farintosh has brought two friends, one more than expected, I fear there will not be room for you at table; so – if you wouldn't mind excusing——

KRUX: [*mortified*] Oh, never mind me, Mrs Sutcliffe; I'm of no consequence.

MRS S: Oh, thank you; so kind of you.

FARINTOSH: [*mistaking* KRUX *for* DR SUTCLIFFE] My dear Doctor, so many thanks. I shall be able to tell you all my admiration during dinner.

[DOCTOR *taps* FARINTOSH, *on shoulder who acknowledges mistake.*]

MRS S: Ladies [GIRLS *rise.*] then, until after dinner, when we will resume our studies.

[GIRLS *curtsey,* KRUX *goes up and leans against desk at back,* FARINTOSH *offers* MRS SUTCLIFFE *his arm, and they go off.* JACK *goes towards* NAOMI, *nodding and laughing and backing towards door at same time, finally knocking up against* KRUX, *who is annoyed.* BEAUFOY's *attention is rivetted on* BELLA. DOCTOR, *at door, coughs.* BEAUFOY *bows, goes to door, looks back and exits; followed by* DOCTOR. *All exeunt. As soon as they are off,* GIRLS *sit down, chatter, talk, and laugh loudly, taking no notice of* KRUX's *authority.*]

KRUX: And they dine without me, and I'd kept such a good appetite, because I knew the dinner was nice. Silence, ladies! Oh, those upstarts – and the guests are as bad as the hosts. Ladies! That old fool and those two young idiots, I don't suppose they could conjugate a verb between them. [KRUX *has a white mark on his left shoulder, as if he had rubbed against a whitewashed wall.*] Ladies! Ladies!! Ladies!!! [*rapping desk*] I must request your attention. Miss Hetty, take your arms off the desk. Miss Laura, heads up! [*The* GIRLS *eat apples, write on slips of paper, draw on slates, &c. They see, as he turns, the white mark on his back, and laugh.*] Silence, if you please.

NAOMI: He's been powdering himself for dinner.

[*They laugh.*]

TILLY: It's not powder, it's flour – he's been kissing the cook.
NAOMI: Oh! how I pity the cook.

[*They laugh.*]

KRUX: Silence, ladies; we will resume our studies in geography. Miss Laura, will you tell me in what country we left off yesterday?
LAURA: [*half asleep*] In bed.
KRUX: Nowhere near it – we left off in South America. Miss Amelia?
MILLY: We left off in the mountains?
KRUX: What mountains.
MILLY: The Alps.
KRUX: Wrong.
KITTY: The Apennines.
KRUX: Wrong.
TILLY: The Pyrenees.
KRUX: Wrong.
CLARA: The Tiber.
KRUX: No – the Chimborazo. Where are the Chimborazo mountains, miss?
LITTLE CHILD: Wherever you please, sir.
KRUX: That's a nice child – she's respectful, though she's stupid. What is the height of the Chimborazo, Miss Naomi?
NAOMI: I don't know.
KRUX: Answer me, miss.
NAOMI: I can't.
KRUX: Why not?
NAOMI: Because I can't. I feel as if I could cry my eyes out.
KRUX: You're hysterical, and should go outside and have your head pumped on; but to resume – [*Turns up stage and shows white on coat again –* GIRLS *laugh.*] – what are you laughing at? There is nothing to laugh at in me, I should think.
TILLY: You've got your coat all over white.
KRUX: Oh, Bella, fetch me a brush. [BELLA *pauses.* GIRLS *look indignant, and* NAOMI *slaps book on desk.* KRUX *looking tri-*

umphant.] Didn't you hear me? – fetch me a brush. [BELLA *goes off.*] What is the height of the Chimborazo mountains?

CLARA: Four hundred miles – [*laugh*] – no, I mean four hundred yards. I made a mistake.

KRUX: Wrong again – mountains of that height do not exist. The height of the Chimborazo is about one mile.

[BELLA *returns with brush, which she offers to* KRUX.]

KRUX: Oh, brush me! [*A pause –* BELLA *stands motionless.*] Did you hear me? Brush me!

[BELLA *crosses up stage, and places the brush on desk.*]

BELLA: [*facing him*] I can't do that.

GIRLS: [*murmur*] What a shame.

KRUX: [*savagely*] Silence in the class. [*to* BELLA] Do you know who I am?

BELLA: I'm not a servant.

KRUX: [*with a sneer*] Not a servant. If you shell peas you can brush coats. Then, pray, what am I?

NAOMI: [*who has endeavoured to restrain herself but failed*] You're a beast! Bella is here to teach ladies, not to brush blackguards. Insulting our Bella! Girls, don't stand it. [*Throws book at him; all the other girls rise and are about to throw books, &c., at* KRUX, *as enter* DR SUTCLIFFE, *holding up his hands,* MRS SUTCLIFFE, LORD BEAUFOY *and* JACK POYNTZ. FARINTOSH *at door with napkin round his neck.* GIRLS *resume their seats as if studying.* NAOMI *hides her head behind slate, which has a comic drawing in chalk of* KRUX *upon it, and* BELLA *kneels at feet of* DR SUTCLIFFE.]

END OF ACT II

ACT III

SCENE I – *The Grounds of Cedar-Grove House. Evening. Stage half dark.* LORD BEAUFOY *discovered, seated on garden chair. Piano heard playing in house, and a joyful shout of laughter from the* GIRLS *as curtain rises.*

LORD B: 'Pon my word, this is a very pretty place; so secluded, rustic, and all that. People seem to pass their lives so innocently, so different from Paris, or Vienna, or any big city. After all, big cities are only agglomerations of brick and mortar, while the country is made up of trees, and fields, and flowers, and birds, and mushrooms, and truffles, and the rest of it. There's better shooting in the country, too. The dinner was very good, and [*meditating, looking up*] it's eighty something miles from here to the moon – eighty—— something, I forget the odd thousands and hundreds. [*Rises and wanders towards* R.] Singular little girl, that – fresh as nature and artless as moss. [*plucking a piece of moss from walls of steps, dreamily*] I wonder who she is, in her nice quiet grey dress, so different from those young persons in Paris, and the tremendous tame tiger lilies one meets in town. [*Leans against swing.*] Ah! simplicity – beautiful simplicity! How you are neglected in this nineteenth century! She doesn't seem to be a boarder like the other girls. I don't care for that Miss Tighe. Poor Uncle Beau, he'll be disappointed in that match again. Jack's got my cigar-case. [*feeling in his pocket*] I must find him. [*Enter* BELLA, *a large jug in her hand*] I beg your pardon. [*nearly running over her*]

BELLA: Oh! my lord, you nearly made me drop the jug.

LORD B: I'm very sorry.

BELLA: It's of no consequence.

LORD B: [*following her*] May I ask where you are going?

BELLA: I'm going for some milk, my lord.

LORD B: Alone?

BELLA: Yes.

LORD B: But do you feel equal to the task of going for milk without an escort?

BELLA: Oh, yes! Cook has used more milk than they expected; and so——

LORD B: The deficiency has to be supplied. [*leaning on back of chair facing* BELLA] But it seems so odd that you should have to go for milk. I thought that in the country they always carried about milk in cows. I mean that they had it on the premises, and drew it up in a bucket from a well.

BELLA: Drew milk from a well!

LORD B: No, no; of course – not milk, that's water; though sometimes the two things do get mixed up in one another. But couldn't they send a servant?

BELLA: They're all busy, and I'd nothing else to do.

LORD B: Very amiable of you; but perhaps you find it amusing.

BELLA: No, my lord; but I'm not a boarder here.

LORD B: No?

BELLA: No! Mrs Sutcliffe took me into the house out of charity.

LORD B: [aside] God bless Mrs Sutcliffe.

BELLA: And to please the Doctor.

LORD B: Ah! I meant God bless the Doctor.

BELLA: So, of course, I try to make myself as useful as I can, my lord, in return for their kindness.

LORD B: And your father and mother, do they approve?

[*The piano is again heard playing in the house.*]

BELLA: I have neither father nor mother.

LORD B: An orphan?

BELLA: Yes.

LORD B: What an interesting girl!

BELLA: I never knew my parents. My mother died in the village close by, when I was quite a baby, and then the poor woman where I was left, Mrs Marks, brought me up till I was nine years old.

[*The moon shines brightly from this time from behind the house.*]

LORD B: Is that Mrs Marks still living?

BELLA: No, my lord; she died two years ago.

LORD B: [aside] Confound these good folks, they always die; but I suppose it is to make room for the bad ones.

BELLA: It was my first sorrow. Then I came here and——

LORD B: You are an excellent scholar——

BELLA: I have tried to improve myself in order that when I am older I may no longer be a burden.

LORD B: And who in the school is your most particular friend?

BELLA: Nummy.

LORD B: Nummy! – what a singular name.

BELLA: I mean Naomi – Miss Tighe – we're the best friends in the school.

LORD B: She's very rich – is she not?

BELLA: Very; indeed she's as rich as she's good, so you may fancy what a lot of money she has. She, too, is an orphan like me; perhaps that's the reason we're so fond of one another; though we're very different in some respects – for she is wealthy and I am – not.

LORD B: Not wealthy [*aside*] How these great natures misunderstand themselves.

BELLA: But I'm forgetting my errand. [*She runs up and opens door in wall.*]

LORD B: Oh, never mind the milk; let it bring itself. I mean – is it far to the moon?

BELLA: Eh?

LORD B: I mean is it far to the milk?

BELLA: Only across the field.

LORD B: That's a pity. [*after a pause*] May I be allowed to accompany you?

BELLA: Oh, my lord, so much trouble.

LORD B: No trouble. The milk here is so pure it's a pleasure to walk with it. What a lovely night, so bright and—— How far did you say it was from this grass plat to the moon?

BELLA: Two hundred and thirty-six thousand eight hundred and forty-seven miles.

LORD B: It's a long way.

BELLA: It's very kind of the moon to shine down here such a distance.

LORD B: Not at all – the grass plat is so soft and pleasant the moon can't help it. May I carry the jug?

BELLA: Oh! my lord——

LORD B: I should like it above all things. [*Takes jug.*] Thanks. Will you take my arm?

[*Church clock strikes eight very distinctly.*]

BELLA: My lord! I don't like to——

LORD B: You shouldn't take dislikes so suddenly.

BELLA: [*taking his arm*] Oh, it isn't that.

[*The piano stops playing.*]

LORD B: What long shadows the moonlight flings. See – there I am.

BELLA: But so tall – so high.

LORD B: And there you are.

BELLA: But not so tall as you are.

LORD B: And yet you're nearer the skies – see! [*moving*] Now we're far apart.

[*The moonlight throws long shadows from* R. *to* L.]

BELLA: And now – [*moving*] – we're joined together. Wonderful things, shadows, are they not?

LORD B: Yes, when they lie before us.

BELLA: I often wonder what they're for – what they mean?

LORD B: No one can tell, except poets, and painters, and lovers; and they know all things, and what they don't know they feel. See, we are divided again.

BELLA: No. [*placing her hand on jug*] The jug unites us.

LORD B: Only for the moment – [*piano music again; the plaintive character of which is changed at their exit to a lively tune, to bring on* JACK.] Only for the moment.

> [*Exeunt, through door in wall. Enter* JACK, *smoking; he goes to swing, and sits in it.*]

JACK: [*after swinging*] Very nice girls these, particularly that Miss Tighe. Girl of spirit; pitched into that infernal teacher; quite right. [*Stop the music.*] She's rather pretty, too; I wonder if she's clever; the two things don't often go together. When Nature makes a pretty woman, she puts all the goods into the shop-window. I wonder where she is. They were all walking about just now. My short day in these female infantry barracks has quite impressed me. Seeing a lot of pretty girls accidentally makes one feel like – going to church when you're not used to it. Let me see, what's the quotation? – oh – "Those who went to cough remained to pray." [*Enter* NAOMI, *her dress, lined with white, over her head, so that she looks like the traditional ghost. She stands motionless.*] Here's a ghost; now really this is pleasant. I'm fond of ghosts, particularly ghosts in petticoats. If you are the departed spirit of any late friend, come back to earth to tell me that you've left me money, please mention it at once.

NAOMI: [*lowering her dress from her face*] Weren't you frightened?

JACK: Awful! I'm a very timid man.

NAOMI: I've been in the Shrubbery, frightening the girls, but it's very slow work; I'd rather talk to you.

JACK: I feel flattered in the highest degree.

NAOMI: Now don't go on like that; if you do, I shall run away. [*She goes out at door in wall, and shuts it; then opens it a little way, peeping in.*] You mustn't come after me.

JACK: Not for worlds.

NAOMI: [*going, then returning*] I can't understand you at all.

JACK: Why not!

NAOMI: You talk so oddly. You seem to tell truths as if they were not true, and fibs as if they were truths; but I like to hear you.

JACK: To hear me tell fibs or the truth?

NAOMI: Both. Go on; tell me something.

JACK: What about?

NAOMI: About yourself.

JACK: Really, the subject is so barren.

NAOMI: What are you?

JACK: Nothing; it's the occupation I'm most fitted for.

NAOMI: But you must be something.

JACK: No; I'm only myself.

NAOMI: Were you ever anything before you were what you are now?

JACK: Eh?

NAOMI: I mean – what used you to be?

JACK: I used to be – a little boy, but I got nothing for it – not even the birch.

NAOMI: Lord Beaufoy said you'd been in the army. [*looking at him admiringly*] Were you a horse soldier or a foot soldier?

JACK: Foot – a very foot soldier.

NAOMI: And he said you were in the Crimea.

JACK: Yes; I was there.

NAOMI: Were you at the Battle of Inkerman?

JACK: Yes.

NAOMI: Then, why didn't you mention it?

JACK: Hardly worth while; so many other fellows were there.

NAOMI: Did you fight?

JACK: I was forced to.

NAOMI: Did you like it?

JACK: No; detested it.

NAOMI: Then why did you do it?

JACK: I was hired for the purpose; besides, I hadn't pluck enough to run away.

NAOMI: Did they give you much money for fighting?

JACK: Not much; but if they gave me very little money, I did very little fighting, so I was quite even with them in that respect.

NAOMI: I wish I was a man!

JACK: I don't.

NAOMI: Why not?

JACK: You're so much nicer as you are.

NAOMI: If you say that I'll run away.

JACK: Then I won't say it. I'll keep on not saying it. [*aside*] Jolly girl for an heiress!

NAOMI: [*aside*] He's beautiful; he's lovely, perfectly lovely. [*aloud*] Are you fond of reading?

JACK: Um – yes – middling.

NAOMI: I am. Did you ever read "Othello"?

JACK: Yes; I don't consider it nice reading for young ladies.

NAOMI: Othello used to tell Desdemona of all the dangers he had passed, and the battles he had won.

JACK: Othello was a nigger, and didn't mind bragging.

NAOMI: Still it must have been very pleasant for Desdemona.

JACK: A black man!

NAOMI: Yes; it must have been like looking at your husband through a piece of smoked glass.

JACK: As if he were a planet.

NAOMI: A heavenly body!

JACK: More like an eclipse. Shall we walk? [*offering his arm*] May I be
    allowed?

NAOMI: I don't like to.

JACK: You'll find it go very easy. [*Music of piano in house.*] Am I too
    tall? [*as she takes his arm*]

NAOMI: No; I like to look up. And you've never been anything at all?

JACK: Never!

NAOMI: Not even married?

JACK: Not even married. Melancholy waste of time, isn't it?

NAOMI: [*looking up*] I know what could be made of you.

JACK: What?

NAOMI: You'd make a capital belfry.

JACK: Am I so deserving of a rope? Then you should be the belle.

NAOMI: Yes; I'd be the belle, and my tongue should go ding dong.

JACK: Yes; you should be a ding dong; a *dindon*, a *dindon truffé*.

> [*Exeunt into Shrubbery. The door in the wall opens,
> and* LORD BEAUFOY *and* BELLA *appear*, LORD BEAUFOY
> *with the jug.*]

BELLA: We're soon back.

LORD B: I'm sorry to say we are.

BELLA: So, if your lordship will give me the jug——

LORD B: Must you leave me?

BELLA: I must take the milk to the kitchen.

> [*Enter* KRUX *from behind house. The music stops.*]

LORD B: Just as she was beginning to be so charming. [*Sees* KRUX, *who
    comes down.*] Oh, here, you'll do. [*offering* KRUX *jug*] Take this
    to the kitchen, will you?

BELLA: Oh, no!

KRUX: [*indignant*] Me – me – milk – me?

BELLA: I'll take it, my lord. [*Takes jug.* LORD BEAUFOY *turns.*] I shall be
    back directly.

LORD B: [*aside to her*] I shall wait here.

> [*Exit* BELLA. KRUX *following her down.* BEAUFOY *goes to
> swing.* KRUX *then crosses to* BEAUFOY *with mock
> deference.*]

KRUX: My lord! Such invidious distinctions——

LORD B: Pardon me. Mr——

KRUX: Krux, my lord.

LORD B: Krux, I mistook you in the dark for——

KRUX: One of the female servants – very natural, my lord. Beautiful
    evening!

LORD B: Beautiful! Good-night!

KRUX: Good-night, my lord! [*aside*] Ahum! – aha!

> [*He pretends to go off behind house. Enter* BELLA, *running; she stops short on seeing* LORD BEAUFOY *– she is out of breath.*]

LORD B: I'm so glad you've come back.

BELLA: I made all the haste I could.

LORD B: The Shrubbery runs nearly round the whole garden, does it not?

BELLA: Yes, my lord.

LORD B: [*Offers his arm, which she takes. Pause.*] You're sure that when I go away to-night you won't quite forget me.

BELLA: Oh, yes! On a first acquaintance, and in so short a time, I never——

LORD B: Never——

BELLA: Liked to hear anybody talk so much. You're the first lord I ever saw.

LORD B: And you're the first little lady I ever took a liking to. And I shall be so sad at leaving you.

BELLA: Sad, my lord!

LORD B: Really.

BELLA: Why?

> [*They walk off into the Shrubbery. Enter* KRUX, *from behind house.*]

KRUX: Where's Mrs Sutcliffe? Where's Mrs Sutcliffe? [*peering into the darkness*] So you wouldn't brush me, Miss Bella, wouldn't you, and my lord takes me for a female servant! Very good – we'll see – we'll see.

> [*Exit* KRUX. *Enter* SCHOOLGIRLS *from different entrances.*]

MILLY: Where is that Naomi?

CLARA: And Mr Poyntz? The little flirt!

KITTY: To keep him to herself!

MILLY: I hate such selfishness!

HETTY: So do I. When one gets hold of a lord, one ought to divide him fairly, like a cake!

> [*Enter* TILLY *from Shrubbery.*]

TILLY: Girls! Girls!

GIRLS: What?

> [TILLY *points, and* GIRLS *retire into shadow.* LORD BEAUFOY *and* BELLA *cross – his arm round her waist. They walk slowly, and are quite silent. Clock strikes nine very distant.*]

TILLY: [*after a pause*] Well!
MILLY: There!
KITTY: I never!
CLARA: Nor I; but I should like to——
LAURA: So should I.
MILLY: What?
LAURA: To go to sleep.
TILLY: That artful Bella!
MILLY: Hush!

> [KRUX *appears at the entrance of the Shrubbery.* JACK *appears from the same entrance with* NAOMI, *and pushes* KRUX *on one side.*]

JACK: Take care – thank you.

> [JACK *crosses with* NAOMI, *and off.*]

TILLY: Ah!
MILLY: Oh!
ALL THE GIRLS: Well!
MILLY: Oh, those two!
CLARA: You mean those four.
LAURA: [*sleepy*] Twice two are four.

> [*Enter* FARINTOSH *agitated – a letter in his hand. Enter* DR *and* MRS SUTCLIFFE.]

MRS S: ⎫ Only another hour!
DR S: ⎬ A glass of sherry or a sandwich?
FARINTOSH: ⎭ My dear friends excuse me——
This letter, which my man has just brought me, is most important. If I drive home immediately, he can put my things together, and we can catch the next night train to town.
MRS S: But——
FARINTOSH: Forgive me, I entreat, and let me thank you for a most charming and instructive day – instructive day; but this is imperative – imperative; the – the – search of a life, of my whole life, indeed; the news has so agitated me that – I – I feel quite – quite agitated. Where is Arthur?

> [*During this* JACK *and* NAOMI *have entered, and also* VAUGHAN, LORD BEAUFOY *and* BELLA – KRUX *following.*]

FARINTOSH: [*mistaking* JACK *for* ARTHUR] Oh, Arthur, here you are; important business takes me to town to-night, so I shall take the carriage; you and your friend can walk home – the night's very fine, very fine; and apropos of your friend, Mr Poyntz, the girls tell me that he's been seen paying too strong attentions to Miss Tighe, whom I had hoped you would have shown some, some – and I consider your friend's conduct very reprehensible, very reprehensible. [*Shakes his hand.*] God bless you!

JACK: So many thanks – a charming day!

NAOMI: And a most charming evening!

MRS S: Delighted to see you at any time, Mr Poyntz.

FARINTOSH: Poyntz. [*crossing to* LORD BEAUFOY *and mistaking him for* JACK] Of course, Mr Poyntz, I need not say that my box is at your disposal so long as you choose to remain to shoot here – to shoot here. One word – these schoolgirls have wonderful eyes; they see everything, like me; and they tell me that Arthur has paid not the slightest attention to any one of them, except a Miss Bella something; now he shouldn't have done that, should he? Very wrong of him, very wrong. So, once more, [*to* DOCTOR *and* MRS SUTCLIFFE] my dear friends, adieu! and wish me good luck in my search. [*Brings* DR SUTCLIFFE *down, mistaking him for* MRS SUTCLIFFE.] My dear Mrs Sutcliffe, I must tell you one thing – but not a word to Theodore, not a word to Theodore – poor Theodore, I think he is looking very ill – very ill indeed. I noticed at dinner, too, that he drank too much, much too much; digestion going – poor Theodore, digestion going; take great care of him or you'll lose him, you'll lose him. Young ladies, good-night, and – and – and bless you all, very much. Receive the thanks of a man old enough to be – to be the father of anyone here, my dear friends, the Dr and Mrs Sutcliffe excepted; and I feel as if I were their child, I do indeed. [MRS SUTCLIFFE *indignant.*] Now – [*taking* KRUX's *arm, mistaking him for* VAUGHAN] – to the carriage, and home quickly. I beg your pardon. [VAUGHAN *offers his arm.*] Oh, thank you – thank you – Good-night! – good-night!

> [*They go off.* DOCTOR *and* MRS SUTCLIFFE *and* KRUX *exeunt.* JACK *and* LORD BEAUFOY *take their leave of* BELLA *and* NAOMI, *and go up stage and the other* GIRLS *cross over and converse together.*]

JACK: Arthur, you've been paying too much attention to that little girl – I'm surprised at you!

LORD B: Not more than you've been paying to the little heiress!

JACK: But heiresses are heiresses; and, of course, to heiresses one's attentions are always the correctest thing possible.

LORD B: Give me a cigar and a light. [*They light cigars from each other's cigars.*] Do you think I've behaved badly?

JACK: Very: walking her about and spooning her; I shall keep my eye upon you; you belong to the old Satanic school.

LORD B: And you to the modern cynical.

JACK: Poor little thing, like Faust and Marguerite.

LORD B: And you're the Mephistopheles.

JACK: Mephistopheles be——

LORD B: Unnecessary; he is already. [*to* GIRLS] Once more ladies, good-night! [*looking to* BELLA] I trust I may say, *au revoir*.

> [JACK *and* NAOMI *exchange glances. Exeunt* JACK *and* LORD BEAUFOY, *at gate.* NAOMI *and* BELLA *watch them out.*]

ALL THE GIRLS: [*Cross to and attack* NAOMI *and* BELLA.] Well, I'm sure, I——

> [*Enter* MRS SUTCLIFFE, DR SUTCLIFFE, *and* KRUX. GIRLS *stop suddenly.*]

MRS S: Oh, Mr Krux – [*agitated*] – if it should be true – [*Sinks on garden seat, almost fainting –* BELLA *takes her hand; she repulses her.*] – Don't touch me – how dare you? You, whom I have reared out of charity, how have you behaved this night? Your conduct towards Lord Beaufoy is known to me – touch me with your hand – or, rather, yes – give it me. [*Takes* BELLA's *hand.*] Where did you get that ring?

BELLA: [*trembling*] Lord Beaufoy gave it me.

GIRLS: Lord Beaufoy!

KRUX: I told you – I told you!

MRS S: You have been watched, you wicked creature!

KRUX: [*aside*] Yes, I did that. [*proudly*]

MRS S: Walking alone, and talking to Lord Beaufoy.

NAOMI: But there's no harm in that – I was walking and talking with Jack.

GIRLS: Oh!

NAOMI: Mr Poyntz! Mr Poyntz, and I'm sure——

MRS S: Silence, Miss Tighe. Little did I think when I took you into my house I was nourishing a serpent in my bosom.

DR S: My dear!

MRS S: Silence, Theodore! Young ladies, to your dormitories.

> [GIRLS *cross silently.* NAOMI, *trying to get a word with* BELLA, *is prevented by* MRS SUTCLIFFE.]

BELLA: [*to* GIRLS] Good-night! Wish me good-night!

MRS S: Don't stir! You abandoned girl, do not dare to address any of the young ladies.

> [*She motions to* GIRLS *to go. Exeunt* GIRLS.]

NAOMI: I will!

> [*She kisses* BELLA, *and as she goes off, turns and makes a grimace at* KRUX.]

KRUX: Hussy! Too proud to brush her betters.

MRS S: You leave this house to-morrow morning. The man will drive you to the station, and, in London, you can go, for one month only, to my friend Mrs Stanton. By that time you may find some situation. You to dare, under my very eyes, to cast out lures to my guests. You——

DR S: My love!

MRS S: [*violently*] Theodore, silence!

DR S: [*in a subdued passion*] Amanthis, hold your tongue! [MRS SUTCLIFFE *dumbfounded.*] The pupils are not here now, and I will speak. [*to* BELLA] Tell me, Bella, did Lord Beaufoy give you that ring?

BELLA: Yes.

DR S: And why did he give it you?

BELLA: I must not tell you that.

KRUX: There!

DR S: [*turning and raising his stick*] Out of my sight, or I shall strike you. [*Exit* KRUX, *hastily.*] Did Lord Beaufoy tell you that he loved you?

BELLA: Yes.

MRS S: I said so.

DR S: Good heavens! what harm is there in that? – perhaps he spoke the truth. 'Tis easy to love Bella – I love her!

BELLA: [*gratefully*] Oh, Doctor!

MRS S: Take me into the house, or I shall faint.

DR S: You are harsh and cruel.

MRS S: [*weeping*] Oh, Theodore, you no longer love me.

DR S: No dear – I mean – yes – I——

MRS S: Go, go, leave me – the same as thirty-five years ago!

> [*Exit* MRS SUTCLIFFE.]

DR S: [*following her*] My love – Amanthis!

> [*Exit* DR SUTCLIFFE.]

BELLA: Was I so wrong to listen to him? Is it so wicked to wear the ring he gave me? If I thought so, I'd – [*About to throw it off, retains it.*] – No, it seems to comfort me. And to-morrow I must go. Must I leave you, my dear home? – the only home I ever knew – and my companions, and the old servants who have been so kind to me? What will become of me – how can I face the world alone? [*sobbing, sinking on her knees*] I am thrust forth – alone – alone – alone!

[*During the last few words* NAOMI *has opened the window and appeared on balcony.*]

NAOMI: Not alone, dear – I'm here, and I'll go with you. Here's my jewels – [*Throws down small parcel on stage.*] – and my purse. There's more than fourteen pounds in it – [*Descends staircase.*] – and we'll go together; and never, never will we be separated in this world, until death do us part.

[*The two* GIRLS *embrace each other, and sob as they kneel upon the ground.*]

BELLA: No, no, Naomi.
NAOMI: [*fondling*] I will – I will – I will!

[LORD BEAUFOY *appears on wall, near tree,* JACK *watching him at wall. Tableau.*]

END OF ACT III

ACT IV

SCENE I – *Same as Act III. Morning. Discovered –* GIRLS *ut play: Skipping rope, battledore, hoops, &c.* NAOMI TIGHE *sitting apart, pale and melancholy.*

MILLY: Naomi, will you play?

NAOMI: I've got a headache.

TILLY: Thinking of Bella?

NAOMI: Yes; thinking of Bella.

CLARA: Poor Bella!

NAOMI: I wonder where he is!

GIRLS: *He* is?

NAOMI: I mean *she* is – how could Bella be a *he?*

MILLY: You've never been well since she went away.

TILLY: And that's just six weeks ago.

NAOMI: Six weeks to-day. [*Sighs. All the* GIRLS *mimic and laugh.*] You're an unfeeling set of brutes; and, if you tease me, I'll slap your faces.

TILLY: [*Crosses to* NAOMI.] Really, Miss Tighe, you should remember that you are with white young ladies, and not among your blackamoor negroes, now. I should like to see you slap my face.

NAOMI: You shall feel me do it in a minute! Oh, I wish Bella was here.

TILLY: Bella was a servant.

NAOMI: She was not.

TILLY: She was.

NAOMI: She wasn't.

TILLY: She was.

NAOMI: She wasn't.

TILLY: Sighing about a little kitchen girl, because she was useful to you. Girls, did you like Bella?

GIRLS: U – m. N – o!

MILLY: She hadn't spirit enough for me.

KITTY: She was so stupid.

CLARA: She was too clever for me.

LAURA: I didn't care much for her, because she was so terribly wide awake .

HETTY: [*in swing*] I liked her.

GIRLS: Why?

HETTY: Because she used to give me her bread and butter.

[GIRLS *laugh – school-bell rings.*]

HETTY: O, there's breakfast.

NAOMI: I shan't go in to breakfast. Mrs Sutcliffe said that when I had my headaches I might stop out here for the fresh air.

[*All laugh.*]

TILLY: Fresh air! Fresh—— [*pretending to see her*] Oh, here's Bella!

NAOMI: [*turning*] Eh!

[GIRLS *laugh, and exeunt.*]

TILLY: [*going. Returns and gives* NAOMI *a sweet.*] Never mind the sneerers. There's an acid drop.

[*She gives her one, and goes.*]

NAOMI: I wish I'd been a boy! I don't see what use girls are – boys are so much more manly. [*Rises, looks round to see if she is unobserved – sits on garden seat, then draws letter from her bosom, and reads*] "My dear, dear Naomi!" [*Laughs, blushes, and hides her face in her hands.*] – "My dear, dear Naomi! – [*Business repeated.*] "My dear, dear Naomi!" – I read that so often that I hardly ever get to the rest of the letter – "Though I have no business to write to you," – such nonsense – "I cannot refrain from sending you these few lines, to tell you what I have been about since my last. You see, my love" – [*Laughs again.*] "You see, my love" – how well he does express himself, to be sure. He's quite an author – "You see, my love, I thought it necessary to see your guardian before I renewed my correspondence with you, because you are so young." – I hate that; Jack's always flinging that in my face. People can't be born grown up, can they? No! I wish I was as old as Mrs Sutcliffe; then people couldn't say I was too young – "However, Mr Farintosh was so ill that he couldn't see anybody. The poor old fellow had a sudden attack, and for three days his life was despaired of. However, he is now better. I saw him yesterday; he could hardly speak, but, as good fortune would have it, one of your guardians was with him, so I was introduced; and I am to dine with him to-morrow." – I wish I was my guardian, to have my Jack to dine with him; but I daresay he won't appreciate him; it requires great intellect and good taste to understand Jack – "I have not heard a word of your friend, Bella, beyond what I have told you; she arrived safely at Mrs Stanton's, where Mrs Sutcliffe sent her, and three days after she disappeared. Mrs Stanton is of opinion that she has not gone to any situation. I have again tried to find Lord Beaufoy, but without success. So, dearest," – oh, that's beautiful – "So, dearest, wish me luck to-morrow at dinner, where I will feign all the interest in the money market, and the tallow ditto, and in hides, cochineal, indigo, and grey shirtings, which these interesting topics are calculated to inspire" – he spells cochineal with two e's, but affection is superior to

orthography, and I love him all the better for his bad spelling –
"And now, dearest Naomi, to talk about ourselves. When I
first saw you I looked at you with curiosity, because I had
heard that you were very rich; but when I left you that evening
I felt that I was in love," – ah [*sighs*] – "and since I left you I am
as unhappy as a sailor without a ship. You know that I am
poor;" now he's going to talk rubbish again, what has that to
do with it? £10,000 couldn't look, and walk, and talk as he
does. £10,000 couldn't have been fighting in the Crimea.
£10,000 couldn't put his arm round your waist and squeeze
you, could it? [*fiercely, then subsiding into gentleness*] No! –
"but I love you, fondly, truly, and devotedly [*beginning to cry*];
and if I am happy enough, through old Farintosh's in-
tercession, to please your guardians, the conduct of my life
shall prove the truth of your affectionate and faithful Jack." –
[*crying*] – that's real poetry – "Your affectionate and faithful
Jack."

> [*She cries in her pocket-handkerchief.* JACK *looks over
> wall.*]

JACK: [*whispering*] Naomi.

> [NAOMI *starts.*]

NAOMI: Is it you? [*hiding letter.* NAOMI *opens gate. Enter* JACK, *with
muddy boots, &c.; they come down stage and look at each other.
A long pause.*] Well, what have you to tell me?
JACK: Loads; but now I see you I forget it.
NAOMI: When did you come?
JACK: By the night train. I walked from the station here, over the
fields.
NAOMI: Then you haven't been in bed all night?
JACK: No.
NAOMI: [*aside*] What devotion. [*Sits. Another pause.*] Why did you
come so suddenly, without letting me know?
JACK: [*fetching chair and sitting* L. *of* NAOMI] I called yesterday at old
Farintosh's, and the servant told me that he had started for his
box here; so I came on by the night train, because I knew,
Naomi, that he would bring me with him, and that I should
see you; so I wandered about, waiting for him, for I know he'll
be here shortly; but I couldn't resist looking over the wall
and——
NAOMI: Here I was. [*another pause*] Are you quite well?
JACK: Quite; are you?
NAOMI: Yes, thank you. [*another pause*] When sweethearts meet after
a long absence their conversation is so interesting, isn't it?
Then you've had no breakfast?

JACK: No.

NAOMI: Neither have I. What sympathy! But what can old Farintosh want so particularly with the Sutcliffes?

JACK: I don't know; but tell me what has happened here since——

NAOMI: Since Bella left? Oh, Mrs Sutcliffe was very ill, and the Doctor has been very cross. [*whispering*] The other day I overheard him talking about Mr. Krux, and he said, D – a – m. Dam!

JACK: Tremendous!

NAOMI: But my guardians – what did they seem to think of you?

JACK: They're both City men, and they can't think. By-the-way, do you know how old you are?

NAOMI: Yes. Eighteen.

JACK: No; you're nearly twenty-one. Your guardians told me that you were so forward, and they didn't know where to send you, so they deceived you on the point of age intentionally.

NAOMI: What a shame, swindling a girl out of three years in that way. And Bella——

JACK: Poor girl!

NAOMI: I loved her so much, and she's never written a word to me. I think it pays best to put all your love upon a man – girls are so deceitful, and men are quite the contrary.

JACK: Some men. There are men, and – individuals.

NAOMI: Will you always be good to me?

JACK: I'll try.

NAOMI: I should like you to be bad, though, sometimes.

JACK: Why?

NAOMI: Because then I should have the pleasure of forgiving you.

JACK: [*rising and putting chair back*] I think I shall be able to accommodate you, as far as that goes.

NAOMI: Jack, when a girl is in love, why do they call her spoons?

JACK: Because she's so often carried to the lips.

> [JACK *is about to kiss* NAOMI *as* KRUX *enters.* NAOMI *crosses to* L.]

KRUX: Miss Tighe. How do you do – I hope I have the pleasure of seeing you in health?

JACK: Quite.

KRUX: I'm quite well, thank you.

JACK: I didn't ask the question.

KRUX: I did not know that you were here.

NAOMI: That's not the only thing he don't know.

JACK: I came to tell the Doctor that Mr Farintosh is expected at the lodge, and seeing the gate open——

KRUX: The gate open! tut, tut, tut. Now who could have opened the gate?

NAOMI: The cat.

KRUX: The cat – what cat?

NAOMI: [*crossing to* KRUX] A cat I keep to scratch spies' eyes out. [*to* JACK] You've been in the army – tell me, would it be wrong to kill Mr Krux?

JACK: By no means.

KRUX: Mrs Sutcliffe sent me to tell you that Mr Farintosh had arrived.

JACK: ⎫
NAOMI: ⎭ Arrived!

KRUX: Yes, and here he is.

JACK: [*to* NAOMI] You'll hardly know the beau again. Since his recovery, he no longer dresses himself in the latest mode, but goes about like any other old gentleman, and looks much the better for it.

> [*Enter* DR SUTCLIFFE *and* MRS SUTCLIFFE, *both very grave.*]

JACK: My dear Doctor and Mrs Sutcliffe, so glad to see you. I got here before Mr Farintosh, and was just going——

MRS S: [*saluting* JACK – *seeing* NAOMI *about to go*] You may remain, Miss Tighe; Mr Farintosh wishes to see you.

> [NAOMI *delighted. Enter* FARINTOSH, *his appearance entirely altered – silver hair, whiskers, and his dress appropriate to his age.*]

FARINTOSH: My dear Miss Tighe, your guardians send you their love. Eh, Poyntz, you here! – How's that? How's that?

JACK: I came down by the train, because I heard you had come on here.

FARINTOSH: Very kind, very kind.

JACK: And while I was waiting about——

KRUX: The garden gate was opened by the cat!

DR S: ⎫ Eh?
MRS S: ⎭ What?

JACK: I – I – I saw the cat outside waiting to come in, so I opened the gate for him or her!

KRUX: From the outside?

JACK: No; I was lifting the animal over the wall, when seeing Miss Tighe in the garden——

NAOMI: I opened the gate; Mr Krux, you can shut it.

> [KRUX *shuts gate, and then comes down.*]

MRS S: Mr Poyntz, let us thank you for the efforts you have made to find that poor girl.

FARINTOSH: Yes, yes; a sad affair – a sad affair.

DR S: A child I was so much attached to!

KRUX: So was I!

> [DOCTOR *gives* MRS SUTCLIFFE *chair.* DOCTOR *sits between her and* FARINTOSH, *who sits on chair which* JACK *takes from* KRUX, *who was about to sit on it close by swing.*]

DR S: We have only just broken the news to our old friend.

FARINTOSH: [*to* JACK *slyly*] It appears that the young lady went off with somebody who was not a young lady. These things happen – girls are but girls; we must not expect them to be angels.

KRUX: [*shaking his head*] If you do you'll be disappointed – continually disappointed.

FARINTOSH: However, my dear friends, the news I bring will, I am sure, give you pleasure even in the midst of your grief. You know, Theodore, that my poor son [*with emotion*] died without my forgiveness – my boy died leaving a wife and child. For years I have been in search of them, but owing to the frequent names assumed by poor Fred for the sake of avoiding creditors, and to his having been some time abroad, I could find no traces either of my daughter-in-law or my grandchild. At last they are found.

DR S: My dear old friend, receive my congratulations.

MRS S: And mine.

NAOMI: [*crossing to* FARINTOSH] Oh, I am so glad, it must be so beautiful to have a father!

FARINTOSH: [*taking* NAOMI's *hand*] My dear child, you shall soon see our meeting. As I said, my lawyer has traced them out; my daughter-in-law, poor Fred's wife, is dead.

KRUX: I congrat——

> [JACK *stops* KRUX.]

FARINTOSH: But her child lives – lives – lives! – my dear friends, lives to be a central object of my affections – lives to be a solace and a comfort to the few years yet remaining to me; for I have been a foolish, vain old fellow, and tried to pass for a young fop, when I was really an old fool. I thought of all this, night and day, as I lay in bed, when they told me I was dying, and the hardest pang of all was that I should not live long enough to see my grandchild – but I recovered; I was never better – never so thankful – or so well.

DR S: We are so pleased.

MRS S: Your happiness compensates us for our grief.

FARINTOSH: My dear friends, if you had children, or if you ever have –

but I suppose that is almost past hope now – you could imagine my joy. You shall witness it. I invited you on purpose, for my granddaughter is here.

JACK: Here!

FARINTOSH: Yes.

NAOMI: Here! Is it Milly, or Tilly, or Laura, or Clara, or Hetty, or Kitty?

MRS S: Did you bring her with you?

FARINTOSH: What! Didn't I tell you? What a stupid old man I am. Now comes the tremendous and delightful surprise. My poor boy's last alias was Mountain – his wife's maiden name. Pursued everywhere by creditors, she retained the name after his death. Mrs Mountain, as she called herself, died in the village here, close by. Her child was left to an old woman named Marks, who brought her up, till you – you adopted her – you best of men and women. You, my old college chum – [*shaking* DR SUTCLIFFE's *hand*] – and you my old sweetheart. [*kissing her hand*] She is known here by the name of Bella Marks. I suppose I saw her when I was here a month ago, but I did not remember her among so many. Perhaps – ah, me! – I did not notice her. Now, where is she? This is the supreme moment of my life. Give her to me! I can contain myself no longer! My heart is hungry for her! Call Bella – my grandchild – call her – give her to me! [*All aghast. A pause.*] What is the matter with you? Isn't she at home? Is she out on a visit? If so, never mind, send for her! [NAOMI *bursts out sobbing.*] My child! [*A pause.*] She's not – dead! [NAOMI *gives him her hand.*] No! no! Thank heaven! Well, then – what – what – what – what – [*getting alarmed*] Tell me – tell me——

[*A pause.*]

KRUX: [*with concealed triumph*] Sir, if no one else will tell you, I will.

FARINTOSH: Go on.

KRUX: Your granddaughter left here six weeks ago. It seems that, in mentioning to you the fact of a pupil who was missing in London, Mrs Sutcliffe has not mentioned her name. [MRS SUTCLIFFE *indicates that she has not.*] The girl whom she has told you of, who eloped clandestinely, was Bella Marks – I should say, is Bella Farintosh, your granddaughter.

FARINTOSH: [*seizing him by the collar*] You lie! I'll throttle you! I'll kill you! [JACK *releases* KRUX *from* FARINTOSH, *twisting* KRUX *into* L.H. *corner.*] It's not true! Theodore, my friend, say it's not true! Jack! my child! Speak! speak!

[DOCTOR *and* MRS SUTCLIFFE *take his hands. He sinks into a chair. They surround him.*]

KRUX: [*frightened*] It is quite true – upon my honour as a gentleman.

DR S: My dear friend!

FARINTOSH: To find her, but to find her – lost!

DR S: It may not be as we suppose.

MRS S: My husband went to London to seek out——

FARINTOSH: And the name of – of the man – she was supposed to accompany. [*Another pause.*] His name? You may tell me – I can bear it now. His name, I say?

KRUX: Lord Beaufoy.

FARINTOSH: [*his hands hiding his face*] My nephew!

[*A ring heard at the gate.* KRUX *opens it.*]

KRUX: Lord Beaufoy!

[*Enter* LORD BEAUFOY. KRUX *shuts gate.*]

KRUX: Lord Beaufoy.

LORD B: [*radiant*] My dear uncle, Doctor, Mrs Sutcliffe, Jack. [*smiling and affable. Pause.*] Why, what's the matter?

DR S: [*rising*] My Lord Beaufoy, we believe that you, and you only, can tell us the hiding-place of Bella Marks.

NAOMI: [*crying*] My dear Bella!

KRUX: A most improper young person.

LORD B: The hiding place of Bella Marks! Yes, I admit I know it – what then?

DR S: What then! [*calming himself*] But I forgot, Lord Beaufoy – you are ignorant that——

FARINTOSH: [*rising*] Let me tell him, Theodore. You are ignorant that Bella is my granddaughter and your cousin.

LORD B: No; two days ago my lawyer, who, as you know, is also yours, informed me of the fact.

FARINTOSH: And fearing that I should alter the disposition of my property, you accomplished this ruin for revenge.

LORD B: Not so; when Miss Farintosh left Mrs Stanton's, I believed her to be only Bella Marks.

FARINTOSH: [*advancing*] Then all may be repaired. Arthur – my nephew – you – you know I'm very rich; my granddaughter shall inherit all I have – I can't last long. Let me implore you, marry her.

LORD B: Marry her? Impossible!

FARINTOSH: Impossible?

LORD B: Yes; I cannot.

FARINTOSH: Why not?

LORD B: I am already married.

JACK:
FARINTOSH: } Married?

FARINTOSH: Secretly?

LORD B: Yes, secretly.

> [FARINTOSH *sinks again into chair.*]

FARINTOSH: My punishment! My punishment!

LORD B: And apropos, Jack——

> [*All in consternation.* LORD BEAUFOY *turns to* JACK.]

JACK: Lord Beaufoy, understand that from this time we are strangers. My contempt for you is too deep for utterance.

LORD B: You shall apologise to me for those words.

JACK: Apologise?

LORD B: And be sorry that you used them. Your [*to* JACK] indignant virtue amuses me; and so does yours [*to* DR SUTCLIFFE] and [*to* FARINTOSH] yours. [*to* JACK] I thought you were a cynic; you used to profess that no occurrence on this earth could be of the slightest consequence. Was your cynicism only a sham? If so, how do you defend it? If mock virtue be a bad sort of hypocrisy, what is mock vice? For you – [*turning*] – how can you reproach me? Bella is contented and happy. [*to* MRS SUTCLIFFE] She does not fetch or carry like a servant. She rings bells – she does not answer them. [*to* FARINTOSH] Your paternal interest is a somewhat sudden spasm of affection. You lived the last eighteen years happily without her – whence this new-born feeling? Am I to suppose it is compensation, or too late remorse? or a desire to be attended by a nurse who takes no wages? Why has this neglected child become so suddenly an object of such tenderness? Not because she has been poor, unloved, and unprotected, but because she is the grandchild of a rich, proud gentleman, who has forgotten his duty to her for twenty years, to remember it during his seventy-first.

DR S: [*crossing to him, and speaking in a whisper*] Lord Beaufoy, ladies are present; I am an old man; if you do not instantly quit this place, by heaven! I'll conduct you by the collar.

> [*Enter all the* YOUNG LADIES. *Hats on, as from their morning walk.*]

MILLY: Oh, Mrs Sutcliffe, we saw such a lovely carriage and footmen, coming towards the school.

> [GIRLS *indicate they see* LORD BEAUFOY *and* JACK.]

LORD B: [*to* DOCTOR] I will go without assistance – but before I go, Mrs Sutcliffe, let me present you to – Lady Beaufoy! [*opening gate, and discovering* BELLA, *dressed as a bride; two footmen attending her.* LORD BEAUFOY *brings her down.*] My wife and your grandchild.

FARINTOSH: My child – my dear – dear grandchild!

[*He embraces her.*]

MRS S: [BELLA *goes to* MRS SUTCLIFFE.] My favourite pupil! [*kissing* BELLA]

NAOMI: [*hysterical*] Please pass her round! I want to kiss her, too! [BELLA *crosses to* NAOMI, *embracing her.*] Oh, my darling – my darling, my true, real lady!

[FARINTOSH, *in his excitement, kisses* MRS SUTCLIFFE. *Everybody astonished.*]

DR S: My dear, for thirty-five years——

FARINTOSH: But, my dear Arthur, how could you be so cruel?

LORD B: My dear uncle, how could you be so suspicious? Knowing that you wished me to marry, in what conventional cant calls my own rank, I prevailed on Bella, who reluctantly consented to become my wife; knowing that once married not even an archbishop could unmarry us, imagine my delight when, on our return to town, my lawyer informed me that, unknowingly, I had married my own cousin.

NAOMI: Of course, you're cousins – it isn't unlawful for – no – cousins can marry. That's a real comfort, isn't it?

LORD B: We went to your house; were told that you had flown here; came after you. I wished to present my lady to her friends in proper form, and really your reception was such that I resolved to punish you.

[*Music, "La Cenerentola." Piano.*]

BELLA: [*to* FARINTOSH, *who has resumed seat.*] You will not be ashamed of your grandchild, because she has not been brought up amid the luxury to which she will try to grow accustomed?

FARINTOSH: Ashamed! My – my happiness is only too great.

BELLA: [*to* DR *and* MRS SUTCLIFFE] And you, my dear, kind friends, to whom I owe everything, will forgive me for the suspense I have caused you? I would have written, but my lord——

LORD B: [*correcting her*] Arthur.

BELLA: Arthur wished me to keep silent, and——

DR S: The end crowns the work!

MRS S: My sweet darling, I had no apprehensions; I always knew that your destiny would be a high one.

BELLA: [*to* NAOMI] And you'll come and pass your holidays with me?

NAOMI: Yes, dear; and you shall show me all your new things.

DR S: [*surrounding* LORD BEAUFOY] I have to ask your lordship's pardon.

JACK: [*ditto*] I could bite my tongue off, Arthur, for what I said just now.

LORD B: Not another word; you were all quite right. I told you, Jack, you would be sorry.

[*Music ceases.*]

BELLA: Mr Krux, I am sure you wish me every happiness.

KRUX: Every happiness, Miss Bella.

NAOMI: [*angrily*] Lady Beaufoy. Do you know who you are talking to? Lady Beaufoy.

DR S: Mr Krux, if you would like to take your usual walk don't let regard for us prevent you.

KRUX: Thank you, Dr Sutcliffe, I——

> [*He bows to characters, then going up bows to the two* FOOTMEN, *who are standing on either side of gate, and goes off by gate.*]

NAOMI: [*quickly*] Jack, do you love me?

JACK: Naomi!

NAOMI: Then run after Mr Krux, and give him a good thrashing. You won't mind, will you?

JACK: It will be a pleasure.

> [*Exit* JACK *after* KRUX. *Immediately after,* KRUX's *hat comes flying over wall.*]

TILLY: [*who has been reading book*] "Cinderella was then conducted to the Prince, who asked her to accept his hand. The marriage ceremony took place in a few days; and Cinderella gave her sisters magnificent apartments in the palace."

MILLY: "And a short time after married them to two great Lords of the Court."

ALL THE GIRLS: [*surrounding* BELLA, *who is sitting on stage by swing*] Oh, my lady!

NAOMI: It's just like the story – [*looking off*] – Prince, carriages, footmen, and all. [*taking up pumpkin*] And to think that this [*the pumpkin*] should ever grow into that.

> [*Pointing to* FOOTMEN, *and placing pumpkin at the feet of* FOOTMAN.]

FARINTOSH: And, in this fairy story, what am I?

NAOMI: You? – you're the godmother.

LORD B: [*taking parcel from* FOOTMAN] Knowing my wife's talent for narrative, I have here something I could only offer to her on the spot.

BELLA: Another present!

LORD B: [*opening case*] A pair of glass slippers.

GIRLS: Oh!

[*They surround him. Re-enter* JACK *through gate in wall,* NAOMI *meeting him.*]

NAOMI: Did you do it?

JACK: Yes.

NAOMI: Did you hurt him much?

JACK: He said I did; and I believe he spoke the truth.

FARINTOSH: [*taking the hands of* DOCTOR *and* MRS SUTCLIFFE] See, my friends, how a good deed germinates into a great one. Your past kindness to a friendless orphan girl is the cause of all our present happiness.

DR S: No, no, not so; your nephew's nature is an exceptionally fine one. He is in the highest sense of the word a gentleman; and there is no sight under the sun finer than a true gentleman.

FARINTOSH: Except one.

DR S: Eh?

FARINTOSH: A true lady!

DR S: So many things are required for the composition of the real thing. One wants nobility of feeling.

FARINTOSH: A kind heart.

DR S: A noble mind.

FARINTOSH: Modesty.

DR S: Gentleness.

FARINTOSH: Courage.

DR S: Truthfulness.

FARINTOSH: Birth.

DR S: Breeding.

MRS S: And, above all, – School!

[*As* LORD BEAUFOY *stoops to fit on slipper,* NAOMI *having taken off* BELLA'*s satin shoe, the Curtain falls. Music.*]

CURTAIN

BIRTH

Produced at the New Theatre Royal, Bristol, on 5th October, 1870.

CAST OF CHARACTERS

Earl of Eagleclyffe	Mr H. Vincent
Paul Hewitt	Mr J. H. Slater
Jack Randall	Mr E. A. Sothern
The Duke	Mr T. A. Palmer
Stanton	Mr Brooks
Dick	Mr Stanley
Tom	Mr Hosegood
Harry	Mr Thomas
The Lady Adeliza	Miss Louise Willes
Sarah Hewitt	Miss Amy Roselle

Forgemen, workmen, servants, volunteers

Act I
THE FACTORY. – *In the Valley! Exterior of Office.* – MORNING.

Act II
THE CASTLE. – *On the Heights!! Banquet Hall.* – EVENING.

Act III
THE KEEP. – *In the Depths!!! Ivy-covered Ruins.* – NIGHT.

Modern Costumes. Time of Representation, two hours and a quarter.

BIRTH

ACT I

SCENE I – *The exterior of the office of* PAUL HEWITT's *works. A wall crosses the back of the stage, in which are large green wooden gates, like folding-doors. Wall down* R.H., *containing small gate. On* L.H. *an office, built chiefly of glass, from which a verandah and pillars, ornamented with creepers, is built out on stage. Door* L.H., *leading into office under verandah; tables, two or three garden chairs, and a davenport. A table, with tumblers and decanter of water. On stage, a carpet, painted like gravel. The whole looking new. On the cloth, high chimneys, hills, a wood. The castle on an eminence.*

> [*Enter* PAUL, *letters in his hand, followed by* STANTON, *a clerk.*]

PAUL: This is for Mr Carter [*giving letters, &c.*], that for Mr Swayne.

STANTON: And about the order from Tipps and Co.?

PAUL: Ask my sister.

STANTON: And young Delve's design for——?

PAUL: Ask my sister. Is everything ready for the friend we expect to-day?

STANTON: Yes. Miss Sarah saw to that.

> [*Noise without.*]

PAUL: What's that?

STANTON: It's the Duke.

PAUL: Crazy old vagabond! What does he want here?

STANTON: Oh, nothing – but to make himself disagreeable. He came into the yard, and began sneering and jeering, and one of the boys threw a cinder at him, and he threatened to shoot him.

PAUL: Has he got his gun then?

STANTON: Yes; and the men got round him, and Billy Purvis wanted to fight him.

PAUL: I'll have no fighting here. This is a factory, not a Fives' court. I particularly desire that no one employed here meddles with anyone belonging to the Castle. Send the old ruffian off the premises.

> [*Exit* STANTON.]

PAUL: [*bitterly*] The Castle! Another month, and the affair will be settled; and they will be – gone. [*with sadness*] I must forget them, though they will not forget me.

[*Exit* PAUL.]

[*Murmurs without.* Go out! Turn him out! Get out, &c. *The* DUKE *appears at door, menacing* DICK, TOM, HARRY, *and* FORGEMEN, *who follow him, with the butt of his gun.*]

DUKE: [*an old man of seventy, in velveteen coat, and red waistcoat, high gaiters, white hair, and long moustaches, also white; his manner soldier-like, distinguished, and haughty; his attire, poor, but not ragged; a picturesque, bronzed figure*] I'll go when I please. I'm only used to receive orders from gentlemen – not from such as you!

DICK: Mr Paul says you're to leave the works.

DUKE: [*with contempt*] Mr Paul!

DICK: Yes. What have you got to say against him? Go out! [*The* DUKE *holds up his gun.*] You murdering thief – would you dare to fire? Take the gun from him, lads.

[*The gun is seized from the* DUKE. *The* FORGEMEN *surround him. He is thrown on the ground. At this moment enter* JACK RANDALL. *He knocks aside two or three men, and stands over* DUKE.]

JACK: What are you about? Twenty to one.

TOM: Who are you?

[*The* DUKE *rises.*]

JACK: Not much. Only a man – but I am *that*. What are you?

FORGEMEN: Smash him! Get out!

[*As they are about to hustle* JACK, SARAH *appears.*]

SARAH: [*on threshold*] What's all this?

FORGEMEN: [*quieted*] Miss Sarah!

JACK: Sarah! That must be Paul's sister!

[*During this the* DUKE *bears himself with great dignity, and shows no sign of fear.* PAUL *enters, and passes* SARAH.]

PAUL: What is this?

DICK: [*his face to* PAUL; *his back to* JACK *and the* DUKE] It's that murdering vagabond.

PAUL: Which murdering vagabond?

DICK: [*seizing* JACK, *and bringing him to the front*] This.

JACK: Me!

PAUL: My dear Jack.
JACK: Paul.

[*They shake hands.*]

PAUL: [*crossing to the* DUKE] How is it, Duke, that you will continue to insult my men? They never insult you.
DUKE: They do! Their very presence is an insult.
DICK: ⎫ Pitch him out!
TOM: ⎬ Chuck him in the cinder heap.
HARRY: ⎭ Break his neck.
JACK: Fine old fellow! [*to* PAUL] Is he mad, or only a patriot?
PAUL: [*taking the* DUKE's *gun from* FORGEMEN, *and returning it to him; the* DUKE *does not take it.*] Now leave the works!

[*The* DUKE *indicates that he will not stir.*]

DICK: ⎫ With a sound thrashing –
TOM: ⎬ With sore bones –
HARRY: ⎭ After a moulding.
PAUL: Silence! I'm master here.
TOM: We won't be insulted.
FORGEMEN: No.

[*Surrounding the* DUKE. *Factory bell rings. A pause.*]

PAUL: [*after looking at his watch*] Dinner!
FORGEMEN: Dinner!
JACK: And beer. [FORGEMEN *pause.*] At my expense.

[*The* FORGEMEN *go off.*]

JACK: I thought the beer would settle them. One glass of "bitter" makes the whole world kin.
PAUL: Now, Duke, take your gun, and here are five shillings. [*offering them; the* DUKE *refuses*]
DUKE: I only take money from my master, as you from yours.
PAUL: [*smiling*] Who is my master?
DUKE: The Devil!
PAUL: The Devil?
JACK: He's such a large employer of labour. He's everybody's master.
DUKE: Look round you; where all used to be rock, and moss, and trees [*pointing to chimneys*], now smoke, fire, cinders, ashes!
SARAH: He means the works.
JACK: Well, they do smell a little sulphury.
PAUL: But a thousand hands are employed; and their wives and families live in abundance – on land that only teemed with rabbits and wood-pigeons.
DUKE: What matter?
JACK: He doesn't like wood-pigeons.

SARAH: [*picking up money*] Now, Duke, you'll take this money from me——

DUKE: No!

SARAH: As far as old Nanny's; she is sick. Give her my love, and I hope she's better.

[*The DUKE takes money.*]

JACK: [*aside to* PAUL] Will he give it her?

PAUL: Every copper. I'd trust him with untold gold.

JACK: Then he *is* mad!

[SARAH *takes gun from* PAUL, *and hands it to the* DUKE, *who takes it gently.*]

DUKE: You're good, because you're a woman.

JACK: He's *very* mad!

DUKE: [*crossing to* PAUL] But you have no right here. My master is a great earl; his sister is a noble lady: if harm come to him, or to her, neither the smoke, nor the fire, nor the engines, nor the rest of these accoutrements of hell can make up for it.

[*Exit* DUKE.]

PAUL: Now, Jack, let me introduce you to my sister.

SARAH: I am always glad to know any friend of my brother's.

JACK: And I'm always glad to know any sister of anybody's. [*shaking hands with* SARAH] I wish I had a sister.

SARAH: Why?

JACK: I don't know; for many reasons. A sister is a sort of sweetheart, who don't require attention; a kind of housekeeper, whom you can't fall in love with; an agreeable spinster, whom you can't marry. In short, a sister is as nice as – as somebody else's wife, without being so dangerous. But that extraordinary old man. What is he?

PAUL: The Duke.

JACK: What duke?

SARAH: His Grace the Gamekeeper of the Castle.

JACK: The Castle?

PAUL: [*pointing*] Yes. You see it there.

JACK: Embosomed in trees – a noble building. But surely that velveteeny old man cannot be the owner of——

PAUL: Owner! – no. He represents the feudal serf, as his chief represents the feudal sovereign, of the good old days. The old fellow has been a soldier in the late lord's time, and in his father's; a slaughterer for sixpence a day. He is now – having retired from the lofty profession of human butchery – a privileged vagabond, whose only employment is to shoot pheasants and to hate me.

JACK: Hate you. Why?

PAUL: Because I am *not* a lord, because I *am* an inventor, and because I am prosperous.

SARAH: There is between us and the grand folks at the Castle a tremendous feud.

JACK: Who are the grand folks?

SARAH: The Earl of Eagleclyffe.

PAUL: And his sister, the Lady Adeliza.

JACK: Oh! There is a lady – is there?

SARAH: Yes – and I detest her.

JACK: [*aside*] Naturally. But go on.

PAUL: Briefly, then – if it interests you: Years ago, my father and this man's grandfather began the quarrel. My father was fortunate, and I have been fortunate; and we have always been eyesores and abominations in the eyes of the Eagleclyffes. As we grew richer, they grew poorer, and bit by bit we bought the land which they were compelled to sell. Then began the rivalry. If they gave a new window to the church – for which they did not pay – my father built a chapel of ease. I offered this present Earl, who has been in the army, the command of the volunteers which we send out from the works here. He declined it because I was captain. Year by year he has become more embittered against me. He has become poorer. He will repent it. I am surrounding him, and he will in time learn that bows and arrows are no match for weapons of modern calibre.

[PAUL *offers* JACK *chairs from verandah. They sit.*]

SARAH: One of the reasons why the Eagleclyffes – these noble paupers – hold our mushroom money-bags in contempt is, that we have no birth – that we are not persons of blood.

PAUL: The Eagleclyffe faith is that everybody must be born.

JACK: Why that seems reasonable enough. Unless people were born they could never make a figure in the world.

SARAH: [*with contempt*] Everybody is born.

JACK: Yes, many are born, but few get married.

SARAH: But with the Eagleclyffes, birth comes before marriage.

JACK: And afterwards, too, I hope. Then this Earl——

SARAH: Is a brute.

JACK: Is he young?

SARAH: About five-and-thirty.

JACK: Good-looking?

SARAH: Very; almost handsome.

JACK: Then you've seen him?

SARAH: Often.

JACK: And the Lady Hildefonza——

PAUL: Adeliza.

JACK: Adeliza. Is she handsome?

SARAH: I think not.

JACK: Ah! Ugly?

PAUL: No. Beautiful.

JACK: Have you seen her often?

PAUL: No: seldom. But what is the use of talking of such out-of-date ornaments? I have often met her riding. She wears an eagle's plume in her hat, and sometimes the Duke trots after her on a pony. The old man worships her. It is a good trait in his vagabond character.

[SARAH *watches her brother.*]

JACK: Did you ever speak to her?

PAUL: No.

JACK: I've an idea. This Earl of Eaglefeather——

SARAH: Eagleclyffe.

JACK: Eagleclyffe – is thirty-five. Lady Anna Melinda——

PAUL: Adeliza.

JACK: Adeliza – is——

PAUL: Three-and-twenty.

SARAH: More.

JACK: Give her a year or two, and say three-and-twenty. Given, The feud between you two – that is, you four; you two twos. Required, How to make it cease. You [*to* SARAH] marry the Earl. You [*to* PAUL] marry the lady. [PAUL *and* SARAH *start from their chairs. After a pause*] What have I said?

[PAUL *and* SARAH *begin to laugh uneasily, each regarding the other.*]

PAUL: Ha! ha! ha!

SARAH: Ha! ha! ha!

JACK: [*after a pause, rising*] Ha! ha! ha! I publish the banns of marriage between the most high Earl of Eaglenest, and the most beautiful Miss Sarah Hewitt; also, likewise, and to save time – and temper – I also publish the banns of marriage between the Lady Adeliza de Somebody and Paul Hewitt, iron-master. If any of you should know any just cause or impediment why these four persons should not commit——

PAUL: ⎫
SARAH: ⎬ [*uneasily*] Ha! ha! ha!

PAUL: Why, she thinks I'm a stoker.

SARAH: And he thinks me a scullery-maid.

JACK: Why?

SARAH: Because we have no birth – we are not of gentle blood. But I must go. Paul will show you to your room.

[*Exit* SARAH.]

PAUL: [*seating himself*] Now, Jack. It is years since we met. Let me say how glad I am to see you. You told me in your letter that since we parted——

JACK: [*seating himself*] At old Prosser's school; where you got the prize for mathematics, and I was expelled. Oh, since then all sorts of things have happened. I have been ruined.

PAUL: Your father left you——

JACK: Yes – but all that went.

PAUL: Went – where?

JACK: Everywhere. I lost heart, health, spirits, money – everything.

PAUL: I heard of some turf exploits of yours. You were——

JACK: Yes. I was – very much so.

PAUL: You found trainers and jockeys to be more expensive animals than even the horses.

JACK: The folks I found most expensive were not exactly jockeys; if they had been, they would have ridden side-saddle; and that is against the laws of the Jockey Club. But the laws of the Jockey Club are to be altered, so perhaps they'll bring in a side-saddle clause. However – suffice it – here I am – with just enough to be able *not* to live upon.

PAUL: What do you intend to do?

JACK: Work.

PAUL: That's right. Have you chosen your walk in life?

JACK: Yes. It's anything but a walk over.

PAUL: What trade?

JACK: It isn't a trade.

PAUL: Profession?

JACK: It's not a *regular* profession.

PAUL: What is it?

JACK: Literature.

PAUL: But have you the requisite ability?

JACK: How should I know? That's for the public to find out – not me.

PAUL: Are you going to write History?

JACK: No, slow.

PAUL: Essays?

JACK: No go.

PAUL: Novels? [JACK *shakes his head.*] What then?

JACK: Plays!

PAUL: Plays?

JACK: Yes, comedies. I want to write a comedy.

PAUL: Well, write one. I should think it is easy enough. You've only to be amusing, spirited, bright, and life-like. That's all.

JACK: Yes, that's all. You see, there is one capital thing in being a dramatist. There is no competition. Nowadays there are no dramatic authors – so they say.

PAUL: That is a good thing.

JACK: Then [*thoughtfully*] there are no actors.

PAUL: No actors?

JACK: No actors; at least, so they say.

PAUL: What, the actors?

JACK: Oh, no, not the actors; they say they're better than ever.

PAUL: Well, at this end of the world, with my nose in my furnaces, I know nothing of such matters; but I suppose, according to the laws of supply and demand, that as there are no authors and no actors there are no theatres.

JACK: Oh, yes, there are lots of theatres. They build a new one every month.

PAUL: Every month! And what do they do with it?

JACK: Do with it! Open it.

PAUL: And what then?

JACK: Shut it. What are theatres for but to open and shut, like telescopes, taking a sight at society a long way off? What the public wants is novelty – a good novelty.

PAUL: Exactly.

JACK: The difficulty is, where to find it.

PAUL: To find a public?

JACK: No, that's another difficulty; but it's a splendid thing when you do find it.

PAUL: What, a good novelty?

JACK: No; a public. If you find one, you're sure to find the other. What they require is the new.

PAUL: [*misunderstanding*] The nude!

JACK: [*impatiently*] No; the new. The nude isn't the new. The nude is as old as Adam – or Eve – in their original costume. However, the stage wants a dramatist; and I'm a dramatist who wants a stage; so I'm going to write a comedy, as I say, *au naturel*.

PAUL: How d'ye mean – *au naturel*?

JACK: I mean, to write raw! from the life. You know I'm a good shorthand writer?

PAUL: Yes; I remember.

JACK: [*producing book and pencil*] I can write as fast as any man can talk; and I can beat a man with a stutter by two syllables a second. Now, supposing I hear anything that would do as an outline for the plot of a comedy – say, for instance, that you told me just now about your feud with the Earl of Eagleberry – I write down [*writing*]: "Earl lives in castle on a hill – with his sister. Iron-master lives in valley – with his sister. The two men dislike each other; the two girls detest each other with an intensity known only to good women, who have been well brought up. By continued mutual annoyances they——" [*starting up, struck by a sudden thought*] Eureka!

PAUL: What!

JACK: I've found it.

PAUL: Found what?

JACK: The plot for my new comedy.

PAUL: I'm glad to hear it. Will you drive over with me to Beckley to meet my lawyer from London? [JACK, *absorbed, nods.*] I'll give orders to have the mare put to.

[*Exit* PAUL.]

JACK: [*absorbed, writing*] The Earl of Eaglecock [I'll call him Lord Featherherring] looks down with scorn on his immediate neighbour, Paul Hewitt. I'll call him Peter Stewpan. Lord Ravendevil meets Peter Fryingirons at a public dinner, and the noble lord pulls Peter Toastingfork's nose because Peter began his soup before the Archbishop of Everysee had said grace. Good! That's social and fashionable. Peter retorts with a butter-bowl full of lobster-sauce, misses Lord Bantampoodle, and hits the Archbishop. [*pausing*] No. You couldn't have an Archbishop on the stage, except in an historical play. The Lord Chamberlain wouldn't license an Archbishop. It won't do. [*Tears leaves out of book.*] Still, there's something in it. Let's try again. [*writing*] Lord Gamebag loses £500,000 to Peter Curlingtongs, at poker. He offers Peter to mortgage the estate——

[*Enter* PAUL.]

PAUL: Now, Jack, the trap's ready – are you?

JACK: Quite. I've got a fit of composition on me. [*writing*] Lord Fitzpheasantfeathers is a noble lord – living on a hill——

[*They go off.* JACK *composing.* SARAH *appears, a "Peerage" in her hand.*]

SARAH: My brother gone – and I suppose taken his eccentric friend with him. [*Opens "Peerage," and reads.*] "Eagleclyffe, Earl of, Stormont. Cecil Arthur Tudor Stormont, fourteenth earl, K.B., V.C.; born June the 10th, 1835. Succeeded his father in 1847 – was educated at Eton, and Christ Church, Oxford – is a lieutenant-colonel in the army, was a page of honour to the Queen, 1846–52. Sister living. Adeliza Elinor." Pah! "Patron of eleven livings – Beckley, Barrow-mud," um – ah. "Creation, 1465. Earl of Eagleclyffe – arms." Ah! I never can understand that. "Seat, Eagleclyffe, Loamshire. Town residence, Long's Hotel. Club, Carlton." [*throwing down book in pique*] What rubbish all that is! I've no patience. What a fuss about ancestors – as if everybody hadn't ancestors – of some sort or another. And if everybody has had ancestors, what can it matter who they were?

[SARAH *sits down at davenport and re-peruses "Peerage". Enter* DICK.]

DICK: The Earl of Eagleclyffe.
SARAH: [*closing book quickly, and turning round*] Who?
DICK: The Earl of Eagleclyffe.
SARAH: From the Castle?
DICK: From the Castle.
SARAH: [*mechanically*] Cecil Arthur Tudor Stormont, fourteenth earl.
    What does he want?
DICK: He wants to see Mr Paul.
SARAH: My brother is out.
DICK: So I told him. Then he said he'd like to speak to you.
SARAH: [*astonished*] To me! [*flushing with pleasure; then, with a sort of spite*] I won't see him. [DICK *is going off.*] Stop! Yes, I will see him.
DICK: Shall I send him round to the great gate?
SARAH: No. I'll see him here. This is quite good enough for a lord.
    [*Exit* DICK.] I'll show him that Sarah Hewitt, of the Works, thinks no more of a lord than of a lump of cinder.

[*She goes to davenport, puts "Peerage" into it; takes out a mirror, and sets herself to rights. Enter the* EARL OF EAGLECLYFFE. SARAH *sits with her back to him. A pause.* EARL *coughs.*]

SARAH: [*still with her back to him*] Is that you, Dick?
EARL: No; it's not Dick. It's me.
SARAH: [*her back still towards him*] And who are you?
EARL: Lord Eagleclyffe, from the Castle.
SARAH: [*turns, rises, curtseys, and then says, dryly*] Happy to make your lordship's acquaintance. [*The* EARL *wears a shooting-dress, bearing the marks and stains of time. His manner is that of a rather old-fashioned patrician than of a modern man of fashion. It is requisite that no foppery, or swelldom of dress or manner be assumed. After a pause*] Won't you sit down?
EARL: [*taking chair*] Thanks, I will; for I'm tired.
SARAH: [*seating herself*] Will you take anything to drink?
EARL: [*puzzled by his reception*] Not anything, thank you. [*a pause*] Mr Hewitt's not at home?
SARAH: No; but I am.
EARL: So I perceive.
SARAH: I was told that you wanted to speak to me.
EARL: I did.
SARAH: You'll excuse my hurrying you, but I have business which—
EARL: I'll be brief. I came to see Mr Hewitt on business – and to offer you an apology.

SARAH: For paying me a visit in that dress?

EARL: No; for a servant of mine.

SARAH: For a servant! Oh!

EARL: Yes; Duke.

SARAH: A duke a servant?

EARL: My gamekeeper.

SARAH: I thought you said a duke?

EARL: The old man's name is Duke. He has been well educated, and has a certain proud, soldier-like air. I suppose that is why they call him Duke.

SARAH: Oh! I never supposed he was a real duke.

EARL: Why not?

SARAH: He appears to be useful and intelligent.

EARL: Have you met many dukes?

SARAH: Let me see. No; not many.

EARL: I thought you spoke from hearsay. However, I must ask you to excuse my old servant and friend. For Duke is a remarkable man. When a soldier, he——

SARAH: I dislike soldiers.

EARL: I'm sorry for that, for I am a soldier.

SARAH: I know that. And you have been a Buttons.

EARL: A Buttons!

SARAH: Yes; a page to the Queen.

EARL: To the Queen? Oh, yes.

SARAH: I knew it was something of that sort. Page or Buttons. I always call them Buttons.

EARL: [aside] What an extraordinary girl! She can't mean to insult me. [aloud] However, let me apologise for Duke. He was wounded severely in the head in the Peninsula. At Talavera, my grandfather, in command of a small body of cavalry, was shot, and fell beneath a heap of slain. All believed him dead except Duke – who was in his troop. He sought for a whole night and the next day – and at last found him.

SARAH: [interested] Dead!

EARL: So all believed – except Duke, who tended him day and night – night and day – and by dint of a devotion seldom seen in those days of modern improvement, restored him to life. Since then Duke has never left the family, but has stayed with it during its fallen and falling fortunes. In another battle, he received a sabre-cut here. [pointing to the back of his head] The blow at times renders him more than eccentric. I hear that he has been the cause of some trouble to you and to your brother, and I ask you to forgive him. He has ancient prejudices. He has been bred in a camp, and not in a furnace; we cannot all have the good fortune to devote the energies of our lives to the improvement of drainage, or the laying down of gaspipes.

[SARAH *rather disconcerted. As* EARL *rises, his gun falls.*]

SARAH: What's that? A gaspipe?

EARL: No. It takes the liberty of calling itself a gun. [*taking it up*] It's a Manton.

SARAH: Are you sure it is not a bow and arrow?

EARL: It is old-fashioned – but it shoots well.

SARAH: [*taking double-barrelled breech-loader from wall*] You see this?

EARL: Yes.

SARAH: Do you understand the theory of percussive power?

EARL: No.

SARAH: I thought not. It will be no use my trying to explain it to you. This is what we poor moderns call a breech-loader. You open the gun so. [*She opens breech-loader.*] You see the trigger is protected here, and the lock works perfectly. The cartridge is placed so. As you see, it contains a double cartridge. There's only one trouble in loading. The ramrod is abolished, which is a capital thing, because the ramrod is liable to break. The barrel is grooved – that is, as you call it, rifled: and the cartridge is larger than the barrel, and would not pass through it but for the powder, which is percussive, so that the shot, if it takes effect, is deadly. Now for the sight. Indeed, the sight is the only novelty in this rifle, and has been sent down for my brother's approval. [*She puts the rifle to her shoulder. The* EARL *places his head so that it is close to hers*] Now, look at your sight. Take your head away; you are looking at my sight, not yours. Now, you see——

[*Their heads close together, as they turn, the muzzles of their guns are pointed at* JACK, *who enters.* JACK *exits behind door hastily.*]

JACK: [*from the outer side of door*] Don't fire. I want to come in.

SARAH: It's Mr Randall.

[*She crosses and opens door. Enter* JACK, *his hat smashed, clothes disarranged.*]

EARL: Randall – Jack Randall?

JACK: Yes; Jack Rand – eh! [*recognising* EARL] What! Cecil Stormont?

SARAH: Cecil Arthur Tudor Stormont, Earl of Eagleclyffe. Do you know him?

EARL: [*shaking hands with* JACK] We are old schoolfellows.

JACK: Eagleclyffe Stormont, of course. I forgot the family name.

SARAH: [*aside*] He is a very nice man, this Mr Randall. Knows good sort of people.

EARL: And why are you down here?

JACK: I'm writing.

EARL: Writing!

JACK: Yes; a comedy. By the way, seeing you unexpectedly – very good incident.

[*He takes out book, and writes shorthand.*]

EARL: You must come and see us at the Castle.

JACK: What, are *you* the grim Earl? By Jove! *Apropos*, Miss Hewitt, there's a lady will be here directly.

SARAH: A lady!

JACK: Yes. As Paul was driving me along one of those roads he has cut out of the hill-side, we saw a lady on horseback, followed by a groom.

EARL: Eh?

JACK: At sight of us the lady's horse swerved, and the lady was nearly off his back. Nice girl – good horse – chestnut – black mane – well-fitting riding habit – good action, and a green veil. Quick your brother jumps out of our trap, and runs to the lady's rescue. The mare in the trap reared up, and then she, and the trap, with me in it, rolled down the hill-side. Capital incident, wasn't it?

EARL: ⎫
SARAH: ⎬ Go on.

JACK: The lady had nearly fainted. I got up. Paul was supporting her – bending over her tenderly, just as in a work of fiction. If it hadn't happened, I should have thought that I had written it myself. The groom and I got the gig right. It was a small tumble. Paul placed the lady in it, and is walking her here.

EARL: Here!

[*The double doors open, and discover* PAUL, *and* LADY ADELIZA *in a riding-habit.* PAUL *is without his hat, and is supporting her. The* GROOM, WORKPEOPLE, FORGEMEN, *and* WOMEN *at back. Picture. Music piano till end of Act.*]

JACK: [*taking notes*] Very good position. Paul supports lady. Groom near her, looking like a fool. Workpeople at back, not knowing what has happened, or what is going to happen, blank and uninteresting, just like on the stage.

EARL: [*going to her*] My sister!

JACK: His sister! [*taking notes*] Very good.

SARAH: The Lady Adeliza Elinor.

[EARL *and* PAUL *bring down* LADY ADELIZA, *the* GROOM *and the* WORKPEOPLE *advance with them.* SARAH *places a chair. The stage at back left open.*]

EARL: [*stiffly*] Mr Paul Hewitt, I believe.

[PAUL *bows stiffly*.]

JACK: [*aside, taking notes*] Stiff, stiff; they don't like each other.

EARL: Let me thank you for the aid which——

PAUL: No thanks are due, Lord Eagleclyffe.

LADY A: [*to* SARAH, *languidly*] To whom am I indebted for——

JACK: [*aside*] Now the women will snub each other.

SARAH: [*stiffly*] I am Sarah Hewitt, of the Works. [*with sweetness*] I hope you are not hurt, Lady Adeliza Elinor?

JACK: [*aside, taking notes*] No, they don't; singular, and quite a novelty.

PAUL: ⎱ Is there anything I——
SARAH: ⎰ Is there anything we——

EARL: Nothing, thank you.

JACK: Cecil won't have the coal-smoke at any price.

SARAH: Will you repose in my room?

LADY A: No, thanks. [PAUL *disappointed*.] If I might ask you for a glass of water.

> [*Noise of carriage at back.* SARAH *is about to fetch water from table.* PAUL *passes her, fills tumbler, and presents it to* LADY ADELIZA. *At this moment* DUKE *enters quickly; his hand touches* PAUL'*s arm, and the water is spilled on the ground.* LORD EAGLECLYFFE'S FOOTMEN *and* SERVANTS *fill up the gate.*]

DUKE: [*saluting*] Your ladyship's carriage!

> [DUKE *looks defiantly at* PAUL. EARL *takes* LADY ADELIZA *up. They turn to bow to* PAUL, *and* SARAH. *The* WORKPEOPLE *and the* EARL'S SERVANTS *mutually defiant and contemptuous.* JACK *taking notes.*]

> *Picture – Drop quickly.*

END OF ACT I

ACT II

SCENE I – *The Banquet-hall at Castle Eagleclyffe, of the 16th century. Rafters in roof. Doors at back, open, showing steps descending into garden. Distant country beyond. The stage sunk, so that the effect is, that the garden is reached by means of steps out of sight of the audience. A pile of boxes, bales, &c. A few old-fashioned chairs.*

> [*Discovered, the* EARL, *seated, his back to the audience.* DUKE, *leaning against door, his head bent, his arms folded.*]

EARL: Duke!

DUKE: [*advancing*] My lord!

EARL: Is everything ready? [DUKE *assents*] The old post-coach?

DUKE: Everything.

> [*The* EARL *sits on chair, and covers his face with his hands.*]

DUKE: Don't give way, Lord Cecil, for now I think you are again little Lord Cecil, whom I taught to ride and to shoot; don't give way.

EARL: [*rising and wiping away his tears*] Not before any one but you, Duke.

DUKE: My lady!

> [LADY ADELIZA *ascends steps in a carriage dress.* LORD EAGLECLYFFE *goes to her.*]

EARL: [*assuming cheerfulness*] Well, Adeliza! come for our promised walk?

LADY A: Our last round the grounds?

EARL: We'll pluck a bouquet from the old parterres.

LADY A: That we may look on the flowers when they are withered, and we are far away.

EARL: Duke, see that everything is put into the carriage; and now, sister, let's visit the kennels, the stables——

LADY A: And all the play places of our childhood, for the last time.

> [*They descend the steps and disappear.*]

DUKE: [*aside*] For the last time! And these paltry intruders who dare displace the lords of the soil! – What are they? Are they iron, that no steel can pierce them? Are they stone, that no flame can burn them? Perhaps not – perhaps not!

> [*Exit* DUKE. *Enter* JACK *and* SARAH.]

SARAH: [*as if continuing the conversation*] But you think so much of him.

JACK: An old schoolfellow.

SARAH: And because he was born a lord.

JACK: But he can't help that.

SARAH: It's so easy to be born a lord.

JACK: On the other hand, it's equally easy not to be born a lord –
indeed, more so. Thousands of people are doing it at this
moment. Besides, Cecil——

SARAH: [*interrupting*] Cecil Arthur Tudor Stormont, fourteenth
earl——

JACK: A splendid fellow!

SARAH: Why? What has he done?

JACK: Everybody – I mean everything – everywhere.

SARAH: I don't like him.

JACK: [*aside*] She asserts that so often that it can't be true. If I could
knock up a marriage between them, what an incident for the
comedy! I will – I'll *make* her like him.

SARAH: The aristocracy of birth is such humbug.

JACK: And the aristocracy of genius?

SARAH: Very often humbug too.

JACK: But considered in the light of poetry?

SARAH: I hate poetry.

JACK: [*aside*] Hate poetry! A woman hate poetry! A girl with such a
complexion hate poetry! She deserves to be doomed to a bad
milliner. [*aloud*] You hate poetry, do you?

SARAH: Yes; it's rubbish.

JACK: [*piqued*] Oh, poetry is rubbish, is it? [*aside*] Now I will be
revenged. She *shall* like Cecil despite herself. [*to her*] You
never read poetry, do you?

SARAH: [*emphatically*] Never!

JACK: [*aside*] Then I'm all right. Let me see; what shall I tell her? Oh!
I've got it, if I can remember the siege of Ismail in Byron's
"Don Juan," [*aloud*] Did you never hear of Eagleclyffe's
splendid conduct at Ismail – I mean Sebastopol?

SARAH: No.

JACK: You know they stormed the town?

SARAH: Yes.

JACK: Well, Eagleclyffe's regiment was in front when the town was
entered. [*aside*] Despises poetry, does she? I'll read her a
lesson. [*declaiming*]

"The town was enter'd. First, one column made
    Its sanguinary way good; then another.
The reeking bayonet and the flashing blade
    Clash'd 'gainst the scimitar; and babe and mother
With distant shrieks were heard Heav'n to upbraid.
    Still closer, sulphury clouds began to smother

The breath of morn and man, where, foot by foot,
The maddened Turks——"

SARAH: Turks?

JACK: I mean Russians——

"——their city still dispute."

SARAH: But that's rhyme.

JACK: You mean poetry.

SARAH: They're the same things.

JACK: Not quite. But sometimes I can't help speaking in rhyme.

SARAH: Tell me about Lord Eagleclyffe.

JACK: [*remembering*] Well, you know they took Sebastopol – they took the city – Eagleclyffe, and a few thousand others. [*aside*] I mustn't make any more rhymes, or she'll find me out. [*to her*] "The city's taken – only part by part –"

"And Death is drunk with gore: there's not a street
    Where fights not to the last some desperate heart,"
        I mean individual –
"For those for whom it soon shall cease to" – throb.
    "Here War forgot his own destructive" – science.
"In more destroying nature; and the heat
Of carnage, like the Nile's sun-sodden slime,
Engender'd monstrous shapes of every crime."

SARAH: But that is rhyme again!

JACK: I know; I can't help it. I'm sometimes taken so. [*aside*] Now I'll hit her.

SARAH: I haven't heard anything about Lord Eagleclyffe yet.

JACK: He's coming –

"He – Eagleclyffe – went –
Upon a taken bastion, where there lay
    Thousands of slaughtered men; a yet warm group
Of murdered women, who had found their way
    To this vain refuge, made the good heart droop
And shudder: while [*with pathos*] as beautiful as May
    A female child of ten years tried to stoop,
And hide her little palpitating breast
Amidst the bodies lull'd in bloody rest."

SARAH: [*affected by the narrative, sitting down and hiding her eyes with her hands*] A child in the midst of all that carnage!

JACK: [*aside*] Now I have got her; she thinks poetry rubbish, does she? [*declaiming loudly*]

"Two villanous Cossacques pursued the child
    With flashing eyes, and weapons match'd with them.

The rudest brute that roams Siberia's wild
  Has feelings pure and polish'd as a" – diamond.
However, no matter about that: –
"The Cossacques' sabres glitter'd o'er her – the child's
  – little head,
  Whence her fair hair rose, twining with affright;
Her hidden face was plung'd amidst the dead;
  When Juan" – I mean Eagleclyffe, "caught glimpse
  of this sad sight."

I won't tell you, Miss Hewitt, what he said, because it was
rude. But what he did was –

"To cut down and lay upon their backs.
  The readiest way of reasoning with Cossacques."

SARAH: [*rising, interested*] He did?
JACK: Yes. "One's hip he slashed, and split the other's shoulder."
SARAH: Cecil Arthur Tudor Stormont, fourteenth earl!
JACK: "And rais'd his little captive from the heap a moment more had
  been her tomb."
SARAH: And what became of the child?
JACK: [*with pathos*] The Moslem orphan – I mean the Russian orphan
  – went with her protector. She was harmless, houseless,
  helpless, all—— All her friends, family, had perished on the
  field. Her place of birth was but a spectre of what it had been.
  There hoop and ball and play was heard no more, and Juan – I
  mean Cecil, fourteenth earl – wept and made a vow to shield
  her – which he kept.
SARAH: [*deeply interested*] He kept the girl?
JACK: She was only a child.
SARAH: What a noble fellow!
JACK: [*looking down on her, aside*] Poetry rubbish, is it? Muses, I have
  avenged you! A devilish good incident.

[*He takes out book, and writes.*]

SARAH: [*after a pause*] What became of the child?
JACK: [*having entirely forgotten his story in some new notion*] Child? –
  what child? Oh – oh! the child, to be sure – she – she's married.
SARAH: To whom?
JACK: [*bothered*] To whom? – to – to – to——

[*Enter EARL and LADY ADELIZA.*]

JACK: I have just driven over with Miss Hewitt.
SARAH: [*interrupting*] With a message from my brother. If it should
  give Lady Adeliza any inconvenience to leave the castle to-
  day, any other time that she may choose to appoint——

EARL: [*interrupting*] Thanks, Miss Hewitt, for your kindness and [*a little stiffly*] – for your brother's. My sister sleeps to-night at our old friend, Justice Parsons'. For the next ten days I mean to take up my abode at the old tower, which a year ago I put into repair. Good shooting, Jack. Come and see me.

LADY A: The old tower – the keep! that is, as we say, you beg an audience of the White Lady.

JACK: The White Lady?

LADY A: A family legend.

JACK: [*eagerly*] A legend!

EARL: Yes; a legacy from the next world – the only legacy likely to be left us. I couldn't raise money on it, or I would.

JACK: [*making notes*] Give a shadow as security! Raise wind on air! Very good!

SARAH: But what is it?

EARL: Our own private and particular ghost.

SARAH: A ghost! Is she patrician?

JACK: I don't think ghosts hold rank in the next world. No one would think of taking precedence of a spectre.

SARAH: Shall I find the White Lady in the Peerage?

EARL: No.

SARAH: Where then?

EARL: In the moonshine.

SARAH: Much the same sort of place.

EARL: How so?

SARAH: Um! dubious, half dark, and shadowy.

EARL: But casting a lovely light on the objects below it.

LADY A: And making mud look like silver.

SARAH: But tell us all about it.

EARL: [*to* LADY ADELIZA] Sister, you preserve those old-world histories better than I.

LADY A: Well, centuries ago——

JACK: Ay, in the days of "once upon a time."

SARAH: Before railways, telegraphs, and civilisation.

EARL: When a tinker was called a tinker, and not an engineer.

SARAH: When men fought like savages, with bows and arrows, and leaders of armies wore suits of tin for fear they should be hit.

EARL: When the foolish world reverenced religion and chivalry.

JACK: And foolish people held it to be rude to interrupt a lady.

LADY A: When Coeur de Lion was fighting in France, a gentle lady was betrothed to a young knight [JACK *takes notes*.]; but he was false to her.

JACK: As usual.

SARAH: Like the men.

LADY A: A few days before the marriage was to have taken place, he fled to France, where he was wounded.

SARAH: Serve him right.

JACK: Serve him with notice of an action for breach of promise.

LADY A: Then thoughts of his old love came back to him. He sought her out, and they were married secretly in the chapel in the old castle. As the knight recovered, he and his young bride met nightly on the rampart. There the lady's brother, the chief of the family, who knew not that the unhappy pair were man and wife, encountered them. With one loud oath, he raised his sword to strike the young knight down. The bride threw herself between them, and holding up her arm to shield the blow from her husband's heart, received the stroke, and fell dead upon the chapel stones.

[*A pause. Enter* DUKE. *He listens.*]

And ever since, when any event of moment is about to happen to the family, or any disaster to befall their enemies, a female figure, attired in white, is seen in the moonlight, flitting down the steps of the old tower, and on the broken wall of the ruined chapel, her arm raised, as if in the act of warding off a blow.

[SARAH *interested. A pause.*]

JACK: [*after having taken notes*] Have you seen her lately? I mean, has she been seen lately?

DUKE: [*advancing*] Yes. I saw her.

JACK: ⎫
SARAH: ⎬ You?
LADY A: ⎭

JACK: When?

DUKE: Last night!

EARL: Impossible!

DUKE: It's true, my lord. I was passing by the lane below the tower, and I happened to look up, and there I saw the figure of a woman.

JACK: A woman in white? Wilkie Collins! Is it possible?

DUKE: Yes; [*raising his arm*] her right arm raised so.

JACK: [*taking notes*] This is a perfect gold mine of incident.

SARAH: Did the ghost – walk?

DUKE: No.

EARL: [*who has seemed highly amused*] No; she wouldn't move.

JACK: But where was this? – upon the platform where you watched? I mean——

DUKE: It stood on the broken steps leading up to the old tower.

LADY A: Cecil.

SARAH: My lord, do you believe this?

EARL: [*laughing*] Of course I do. I am sure he saw it.

JACK: *You* believe it?

DUKE: Don't doubt me, because I am old. The White Lady is walking, and it bodes that some change shall happen to the family; it bodes, too, that to the foes of the old Eagleclyffes, danger shall come, and death.

SARAH: To whom?

DUKE: To——

[SERVANT *announces* "Mr Paul Hewitt." *Enter* PAUL.]

PAUL: Lady Adeliza – Lord Eagleclyffe – I have to apologise——

EARL: No apology is necessary, Mr Hewitt. You are in your own house.

PAUL: My sister was the bearer of a message.

LADY A: [*gently*] For which we have to thank you.

EARL: [*stiffly*] And, at the same time, to regret that we must decline your offer. [PAUL *bows*.] We quit Eagleclyffe in half-an-hour. Everything is left standing according to our contract. For these [*pointing*] I will send to-morrow. There are only a few broken-down family relics and heirlooms, to which I am foolish enough to attach a sort of value – old iron – not worth a pound – commercially – at the marine stores or the rag-and-bottle shop.

JACK: [*who has been taking notes, to* DUKE] Was the White Lady tall or short? Ah, medium height. Better been tall – more impressive.

PAUL: [*hesitating*] I regret to say, Lady Adeliza, that my people at the works insist on making my – entry – into the Castle – the occasion of a sort of ceremony – a rejoicing.

JACK: [*coming down*] Yes; Paul tried to put a stop to it – and so did Miss Hewitt; but the workmen wouldn't hear of it. They're coming – workfolk, volunteers – all.

EARL: Welcome the coming – speed the parting – host, Adeliza.

[LADY ADELIZA *rises*.]

JACK: Cecil, before you go, I wish you'd take me to the picture gallery, and tell me that history of old Baron Marmaduke.

EARL: With pleasure.

SARAH: May I come, too?

EARL: I shall only feel too——

JACK: Of course, too – too – happy. Let the last Eagleclyffe give his arm to the – first Hewitt. [EARL *offers his arm to* SARAH, *which* SARAH *takes*.] So. I'll follow.

EARL: [*to* SARAH] You are going to be introduced to some very old-fashioned people.

SARAH: Never mind. I like old fashions when I'm not forced to wear them myself.

[*Exeunt* EARL *and* SARAH.]

JACK: Oh, if I could only marry them, it would be such a capital incident for my comedy! [*observing* PAUL, *then* LADY ADELIZA, *who is looking off.*] And if I could marry *them* – the double event. Lady Adeliza. [*She turns.*] Mr Paul Hewitt wishes to speak to you.

[LADY ADELIZA *is agitated.*]

LADY A: I – I would rather not.

JACK: Eh! No! Why?

LADY A: I feel – half afraid of him.

JACK: [*aside*] That's a good sign. [*aloud*] Because he is the brutal intruder who——

LADY A: No; but my first impression of him was when a row of cottages near to his——

JACK: Works.

LADY A: Works – caught fire. It was night, and I saw him on the roofs, among the flames. He seemed, as he stood there, calm and fearless, ordering his men to vanquish the fire, to be in his own element. It was as air and ocean to the sailor.

JACK: [*aside*] That's very good. [*taking notes, unseen by* LADY ADELIZA] First impressions – night – flames – master-spirit. [*to* LADY ADELIZA] I'm waited for in the picture gallery.

PAUL: [*as* JACK *passes him, taking his arm*] Shall I——

JACK: [*disengaging his arm*] No. [*aloud*] Lady Adeliza wishes to speak to you. [*aside to* PAUL] Propose to her – propose to her – now, at once. [*aside*] What an incident! If I can only fan these two into a flame! Now I'll go, blow the bellows, and boil up a gallop for the other pair, and so I'll make my comedy as I go on.

[*Exit* JACK, *making notes.*]

PAUL: [*advancing*] To speak to me?

LADY A: What can he have to say?

[*They stand opposite each other, embarrassed for some time.*]

PAUL: [*with repressed agitation*] Lady Adeliza, I owe an apology for my presence here – indeed, to speak the truth, I feel somewhat of an intruder. But circumstances must plead my excuse. I should not have dared to have sought this interview if – if—— [*breaks down*]

LADY A: You are very kind, Mr Hewitt; but it is we who are the intruders. What can be sold of the estate you have purchased; what cannot be sold from it you have – hired – for the present. [PAUL *winces at the word* "hired".] Let me now thank you for saving me on the day when my horse——

PAUL: Not a word of thanks, Lady Adeliza; [*approaching her*] although your offering them emboldens me to ask one favour.

LADY A: A favour!

PAUL: A great favour – that your ladyship will kindly take away with you any familiar object – any picture – anything to which you have become accustomed by association.

LADY A: There is nothing, thank you. I am associated with all here – the woods – the rocks – the river. I cannot take them away.

PAUL: [*after a moment's pause, advancing, and speaking tremulously*] Then why leave them?

LADY A: Why leave them?

PAUL: Yes.

LADY A: [*tremulously*] I do not understand you.

PAUL: Lady Adeliza, I hardly know how it is that I am here, still less do I know what gives me boldness to speak the thoughts that have so long lain dormant – but please to understand that I do not say this because I am rich and you are poor; but for the last five years I have watched and followed your steps, as you know [*She averts her head.*] because, Lady Adeliza, I have dared to love you! [*a pause*] My love dates from our childhood. Since then I have never ceased to think of – to dream of you, as the distance between us was widened by the prejudices of our families. I admit your exalted station; and it is only now, I know not why, that I dare to tell you I love you. I have in some wild, mad moments dared to think that the avowal would not be entirely distasteful to you. If it is, pardon me – I withdraw it, and ask your forgiveness for my presumption. But if you should not think that I presume too much, and that you could remain here amid the woods, and rocks, and rivers your presence has consecrated from your childhood, stay here – remain in the castle – be its mistress – let me be your slave!

> [*During the last few lines, the* EARL *has entered, and has overheard* PAUL's *avowal. He comes forward, and takes* LADY ADELIZA's *hand.*]

EARL: [*with apparent unconcern*] Come and see the volunteers, as they march towards the castle: it would make a pretty sketch.

> [EARL *takes* LADY ADELIZA *up steps, she descends until out of sight.* EARL *returns and speaks to* PAUL *with intense emotion, but not loudly.*]

EARL: Mr Hewitt, you are a rich man, you are a scoundrel! I overheard your offer to my sister. As I have no wish to make a scandal, I forbear to horsewhip you. If you were a gentleman I would fight you; but in these days of glorified tinkerdom, when coal-smoke is superior to chivalry, I dare not, willing as I am to waive the question of rank, ask you to meet me, for my instinct tells me that all upstarts are cowards.

PAUL: [*after a moment's pause of pain*] Lord Eagleclyffe, you lie!

EARL: Lie!

PAUL: Your contempt for me is too thorough. Much as you may despise coal-smoke, a steamboat will convey us to Belgium or France – we can fight there; or are you a specimen of the modern aristocrat – at one and the same time a bankrupt, a beggar, and a braggart?

> [EARL *seizes him by the arm,* PAUL *seizes* EARL *by the throat.* JACK, *who has ascended the steps, comes between them.*]

JACK: What's this?

> [*They release each other.*]

EARL: Randall, that canaille has dared to propose marriage to my sister!

JACK: [*to* PAUL] Quite right. [*aside*] What a splendid incident!

EARL: Quite right!

JACK: [*to* EARL] I mean quite wrong.

EARL: And I, I am ashamed to say, have not chastised his presumption.

PAUL: Chastised!

JACK: [*to* PAUL] Quite right!

EARL: We can go abroad——

PAUL: And fight!

JACK: Quite right! A splendid incident! A duel – birth! – wealth! – brother! – proud lover! Fight it out, by all means, my dear fellows. [*He shakes hands with both of them.*] God bless you both, and curse the other side! [*suddenly recollecting*] No, stop! you are both my friends. I cannot look calmly on and see—— [*aside*] What a dreadful thing when one's duty to one's friends as a man, and one's duties to the public as a dramatist, run different ways! If one shot the other, the success of my comedy would be ensured. Comedy? no; tragedy – no, drama – no, never mind what. Write the piece first, let them call it what they like afterwards. [*to* EARL] But Lady Adeliza!

EARL: My sister's name must not be mentioned in the presence of that fellow!

PAUL: Lord Eagleclyffe, you are a peer, try and be a gentleman!

EARL: What!

> [*A volley heard without.* LADY ADELIZA *and* SARAH *appear on steps.*]

LADY A: They are here!

EARL: [*to* PAUL *and* JACK] Not a word!

JACK: Not a syllable – to anybody [*aside*], except the British public.

> [*Enter* STANTON, *the* VOLUNTEERS *and the* WORKMEN. *They arrange themselves on the left hand.*]

PAUL: Welcome!

> [*Enter* SERVANTS – Butler, Coachman, Footman, Housekeeper, *&c., all old and white-haired.*]

EARL: [*shaking hands with them*] My good old friends!

SERVANTS: God bless you, my lady and my lord.

EARL: [*shaking hands with them all round, much affected*] Good-bye, friends, and thank you for many years of faithful service done to me and mine. In Mr Paul Hewitt, of the works, you will find, I am sure, as kind a master, and a cleverer one than I have been. For all shortcomings of temper, for all that I have done to wrong or to injure you – if by word or deed I have ever injured you – I ask your pardon. Most likely, I and my sister are the last of the Eagleclyffes who will ever utter orders here. Good-bye! Thank you, and God bless you! Is the carriage ready?

> [*Enter* DUKE, *who signifies assent.*]

EARL: [*affected, but bearing up.* LADY ADELIZA *affected*] Once more, old friends, good friends, tried friends – good-bye.

> [*He bows slightly to* PAUL, *deeply to* SARAH, *shakes hands with* JACK, *cordially, and bows stiffly to the* VOLUNTEERS *and* WORKMEN, *and taking* LADY ADELIZA *on his arm, disappears down the steps. After a pause the old* SERVANTS *follow them, the women crying.* LADY ADELIZA *and* PAUL *take leave of each other mutely.* DUKE *eyes* PAUL *menacingly.*]

JACK: [*takes out his note-book, and tries to write*] I can't see, – my tears flood my eyes. This will never do for a comedy. Why, it's a tragedy of the deepest description.

STANTON: [*dressed as sergeant of Volunteers*] Mr Paul, we congratulate you. The castle is yours at last.

> [WORKMEN *shout.*]

PAUL: In my own right, as my father wished; and yet I feel like a murderer.

SARAH: [*sadly, wiping her eyes*] I am not so happy as I thought I should be; I don't think women should always have their own way.

PAUL: [*aside*] She gave me no answer.

SARAH: [*aside*] He's gone.

JACK: [*rising*] This is cheerful.

> [*Re-enter the old* BUTLER.]

BUTLER: My lord – I beg pardon, I mean, sir – the dinner is ready in the garden.

> [VOLUNTEERS *and* WORKMEN *shout.*]

JACK: These fellows' stomachs are insatiable.

PAUL: Come, my friends. [*aside*] And this is the happy day I have so long promised myself.

> [*Exeunt* SARAH, *with* PAUL, *down steps, then the old* SERVANTS, *then the* VOLUNTEERS, *leaving* JACK *on the stage.*]

JACK: Comedy! It is a domestic drama. [*He rises and tears notes, throwing them into the old-fashioned fireplace.*] It will never do. I must give it up. If I am to write for the stage, I won't attempt anything new. I will write in the good old conventional groove in which my good old great grandfathers wrote before me. [*as if inspired*] I know what I'll do! I'll write a good old legitimate comedy on the good old legitimate principle. I'll crush these modern impostors! It is so pleasant to crush a modern impostor. It's an odd thing, now; but why should it be more pleasant to crush a modern impostor than an old one? Let me see. In my new comedy, that is, in my new *old* comedy, there must be a baronet – and, of course, being a baronet, he must be an old man. In old comedies baronets are always old men – a young baronet would have smashed any old comedy – and he must have a son who is old enough to get married. Let me see – shall the baronet be bluff and hearty, or shall he be senile and tottering? I'll have him bluff and hearty. [*imitating the bluff and hearty in the old conventional comedy*] "Blood and thunder, sir! You shall marry her – don't talk to me! Capons and flagons! Don't talk to me; you *shall* marry her – to-morrow – to-*morrow*, sir! Do you hear me? And by gad, sir, if I wish it, you shall trundle her from church in a wheelbarrow. You dog! you rascal! you puppy! you – you – you – you – you – wagh! – wooh! – booh! – bash! – bosh!" That's the sort of thing. Yes, very good – very good, indeed. I must pepper it with impropriety, and make it hot and strong with Holywell Street wit. Then the baronet's son: because he is five and twenty he must flourish his pocket-handkerchief, talk in a high falsetto voice, show his teeth, and wag his head. [*imitating light comedians of the past age*] " 'Fore Heaven, if my old dad and her guardian cannot agree – rope ladders and Gretna Green! –

by Cupid and Hymen! – by Mercury and Mars! – I'll order a post-coach, and with Sacharissa by my side, and my man in the rumble, ride, at the rate of fifteen miles an hour, to endless happiness. Ha! ha! ha!" [*He crosses the stage, laughing.*] Then the guardian, who has the care of the young lady, and who is in love with her himself – a young rascal about ninety. [*imitating a tottering old man*] "Aye, aye, aye, aye, aye, but it is a pretty one, and its guardy will make it happy, and it won't think of the young men. It shan't think of the young men. Adad! if it does I'll lock it up, and give it bread and water; I'll sta-a-a-a-rve its pretty flesh, and when – and when it's cured of love, I'll take it to the church and marry it. Adad! I feel as young as any wanton boy of fifty of them all." La! la! la! la! [*dancing*] Oh, yes, I'll go in for a new-old comedy; it's very easy, and one likes to be a bulwark against modern innovations. I'll make out a list of characters. Sir Furious Fiftybottle – yes, good. [*taking notes*] That's the baronet. Sir Skeleton Skagglemaggle – that's the miser and the guardian. Then a virtuous farmer – um! Pleasant Weathers, a shepherd.

[*Exit, taking notes. Cheers without. Enter* SARAH.]

SARAH: [*pensive*] How those common people do eat! It's awful! To see eighty or ninety – I should say 160 or 180 – jaws all going at once; it's like machinery. After all, there is *something* in birth. I was very much impressed by that picture-gallery. There they were – knights, generals, judges, statesmen, squires, ladies, all dead, and living. Mute in their graves, their eyes open, as if they said, "We have lived, and moved, and spoken; we shall move and speak no more; but we shall live on for ever, and watch the world we've left." It was like reading the history of England in one family face. Paul and I have no ancestors, except our father and mother. One can't buy forefathers, and it's no use advertising for 'em. [*with some contempt*] Why, if our ancestors got the papers, few of them could read the advertisement.

[*Stage grows gradually darker, and continues to grow darker until the end of the scene. Enter* EARL.]

EARL: I left my pistol-case. [*finding it on the pile of things*] Oh! here it is. What a fool I was to lose my temper with this auriferous stoker. [*walking about*] I only made him of consequence by putting him on a level with myself. However, if he should consent to fight, I cannot retract. Ah! my poor sister. He has a sister, too – very interesting girl. [*As he goes up stage, he meets* SARAH; *she sees him and starts.*] I beg your pardon, did I frighten you?

SARAH: You did. I thought you were a ghost.

EARL: I wish I was.

SARAH: I was afraid – I mean, that I thought that you had gone.

EARL: I returned for something that I had forgotten.

SARAH: I wish you would take something away with you as a souvenir.

EARL: There is nothing I want to take away. [*aside*] Except you.

SARAH: I know why you won't.

EARL: Why?

SARAH: Because you despise us; because, though we have wealth, we have no birth.

EARL: My dear Miss Hewitt, you mistake me.

SARAH: No, I don't; and it is very unkind of you. You might have been born humbler than you are. You might have been born a blacksmith, or, even worse, you might have been born a girl.

EARL: [*seriously*] Those accidents will happen in the best regulated families.

SARAH: Then do take something, if only for my sake.

EARL: I will take something – for your sake; I will take away with me—

SARAH: What?

EARL: The memory of the tones of your voice, of the sweet expression of your face, which I may never see again, as by this wasting light I bid you a last adieu.

> [*He kisses her hand, and goes up the steps, leaving her* C. *of stage.*]

SARAH: Don't go!

EARL: [*coming back*] I must; why should I stay?

SARAH: I don't know; but I have so long thought of the castle in connection with you and your family, that when you have gone the castle will not seem like itself.

EARL: When away from here – and from you, I shall not feel like myself. No matter, better feel like somebody else.

SARAH: Why?

EARL: My own individuality does not please me. Good-bye, Miss Hewitt. I wish you every happiness.

SARAH: And I you.

EARL: I'll ask you one favour.

SARAH: Yes?

EARL: Walk with me as far as the garden-gate. I shall treasure my last look of Eagleclyffe if only in memory of my escort.

> [*They exeunt down steps. Enter* PAUL. *Cheers without,* "Hip! hip!" &c.]

PAUL: [*mournfully*] As I used to say when I was a boy, I am king of the castle! And she has left it, and her brother dared to outrage me because I stood on the floor that had been his, and was mine, and offered love to his sister [*going up towards steps. Cheers without.*] At last my father's dream and my own dream is accomplished, and I stand in Eagleclyffe Castle, master of all.

> [*A shot heard.* PAUL *falls. He falls behind the pile of boxes, &c., in the centre of the stage, so that his body is not seen by the audience. Cheers without. Enter* JACK.]

JACK: Those fellows will never leave off drinking, or shouting, or shooting. On second thoughts I won't write that new old comedy. No; I will write a new new one instead. [*looking back. The garden is now suffused with moonlight.*] What a beautiful night! [*walking towards the back*] Nice sort of a night for something to happen – something uproariously funny – something highly comic. If I could only tumble on a really comic incident. [*His foot touches the body of* PAUL.] Hallo! what's this? Now, my friend, get up. One of the forgemen who has been enjoying himself too much. Oh, alcohol! alcohol! what a foe thou art to the perpendicular. People ought not to get drunk now-a-days. What's your name? Speechless! Could anybody be as drunk as you are? [*bending over* PAUL, *and touching him with his hands. Starting back with horror, and raising his hands*] Blood! he's wounded – and – help! help! [*shouting*] Murder! rescue! What an incident! [*taking out his note-book*] No; I must not do that. [*putting away note-book*] I'll save his life first, and dramatise it afterwards. Lights! lights! lights!

> [*Enter* SERVANTS, *with lights,* WORKMEN *and* VOLUNTEERS. *Stage lighter.*]

JACK: [*recognising* PAUL] Paul! [*to others*] Mr Paul, your master, has been wounded.

> [*Enter* SARAH.]

SARAH: What is all this?

> [*As she advances, two or three interpose.*]

JACK: For heaven's sake not a word, or you will frighten her to death!

> [*Enter* STANTON, *who goes to* SARAH.]

STANTON: Miss Hewitt, this is strange news! Your brother tells me he wants to fight a duel with Lord Eagleclyffe.

SARAH: What?

DICK: Why, here lies Mr Paul, wounded.

SARAH: [*screams*] By Whom?

STANTON: Perhaps by Lord Eagleclyffe!

SARAH: No!

STANTON: Why not? – they had quarrelled.

SARAH: Lord Eagleclyffe is incapable——
JACK: [*interrupting*] Who is it then?
DICK: Perhaps you!
JACK: Me!
DICK: You didn't like Lord Eagleclyffe leaving the castle.

[STANTON *takes* JACK's *note-book out of his hand.*]

STANTON: I can't read it. [*to* WORKMEN] Take him to the justice's!
[JACK *is seized.*] As to this note-book, perhaps it may throw
some light on the subject.
JACK: [*screaming*] Give me back my note-book! Take my life, but
spare my comedy!

[*His note-book is passed from hand to hand. He is taken
off in custody on* MEN's *shoulders.* SARAH *rises and looks
round as the curtain falls.*]

END OF ACT II

ACT III

SCENE I – *Ivy-covered ruins and grass plot, supposed to have formed the old courtyard of the castle; the chapel at the back. The tower to be new [i.e., restored], and to look habitable. The door practicable. No moon in the cloth. The moonlight to be on the grass. The ivy to be real ivy, and the grass to be grass matting – not painted. The* DUKE *enters, looks about him nervously, and appears in a state of great agitation. He knocks at the door of the tower.*

EARL: [*within*] Who's there?

DUKE: I, my lord.

[EARL *opens door of tower, and enters.*]

EARL: Why were you not here before?

[DUKE *sits down on bank, overwhelmed with agitation.*]

EARL: What's the matter?

DUKE: [*rising*] My lord, I rode here on the old grey mare, and brought Hotspur with me.

EARL: At this time of night! – what for?

DUKE: Because, I beg, I beseech your lordship to mount quickly and to ride with me.

EARL: Duke, my poor fellow, you are in one of your old humours. Where should I ride to?

DUKE: Anywhere – from here!

EARL: Why?

DUKE: There's danger.

EARL: What danger?

DUKE: [*hesitating*] The – the – the White Lady has been seen.

EARL: [*laughing heartily*] The White Lady! Ha! ha! ha! [DUKE *looks cautiously through window.*] Well, well, well – I know she is – I was sure of it.

DUKE: If you doubt me, come and see yourself, my lord.

EARL: Not the least occasion. I know the White Lady is there at the top of the turret.

DUKE: You do? You know it?

EARL: Yes, I know it, because I put her there myself.

DUKE: You, my lord!

EARL: Yes, me. Don't you recollect three years ago, the vagabond boys of the village got into the window and stole two guns and some powder. Since I have had the place done up, and a new door, and a new lock, I have dressed up a gunstock in white clothes, which makes a good scarecrow, and which the boys take for the ghost – I mean for the White Lady.

DUKE: Your lordship did that! [*Turning his back to audience, looks through window.*] And you think that white shadow that I now see is no other than the scarecrow your lordship placed there?

EARL: I am sure of it. Look again, Duke, and you will find that your White Lady does not walk.

DUKE: [*looking*] She walks – she moves! She is coming this way! [EARL *laughs.*] She is here!

> [*The figure of* SARAH, *a white shawl enveloping her, is seen to pass the broken windows of the chapel.*]

EARL: [*seeing figure pass*] The White Lady!

DUKE: Warns the last Eagleclyffe, the head of the house, to fly! – that there is danger!

> [EARL *goes up to archway.* SARAH *appears in archway.*]

SARAH: [*using the action with her arm*] Fly, there is danger!

EARL: Miss Hewitt!

DUKE: [*surprised*] His sister!

SARAH: [*hurriedly*] Lord Eagleclyffe, my brother has been shot. Happily, he is only wounded, and the wound but slight. There is no cause for alarm; but our workpeople are excited. They have heard of your quarrel with my brother, and it has excited them. They are coming this way to wreak their vengeance upon you.

EARL: Your brother shot?

SARAH: Yes. They call it an attempt to murder.

EARL: And they dare to accuse me?

DUKE: [*aside*] Great Heaven, to accuse him!

EARL: Duke, ride to Mr Parsons, the magistrate, and tell him that at eight o'clock to-morrow morning I shall be with him. Tell him that there is an attempt to murder to investigate, and that the victim of the outrage is Mr Paul Hewitt. Go quickly.

DUKE: [*touches his hat. Then to* SARAH] Your brother is not killed then?

SARAH: No.

DUKE: Thank Heaven! To Justice Parsons, my lord? I'll ride there directly. Not dead! Thank Heaven!

> [*Exit* DUKE.]

SARAH: Lord Eagleclyffe, you must think me a strange bold, forward girl, to come here at the dead of night to give you this warning.

EARL: I took you for a ghost. I am delighted to find that you are flesh and blood.

SARAH: I know our workpeople – their devotion to my brother – their detestation of you. They will tear you to pieces if they find you.

EARL: And you came here to warn me of my danger?

SARAH: Yes.

EARL: Then you do not believe me guilty.

SARAH: [*indignant at the supposition*] Of cowardly assassination?

EARL: Why not?

SARAH: I knew it because – because I knew it. My instincts told me you could not be guilty.

EARL: But why not?

SARAH: Because you are a gentleman.

EARL: Ah! Then you acknowledge——

SARAH: That a gentleman is a man – like any other man. Yes!

EARL: And that he is not disgraced by having ancestors?

SARAH: A man cannot help his ancestors.

EARL: And his ancestors cannot help him. Then you admit that birth——

SARAH: I didn't come here to talk of birth, but in fear of death. See, the workpeople are coming here! I see their torches in the valley. Cecil Arthur Tudor, fourteenth earl, on my knees I implore you to fly!

EARL: Fly from an unjust accusation! The very reason I must remain. It grieves me to oppose you, but if all the workpeople that ever sweltered in a forge were to come here and tear me to pieces with red hot pincers I should stop.

SARAH: Go! Go!

EARL: With an accusation of murder hanging over me? Why, they would say my flight proved my guilt.

SARAH: [*after a pause*] I never thought of that.

EARL: But tell me, why this interest in me? Is it – is it [*lowering his voice*] because you love me?

SARAH: [*hiding her face in her hands*] Yes! I tell you the truth though I am a woman.

EARL: [*embracing her*] Sarah!

[*Noise of voices at a distance.*]

SARAH: They are coming!

EARL: They must not see you here.

SARAH: Why not?

EARL: Your presence at this time of night——

SARAH: [*proudly*] My reputation needs no defence.

EARL: I am not thinking of you.

SARAH: Of whom then?

EARL: Of myself.

SARAH: Yourself?

EARL: Yes; among your own people your reputation is enough defence; among mine you are a stranger, and no tinge of suspicion must cling to the lady who will some day, I hope, honour me by becoming my wife.

SARAH: [*with transport*] Your wife!

EARL: With your consent [*clamour outside*]; give it me now? [*taking her hand*]

SARAH: [*throwing herself into his arms*] Cecil Arthur Tudor Stormont, I'd die for you.

> [*He opens door of turret and brings out a gun with him.*]

SARAH: [*stopping him*] But, Cecil, have you no fear?

EARL: Fear! With your love to guard, and the hope of future happiness to inspire me!

SARAH: Are there any other guns in here?

EARL: Yes.

SARAH: I'll load them for you, and hand them out to you by the door.

EARL: Thanks. [SARAH *goes in*, EARL *closes door*.] What a singular girl! What a divinity! What a wonderful night! I feel that I adore her, and her brother whom I last night wanted to fight—— what fools we men are when we are in love. I'll call her the White Lady for the rest of my life. She'll be a white lady in reality, not an unsubstantial spectre.

> [*A female figure, dressed in white, appears on the tower; it waves its arms, as if warding off a blow.* EARL *sees it and starts.*]

EARL: Gracious heaven! what does this mean? This must be some impostor. [*raising his gun*] Whatever you may be – whether of this planet or any other, answer me, or I'll fire.

> [*The* White Lady, *turning round to the audience, reveals the features of* JACK RANDALL.]

JACK: Don't fire – I'll come down.

EARL: Jack!

JACK: Hush! I am the White Lady keeping off the crowd below. I'll tell you all about it by-and-by.

> [JACK *walks about to and fro on the ruined wall, now and then raising his arm. Clamour without.* JACK *raises his arm. A shot heard without.* JACK *ducks, and falls down without dignity.*]

EARL: Are you hurt?

JACK: [*coming through broken window*] No.

EARL: What's the matter?

JACK: I will deliver myself in verbal stenography. Paul Hewitt has been shot. I was suspected of shooting him.

EARL: You?

JACK: Yes. I was sorry for it as an individual, but it gratified me as a dramatist. The crowd lugged me off to a magistrate. No evidence being found against me, they discharged me. Innocent, innocent – by the bright heavens above, innocent! Then the mob insisted that as Paul was shot, you shot him; and knowing that you had come to this place, they resolved to come after you and execute lynch law. All this I learned at the public-house. I bribed the chambermaid – a small girl with a large dialect – to let me have these clothes. I hired a horse, galloped here, not knowing the road, but keeping the keep in view all the way, I found the place, put on the petticoats to try whether the White Lady would not keep them back.

[*Noise without as the mob approach.*]

JACK: They are there! My horse is just below – mount, fly! [*putting off his female habiliments, and pointing to them as they lie on the stage*] The White Lady implores you!

EARL: Fly! I'd see you, the White Lady, and all the vagabond mobs who ever howled down an innocent man at the devil first.

JACK: You remain here and perish. Very good – it's devilish good, and a capital incident. Here they are.

[WORKMEN, VOLUNTEERS, *old* SERVANTS, *with six or eight torches, appear through arches, &c.*]

EARL: Whom do you want here?

JACK: This is a capital incident. [*Takes notes.*] First rate!

STANTON: [*advancing*] You are Lord Eagleclyffe?

EARL: Yes. Who are you? You're not a servant of mine.

JACK: [*taking notes*] Very good.

STANTON: Mr Paul Hewitt has been shot, and you are suspected to be the man who shot him.

EARL: Who accuses me?

WORKMEN: We do! we do!

EARL: The man who says I ever shot a man except in fair fight and on duty is a liar. [*to* STANTON] Have you a warrant for my apprehension?

STANTON: No.

EARL: Then who dares lay a hand upon me?

WORKMEN: [*advancing*] We do.

EARL: [*clapping his hand on his musket*] Touch me who dares!

JACK: Stop a moment. Stand as you do now – in the interest of the drama. [*taking notes*] This is capital.

EARL: I am here on my own land – the last half-acre that remains to me. You are committing a trespass. If I live to survive this night I will bring an action against you. Get off my land, you dirty swarm of suspicious vagabonds! Who dares to lay a hand upon me, I'll put a bullet into.

WORKMEN: Bring him along.

[*Enter* LADY ADELIZA, *through archway.*]

LADY A: Cecil!

EARL: Adeliza, have you heard the charge against me?

LADY A: Yes; and came here to disprove it.

JACK: Very good indeed – a capital picture. [*Three or four of the* SERVANTS *of the* EARL *cross to the other side.*] Bravo! bravo! it's like a family feud – Montagues and Capulets – Guelphs and Ghibellines – a drama – not a comedy – distinctly a drama.

LADY A: You a murderer, my dear Cecil? The thought is too absurd. Why, Mr Hewitt, who was insensible for a time——

EARL: [*anxiously*] Yes?

LADY A: [*with her eyes on the ground*] Is well enough to drive me here—

PAUL: [*entering, with his arm in a sling, taking off his hat to the* EARL] And to offer apologies to Lord Eagleclyffe if anybody connected with the works should have inconvenienced him. [*turning to* WORKMEN, *who shout. Stage during this grows gradually lighter. Effect of morning upon the horizon cloth.*] The man who shot at me is now in custody.

WORKMEN: Who was it? Who was it?

LADY A: Duke!

STANTON: The gamekeeper?

LADY A: Yes.

EARL: Duke! Fire at a man from a cover! I can't believe it.

LADY A: The poor old man is mad. I was staying with our friend Justice Parsons when he came to deliver himself up. He confessed that he knew not what impelled him to the act, but that he saw Mr Hewitt standing alone, and, as it were, despite himself he fired at him. After securing him, Mr Parsons drove me into the village, where I found Mr Paul Hewitt, and heard of the arrival of these men, whom I thought would make speedy work of you. Mr Hewitt then insisted on coming here to rescue you, and [*with bashfulness*] I accompanied him.

EARL: [*advancing, offering his hand to* PAUL] Mr Hewitt, let me thank you.

> [*During this the* WORKMEN, VOLUNTEERS, *&c., are all in front of the stage in a line with the principal characters.*]

JACK: Very good, very good, very good! It would have been better if Paul had been killed – better for the drama. [*reflecting*] No, yes, no, yes, yes! [*taking notes.*] Let it go down as it is.

EARL: [*turning to* JACK] Send these vagabonds away!

JACK: Who?

EARL: These rascals – they have no business here.

JACK: One moment. [*finishing his notes. Oratorically*] My excellent
friends, tillers of the soil. No! I don't mean that. Divers in the
mine, swart fishers in subterranean seas, who bring diamonds
to the light of day – you have this day – but no, this night, no,
early to-morrow morning – never mind – [*getting bothered*]
nobly vindicated the sovereignty of the people, the people
who are the cause of everything and something more. [*Slight
cheers.*] Who is it makes the bread? The people! Who is it that
brings down the price of bread? The people! Who eats it? The
people! Who works for wages? The people! Who spends
them? The people! Who killed Cock Robin? The people! – no,
I don't mean that – I won't flatter you, I won't make dramatic,
I mean political, capital out of you, but I say without fear of
contradiction, that you are the noblest, the grandest, the most
self-sacrificing creatures in the world! [*Cheers.*] Still, this is a
family party. Mr Paul Hewitt, and the man who, until a
universal Republic, one, many, various, and indivisible, wipes
away such absurd distinctions, I will still call the Earl of
Eagleclyffe, wish to have a long talk together. Will you retire?
Lord Eagleclyffe, I know, has some excellent wine in his
cellar, which, in the absence of that best of spirituous liquors,
beer, perhaps you will allow me to offer you.

[*Loud cheers. The* WORKMEN *retire to the back of
stage.*]

EARL: Mr Hewitt, permit me to offer you the small hospitality I can. If
you will come into the keep there is an armchair at your
service. [*suddenly recollecting*] But Sarah?

PAUL: Thanks, Lord Eagleclyffe, but I prefer returning. My sister
will be anxious to see me.

EARL: [*after thinking*] You can tell her the good news here.

[*He opens the door. Enter* SARAH. *All surprised.*]

PAUL: Sarah here!

JACK: His sister locked up in the castle! [*taking notes*] It's like one of
the old pieces.

PAUL: [*displeased*] My sister here in the tower!

EARL: With me – yes. [JACK *confers with old* SERVANTS, *who go into the
tower. Stage light.*] She heard that your people were bent upon
having my blood in revenge for my supposed attack upon you.
Prompted by her own goodness, she came to warn me. Mr
Paul Hewitt, you made my sister an offer of marriage. You are
rich, powerful, master of half the county, and I am poor, not
even owner of a blade of grass, save this I stand on. Permit me
to have the honour of asking for your sister's hand in
marriage?

JACK: [*taking notes*] Capital! [*wiping his eyes*] Very effective comedy – no, melodrama – no, bother!

PAUL: Lord Eagleclyffe, and you, sister, what do you say?

SARAH: I say, yes. I love him, and I should like to be Lady Cecil Arthur Tudor, fourteenth countess.

EARL: [*smiling, to* SARAH] They will say I married you for money.

SARAH: They will say I married you for rank. Let those people who despise rank despise it – I like it. I confess, I am thoroughly converted.

PAUL: [*smiling*] From conviction?

SARAH: No. From love! Now, Cecil, tell me – about that child?

EARL: What child?

SARAH: The child you saved at the storming of Sebastopol.

EARL: [*surprised*] Eh?

JACK: [*interposing*] Don't mention that to him.

SARAH: Why not?

JACK: It hurts his feelings; the child died.

SARAH: Died?

JACK: Cold in its head, and – now there is only one thing wanting.

EARL: What's that?

JACK: Don't you see? You, Cecil, are going to be Paul's brother-in-law. One good brother-in-law deserves another. Don't you understand? Supposing that I were Mr Paul Hewitt, labouring under the disadvantages of holding half a county and the works that bring in some fifty or sixty thousand a year, I know I have no birth, but still I have the audacity to ask the honour of the hand of your sister, the Lady Adeliza.

EARL: Is this so?

> [PAUL *signifies assent.* EARL *shakes hands with* PAUL. *During the following speech, three or four of the old* SERVANTS, *who have entered the Keep, come out with bottles, which they distribute.* VOLUNTEERS *sitting upon the grass.* SERVANTS *proceed to uncork bottles.*]

JACK: Bless you, my children. The White Lady blesses you! Bravo! bravo! Two marriages. It's a comedy – it's not a drama – it's a comedy!

CURTAIN